CRITICAL MUSICOLOGY AND THE RESPONSIBILITY OF RESPONSE

Why does music move us? Lawrence Kramer suggests we should ask this old question in a different way: what is responsible for our response to music, and to what is our response responsible? The essays in this outstanding collection try to answer this question amongst many others, and by finding cultural meaning in music they exemplify the critical turn in musicology. Sixteen essays have been selected, most of them previously published, from the late 1980s to the present day. These are prefaced by an excellent introduction which traces the intellectual development of critical musicology and discusses the part these essays have had to play in that movement.

ASHGATE CONTEMPORARY THINKERS ON CRITICAL MUSICOLOGY

The titles in this series bring together a selection of previously published and some unpublished essays by leading authorities in the field of critical musicology. The essays are chosen from a wide range of publications and so make key works available in a more accessible form. The authors have all made a selection of their own work in one volume with an introduction which discusses the essays chosen and puts them into context. A full bibliography points the reader to other publications which might not be included in the volume for reasons of space. The previously published essays are published using the facsimile method of reproduction to retain their original pagination, so that students and scholars can easily reference the essays in their original form.

Titles published in the series
Music and Historical Critique: Selected Essays
Gary Tomlinson

Titles to follow
Selected Essays of Nicholas Cook
Selected Essays of Simon Frith
Selected Essays of Richard Leppert
Selected Essays of Susan McClary

Critical Musicology and the Responsibility of Response

Selected Essays

LAWRENCE KRAMER
Professor of English and Music, Fordham University, USA

ASHGATE CONTEMPORARY THINKERS ON CRITICAL MUSICOLOGY

ASHGATE

© Lawrence Kramer 2006

All rights reserved. No part of this publication may be reproduced, stored in a retrieval system or transmitted in any form or by any means, electronic, mechanical, photocopying, recording or otherwise without the prior permission of the publisher.

Lawrence Kramer has asserted his moral right under the Copyright, Designs and Patents Act, 1988, to be identified as the author of this work.

Published by
Ashgate Publishing Limited
Gower House
Croft Road
Aldershot
Hampshire GU11 3HR
England

Ashgate Publishing Company
Suite 420
101 Cherry Street
Burlington, VT 05401-4405
USA

Ashgate website: http://www.ashgate.com

ISBN-13: 978-0-7546-2664-0

British Library Cataloguing in Publication Data
Kramer, Lawrence, 1946–
 Critical musicology and the responsibility of response : selected essays. – New ed. – (Ashgate contemporary thinkers on critical musicology)
 1. Music – Psychological aspects 2. Musical criticism
 I. Title
 781.1'1

US Library of Congress Control Number: 2006935179

Printed and bound in Great Britain by TJ International Ltd, Padstow, Cornwall

Contents

Acknowledgements		vii
Introduction		ix
Selected Bibliography		xvii
1	Tropes and Windows: *An Outline of Musical Hermeneutics* (1990)	1
2	Decadence and Desire: The *Wilhelm Meister* Songs of Wolf and Schubert (1987)	21
3	Dangerous Liaisons: The Literary Text in Musical Criticism (1989)	35
4	Music Criticism and the Postmodernist Turn: In Contrary Motion with Gary Tomlinson (1993)	45
5	Charging the Canons (1994)	57
6	The Strange Case of Beethoven's *Coriolan*: Romantic Aesthetics, Modern Subjectivity, and the Cult of Shakespeare (1995)	69
7	The Harem Threshold: Turkish Music and Greek Love in Beethoven's "Ode to Joy" (1998)	95
8	Primitive Encounters: Beethoven's "Tempest" Sonata, Musical Meaning, and Enlightenment Anthropology (1998)	109
9	Tolstoy's Beethoven, Beethoven's Tolstoy: The *Kreutzer* Sonata (1998)	145
10	Like Falling Leaves: The Erotics of Mourning in Four *Drum-Taps* Settings (2000)	163
11	Chopin at the Funeral: Episodes in the History of Modern Death (2001)	179
12	Recognizing Schubert: Musical Subjectivity, Cultural Change, and Jane Campion's *The Portrait of a Lady* (2002)	209

13	Haydn's Chaos, Schenker's Order; or, Musical Meaning and Musical Analysis: Can They Mix? (1992; 2003)	237
14	Speaking Melody, Melodic Speech (2005)	263
15	"Longindyingcall": Of Music, Modernity, and the Sirens (2006)	281
16	"Au-delà d'une musique informelle": Nostalgia, Obsolescence, and the Avant-Garde (2006)	303
Index		317

Acknowledgements

The author and publisher wish to thank the following for permission to use copyrighted material:

Current Musicology for 'Music Criticism and the Postmodernist Turn: In Contrary Motion with Gary Tomlinson', **53**, 1993, pp. 25–35.
Note: Gary Tomlinson's original article and his response to Lawrence Kramer appear in G. Tomlinson, *Music and Historical Critique: Selected Essays*, Ashgate, 2006.

Editions Rodopi for 'Speaking Melody, Melodic Speech' in *Word and Music Studies 7*, ed. Suzanne M. Lodato and David Francis Urrows, 2005, pp. 127–43.

Indiana University Press for '"Longindyingcall": Of Music, Modernity, and the Sirens' in *Music of the Sirens*, ed. Linda Phyllis Austern and Inna Naroditskaya, 2006, pp. 194–215.

Oxford University Press for 'Charging the Canons', *Journal of the Royal Musical Association*, **119** (1), 1994, pp. 130–40; 'The Strange Case of Beethoven's *Coriolan*: Romantic Aesthetics, Modern Subjectivity, and the Cult of Shakespeare', *The Musical Quarterly*, **79** (2), Summer 1995, pp. 256–80.

Taylor and Francis Ltd for 'Like Falling Leaves: The Erotics of Mourning in Four *Drum-Taps* Settings' in *Walt Whitman and Modern Music: War, Desire, and the Trials of Nationhood*, Garland Publishing Inc., 2000, pp. 151–65.

The Regents of the University of California, University of California Press for 'Tropes and Windows: *An Outline of Musical Hermeneutics*' in *Music as Cultural Practice, 1800–1900*, 1990, pp. 1–20; 'Decadence and Desire: The *Wilhelm Meister* Songs of Wolf and Schubert', *19th-Century Music*, **10** (3), Spring 1987, pp. 229–42; 'Dangerous Liaisons: The Literary Text in Musical Criticism', *19th-Century Music*, **13** (2), Autumn 1989, pp. 159–67; 'The Harem Threshold: Turkish Music and Greek Love in Beethoven's "Ode to Joy"', *19th-Century Music*, **22** (1), Summer 1998, pp. 78–90; 'Tolstoy's Beethoven, Beethoven's Tolstoy: The *Kreutzer* Sonata' extracts from *After the Lovedeath: Sexual Violence and the Making of Culture*, 1998; 'Chopin at the Funeral: Episodes in the History of Modern Death', *Journal of the American Musicological Society*, **54** (1), Spring 2001, pp. 97–125.

The University of Chicago Press for 'Recognizing Schubert: Musical Subjectivity, Cultural Change, and Jane Campion's *The Portrait of a Lady*', *Critical Inquiry*, **28**, Summer 2002, pp. 25–52.

University of Nebraska Press for 'Primitive Encounters: Beethoven's "Tempest" Sonata, Musical Meaning, and Enlightenment Anthropology', *Beethoven Forum* 6, ed. Glenn Stanley, 1998, pp. 31–65.

Walter de Gruyter GmbH and Co for 'Haydn's Chaos, Schenker's Order; or, Musical Meaning and Musical Analysis: Can They Mix?' (1992; 2003) in *Regeln der Bedeutung* [Rules of Meaning], ed. Fotis Jannidis et al., 2003, pp. 486–511.

Illustrations

Centre des Monuments Nationaux, Paris for Figure 1 in chapter 11: Nadar, "*Paris, catacombs: façade avec ornamentation de tibias et de crânes*". Arch. Phot. Coll. MAP.

Fogg Art Museum, Harvard University Art Museums for Plates 1 and 2 in chapter 8: Joseph Vernet, *Tempest by Moonlight [Storm in the Moonlight]*, engraving by Jean-Jacques Flipart (1771).

Fogg Art Museum, Harvard University Art Museums for Figure 6.1 in chapter 15: Edward Burne-Jones, *The Depths of the Sea*.

Houghton Library of the Harvard College Library for Figure 2 in chapter 11: "La Morgue, Quai Notre Dame", plate between pages 62 and 63, from Augustus Pugin, *Paris, Its Environs Displayed in a Series of Two Hundred Picturesque Views*, London: Jennings and Chaplin, 1831. Typ 805.31.7155 v.1, Department of Printing and Graphic Arts, Houghton Library, Harvard College Library.

The Huntington Library, San Marino, California, for Figure 1 in chapter 13 : Plate at Caput III from Robert Fludd, *Utriusque Cosmi Historia*, 1617–1621, RB338942.

The Morgan Library & Museum, New York, for Figure 2 in chapter 13 : William Blake, *The Ancient of Days* (1794), frontispiece to *Europe: A Prophecy*, PML 77235.

Every effort has been made to trace all the copyright holders, but if any have been inadvertently overlooked the publishers will be pleased to make the necessary arrangement at the first opportunity.

Note

The essay '"Au-delà d'une musique informelle": Nostalgia, Obsolescence, and the Avant-Garde' also appeared in *Musicology* (Belgrade) in 2006.

Introduction

> Considering that one begins to take care of men through sensation, by getting them to see beautiful forms and figures and hear beautiful rhythms and melodies, [Pythagoras] began education with music, with certain melodies and rhythms, thanks to which he . . . restored harmony to the soul's faculties, as they originally were.
>
> —Iamblichus[1]

Why does music move us?

This is perhaps the oldest of musical questions, and its rich tradition of answers has tended to dwell on the traits that might be responsible for music's traditional powers: to involve the senses, to stir up feeling, to touch the spirit. Among the most prominent of those traits is the capacity of music, even vocal music, to communicate without language. Especially since the mid eighteenth century, this capacity has been at the center of both casual and systematic thinking about music. It is the basis for the common idea that music's expressiveness begins where that of words breaks off. It supports the widespread supposition that music is in essence non-referential, and therefore has no meaning in the everyday, semantic sense of the term.

This semantic absence has not historically functioned as a sign of lack, which is one key to its cultural value. On the contrary, this absence in music has marked the site of a lack in the order of language, and one that music alone can make good. Precisely because language is so rich, so obviously rich, in signification, it constantly challenges us to interpret it. At both its best and its worst, language withholds a part of itself from those it addresses. But the music that moves us seems to do just the opposite. It seems just to pour itself into our ears; we take it in without hesitation and without reserve. (Music that does *not* move us has the opposite effect; it bothers us like a stream of words we can't understand.) This capacity to be, or seem to be, apprehended directly makes music unique among the arts in its universal appeal. Many people don't read for pleasure, many have no interest in theater or visual art, but almost no one doesn't like, indeed love, some form of music.

Perhaps most of us discover the music we love on just these grounds: the sounds raise an obscure resonance in us and we are never the same again. Many of us can date this experience of musical initiation to a single event; mine came about in my teens as the result of a mistake, the purchase of a couple of classical LPs that no one in my family ever listened to—no one but me. Beethoven, Schubert, and Tchaikovsky just dropped in like uninvited guests, but I took it upon myself to ask them to stay. The opening measures of Schubert's

---

[1] Ca. 300 CE; quoted in Michel Foucault, *Hermeneutics of the Subject: Lectures at the College de France, 1981–1982*, ed. Frédéric Gross, trans. Graham Burchell (New York: Palgrave Macmillan, 2001), 62 n.8.

"Unfinished" Symphony can still sound to me like the very threshold where enigma gives way to discovery.

Yet for all that, there *is* a lack in this important cultural system. Or call it an illogic: something that bothered me more and more as my involvement with music grew. The very depth of our attachment to the system means that its basic premise must be false.

If music makes us feel, it cannot be non-referential. The feelings it stirs arise from and refer to the vicissitudes of living. Feelings have histories, both in the lives of individuals and the lives of generations. If music has anything other than an accidental relation to feeling, it has a relation to the histories of feeling. And if that is so, it also has meaning. That meaning must be part of what moves us in music. Apparently, we only think otherwise because the meaning is not expressed in words.

We should therefore ask the old question differently. Not, why does music move us? but: when music moves us, to what are we moved? What is at stake in what we come to feel? And just who do we become, who do we recognize ourselves as being, when music addresses us? What kind of person feels just these things, in just this way? What conception of the person is put into play by the music in question? What does it mean to be a person moved by music, and by *this* music in particular? What is responsible for our response, and to what is our response responsible?

Many questions, then, not one: questions the answers to which are not a paraphrase of the music's content but a description of its action. Each in its own way, the essays collected here try answer some of these questions, and in so doing to acknowledge, in however small a way, the weight of music in the world. The music is what we call classical (it might have been otherwise, though not from me); the essays are interpretive, which means that they are what we have learned to call performative (they could not have been otherwise, though another author might have performed them differently). They are also, among other things, historical, political, cultural, theoretical, and personal. They are representative; they are idiosyncratic. They are metaphorical—and not; they are intent upon musical works—and not, twining through and around one work and another into the worlds where the works arise, and circulate, and signify.

How to sort all this out? When asked to supply the troublesome little biographical sketches that accompany publication in journals or compilations, I usually say that my writing concerns itself with the interactions of music, society, and culture. What I don't say, figuring that it will be obvious soon enough to anyone who doesn't know it already, is that this concern pivots on the expressive content of particular works of music. My studies treat each work that comes their way as a nodal point in a complex network of thought, signification, and action. They ask how and what the work might mean within that network: how the expressive content of this music may both reflect and help produce, both transmit and transform, the general circulation of meaning in a concrete historical situation.

I began asking these questions in earnest during the later 1980s, just at the same time that a substantial group of others, some of whom have since become close friends and colleagues, began to do the same thing in their own terms. The collective result is what is now often called the critical or cultural turn in musicology. (It is also commonly called the New Musicology, although it is no longer new; the term is only valuable as a mark of what seemed new at one time. For some of us, it rather nostalgically marks the enterprising spirit of the

1990 meeting of the American Musicological Society meeting in Oakland, California, where vivid ideas and personalities seemed to loom up on all sides.) At first widely received as an oppositional development, suspect both for its supposedly reductive attitude toward music and for its candid reliance on difficult forms of critical theory, the critical turn has since won recognition, if not from everyone, as essentially ecumenical and open-ended, interested more in incorporating traditional methods than in debunking them.

This incorporation is inevitably hermeneutic. As understood here, critical musicology is an interpretive discipline; it finds cultural meanings in musical works. Its questions and procedures are unlike those of ethnomusicology, but it does resemble a tricky kind of ethnography internal to Western musical culture. It fosters a principled alternation between absorption in the music and reflective distance from it; the distance enables the interpretation that the absorption both incites and inhibits. The two attitudes have no prescribed relationship, and rarely a simple one. Their interplay does draw music closer to language in the sense that the music constructed by critical musicology as its object of understanding demands to be understood interpretively. But the same music retains every one of its traditional powers, and every bit of them; interpretation may complicate musicality, but has neither the will nor the skill to abrogate it.

This is not an untroubled identity, nor should it be. Even aside from the traditional viewpoints that deny meaning to music in any meaningful sense, meaning itself is not beyond suspicion. That is part of its nature, present at any time, but it is a quality that may seem to have a special salience at the present time. Meaning is too easy to fix in every sense of the term, and the sense that the fix is in is ubiquitous today. Far too often, given the ever-evolving possibilities of its political and technological management, meaning today seems far less the product of the pursuit of truth than of the protection of interests, ideologies, or dogmas. Meaning is tailored to these ends either cynically or, worse yet, credulously. In this climate of thought the best course to take with music might seem the very opposite of hermeneutic. Why not take advantage of music's traditional immunity from meaning and rely on it as a bulwark against deception and bad faith?

Why not, indeed. To a limited degree, that recourse seems eminently justified. It is especially so, perhaps, with classical music, which often, in principle, resists and eludes the heightened attention it demands of its listeners. There are times when denial of meaning is denial of coercion. But it makes no sense—literally refuses to make sense, abdicates the responsibility of making sense—to open our ears in order to shut our eyes. Meaning may be corrupted, but it is not therefore corrupt. Meaning may be unverifiable, but it is not therefore false. Meaning may be suspended in certain circumstances, but it is not therefore expendable. In the long run, I suppose, this is simply an article of faith, but in the long run meaning must be reckoned with. And this is as compelling a principle with music as with anything else.

Reckoning with musical meaning may involve multiple interlocking issues of composition, performance, reception, and reproduction. In the long run, however, and sometimes in the short, it leads to an encounter with the musical work. It is notoriously hard to say just what a "work" of music is, especially since the category itself is historical, and therefore variable. I use it here in a broad sense to designate the repeatable and relatively stable form through which a particular musical action is realized and identified.

Unlike its literary counterpart, the musical work has no familiar family of tropes to represent it. The nearest equivalent is the shopworn figure of the masterpiece, which actually embodies an artisanal ethos quite remote from musical practice (Wagner's Nuremberg aside). The core literary trope is the monument, a metaphor of classical origin well exemplified by Milton's memorial tribute to Shakespeare: "What needs my *Shakespeare* for his honour'd Bones / The labour of an age in piléd Stones? / . . . / Thou in our wonder and astonishment / Hast built thyself a live-long Monument."[2] The work in this guise both fixes memory and imparts authority to it, but it does so, as Milton's sonnet suggests, in terms that undo the mortuary quality of the monument; the words of the work make memory come alive in the forms of wonder and astonishment. The monument of a Shakespeare is non-material to the extent that words themselves are.

This effect of a "livelong monument" is even stronger with fully scored music, in which each performance reanimates the sounds encoded in the score. The musical work is, at one level, a model of living memory, each performance of which reanimates every prior performance and posits its own potential reanimation in future performances. The lack of tropes for this is perhaps as telling as an abundance of them would be. The literary work incites or conjures memory; the musical work embodies it. The literary work is a mediation; it cannot do without tropes. That's why Milton invokes a monument to deny that Shakespeare needs one. The musical work is, or seems, the very substance of what elsewhere must be mediated. Any trope other than that of the work alone would be superfluous for it.

The task of interpreting such a work—semantically, that is, though there is a real continuity with the common musical sense of realization in performance—raises two large theoretical questions. First there is the status of the work as an ideal object, a definite but non-material something, never graspable even when it is most fully present. What is it that we understand when we understand a musical work? Second there is the status of interpretation as cognition, and more particularly of musical cognition. In what sense can words, the essential instrument of interpretation, translate meanings formed in the non-verbal, seemingly non-referential medium of music? This cognitive question subdivides into the question of means (What is it we interpret in the music? How do we know what we know about it?) and the question of content (When we put words in music's mouth, what kinds of things should we ask it to say?).

Challenges to the concept of the musical work generally involve exacerbating one of these questions. The status of the work comes into doubt when suspicion falls on its apparently fixed and therefore authoritative form, behind which there lie obscured the variant and discarded versions, editorial collaborations and redactions, and other vagaries of transmission and reproduction. The result of this concealment may be the investment of a spurious authority in fixity itself. The question of interpretive means arises in critiques that treat the notion of the work as an abstraction from the richness of multiple performances or even from the ambiguity that is part of any score. Here is false fixity again in a new guise, one of the many deceptive faces of reification. (But who is fooling whom? Perhaps the critique is imposing the masks it tears off; perhaps it forgets, or fails to recognize, that performance can be regarded as a one-

---

[2] "On Shakespeare," Milton, *Paradise Regained, The Minor Poems, and Samson Agonistes*, ed. Merritt Y. Hughes (New York: Odyssey Press, 1937), 177.

sided reduction of the rich potentiality inscribed in the work, and the ambiguities of the score taken as an open invitation to interpret in highly audible ways. But I digress.) The question of content emerges in critiques that regard the musical work as a device for accumulating and distributing cultural capital, so that any putative meaning is no more than an ideological bargaining chip.

None of these challenges is new; the elements of all of them may be found in Roland Barthes's famous essay of 1967, "From Work to Text."[3] Barthes denounces the work as a fixed, dead, consumable, "computable" form in contrast to the text, or Text, as a changing, living, unpossessable, incalculable process. The work killeth; the Text giveth life. Even Barthes, however, draws back from the sheer poststructuralist intoxication of this idea, which he presents as an instrument of liberation. The Barthesian Text is at once the battle cry of a radical anti-authoritarianism and a bellwether in the process of secularization that was about to overtake European culture at large; its effect is reminiscent of Walter Benjamin's linking of surrealism, some forty years earlier, to drug-intoxication on one hand and hatred of Christianity on the other—a topic in the most recent of the essays collected here; and it precedes the turn of such widely read thinkers as Derrida, Zizek, Badiou, and Agamben to religious texts precisely at the point of apparent no return for European secularization. The Text is dazzling, but bedazzlement is just a step away from vertigo; it demands another step—backwards.

Barthes's critique thus contains the principle of its own undoing; it recoils at the limit of its extremity. Somewhat confusedly, and no doubt indifferent to the confusion, Barthes acknowledges that, despite his own sorting out of various writings into one category or another, such sorting is actually impossible. The status of work and Text is finally determined not by what is written but by how it is read. This admission allows us, if not Barthes, to conceive the work along sinuous lines that do not require fixity of either form or meaning. The work becomes fluid. The intimidating trope of monumentality dwindles in favor of the work as something done rather than something made, a focused form of the necessarily unfinished activity of animating cultural memory and drawing meaning from it.

So understood, the work appears not as a fictitious object, but as the relatively stable point of reference in a system of repetition, transmission, distribution, adaptation, and commentary. The work in this sense is not degraded but enhanced by the various indeterminacies of edition, performance, notation, and version. To adapt Barthes's terms, such a work exists only insofar as it is textualized, but without being vaporized into a haze of pure textuality. It exists, moreover, only insofar as it is reproduced and discussed, treated as the referent of a name. This treatment is what allows the work, as the first chapter of my *Music as Cultural Practice*, reprinted here, puts it, to attract meanings that form "part of the general circulation of regulated practices and valuations—part, in other words, of the continuous production and reproduction of culture."

This brings us back to the cognitive problems of interpretation. These, we might recall, divide readily into issues of means and content, although each is always involved with the

---

[3] Roland Barthes, *The Rustle of Language*, trans. Richard Howard (Berkeley: University of California Press, 1986), 56–64.

other. I have gone into these issues in detail in other places (among them several of the essays in this volume); suffice it here to comment on each one briefly.

First, the means of interpretation. Interpretation requires that we travel along the famous hermeneutic circle, the principle that no understanding can arise that does not depend on prior understanding, but that genuine understanding must do more than merely reproduce prior understanding. No explicit criteria can be found for achieving this, only attitudinal formulas like Hans-Georg Gadamer's injunction to put prior understanding "at risk."[4] Of course it is possible to invoke familiar and admittedly indispensable guidelines such as credibility with respect to the source, that is, the interpretation's power to engage richly with both detail and context, but just what that means changes so much from case to case that it is impossible to generalize about it. We cannot help but invoke attitudinal criteria even if in some sense they are not criteria at all. And perhaps the most effective attitudes are those whose expression openly invites interpretation in its own right: just what does it mean, for instance, to put at risk a prior understanding of which one is probably only imperfectly aware?

One injunction I try to follow is to let the interpretation stand to the work as a persona does to a person, that is, as a mask or role in which one both finds oneself and exceeds oneself. Implicit in this analogy are both the claims of history (persons and personae are equally bound by it) and the claim of knowledge (at stake with any persona is the problem of recognition). The latter is especially controversial; for its critics, interpretation variously appears as a mere power play, a blind expression of ideological investment, or a second-order poetry that is at best suggestive and at worst capricious. I've dealt with these cavils in any number of writings; suffice it to say here that the knowledge channeled through cultural works of any kind can be grasped at all only insofar as it is interpreted. In Wittgensteinian terms, interpretation is part of the language-game of cultural production. Interpretation neither contributes to nor hinders the knowledge of cultural works. It *is* that knowledge.

Second, the content of interpretation. All interpretation requires that we go beyond what is apparent, but this is especially so with regard to music, where content of any sort is notoriously under-specified. I have argued elsewhere that this actually makes the interpretation of music paradigmatic for interpretation in general. It is possible to link this idea to the very singularity that is so pronounced in music and apparently so resistant to any interpretation at all. This singularity remains a fundamental part of musical experience, but it does not define or determine that experience, however much it may tempt us to imagine that it does.

According to Emmanuel Levinas, who broaches the question in the sphere of ethics, the responsibility both to feel and to understand arises in the demand that I respond to, be responsive to and therefore responsible for, the call that reaches me from someone else, the Other in a positive, not a stigmatized sense.[5] I fail to answer this call if I do no more than repeat it. Only by venturing forth with an answer that carries both myself and the call into the hermeneutic circle do I do any justice at all to the human connection sought in the encounter. Sometimes, as passages and even whole essays in this collection show, the

---

[4] Hans-Georg Gadamer, *Truth and Method* (1960), 2nd revised edition (1975), trans. Joel Weisheimer and Donald G. Marshall (New York: Continuum, 1996), 265–71.

[5] Emmanuel Levinas, "The I and the Totality" (1954), in *Entre Nous: Thinking-of-the-Other*, trans. Michael B. Smith and Barbara Harshav (New York: Columbia University Press, 1998), 13–38, esp. 25–7, 30–35.

effort to be both responsive and responsible requires me to push to and beyond the limits of exposition, description, and paraphrase (all of them quite necessary; there is no question of that) and to insist on the cognitive as well as the expressive value of evocative or metaphoric writing. In order to heed the call that comes, in order to let it "reach" me in every sense, I may need more than one language in which to frame an answer.

Levinas is concerned with human suffering, and the stakes in the responsibility he describes are far higher than anything posed by our encounters with musical works—as long as those encounters take place in open societies where aesthetic immersion is never a political crime. But works are, after all, composed by people, and our response to them, our response-ability, does count for something in human terms. So the same link that Levinas finds between the ethical and the cognitive does apply, though with lesser urgency, to the encounter with musical and other works of art. The work is in that sense a theater of response, and one that is, perhaps, in any culture worthy the name, indispensable.

As with any essay collection spanning more than a few years, this one shows change as well as continuity and displays a variety of authorial personas none of which perfectly represents the person who crafted them. What links these essays, more than any particular thesis or procedure, is a conviction that the meanings of a culture and the value of its heritage must constantly be tested and developed by thoughtful encounters, and in particular thoughtful *written* encounters, with its particular products. In other words, culture lives by criticism, in as broadly humane a sense of that term as might be mustered. To pursue the work of criticism, whatever the fate of its specific works, is to help sustain the public sphere on which we depend to secure intellectual freedom and promote intellectual honesty. That is one reason why musicology, for me, must define itself, not by how it comes to music, but by how it goes beyond it.

In lieu of a survey or synopsis of the essays, let me try to locate some of the tendencies they exhibit when gathered together.

Both within and among them, there is often a certain vacillation—more deliberate as the texts become more recent—between two approaches to the historical character of the musical work. On the one hand, there is a sense of history based on thematic continuity and narrative consistency; on the other, there is a sense of history primarily attuned to contingency and disjunction. This distinction, of course, is not absolute, nor should it be. The vacillation is the point; it cannot and should not stop. Cannot and should not, that is, if we want historical and critical understanding to form some kind of productive relationship, one that neither blinds itself to the former nor starves the latter. The exact nature of this relationship is necessarily pragmatic and ad hoc; it cannot be made systematic; above all it cannot permit either of its terms to become the high-minded scourge of the of the other.

A frequent topic in this volume is the history of subjectivity, of which the history of music is an essential part. As with history, a certain systematic ambiguity attaches to the conception of subjectivity here, but this time with a definite shift of emphasis. Subjectivity first appears as personal agency, as something in the person that acts, but increasingly comes to be regarded as itself a form of action, and more specifically a form of communicative action in recurrent, relatively stable, but historically bounded forms. So understood, subjectivity is very like the work with which it engages in a mutual address. The subject finds itself mirrored and notated, but also changed, in the ideal object, though the congruity between them is never complete or seamless.

Another trend worth noting is a gradual effort to undo the natural-seeming reliance of hermeneutics on musical analysis, and so to redefine the relationship of meaning and technique more productively. I have dealt with this in several published essays, represented here by the later revision of the first of the series, on Haydn and Schenker.

In addition, there is a growing sense of the importance of relationships extending across media and genres, exemplified most directly by the essays on music in Jane Campion's film version of Henry James's novel, *Portrait of a Lady*, and on the history and meaning of the avant-garde. Together with this concern goes an emergent effort to think speculatively, quasi-philosophically, about music without ceasing to think historically about it.

Finally, an attitude present from the outset grows stronger as the work becomes more recent: the conviction that music, in the field of its interpretation, does not simply reflect historical circumstances and mentalities but rather contributes to their formation and may lead to discoveries about them are not otherwise available. This is a point of view I have shared for many years with Susan McClary, who has been consistently eloquent in its articulation and defense. McClary and I, of course, are not the only ones to think as much, but we have, perhaps, been the ones to think it aloud most often.

My hope is that these essays exemplify a discourse that is increasingly reflective, in ways both small and large, of its own performativity, increasingly willing to be candid about its own conditions of possibility, and yet unwilling on these grounds—universal grounds if any exist at all—to relinquish their claim to credibility: not a claim to truth as such, which at this level of inquiry has no singular form, but to something even more animating and revealing: a truthful account of such things as we might hear.

Selected Bibliography

Books

Why Classical Music Still Matters (Berkeley: University of California Press, forthcoming 2007).

Opera and Modern Culture: Wagner and Strauss (Berkeley: University of California Press, 2004).

Musical Meaning: Toward a Critical History (Berkeley: University of California Press, 2001).

Franz Schubert: Sexuality, Subjectivity, Song (Cambridge: Cambridge University Press, 1998).

After the Lovedeath: Sexual Violence and the Making of Culture (Berkeley: University of California Press, 1997).

Classical Music and Postmodern Knowledge (Berkeley: University of California Press, 1995).

Music as Cultural Practice: 1800–1900 (Berkeley: University of California Press, 1990).

Music and Poetry: The Nineteenth Century and After (Berkeley: University of California Press, 1984).

Edited volumes

Beyond the Soundtrack: Representing Music in Cinema, with Daniel Goldmark and Richard Leppert (Berkeley: University of California Press, forthcoming 2007), with an introduction and contribution (listed below).

Walt Whitman and Modern Music: War, Desire, and the Trials of Nationhood (New York: Garland/Routledge, 2000), with an introduction and contribution.

Schubert: Music, Sexuality, Culture, special issue of *19th-Century Music* (17: 1 [1993]), with an introduction.

Essays not included in this volume

"Melodic Trains: Music in [Roman] Polanksi's *The Pianist*," in *Beyond the Soundtrack: Representing Music in Cinema*, ed. Lawrence Kramer with Daniel Goldmark and Richard Leppert (Berkeley: University of California Press, 2007).

"Value and Meaning in *The Magic Flute*," in *Musicological Identities: Essays in Honor of Susan McClary*, ed. Raymond Knapp, Steven Baur and Jacqueline Warwick (Aldershot: Ashgate, 2007).

"Whose Classical Music? Reflections on Film Adaptation," *Word and Music Studies 9*, ed. David Urrows (Amsterdam: Rodopi, 2006).

"Odradek Analysis: Reflections on Musical Ontology," *Music Analysis* 23 (2004): 287–309, published 2005.

"Music, Historical Knowledge, and Critical Inquiry: Three Variations on the Ruins of Athens," *Critical Inquiry* 32 (2005), 61–76.

"The Kitten and the Tiger: Tovey's Haydn," in *The Cambridge Companion to Haydn*, ed. Caryl Clark (Cambridge: Cambridge University Press, 2005), 239–48.

"Saving the Ordinary: Beethoven's 'Ghost' Trio and the Wheel of History," *Beethoven Forum* 12 (2005), 50–81.

——, shorter version, *Phrase and Subject: Studies in Music and Literature*, ed. Delia Da Sousa-Correa (Oxford: Legenda, 2006), 73–86.

"Analysis Worldly and Unworldly," *The Musical Quarterly* 87 (2004), 1–21, published 2005.

"Music, Metaphor, and Metaphysics," *The Musical Times* 145 (2004): 5–18.

"Musicology and Meaning," *The Musical Times* 144 (2003), 6–12.

"Music, Cultural Mixture, and the Aesthetic," *The World of Music* 45 (2003), 11–22.

"But Not For Me: Pathology, Modernity, and the Lied," *Arbeiten aus Anglistik und Amerkanistik* 28 (2003): 5–15, revised and expanded for inclusion in *Why Classical Music Still Matters*.

"Chopin bei der Trauerfeier. Episoden in der Geschichte des modernen Todes," translated by Heike Wenzler-Ballstaedt from a condensed version of "Chopin at the Funeral: Episodes in the History of Modern Death," in *Chopin 1849/1999: Aspekte der Receptions- und*

Interpretationsgeschichte, ed. Andreas Ballstaedt (Schliegen: Edition Argus, 2002), 197–209, published 2003.

"Signs Taken for Wonders: Words, Music, and the Performative," in *Word and Music Studies 4*, ed. Suzanne Lodato et al. (Amsterdam: Rodopi, 2002), 35–47.

"Musica y poesia: Introduccion," trans. Silvia Alonso, in idem, ed., *Musica y literatura: Estudios comparativos y semiologicos* (Madrid: Arco/Libros, 2002), 29–62.

"A Prelude to Musical Ethics," *Tijdschrift voor Muziektheorie* 7 (2002), 165–73, published with "Variations on a Prelude: Commentary on Lawrence Kramer's Ethical Interpretation of Chopin's Prelude in B♭," by Rokus de Groot, idem 174–81.

"Contesting Wagner: The Lohengrin Prelude and Anti-anti-Semitism," *19th-Century Music* 25 (2002), 190–211, included in *Opera and Modern Culture: Wagner and Strauss*.

"Subjectivity Rampant! Music, Hermeneutics, and History," in *The Cultural Study of Music*, ed. Martin Clayton, Trevor Herbert, and Richard Middleton (New York: Routledge. 2002), 124–35.

"'Little Pearl Teardrops': Schubert, Schumann, and the Tremulous Body of Romantic Song," in *Music, Sensation, and Sensuality*, ed. Linda Austern (New York: Garland Press, 2002), 57–74.

"The Mysteries of Animation: History, Analysis, and Musical Subjectivity," *Music Analysis* 20 (2001):151–76.

"Opera: Two or Three Things I Know About Her," in *Siren Songs: Gender and Sexuality in Opera*, ed. Mary Ann Smart (Princeton: Princeton University Press, 2000), 186–203. Revised and expanded for inclusion in *Opera and Modern Culture: Wagner and Strauss*.

"Ein Phantasiestück zur Jahrtausendwende" [in German], *Archiv für Musikwissenschaft* 57 (2000): 101–107.

"On Deconstructive Text-Music Relations" (adapted from chapter 4 of *Music and Poetry: The Nineteenth Century and After*), in *Music, Culture, and Society*, ed. Derek Scott (Oxford: Oxford University Press: 2000), 173–9.

"Beyond Words and Music: An Essay on Songfulness," in Word-Music Studies: Defining the Field, *Word and Music Studies 1*, ed. Walter Bernhart et al. (Amsterdam: Rodopi, 1999). Revised and expanded for inclusion in *Musical Meaning: Toward a Critical History*.

"Consciousness Redoubled: Music, Race, and Three Riffs on Lenox Avenue," *Lenox Avenue: A Journal of Interartistic Inquiry* 4 (1998): 1–17, published 1999.

"Eroica-traces: Beethoven and Revolutionary Narrative," in *Musik/Revolution*, ed. Hanns-Werner Heister (Hamburg: von Bockel Verlag, 1997), 2:35–48.

"The Waters of Prometheus: Sexuality and Nationalism in Wagner's Ring," in *The Work of Opera: Genre, Nationhood, and Sexual Difference*, ed. Richard Dellamora and Daniel Fischlin (New York: Columbia University Press, 1997), 131–59. Revised for inclusion in *Opera and Modern Culture: Wagner and Strauss*.

"Revenants: Masculine Thresholds in Schubert, James, and Freud," *Modern Language Quarterly* 57 (1996): 449–78. Revised for inclusion in *Franz Schubert: Sexuality, Subjectivity, Song*.

"Hugo Wolf: Subjectivity in the Fin-de-Siècle Lied," in *German Lieder in the Nineteenth Century*, ed. Rufus Hallmark (New York: Schirmer, 1996), 186–217.

"Powers of Blackness: Africanist Discourse in Modern Concert Music," *Black Music Research Journal* 16 (1996): 53–70. Revised and expanded for inclusion in *Musical Meaning: Toward a Critical History*.

——, rpt. in *Best of BMRJ*, *Black Music Research Journal* 22 (supplement 2002), 197–214, juried special issue commemorating the 20th anniversary of the journal, published 2004.

"Performance and Social Meaning in the Lied: Schubert's 'Erster Verlust,'" *Current Musicology* 56 (1994): 5–23. Revised for inclusion in *Franz Schubert: Sexuality, Subjectivity, Song*.

"The Singing Salami: Unsystematic Reflections on the Marx Brothers' A Night at the Opera," in *A Night in at the Opera: Media Representation of Opera*, ed. Jeremy Tambling (London: John Libbey, 1994), 253–65. Revised and expanded for inclusion in *Musical Meaning: Toward a Critical History*.

"[Schumann's] Carnaval, Cross-Dressing, and the Woman in the Mirror," in *Musicology and Difference: Gender and Sexuality in Music Scholarship*, ed. Ruth Solie (Berkeley: University of California Press, 1993), pp. 305–25. Revised and expanded for inclusion in *Musical Meaning: Toward a Critical History*.

"Fin-de-Siècle Fantasies: *Elektra*, Degeneration, and Sexual Science," *Cambridge Opera Journal* 5 (1993): 141–66. Revised and expanded for inclusion in *Opera and Modern Culture: Wagner and Strauss*.

"Felix Culpa: Goethe and the Image of Mendelssohn," in *Mendelssohn Studies*, ed. R. Larry Todd (Cambridge: Cambridge University Press, 1992), pp. 65–79. Revised and expanded for inclusion in *Classical Music and Postmodern Knowledge*.

"The Musicology of the Future," *Repercussions* 1 (1992): 5–18. Revised for incorporation into chapter 1 of *Classical Music and Postmodern Knowledge*.

"*Musical Narratology: A Theoretical Outline*," Indiana Theory Review 12 (1991): 141–62. Revised and expanded for inclusion in *Classical Music and Postmodern Knowledge*.

"Music and Representation: The Instance of Haydn's Creation," in *Music and Text: Critical Inquiries*, ed. by Steven Paul Scher (Cambridge: Cambridge University Press, 1991), pp. 139–62. Revised and expanded for inclusion in *Classical Music and Postmodern Knowledge*.

Music and Cultural Hermeneutics: The Salome Complex," *Cambridge Opera Journal* 2 (1990): 269–95. Revised and expanded for inclusion in *Opera and Modern Culture: Wagner and Strauss*.

"Text and Music: Some New Directions," *Contemporary Music Review* 5 (1989): 143–53.

"Expressive Doubling: Beethoven's Two-Movement Piano Sonatas and Romantic Literature," *Studies in Romanticism* 27 (1988): 175–202. Revised and expanded for inclusion in *Music as Cultural Practice: 1800–1900*.

"'A Completely New Set of Objects': The Spirit of Place in Wallace Stevens and Charles Ives" (adapted from chapter 6 of *Music and Poetry: The Nineteenth Century and After*), in *Critical Essays on Wallace Stevens*, ed. Steven Gould Axelrod and Helen Deese (Boston: G. K. Hall, 1988), pp. 213–29.

"Romantic Meaning in Chopin's Prelude in A Minor," *19th-Century Music* 9 (1985): 145–55. Revised and expanded for inclusion in *Music as Cultural Practice: 1800–1900*.

"The Schubert Lied: Romantic Form and Romantic Consciousness," in *Schubert: Critical and Analytical Studies*, ed. Walter Frisch (Lincoln, Nebraska: University of Nebraska Press, 1985, 1996, pp. 200–238.

"The Mirror of Tonality: Transitional Features of Nineteenth Century Harmony," *19th-Century Music* 4 (1981): 191–208.

"'Syringa': John Ashbery and Elliott Carter," in *Beyond Amazement: New Essays on John Ashbery*, ed. David Lehman (Ithaca: Cornell University Press, 1980), 255–71. Revised for inclusion in *Music and Poetry: The Nineteenth Century and After*.

Review Essays and Shorter Articles

Foreword to Giuseppe Mazzini, *Philosophy of Music*, trans. Emily Ashurst Hawkes (1867), ed. Franco Sciannemeo (Lewiston: Edwin Mellen, 2004).

"Dialogue," interview accompanying the article "Schubert, Kramer, and Musical Meaning," by Matthew Head, *Music and Letters* 83 (2002): 438–40.

"The Narrative Moment," *Lenox Avenue: A Journal of Interarts Inquiry* 5 (1999): 99–101.

"The Real in Embers, the Arts Enflamed," *Modern Language Quarterly* 54 (1993): 285–94.

"Analyzing Analysis, Criticizing Criticism," *19th-Century Music* 15 (1992): 76–9.

"Song and Story" [review essay on Carolyn Abbate, *Unsung Voices: Opera and Musical Narrative in the Nineteenth Century*], *19th-Century Music* 14 (1992): 65–9.

"Schorske's Ring Cycle, Schoenberg's Liebestod" (review essay on Carl Schorske's *Fin-de-Siècle Vienna*), *19th-Century Music* 5 (1981), 76–81.

Musical Compositions (with year of first performance).

Rhapsody for Solo Violin. Purchase, N. Y., 1982.

Moment by Moment for flute, oboe, and piano. New York City, 1983. Commissioned by the Woodstock Chamber Players.

"That Music Always Round Me": *Three Poems of Walt Whitman* for tenor and piano. New York City, 1985. Commissioned by Darrell Lauer, tenor.

"That Stillness in the Air": *Five Poems of Emily Dickinson* for soprano, trumpet, and piano. New York City, 1986.

*Illumination*s for Piano. Annandale, New York, 1986.

Eclogue and Elegy for Clarinet and Piano. New York City, 1986. Commissioned by Paul Gallo.

Break of Day for soprano and orchestra (or piano). Annandale, N. Y., 1987. Commissioned for Lucy Shelton, soprano, by the Hudson Valley Philharmonic Chamber Orchestra, Leon Botstein, music director.

Jornada del Muerto for baritone, chamber ensemble, and percussion. Hanover, N.H., 1988. Commissioned by Dartmouth College.

Thresholds for Orchestra. Woodstock, N. Y., 1989 (revised 1994). Commissioned by the Woodstock Chamber Orchestra.

Ursound for orchestra. Annandale, N. Y., 1992. Commissioned by the Hudson Valley Philharmonic Chamber Orchestra, Leon Botstein, music director.

A Ring of Light, cycle of five songs for voice and piano. Plattsburgh, New York, 1994.

Revenants for solo piano. Hartford, Connecticut, 1998.

Five Songs and an Epilogue from *The Wings of the Dove* for voice and piano. Edinburgh, 2007. Composed for Michael Halliwell, baritone.

CD Recordings

Three Poems of Walt Whitman ("That Music Always Round Me"; 1985), with Joan Heller, soprano, and Thomas Stumpf, piano; published with *Walt Whitman and Modern Music* and also including song cycles by Marc Blitzstein, Kurt Weill, and George Crumb.

Revenants: 32 Variations in C Minor for Piano (1996), computer realization, published with *Musical Meaning: Toward a Critical History*.

CHAPTER 1

TROPES AND WINDOWS:

An Outline of Musical Hermeneutics

The aim of this book is to give practical confirmation to four closely related claims:

1. that works of music have discursive meanings;

2. that these meanings are definite enough to support critical interpretations comparable in depth, exactness, and density of connection to interpretations of literary texts and cultural practices;

3. that these meanings are not "extramusical," but on the contrary are inextricably bound up with the formal processes and stylistic articulations of musical works;

4. that these meanings are produced as a part of the general circulation of regulated practices and valuations—part, in other words, of the continuous production and reproduction of culture.

I am well aware that these claims exceed (and then some) the customary ambitions of what has come to be called musical hermeneutics.[1] Problematical though my claims may be, they are by no

---

1. Critical surveys of the recent literature, as well as important statements of position, appear in Monroe C. Beardsley, "Understanding Music," in *On Criticizing*

2   Tropes and Windows

means merely polemical. Meaning is an irrepressibly volatile and abundant thing; you really can't have just some of it. My purpose here is to appropriate this strength of meaning on behalf of music—and most especially on behalf of textless instrumental music. For if my claims are tenable where music is furthest from language, they will a fortiori be tenable where music and language meet.

One obvious qualification needs to be entered at this point. For present purposes, *music* refers to European art music composed between 1798 and 1888. This restriction is not meant to be exclusionary, however. The following chapters on nineteenth-century topics are to be understood as case studies. The techniques of interpretation that I apply here to nineteenth-century art music are meant to be equally applicable—in hands more competent than mine—to the music of other periods and to music of other sorts.

As to the present chapter, its concerns are with the need to give my claims a *practical* confirmation. All of the claims stand or fall on the possibility of making certain kinds of interpretation. And though interpretive practices benefit enormously from hermeneutic theorizing, a hermeneutic theory is only as good as the interpretations that it underwrites. Freud, whose name will come up more than once in this book, repeatedly insisted that psychoanalysis was unconvincing as a body of theory. Only by *doing* analysis, by engaging in the work of interpretation whether as analyst or analysand, could one be persuaded that Freudian claims are credible—or, as Freud forgot to add, of the reverse. The same is true of musical hermeneutics, which, like psychoanalysis, seeks meaning in places where meaning is often said not to be found. I will, to be sure, theorize a little in what follows, both about music and about interpretation. The value of the theory, though, must rest with the interpretive practices that it empowers.

The essential hermeneutic problem about music is usually put by saying that music is all syntax and no semantics, or that music lacks denotative or referential power, or, to revert to Hanslick's much-quoted aphorism, that "sounding forms in motion are the one and

---

Music, ed. Kingsley Price (Baltimore, 1981), 55–73; and Anthony Newcomb, "Sound and Feeling," *Critical Inquiry* 10 (1984): 614–43. See also the discussion of "expressive potential" in Edward T. Cone, *The Composer's Voice* (Berkeley and Los Angeles, 1974), 158–75.

only content of music."[2] This view—the formalist view that has since Hanslick and even since Kant set the terms for serious thinking about music—rests on an implicit comparison of music with verbal utterance or written discourse. Not surprisingly, music emerges from this contest with language in thoroughly poor shape, conceptually indefinite and semantically impoverished. As Kant puts it,

> Although [Music] indeed speaks by means of pure sensations without concepts, and so does not, like poetry, leave something over for reflection [etwas zum Nachdenken übrig bleiben lässt], yet it moves the mind more variously and, though fleetingly, with more fervor; but it is certainly more enjoyment [Genuß] than culture (the neighboring thought-play excited by its means [das Gedankenspiel, welches nebenbei dadurch erregt wird] is merely the effect of a sort of mechanical [mechanisch] association).[3]

Kant's phrase "leave something over for reflection," however, quietly points up the weakness in the formalist attitude. Where does this incitement to reflection come from when language is in question? Where, for example, does it come from in Kant's own statement? Most obviously, it comes from Kant's truth claims: the assertions that music communicates by means of pure sensations, that poetry communicates by means of concepts, that culture entails a hierarchy of concepts over sensations, and so on. Each of these claims can be elaborated or contested: hence they leave something over for reflection. Yet there is another way to reflect on this text, a hermeneutic way that bypasses truth claims to consider the dynamic elements in the act of writing itself, to treat the text precisely as a *Gedankenspiel*, though not at all a mechanical one.

Kant's labyrinthine series of qualifiers (*ob, zwar, doch, obgleich bloß, doch, aber freilich, bloß*) suggests a struggle to control some very equivocal materials. The suggestion is borne out by the submerged and perhaps inadvertent metaphor of neighboring thought-play that is called on to crown the case against music. Kant sets out to ratify the inferiority of music to poetry as a simple consequence of the supposed inferiority of sensation to reflection. Yet he cannot stabilize

---
2. Eduard Hanslick, *Vom Musikalisch-Schönen* (Leipzig, 1854), 32.
3. Immanuel Kant, *Kritik der Urteilschaft*, sec. 53; from *Sämtliche Werke*, ed. G. Hartenstein (Leipzig, 1867), 5:339.

4   Tropes and Windows

his terms. In particular, he cannot both take music as his instance of pure sensation and still maintain the difference between sensation and reflection. For music, too, provokes the mind to reflect; it excites a neighboring thought-play. As Kant's terms make explicit, the primary features of this form of reflection are intimacy (*nebenbei*) and unruliness (*[ein]-spiel . . . erregt*). The *Gedankenspiel* transfers what is palpable and impulsive in musical sensation to the detached realm of reason, culture, meaning; it intrudes bodily pleasure into the space reserved for thought. Kant later ascribes an explicit bodiliness to the "free play" (*das freie Spiel*) of both tones (*Tonspiel*) and thoughts (*Gedankenspiel*). In music, he adds, "this play goes from bodily sensations to aesthetic ideas . . . and from these back again, but with united force, to the body."[4]

But music and its *Gedankenspiel* inhibit reflection proper, the "true" reflection that for Kant is the bearer of culture. The blockage seems to derive from too much immediacy; the subject of reflection, the Kantian subject of culture, requires a space of detachment in which to operate. In order to safeguard this space, Kant peremptorily severs pleasure from meaning, pronouncing ex cathedra that the *Gedankenspiel* is only the effect of "a sort of mechanical association." This statement shifts the metaphorical ground from the coalescence of mind and body to impersonal mechanism. Kant thus demotes the sensitive body to mere extension in space and pleasurable impulse to simple physical movement. With the same stratagem, he also detaches the quasi-autonomous subject of reflection from the anarchic, pleasure-seeking, decentered subjectivity of *Gedankenspiel*.

In preferring poetry to music, therefore, Kant is striving, indeed rather desperately striving, to shield a group of higher values—culture, reflection, subjective autonomy—from encroachments and appropriations by a group of lower values—enjoyment, sensation, subjective contingency. Music is the loose cannon in this process. Kant treats it as a principle of pleasurable intrusion, so much so that he later compares it to the unwelcome scent of a perfume. In denying meaning to music, Kant not only theorizes but also legislates; he responds less to an absence of thought than to the presence of danger.

---

4. Ibid., 342–43.

Where does our reflection on Kant's text leave us, as would-be interpreters, with regard to music? As far as truth claims go, it leaves us nowhere at all. A certain formalism to the contrary, music does have referential power, even if we are not prepared to be very precise about it. To affirm, for example, that nineteenth-century overtures named for Coriolanus, Manfred, and Hamlet fail to represent those characters seems foolish if not perverse. Yet truth claims are quite another matter. Music—and this is precisely the truth claim of Kant's text—cannot make them. Music may seduce us, but it never makes propositions. And here we must acknowledge the kernel of truth in the formalist position. If meaning begins with (forms around, clings to) a truth claim (implicit or explicit, real or fictive), then music has no meaning in the ordinary sense. One may wish to reinterpret this admission in order to endow music with a higher than ordinary "meaning"; E. T. A. Hoffmann does just that when he claims that instrumental music conveys the sense of the infinite and is therefore the quintessentially Romantic art. Even Hanslick, and later Schenker, make similar moves.[5] The fact remains, however, that on this view music may be spoken of rigorously only in formal terms. Anything else is—at best—inspired impressionism.

Yet to argue that meaning begins with a truth claim is merely to give a restrictive definition of meaning. The hermeneutic approach that we took to Kant's text begins, on principle, somewhere else: on this occasion, with the resonance of a metaphor. In taking up the hermeneutic attitude, we approached the text by assuming that it resists fully disclosing itself, that in certain important respects it is mute, and that we ourselves understand it at first in terms we must work to articulate. To put this another way, we approached the text very much as we would be compelled to approach a piece of "abso-

---

5. E. T. A. Hoffmann, "Beethoven's Instrumental Music," in *Source Readings in Music History: The Romantic Era*, ed. Oliver Strunk (New York, 1965), 35–41. On Hanslick's concept of form as spirit or *energeia*, see Carl Dahlhaus, *Esthetics of Music*, trans. William Austin (Cambridge, 1982), 52–54. Schenker's invocation of Nature as a transcendental category is well known. The kernel of his "higher" hermeneutic is succinctly formulated in the preface to his early *Harmony* (ed. Oswald Jonas, trans. Elizabeth Mann Borgese [Chicago, 1954], xxv): "I should like to stress in particular the biological factor in the life of tones. We should get used to the idea that tones have lives of their own, more independent of the artist's pen in their vitality than one would dare to believe."

6   Tropes and Windows

lute" music. The hermeneutic attitude, which begins to assume its modern form at just about the time that instrumental music begins its cultural ascendancy,[6] works by assigning to discourse the nondiscursive opacity that is supposed to belong to music. We enable the interpretation of a text by depreciating what is overtly legible and regarding the text as potentially secretive, or at least as a provocation to understanding that we may not know how to answer. The text, in this frame of reference, does not give itself to understanding; it must be made to yield to understanding. A hermeneutic window must be opened on it through which the discourse of our understanding can pass.

Once that window opens, the text appears, or at least may appear, not as a grid of assertions in which other modes of meaning are embedded but as a field of humanly significant actions. In the example from Kant, the window opened by the metaphor of neighboring thought-play revealed an intricate spectacle of intrusion and protection in which philosophical judgment, ambivalence about bodily pleasures, and the work of building culture all play a part.

Where, then, to repeat my earlier question, does our reflection on Kant's text leave us with regard to music? As far as interpretation goes, the answer may well be: here, there, and everywhere. Under the hermeneutic attitude, there is and can be no fundamental difference between interpreting a written text and interpreting a work of music—or any other product or practice of culture. This is not, of course, to say that it has suddenly become obvious how to interpret music; what is obvious is that we still lack the techniques for that. But we should now know how to develop the techniques we need; analyzing the hermeneutic attitude at work has given us our clue. In order to practice a musical hermeneutics we must learn, first, how to open hermeneutic windows on the music we seek to interpret and, second, how to treat works of music as fields of humanly significant action.

It will prove convenient to take up these projects in reverse order. Much of my discussion so far has been guided implicitly by a critical adaptation of J. L. Austin's theory of speech acts—a theory in which

---

6. On this topic see Tilottama Rajan, "The Supplement of Reading," *New Literary History* 17 (1985–86): 573–94.

language as action takes precedence over language as assertion. In his book *How to Do Things with Words*, Austin begins by distinguishing between two types of utterance, which he calls constative and performative.[7] Constative utterances make truth claims, and are accordingly evaluated as true or false. Performatives attempt to achieve something, and are accordingly evaluated as successful or unsuccessful. "The path is steep" is a constative; "Be careful: the path is steep" is a performative—namely, a warning. In developing this distinction, Austin deliberately works up to an impasse: he shows that we cannot find a reliable criterion by which to separate constatives from performatives. In particular, any constative utterance can also serve as a performative: in the right setting, "The path is steep" can also be a warning. The constative and the performative thus become dimensions of utterance rather than types of utterance, and to underline this change Austin changes his terminology.[8] The constative dimension is now said to manifest itself in *locutionary meaning*, the claims or assertions that a speech act puts into play. The performative dimension manifests itself in *illocutionary force*, the pressure or power that a speech act exerts on a situation.[9]

Illocutionary force quickly proves to be a very unruly thing. Its relationship to locutionary effects (not meaning, *pace* Austin) is loose at best and highly variable; a speech act may say things that are widely at odds with what it does. Speech acts, moreover, are constantly in danger of going awry, "misfiring," as Austin puts it:

QUEEN
    Do not for ever with thy vailèd lids
    Seek for thy noble father in the dust.
    Thou know'st tis common. All that lives must die,
    Passing through nature to eternity.

---

7. J. L. Austin, *How to Do Things with Words*, ed. J. O. Urmson and Marina Sbisa (Cambridge, Mass., 1962).
8. Ibid., 94–108.
9. Austin also distinguishes between illocutionary and what he calls perlocutionary forces, the former referring to what one does *in* saying something, the latter to the results one achieves *by* saying something. The distinction complicates matters with no very clear gain; I use the term *illocutionary force* to cover both meanings.

8   *Tropes and Windows*

HAMLET
Ay, madam, it is common.

(*Hamlet*, 1.2.70-74)

This famous exchange exemplifies both types of unruliness. Gertrude in all likelihood wants to help Hamlet, but her help shades too easily into manipulation. She tries to control his grief—and his rage—by getting him to consent to some platitudes about mortality. Hamlet pretends to comply, but his withering multiple pun on *common* not only refuses the manipulation but also attacks the manipulator.

Austin is ambivalent about this sort of discursive skittishness; he alternately unleashes and tries to limit the instability of illocution. For present purposes, the most important fact about his proposed limitations is that none of them works. The reason why becomes apparent in a decisive critique of speech act theory put forth by Jacques Derrida.[10] Derrida points out that all acts of communication presuppose the possibility of their repetition in new contexts. In order to function at all, a speech act, like a piece of writing or a visual image, must be *iterable*, that is, capable of functioning in situations other than the occasion of its production, among persons other than those who immediately produce and receive it. In their iterability, speech acts necessarily presuppose the possibility of difference, and hence also the possibility of their being redirected, reinterpreted. The prospect of what Austin thinks of as "misfire," an "infelicitous" deviation from the norm, is actually the norm itself. Even though certain speech acts may, and do, recur in typical settings with typical illocutions, we are not spared by that fact from understanding them anew with each recurrence. Speech acts are radically implicated in the situations that they address; they come to life as a kind of improvisation.

10. Derrida's essay, "Signature Event Context" originally appeared in the short-lived periodical *Glyph*, where it provoked a now famous exchange with the speech act theorist John Searle; the essay is reprinted in Derrida, *Margins of Philosophy*, trans. Alan Bass (Chicago, 1982): 307-30. For a fuller account, see Stanley Fish, "With the Compliments of the Author: Reflections on Austin and Derrida," *Critical Inquiry* 8 (1982): 693-722. For more on the instability of the performative dimension, and on Austin's treatment of it, see Shoshana Felman, *The Literary Speech Act: Don Juan with J. L. Austin, or Seduction in Two Languages*, trans. Catherine Porter (Ithaca, N.Y., 1983).

Tropes and Windows 9

Taken together with Derrida's critique, Austin's theory of speech acts holds great promise for musical hermeneutics. Although Austin privileges what he calls the "speech situation,"[11] speech act theory generalizes easily to cover writing, which also has a busy performative dimension. And although locutionary effects are confined to the sphere of language, illocutionary force need not be. Any act of expression or representation can exert illocutionary force provided, first, that the act is iterable and, second, that in being produced the act seeks to affect a flow of events, a developing situation. In their illocutionary dimension, therefore, speech acts exemplify a larger category of expressive acts through which illocutionary forces pass into general circulation. Musical processes clearly count as expressive acts according to the terms just given. If we can learn to recognize them as such, to concretize the illocutionary forces of music as we concretize its harmonic, rhythmic, linear, and formal strategies, we can then go on to interpret musical meaning.

What techniques can we use to this purpose? An expressive act can be recognized as such only within the situation that it traverses, and here again speech acts enjoy certain advantages. Either their situation is explicit, as in the example from *Hamlet*, or they imply a situation while apparently concentrating on locutionary business, as in Kant's metaphor of thought-play. Unfortunately for the interpreter, these situational signals have no exact parallels in music. They do, however, have inexact parallels—sometimes oblique ones, elliptical, latent rather than manifest, but still and all sufficient to work with.

In recognizing and reflecting on an expressive act, we empower the interpretive process; we open what I earlier called a hermeneutic window through which our interpretation can pass. When it comes to music, at least three types of hermeneutic window are available to us, either as the expressive act to be recognized or as a signpost to such recognition.

    1. *Textual inclusions.* This type includes texts set to music, titles, epigrams, programs, notes to the score, and sometimes even expression markings. In dealing with these materials, it is critical to remember—especially with the texts of

11. Austin, *How to Do Things with Words*, 139.

vocal pieces—that they do not establish (authorize, fix) a meaning that the music somehow reiterates, but only invite the interpreter to find meaning in the interplay of expressive acts. The same caution applies to the other two types.

2. Citational inclusions. This type is a less explicit version of the first, with which it partly overlaps. It includes titles that link a work of music with a literary work, visual image, place, or historical moment; musical allusions to other compositions; allusions to texts through the quotation of associated music; allusions to the styles of other composers or of earlier periods; and the inclusion (or parody) of other characteristic styles not predominant in the work at hand.[12]

3. Structural tropes. These are the most implicit and ultimately the most powerful of hermeneutic windows. By *structural trope* I mean a structural procedure, capable of various practical realizations, that also functions as a typical expressive act within a certain cultural/historical framework. Since they are defined in terms of their illocutionary force, as units of doing rather than units of saying, structural tropes cut across traditional distinctions between form and content. They can evolve from any aspect of communicative exchange: style, rhetoric, representation, and so on.

The loose network of structural tropes operative at any given moment forms a kind of illocutionary environment in which expressive activities of all kinds go forth. Such a network forms an extension, in the expressive/hermeneutic sphere, of what Pierre Bourdieu calls the habitus of the social sphere: "systems of durable, transposable *dispositions*, structured structures predisposed to act as structuring structures, that is, as principles of the generation and structuring of practices and representations which can be objectively 'regulated' and 'regular' without in any way being the product of obedience to rules." The habitus, Bourdieu continues, enables us to form the strategies

---

12. For a discussion of this last type of citational inclusion, see Peter Rabinowitz, "Fictional Music: Toward a Theory of Listening," *Bucknell Review* 26 (1981): 193–208.

by means of which we cope with "unforeseen and ever-changing situations."[13]

For a simple example of a structural trope, consider the citation of one's own earlier work, which in nineteenth-century expressive practice often marks an important moment of reorientation. At the close of *Adonais* (1821), his elegy for Keats, Shelley tries to disentangle himself from "the web of being" and to fasten his desires on death. His success, if "success" is the word, turns on an allusion to his own "Ode to the West Wind":

> I.
> O wild West Wind, thou breath of Autumn's being,
> Thou, from whose unseen presence the leaves dead
> Are driven . . .
>
> V.
> Be thou, Spirit fierce,
> My spirit! Be thou me, impetuous one!
> Drive my dead thoughts over the universe
> Like withered leaves to quicken a new birth!
>
> ("West Wind," 1–3, 61–64)

> The breath whose might I have invoked in song
> Descends on me; my spirit's bark is driven
> Far from the shore, far from the trembling throng
> Whose sails were never to the tempest given;
> The massy earth and sphered skies are riven!
> I am borne darkly, fearfully afar.
>
> (*Adonais*, 487–92)

Condensed in the key words *breath*, *driven*, and *spirit*, the ode's language of rebirth returns as the elegy's language of death. Shelley's self-citation is almost penitential; it recants the text of what has come to seem false hope.

In his String Quartet in A Minor, D. 804 (1824), Schubert makes a similar, if less drastic, recantation. After an unsettled Allegro, the Andante seeks an idealized Biedermeier repose with the help of a

---

13. Pierre Bourdieu, *Outline of a Theory of Practice*, trans. Richard Nice (Cambridge, 1977), 72, 78.

melody borrowed from the incidental music to *Rosamunde*. The third movement then introduces a problematical counterquotation from Schubert's setting of Schiller's poem "Der Götter Griechenlands"—namely, the accompaniment to the line "Schöne Welt, wo bist du?" The force of this new quotation is both to acknowledge the unhappy destiny of all Biedermeier innocence and to withdraw, perhaps self-accusingly, from the illusion of a "schöne Welt" housed in the Andante. Schubert, however, is not quite ready to be borne darkly, fearfully afar. He qualifies his negative gesture with a dialectical irony by making the third movement a minuet—itself a relic of a "schöne Welt" gone by.[14]

Structural tropes operate freely across the entire cultural field. They act independently of received ideas about resemblances among various practices, discourses, and representations, and may even override obvious dissimilarities in style, scope, and context on behalf of shared ways of proceeding, of valuing, of presenting. They may or may not derive from the explicit vocabulary that a historical period uses about itself. Their structuring effect ranges from the local and fragmentary pinpointing of a structural perspective to the large-scale unfolding of a structural rhythm.[15] In their malleability and semantic openness, structural tropes implant the hermeneutic attitude within the object of interpretation itself. As latent hermeneutic windows with a diversity of cultural affiliations, they form something like the body language of an interpretive community.

Recognizing structural tropes is an empirical, even a catch-as-catch-can, matter: no formal discovery procedure is available for them. We can, however, formulate a few rules of thumb. Hermeneutic windows tend to be located where the object of interpretation appears—or can be made to appear—explicitly problematical. Interpretation takes flight from breaking points, which usually means from points of under- or overdetermination: on the one hand, a gap, a lack, a missing connection; on the other, a surplus of pattern, an extra repetition, an excessive connection. In some cases, our effort

---

14. The quotation in the minuet is identified by J. A. Westrup, "The Chamber Music," in *Music of Schubert*, ed. Gerald Abraham (1947; rpt. Fort Washington, N.Y., 1969), 93.

15. On structural rhythms, see my *Music and Poetry: The Nineteenth Century and After* (Berkeley and Los Angeles, 1984), 4–24, 229–30.

to turn these breaking points into sources of understanding may involve no more than reflection on the explicit expressive acts that are particular to the object. Structural tropes tend to appear, to be called on by the interpreter under one name or another, when we widen the scope of reflection: when, guided by the problem posed by the breaking point, we begin to play with analogies and recategorizations, seeking to throw light on one object by seeking out its multiple affiliations with others. The goal of this process, at least its ideal goal, resembles what the anthropologist Clifford Geertz calls a "thick description": an account of "a multiplicity of complex conceptual [read: expressive] structures, many of them superimposed upon or knotted into one another, which are at once strange, irregular, and inexplicit, and which [we] must contrive somehow first to grasp and then to render."[16] Structural tropes, actualized practically and experimentally during the interpretive process, emerge both as means and as ends in our approach to this mode of understanding.

A strategic map for musical hermeneutics might thus read more or less as follows:

1. Locate the hermeneutic windows of the work, starting with the most explicit (textual inclusions) and working up to the least explicit (structural tropes).

2. Identify the expressive acts found among or by means of these materials. Interpret the interplay of their illocutionary forces.

3. Ask whether the formal processes and stylistic articulations of the music can be said, either literally or figuratively, to exemplify the same or associated expressive acts. Interpret the interplay of illocutionary forces as a correlate—loose or tight, whatever seems practicable—of the interplay of musical forces. Where the music is linked to a text, treat the interplay of musical meaning as an appropriation and reinterpretation of the (already interpreted) textual meaning.

---

16. Clifford Geertz, *The Interpretation of Cultures* (New York, 1973), 10. Geertz takes the term *thick description* from Gilbert Ryle, "Thinking and Reflection" and "The Thinking of Thoughts," in *Collected Papers* (New York, 1971), 2:465–79 and 480–96, respectively.

14   *Tropes and Windows*

4. Connect the results to similar interplays elsewhere in the cultural field, freely allowing the activity of musical and nonmusical materials to comment on, criticize, or reinterpret each other as well as to repeat each other.

5. Perform these steps in any order and as often as you like, omitting any that you do not need. Avoid burdening the interpretive process itself with labels like "hermeneutic window" and "illocutionary force" except when there is little other choice. In fact, throw away this map before you use it.

The last step is not a joke, but a sober recognition of the character of interpretation. As I acknowledged earlier, hermeneutic theories can be very useful. Many flexible and powerful ones are available, from the Freudian system of condensations and displacements to the textual codes of Roland Barthes's S/Z. The usefulness of all such theories, however, including the one I have outlined in this chapter, depends on our according each particular theory only a provisional, implicit, occasional authority. To do otherwise leads merely to the conventionalized recycling of theoretical terms in concrete instances, and not to anything we can properly call interpretation. Real interpretation belongs decisively to the sphere of what has been called practical consciousness. However guided it may be by precept, it is learned only by example and performed only by applying tacit, unformalized knowledge to individual cases. The knowledge of how to interpret is social in its structure and origin, the product of a habitus. And such social knowledge, as Norman Bryson puts it, "cannot be abstracted from the situations in which it is revealed *in profiles*, that is, immanently within its contextual embodiment."[17]

Interpretation, accordingly, cannot be regimented, disciplined, or legislated—at least not successfully. As a practice, it is opportunistic, unruly, and contestatory, inescapably committed to both preserving and appropriating whatever it addresses. As nineteenth-century critical thought insisted, especially through the unholy trinity of Nietz-

---

17. Norman Bryson, *Vision and Painting: The Logic of the Gaze* (New Haven, 1983), 70. Bryson borrows the term *practical consciousness* from Raymond Williams, *Marxism and Literature* (Oxford, 1977), 35–42; *in profiles* is from Bourdieu, *Outline*, 18.

sche, Marx, and Freud, interpretation is intimately bound up with questions of power and desire. "Whatever exists," Nietzsche argues,

> having somehow come into being, is again and again reinterpreted to new ends, taken over, transformed and redirected by some power superior to it. . . . The entire history of a "thing," an organ, a custom can in this way be a continuous sign-chain of ever new interpretations . . . a succession of more or less profound, more or less mutually independent processes of subduing, plus the resistances they encounter, the attempts at transformation for the purposes of defense and reaction, and the results of successful counteractions. The form is fluid, but the "meaning" is even more so.[18]

An interpretation unhesitatingly seizes on any association, substitution, analogy, construction, or leap of inference that it requires to do its work. If it is guided by rules, then it partly makes up the rules as it goes along. Not for an idle reason does the term *hermeneutics* invoke the name of Hermes, the wing-shod messenger of Olympus and god of invention, cunning, and theft.

The inherently problematical character of interpretation is perhaps most evident in the paradox that while bad interpretations may be manifestly false, good interpretations can never be manifestly true. Unlike a true account of something, an interpretation can never exclude rival, incompatible accounts. For any given interpretation, an alternative always exists; as we have seen from Derrida's critique of Austin, the availability of alternatives is the very condition that makes interpretation possible. Lacking the power of exclusion, interpretations must convince by other means. My claim in this book is that they convince by their power to sustain a detailed scrutiny of a text that also reaches deep into the cultural context.

Again, unlike a true account, an interpretation cannot stabilize its key concepts—or if you prefer, cannot afford the illusion that concepts are stable in the first place. On the contrary: interpretation can only proceed by intensifying conceptual mobility, by tautening the associative threads between ideas to suggest relationships, by expanding the relationships between ideas to suggest equivalences, by prizing

---

18. Nietzsche, *On the Genealogy of Morals*, essay 2, sec. 12; from *"On the Genealogy of Morals" and "Ecce Homo,"* trans. Walter Kaufmann (New York, 1969), 77–78.

16   *Tropes and Windows*

apart equivalences to locate differences. In the terms provided by Kant's theory of music, we can state the case by saying that interpretation is the art of putting the concepts that Kant cherished into the *Gedankenspiel* that he mistrusted. And if Kant's description of musical *Gedankenspiel* has any credibility, we can even suggest that interpretation is an art modeled on the experience of music.[19]

None of which is to say—emphatically not—that interpretation must forgo all claims to be credible, scrupulous, and rational. What it does say is that these terms are susceptible to continual redefinition, continual transposition to unexpected planes of discourse. In order to present itself as knowledge amid so much volatility, interpretation must meet certain demands—demands for explanatory power, interconnectedness, telling detail, and honesty. Nor is that enough. Responsible interpretation also involves a principled refusal to monumentalize its own efforts, while at the same time sparing no efforts; a willingness to allow the object of interpretation its measure of resistance; a readiness to admit that interpretation, too, is an expressive act, urging truth claims—which is not the same as exhibiting the truth—while also exerting power or pressure on behalf of the interpreter's values.

This interpretive ethic is particularly important when we try to connect the object of interpretation to its cultural/historical situation; no enterprise is more vulnerable to the lure of monumentalization, the illusion that the wavering movement of meaning has been arrested at last. The danger here is to place too much restraint on the language and conceptual reach of the interpreter, as if doing so represents an allegiance to "objectivity" rather than the exercise of illocutionary coercion. A plausible alternative position might be built around Hans-Georg Gadamer's claim that all interpretation necessarily arises through a "fusion" of past and present "horizons" of meanings and presuppositions—though we might see this claim, too, as overidealizing, a rewriting of Nietzsche without Nietzsche's radicalism and risk-taking.[20]

---

19. The role of music, as heard, in providing a model for interpretation was not lost on Kant's contemporaries. For a discussion, see Kevin Barry, *Language, Music, and the Sign* (Cambridge, 1987).

20. Hans-Georg Gadamer, *Truth and Method*, ed. Garrett Barden and John Cumming, from the second German edition (1965) (New York, 1975). For a tren-

My own position was anticipated when, in point 4 of my hermeneutic roadmap, I urged the interpreter to allow musical and nonmusical materials to comment on, criticize, or reinterpret each other as well as to repeat each other. The implication is that we will quickly run aground if we treat the object of interpretation, in this case the music, merely as an instance of anterior claims or forces—merely, that is, as the reflection of some context, however thickly described. In order to release the energies of interpretation, the relationship between the object—call it the music—and its situation must be understood as dynamic. The music, as a cultural activity, must be acknowledged to help produce the discourses and representations of which it is also the product.

This principle is one of the cornerstones of what literary critics have taken to calling "the new historicism," an approach to literary and cultural history that conjoins elements of historicism, cultural materialism, and poststructuralism.[21] That is a large wad of isms, but for present purposes we can set them aside to focus on enabling principles—two in particular. First, the cultural field has no stable or privileged sites of meaning. Meaning is produced everywhere, and, like air or money, it circulates everywhere. Second, the works, practices, and activities—for us, the music—that we address as interpreters are not only the products but also the *agencies* of culture, not only members of the habitus but also makers of it. In recent years, important projects have been outlined for understanding music in its cultural/historical situation, notably by Joseph Kerman, Gary Tomlinson, and Leo Treitler.[22] My purpose in adding my voice to theirs

---

chant, if brief, critique of Gadamer's hermeneutics, see Terry Eagleton, *Literary Theory: An Introduction* (Minneapolis, 1983), 71–74.

21. The best overviews of the new historicism emerge from the field of Renaissance studies, where the new-historicist viewpoint is especially strong. See Louis Adrian Montrose, "Renaissance Literary Studies and the Subject of History," *English Literary Renaissance* 16 (1986): 5–12; Jean Howard, "The New Historicism in Renaissance Studies," *English Literary Renaissance* 16 (1986): 13–43; Jonathan Goldberg, "The Politics of Renaissance Literature: A Review Essay," *ELH* (*English Literary History*) 49 (1982): 514–42; and Edward Pechter, "The New Historicism and its Discontents: Politicizing Renaissance Drama," *PMLA* 102 (1987): 292–303.

22. Joseph Kerman, *Contemplating Music: Challenges to Musicology* (Cambridge, Mass., 1985); Gary Tomlinson, "The Web of Culture: A Context for Musicology," *Nineteenth Century Music* 7 (1984): 350–62; and Leo Treitler, *Music and the Historical Imagination* (Cambridge, Mass., 1989).

18   *Tropes and Windows*

is to urge that this understanding can proceed only if it proceeds in two directions.

"Grau . . . ist alle Theorie / Und grün des Lebens goldner Baum"— said Mephistopheles. This chapter has not paid much attention to particular works of music. The chapters that follow will make good the omission, but I would still like to conclude with one example, a kind of microcosm of musical hermeneutics in action. The example is a particularly suggestive one, in part because it represents a collaborative effort and in part because it focuses on a formal question that *must* receive a hermeneutic answer.

In his *Grande messe des morts*, Berlioz recapitulates the opening section of the Sanctus with a remarkable addition. Shortly after the recapitulation begins, soft strokes on the bass drum and cymbals, the latter allowed to vibrate, begin to set up polyrhythmic patterns and continue to do so until the end. The series of polyrhythms forms an independent, well-organized whole, as if an independent movement for percussion were being superimposed on the Sanctus, a portent of things to come in Elliott Carter. At first, the repetition of a single rhythmic pattern by the percussion articulates 5/2 against the basic 4/4 (mm. 3^3–23^2); next, the polyrhythms become irregular while the rhythmic pattern breaks down (mm. 23^3–33^3); finally, the repetition of a new rhythmic pattern articulates 3/2 against the basic 4/4 (mm. 33^3–47). The overall design is a lucid ABA: metrical regularity–metrical irregularity–metrical regularity reinterpreted.

What are we to make of all this? When I posed the same question to the members of a 1988 colloquium on music and narrative, some compelling answers came to the fore.[23] Reinhold Brinkmann heard the drum-and-cymbal music as a kind of *Klangfarbenmelodie*, something in keeping with Berlioz's exploitation of acoustic space in the Requiem. Anthony Newcomb seized on the fact that the bass drum and cymbals are military instruments, and suggested that the Sanctus incorporates military music in estranged or defamiliarized form, as if to subsume martial strife to religious peace. Christopher Reynolds recalled Beethoven's use of drums and cymbals in the finale of the

23. The conference, organized by Karol Berger and Anthony Newcomb, was held at Stanford University and the University of California at Berkeley in May 1988.

Ninth Symphony. Beethoven, like Berlioz, employs a solo tenor at this point, and does so to set a portion of Schiller's text that is remarkably pertinent:

> Froh, wie seine Sonnen fliegen
>> Durch des Himmels pracht'gen Plan,
>> Laufet, Brüder, eure Bahn.
> Freudig wie ein Held zum Siegen.[24]

The allusion reinforces both the spatial and the military resonance of Berlioz's percussion.

Once we put interpretive materials like this into play, we can also put them together, both with one another and with their formal environment. Take the environment first. The ABA pattern of the percussion "movement" suggests a process of gradual stabilization. The series of polyrhythms first lapses from and then recovers a state of metrical regularity. Moreover, the third part replaces a complex or irregular meter (5/2) with a simple meter (3/2)—a simple meter that can even be taken as an element of the complex one (5/2 = 2/2 + 3/2 in mm. 6–8^2, 16–18^2). And not to stop there, the 3/2 meter is articulated, as Edward T. Cone has observed, by twice-five repetitions of a basic group of three.[25] The five-beat grouping is stabilized by transposition to a higher structural level.

In the presence of so much dynamism, the spatial and military dimensions of this music demand to be understood as a process. The defamiliarization that Newcomb speaks of can be taken to increase as the drum-and-cymbal polyrhythms evolve from an immediate expressive effect to a superimposed "movement" with an autonomous structure. At the far end of this process lies Brinkmann's *Klangfarbenmelodie*: the subtilization of the sound of a military band into sound pure and simple. This sound, especially the swooshing vibration of the

---

24. Glad as His suns fly / Through the glorious order of Heaven, / Run your course, brothers, / Joyfully as a hero to victory.

25. Edward T. Cone, "Berlioz's Divine Comedy: The *Grande Messe des Morts*," *19th-Century Music* 4 (1980): 13–14. Cone understands the percussion "movement" as an instance of a disposition toward reinterpretation, toward the creation of multiple perspectives, that rules both the Mass and Berlioz's music as a whole. This reading is amply congruent with the others developed here. My thanks to Walter Frisch for drawing Cone's essay to my attention.

20   *Tropes and Windows*

cymbals, resonates through the huge performance space demanded by the Requiem—in the case of the premiere, the Church of St. Louis des Invalides in Paris, with its great amplitude and high dome. Thus employed, the performance space becomes an embodiment of the cosmic space invoked by Beethoven's Ninth. The order of the heavens is remapped in the architecture of the church, which on this occasion is also the order of public space and of state authority. (The Requiem was commissioned to commemorate the dead of the 1830 revolution but premiered instead as a memorial for a French general killed in Algeria.) Within the multiple valences of this space, the strife of the world is nullified and one is free to praise God in peace.

It now remains to bring the claims of this chapter to life in more detail, and more than once. I will pause only to risk a personal—or perhaps I mean a political—conjecture. It is scarcely a secret that the extraordinary value ascribed to music, and to the arts in general, during the nineteenth century has lost much of its credibility; not much survives except a certain quantity of impoverished rhetoric. Professional students of all the arts have been increasingly confronted with a sense of cultural marginalization, an unhappy awareness that their work is tolerated rather than encouraged by the academy and by society at large. One response to this state of affairs has been a retreat into ever more arcane languages of inquiry and ever more exclusionary specialities, a result that Nietzsche foresaw as early as the third essay of *On the Genealogy of Morals*. Yet there has also been a more affirmative response, particularly among literary critics. This has taken the form of developing communicative languages of inquiry that empower and even demand the breaking of disciplinary barriers, and of using those languages to (re)open—to discover, construct, provoke—a dynamic, dialogical relationship between cultural processes and cultural products. The growing interest in musical hermeneutics, without which this book could scarcely have been written, is a sign of this same affirmative development struggling to be born in humanistic studies. My purpose here is simply to assist in the birth.

CHAPTER 2

Decadence and Desire: The *Wilhelm Meister* Songs of Wolf and Schubert

The lyrics from Goethe's novel *Wilhelm Meister's Lehrjahren* haunted more than one generation of German composers. What Friedrich Schlegel called their "music and romantic enchantment" prompted important settings from Beethoven, Schubert, Schumann, and Wolf, among others.[1] Hugo Wolf's *Wilhelm Meister* songs are among his finest, but they are exceptional among his fifty-odd Goethe Lieder in one respect. Wolf ordinarily avoided setting texts by Goethe that had already been set by Schubert. The only other exceptions of consequence are *Prometheus, Ganymed*, and *Grenzen der Menschheit:* the trilogy of songs about mortal limits that closes Wolf's Goethe collection, as the trilogy of harper songs from *Wilhelm Meister* opens it.

The standard explanation for this state of affairs, established by Ernest Newman in the biography he published in 1907, three years after the composer's death, is that Wolf would not set a text if he felt that Schubert had set it effectively. Writing as a partisan, Newman takes up the cudgels to justify this practice. His Schubert, naively scribbling pieces in Viennese coffeehouses, failed to understand the psychopathology of Goethe's harper and Mignon, perhaps because he did not trouble to read Goethe's novel, or perhaps because of his inferior "general culture." He set the *Wilhelm Meister* lyrics "in a more or less mechanical

---

[1] Friedrich Schlegel, "On Goethe's Meister," trans. Peter Firchow, rpt. in *German Aesthetic and Literary Criticism: The Romantic Ironists and Goethe*, ed. Kathleen Wheeler (Cambridge, 1984), pp. 59–73; see p. 73.

way, vaguely sensing their underlying emotions but never realizing them in terms of music as profound as themselves. . . . [F]or him they were just pretty poems."[2] Where Wolf unerringly penetrates "into the very depth of Goethe's mood," poor Schubert fails "to get very far beneath the surface of it."[3]

The best of Wolf's later commentators—Frank Walker, Philip Radcliffe, Eric Sams, Mosco Carner—have not fallen into Newman's trap of crassly undervaluing Schubert in order to praise Wolf, but neither have they escaped Newman's frame of reference. The idea lingers that Wolf understood Goethe better than Schubert did, that his settings have a psychological penetration and intensity that Schubert's lack, that Wolf is sophisticated where Schubert is naive.[4] What is most problematical about this point of view is not that it misconceives Schubert, whose songs routinely triumph over the misconception from their place at the center of the repertoire. The real trouble with the critical tradition established by Newman is that it positively inhibits a productive understanding of the relationship between Schubert's and Wolf's settings of the same texts.

That relationship is my subject. My discussion will turn on three claims, all of which run counter to the standard account. First, no composer is responsible to the poet's sense of a text, much less to a commentator's sense of that sense. The composer appropriates the text and makes a song with it. The results need not be "true" to the poet—and rarely are; they need only be convincing on their own terms.[5] Second, Wolf's *Wilhelm Meister* songs are not simply attempts to best or dethrone Schubert's versions: they are attempts to revise or recompose what Schubert wrote. The two composers' songs are bound together dynamically, on both literary and musical planes of opposition. Wolf's songs could supplant Schubert's only at the cost of their own expressive value. Finally, Wolf's rewriting of Schubert's settings depends less on his "understanding"—that is, his interpretation—of particular texts than on his adherence to a culturally ascendent model of human personality that differs from Schubert's. Wolf's expressive differences from Schubert can no more be extricated from late nineteenth-century representations of the self than his purely musical differences can be extricated from the influence of Wagner.

The impetus for hearing a dynamic relationship between Wolf's and Schubert's shared Goethe settings comes from certain developments in literary criticism. In recent years, critics have increasingly concerned themselves with the ways in which literary texts repeat, revise, or reinterpret earlier texts, a situation covered broadly by the term "intertextuality." In the troubled and pluralistic world of contemporary criticism, there are almost as many theories of intertextual processes as there are critics. Texts may be studied through their implication in a variety of literary and cultural codes; through their repeated exposure of their own literariness and rhetoricity; or as vehicles of an Oedipal power-struggle between poets and their precursors.[6] For present purposes, I will simply assume without a *parti pris* that the expressive design of one work of art may include, and even found itself upon, a critical understanding of another. Following Paul de Man, I am persuaded that critical interpretation depends on the same rhetorical and expressive practices that are basic to works of art, so that creative activity and

---

[2]Ernest Newman, *Hugo Wolf* (London, 1907; rpt. New York, 1966), p. 196.
[3]Ibid., p. 192.
[4]Frank Walker, *Hugo Wolf: A Biography* (London, 1951); Philip Radcliffe, "Germany and Austria: The Modern Period," in *A History of Song*, ed. Denis Stevens (New York, 1960); Eric Sams, *The Songs of Hugo Wolf* (London, 1961); Mosco Carner, *Hugo Wolf: Songs* (London, 1982). Jack M. Stein's *Poem and Music in the German Lied from Gluck to Hugo Wolf* (Cambridge, Mass., 1971) should be mentioned here also, but only as a kind of nadir of the Newman tradition. Stein goes Newman one better and condescends to *both* Schubert and Wolf as interpreters of Goethe—thus making it impossible for him to interpret their settings.
[5]For detailed discussions of this issue, see Edward T. Cone, *The Composer's Voice* (Berkeley and Los Angeles, 1974); Steven Paul Scher, "Comparing Poetry and Music: Beethoven's Goethe-Lieder as Composed Reading," *Sensus Communis: Festschrift for Henry Remak* (forthcoming); and chapter 5 of my *Music and Poetry: The Nineteenth Century and After* (Berkeley and Los Angeles, 1984).
[6]These literary approaches may be exemplified, respectively, by Roland Barthes, *S/Z*, trans. Richard Miller (New York, 1974); Paul de Man, *Allegories of Reading: Figural Language in Rousseau, Nietzsche, Rilke, and Proust* (New Haven, 1979); and Harold Bloom, *The Anxiety of Influence* (New York, 1973).

critical understanding are inescapably entailed in each other.[7]

A Short History

Wolf's critical understanding of the Goethe songs that he found problematical in Schubert seems to pivot on Schubert's dramatization of the Romantic ego—the vital core of subjectivity that dominates both literature and philosophy in the first decades of the nineteenth century. According to the literary historian M. H. Abrams:

> In its central tradition Christian thought had posited three primary elements: God, nature, and the soul.... The tendency in innovative Romantic thought . . . is greatly to diminish, and at the extreme to eliminate, the role of God, leaving as the prime agencies man and the world, mind and nature, the ego and the non-ego, the self and the not-self, or (in the favorite antithesis of post-Kantian philosophers) subject and object.[8]

Two consequences of conceiving the subject in these terms concern us at present. The first is a celebration of inwardness in all its forms: memory, self-reflection, imagination, and desire, among others. Recalling his first conscious discovery of these things, Wordsworth writes:

>   Of genius, power,
> Creation and divinity itself,
> I have been speaking, for my theme has been
> What passed within me. Not of outward things
> Done visibly for other minds—words, signs,
> Symbols or actions—but of my own heart
> Have I been speaking, and my youthful mind.[9]

And Novalis, echoing Schiller, claims: "The highest task of education—is to master one's own transcendental self—and at the same time to be the Self of one's Self."[10]

Inwardness, however, also embraces the inwardness of pain. For the Romantic subject, intense mental suffering is as primary as the exhilarations of sentience, and it is equally capable of being idealized. Romantic writers frequently seek in guilt, grief, or despondency the evidence of what Wordsworth called "intellectual strength": an internalized heroism that engenders

> Sorrow that is not sorrow but delight,
> And miserable love that is not pain
> To hear of, for the glory that redounds
> Therefrom to human-kind and what we are.
>   —*The Prelude* (1805), XII, 245–48.

No matter how anguished it becomes, the Romantic ego retains a core of unity, resiliency, and latent power that limits its alienation and blocks its collapse.[11] The figure of Prometheus personified this "patient energy"—what Nietzsche called "the glory of passivity"—for Byron, Shelley, and Goethe. Its other archetypes include wanderers like Coleridge's ancient mariner; heroic artists who "learn in suffering what they teach in song";[12] and marginal figures who suddenly intrude on the eye: beggars, solitaries, obsessives, the silent, the emaciated.

The hurdy-gurdy man of Schubert's *Winterreise* is a marginal figure of this sort: an extreme one, through whom the patient energy of self travels to the border of annihilation. *Winterreise* enacts an ordeal that tests its wanderer-protagonist's ability to endure the endless symbolic repetition of his thwarted desire. In the final song, the almost insentient figure of the hurdy-gurdy man, with his empty cup and mechanical music, beckons toward a subjective void:

> Wunderlicher Alter, soll ich mit dir gehn?
> Willst zu meinen Liedern deine Leier drehn?
>
> (Strange old man, shall I go with you?
> Will your hurdy-gurdy turn to my songs?)

---

[7]See chapter 1 of de Man's *Allegories of Reading* and chapters 2 and 3 of his *Blindness and Insight: Essays in the Rhetoric of Contemporary Criticism* (New York, 1971).
[8]M. H. Abrams, *Natural Supernaturalism: Tradition and Revolution in Romantic Literature* (New York, 1971), p. 91.
[9]*The Prelude* (1805), III, 171–77. Cited from *The Prelude: 1799, 1805, 1850*, ed. Jonathan Wordsworth, M. H. Abrams, and Steven Gill (New York, 1979).
[10]From *Miscellaneous Writings*, trans. Joyce Crick, in *German Aesthetic and Literary Criticism*, p. 88. For the reference to Schiller (and Schiller's reference to Fichte!) see p. 239, n. 4.

[11]But not its death—the exemplary case of Goethe's Werther, Byron's Manfred, and many others, who die in order to affirm themselves.
[12]"Patient energy" is from Byron's *Prometheus*; Nietzsche's phrase is from his discussion of Goethe's *Prometheus* in *The Birth of Tragedy*, trans. Walter Kaufmann in Nietzsche, *The Birth of Tragedy and The Case of Wagner* (New York, 1967), pp. 69–70. "They learn in suffering what they teach in song" is from Shelley's *Julian and Maddalo* (l. 546).

As he sings these closing lines, the wanderer half-consciously opposes the question that they ask and finds a saving scruple of resistance to the lure of his nerveless double. For only here does he abandon the two-measure scraps of jingling melody that have so far matched his song to the mindless turning of the hurdy-gurdy.

As the nineteenth century wears on, however, the Romantic ego wears out. Werther becomes Emma Bovary; Faust turns into Ibsen's Master Builder. Increasingly, the inner resonances of both desire and suffering merge with intimations of solipsism, morbidity, and self-destructiveness. Looking back on the century from the mid-1880s, Nietzsche remarks on "that typical transformation of which G. Flaubert offers the clearest example among the French and Richard Wagner among the Germans, in which the romantic faith in love and the future is transformed into the desire for the nothing, 1830 into 1850."[13] The reflexive awareness, or irony, celebrated by German Romantics like Jean-Paul, Tieck, and Friedrich Schlegel, metamorphoses into a perverse and paralyzing self-consciousness. Thus Baudelaire, in *L'Héautontimorouménos* ("The Self-Tormentor"):

Ne suis-je pas un faux accord
Dans la divine symphonie,
Grâce à la vorace Ironie
Qui me secoue et qui me mord? . . .

Je suis la plaie et le couteau!
Je suis le soufflet et la joue!
Je suis les membres et la roue
Et la victime et le bourreau!

(Am I not a false accord in the divine symphony, thanks to the voracious Irony that shakes me and that gnaws at me? . . . I am the wound and dagger both! I am the slap, I am the cheek, I am the body and the rack and the victim and the torturer.)

Pain becomes a vocation; desire fastens increasingly on images of decline, the "passing sweetness / Of autumn splendor or a setting sun."[14]

---

[13] From *The Will to Power*, trans. Walter Kaufmann and R. J. Hollingdale, ed. Walter Kaufmann (New York, 1968), p. 66.
[14] Text of *L'Héautontimoroumenos* from the complete bilingual edn. of *Les Fleurs du mal: Flowers of Evil*, ed. Jackson and Marthiel Matthews (New York, 1955). "Passing sweetness": my translation from lines 27–28 of Baudelaire's *Chant d'automne*; text from the Matthews's edn.

232

When this devaluation of the ego is coupled with a certain masochistic pleasure, a heightened sensuousness, and a love for artifice, we can begin to speak of decadence: the ethos of Swinburne and Mallarmé, of Klimt and Beardsley, of unfocused eroticism and the archetypes of fatal desire, Salome and the Medusa. In turning now to a comparative account of some representative *Wilhelm Meister* settings by Schubert and Wolf—the harper trilogies and Mignon's *Nur wer die Sehnsucht kennt*—I will suggest that Wolf's critique of Schubert founds itself on the replacement of a Romantic by a decadent model of the self. Wolf's "Schubert" songs, typically for their composer, carry forward a process that begins in music with Wagner and culminates in the self-flagellations of Schoenberg's *Book of the Hanging Gardens* and Berg's *Lulu*.

THE HARPER TRILOGIES

Goethe's harper, the father by incest of Wilhelm Meister's ward, Mignon, is consumed by a remorse that he barely manages to sublimate in his songs, three of which apply covertly to his own sufferings. Goethe gave these songs an independent life by extracting them from the novel and rearranging them to form a lyric trilogy. Free of their narrative context, the poems break the grip of the harper's obsessions and enact an archetypal Romantic progression from self-alienation to self-mastery. *Wer sich der Einsamkeit ergibt* dwells on despair and a longing for death; *An die Türen will ich schleichen* seeks life again through the role of the Romantic wanderer and attains a degree of self-conscious detachment from the pathos that the wanderer evokes in others; *Wer nie sein Brot mit Tränen ass* voices a bitter but dignified accusation of the heavenly powers for their injustice to humanity.

Both Schubert and Wolf set the three poems as a group. Schubert ties them together by setting all three in the same key, A minor. Wolf is more tenuous—or attenuated: he closes the first song inconclusively over bare parallel fifths in the bass, then returns to the same texture as the third song closes a whole-step lower with a decisive full cadence. In the first version of *Gesänge des Harfners*, Schubert followed Goethe's lyric order, but then reversed the second and third songs for the final version, published as op. 12. The change freed him to reconceive Goethe's scenario of self-mastery as a movement toward resignation or stoical acceptance. He reads the *Meister* lyrics much as Friedrich Schlegel does, "as if their sorrow would tear our hearts in two, but this sorrow has the form, the tone, of some lamenting dignity."[15] Wolf, despite his apparent feeling that his settings refer to the half-mad harper of the novel, keeps strictly to the lyric order, but recasts it as a descent into an all-consuming rage of almost infantile ferocity. The disparity between Schubert and Wolf expresses itself most broadly through their tempos. Both composers write the whole harper sequence as slow music, but Schubert's pace quickens a little as the songs succeed each other, while Wolf's remains leaden from first to last.

Goethe's *Wer sich der Einsamkeit ergibt* begins in detachment and ends in despair:

Wer sich der Einsamkeit ergibt,
Ach! der ist bald allein;
Ein jeder lebt, ein jeder liebt,
Und lässt ihn seiner Pein.

Ja! lasst mich meiner Qual!
Und kann ich nur einmal
Recht einsam sein,
Dann bin ich nicht allein.

Es schleicht ein Liebender lauschend sacht,
Ob seine Freundin allein?
So überschleicht bei Tag und Nacht
Mich Einsamen die Pein,

Mich Einsamen die Qual.
Ach, werd' ich erst einmal
Einsam im Grabe sein,
Da lässt sie mich allein![16]

(He who devotes himself to solitude, ah! he is soon alone; everyone lives, everyone loves, and leaves him to his pain. Yes! leave me to my torment! And if I can once be truly solitary, [even] then I will not be alone. A lover steals up and listening seeks if his mistress is alone; so steals over me, night and day in my solitude, pain, in my solitude, torment. Ah! when one day I am solitary in the grave, then it will leave me alone!)

The first stanza portrays the solitary man as a pathetic figure alienated from the life and love that others enjoy. The succeeding stanzas, however, suggest that this alienation is precisely what the solitary desires—a desire the harper acknowledges as his own with the line, "Ja! lasst mich meiner Qual!" It is a desire condemned to frustration. Alone though he may be in a literal sense, the harper finds that his personified torment visits him in secret just as a lover visits his mistress. The presence of others cannot be refused: it reconstitutes itself in the deepest reaches of the self. The simile of the lover suggests that the harper feels the inevitable internalization of others as a sexual violation, an unwanted penetration of the ego, compelled by the alliance between life and love. The harper thus longs for the grave as that fine and private place where true solitude can be at last accomplished.

Goethe's harper, then, is less in flight from his suffering than from the sexualized presence of other selves. By contrast, the harper of Schubert's song wants only to be "left alone" by his unintermitted suffering. A solitary life only heightens his vexed self-awareness, so he turns for mitigation to the solitude of death, in which even sentience leaves one alone. The expressiveness of the song comes chiefly from the quasi-allegorical use it makes of its full cadences, which occur only on the words *Pein*, *Qual*, and *allein*, and which thus create a subtext that outlines the harper's essential conflict as Schubert recreates it.

The first half of the song seems to dramatize a reluctance on the harper's part to admit the reality of his suffering. The opening section divides into a pair of eight-measure periods, with regularly occurring full cadences at mm. 4, 8, and 12. The pain (*Pein*) of the pathetic solitary of the first stanza is referred to over the last of these. The torment (*Qual*) of the harper himself, however, disrupts the periodic rhythm. After a premature full cadence in m. 14, the harper's half perverse, half defiant demand to be left alone with his torment takes the form of an abrupt move onto VI through a local dominant substitute (mm. 15–16). Schubert's harper thus limits, even as he admits, his identification with the generalized figure of the solitary. *Seiner Pein* and *meiner Qual* become antonyms rather than synonyms: the one linked with closure, acceptance, the other with continuation, resistance.

---

[15] *German Aesthetic and Literary Criticism*, p. 73.
[16] Goethe's texts are taken from *Gedenkausgabe der Werke*, ed. Ernst Beutler (Zurich, 1949), I, 345.

In the measures that follow, the harmony becomes digressive. It first skirts the "painful" sonority of the tonic, then passes through it en route to a stronger cadence on VI (m. 25), which accompanies the first half of the simile of the lover. Only as he goes on to apply the simile to himself does Schubert's harper assume the burden of his own torment with a full cadence on the tonic at "mich einsamen die Qual" (m. 31). Heard *subito piano* (then *pianissimo*) after a rending *subito forte on Pein*, this cadence answers the submediant cadence at "Ja! lasst mich meiner Qual" (mm. 15–16) which had evaded the emotional truth and initiated the harmonic digression.

The remainder of the song finds a melancholy peace in the aftermath of this catharsis. Marked "mit leiserer Stimme," it dreams of an easeful death by drawing out the process of closure. In this section, lines of text are repeated for the first time, as if the harper were trying to invoke, to call forth, the mortal solitude that the lines envision. In the process, the cadential allegory of the song is brought to fulfillment. The section consists of two eight-measure periods followed by a brief piano postlude. Each period moves in four measures to a half cadence on the dominant at "im Grabe sein" (V at m. 35, V^6 at m. 43), and in four measures more to a perfect authentic cadence on the tonic closing the phrase "da lässt sie mich allein" (mm. 39, 47).

The relation between the terms singled out by the cadences could not be drawn more directly or simply: death is the dissonance that resolves in solitary rest.

Early in this passage (m. 36), "Da lässt sie mich allein" is set to a startling dissonant outburst that disturbs the gathering calm, and, before it subsides onto the dominant, gives an edge of desperation to the harper's wishful prophecy. But the music quickly hushes itself, and as it ebbs away the finality of the closing cadences merges increasingly with the longed-for finality of the grave. In the end, Schubert's harper sings himself to sleep.

Wolf's setting of *Wer sich die Einsamkeit ergibt* alludes to Schubert's in both detail and design without ever sounding like the earlier song. Like Schubert, Wolf begins with an arpeggiated piano prelude to evoke the sound of the harp and rounds back to the harmony of the prelude near the close; he culls his main accompaniment motif from a snatch of descending melody that Schubert dwells on briefly, then abandons (ex. 1); he even follows Schubert in giving Goethe's resentful "dann bin ich nicht allein" a wistful cast by ending the phrase on a somewhat incongruous cadence to a major key. There is also a parallel in the harmonic drama of the two songs. Like Schubert, Wolf sets "Ja! lasst mich meiner Qual" to an "alienated" harmony (G minor, the nominal tonic, as V of C mi-

a. Schubert, mm. 11–14 (piano only)

b. Wolf, mm. 1–2

Example 1

nor),[17] then finds an answering harmony at "mich Einsamen die Qual" (V^7/V in G minor), which thereupon marks a moment of self-recognition. The effect of these allusions is to incorporate a critical awareness of Schubert into Wolf's expressive design. They establish Wolf's differences from Schubert as explicit acts of revision, and even, as it turns out, of admonishment. The setting of "mich Einsamen die Qual" forms the turning point in this process. Wolf has the voice close this phrase with a sickening descent of a tritone, the most wrenching vocal discontinuity in the song. In so doing, he contradicts the cathartic effect of the cadence with which Schubert sets the same words, and intimates the grim conclusion that the harper's pain can never be mastered.

Wolf's large expressive purpose in *Wer sich die Einsamkeit ergibt* is to revoke the peace of mind that Schubert's harper achieves through the contemplation of his death. Wolf's harper may look forward to oblivion, but he is nonetheless condemned to go on living. His longing for the grave can do nothing to still his unrest: in the final analysis, it *is* that unrest.

Like Schubert, Wolf makes a quasi-allegorical use of full cadences on the tonic to dramatize the harper's quest for assuagement, but his cadential pattern forms a studied antithesis to Schubert's. Of the four full cadences on G minor in Wolf's song, the first two are only fictitiously tonic; their G minor functions as the dominant minor of C minor, which acts throughout as a polar or shadow tonic. As ex. 2 shows, this splitting of the song into competing tonics is the process that calls forth the entry of the voice. The G-minor Neapolitan sixth of m. 1 becomes a German sixth of C minor through the addition of a G♭, so that the cadence at m. 6 hovers somewhere between V^7–i in G minor and V^7/V-v in C minor. This splitting, which is reenacted in mm. 11–14,[18] represents Wolf's version of decadent irony: the quasi-masochistic anguish of a personality that has divided itself into the roles of victim and torturer.

The third G-minor cadence emerges as the harper's thoughts first turn toward the grave. Evolving from a much-prolonged dominant (mm. 18–29, with digressions), the cadence seeks to recover Schubert's association of the peace of death with the release of harmonic tension, but it quickly leads to a reprise of the clash between G minor and C minor (ex. 3). Only with the setting of the last line of text, "Da lässt sie mich allein," is there an uncontested tonic cadence on G minor. As the voice "dies away"—Wolf marks it *ersterbend*, a wishful expansion on Schubert's "leiserer Stimme"—something like peace, repose, release, seems to have been won. Indeed, it is only at this point that the vocal and harmonic cadences coincide, as if the voice finally had made the harmonic repose its own; earlier, the vocal line has either anticipated or followed cadential harmonies.

And then Wolf subverts the whole labor of assuagement with a single stroke. The brief piano postlude seems intent upon echoing the dying fall of the consummating cadence, as Schubert's postlude does. The last two measures, however, intrude the hollow sounds of their parallel fifths and close unexpectedly on the dominant. The music breaks off in the unsatisfied anticipation of a death that lies forever in the future.

The rest of the harper's songs, both Schubert's and Wolf's, steadily work out the emotional logic of the first. Schubert's *Wer nie sein Brot mit Tränen ass* is an unusually protracted song, especially given the brevity of the text, which is matched by Schubert's two earlier settings of it. Schubert requires these antiheavenly lengths in order to play out the drama of the text

---

[17] Wolf's harmony in this passage requires some comment. Mm. 13–14 seem to articulate a full cadence to G minor, but the passage is governed by the German sixth of C minor, which occupies mm. 11³–12, and persists, respaced, through 13¹. (In this context, the D^7 at 13³⁻⁴ becomes a version of the supertonic chord from which the augmented sixth theoretically derives.) Wolf thus evokes the normal expectation for a G-major chord as V, probably preceded by i$^6_4$ of C minor. By moving to V/V and cadencing on G minor, however, he gives the G minor sonority a credible but illusory tonic feeling. If the chord is played in the major, its dominant quality becomes obvious. Another way to understand this passage is to say simply that a tonic G minor appears where a dominant G major is expected. G minor, however, receives no immediate confirmation as a tonic, and turns to a clear G-major dominant in m. 15, followed by a C-minor cadence in m. 16. I prefer to think of the G minor in m. 14 as a purely fictitious tonic; but on either account the G-minor chord comes out sounding defamiliarized, not quite right, and that is what counts in the expressive design of the song.

[18] See fn. 17.

Example 2

Example 3

as an internal rather than an external conflict. Goethe's harper accuses the "heavenly powers" of crassly making guilt the basis of human life:

Ihr führt ins Leben uns hinein,
Ihr lasst den Armen schuldig werden,
Dann überlasst ihr ihn der Pein:
Denn alle Schuld rächt sich auf Erden.

(You lead us into this life, you let the wretched one grow guilty, then you abandon him to pain: for all guilt calls forth its retribution upon earth.)

Schubert is less concerned with the moral force of this accusation than with the psychology of defying a higher power. The gods of Schubert's harper have their power only in the harper's reverence for them; in Freudian terms, they personify the punitive excesses of his own superego.[19] The song, we might say, unfolds not in textual time but in psychological time.

Schubert's design for *Wer nie sein Brot mit Tränen ass* consists of four variations on a single dramatic gesture, followed by a long coda. The gesture is a crescendo of protest at divine injustice which is abruptly curtailed by a terse decrescendo or a *subito piano*. The first three curtailments also coincide with an abrupt cadential turn from minor to major harmony—a Picardy third. This feature has been much criticized as blandly inappropriate to the text.[20] Assuming that Schubert knew what he was doing, however, it makes expressive sense to take the Picardy thirds as gestures of self-restraint. The major cadences block the anger of the crescendos, perhaps with awe, perhaps with a mechanical but psychologically useful expression of piety. The fourth and most powerful crescendo brings with it the harper's climatic outcry, "alle Schuld," set to a wrenchingly discontinuous harmony that just happens to be in the tonic (ex. 4: A♭ major, approached abruptly from B♭ minor, left unrationalized, and given dominant support in mm. 49–50, is reinterpreted enharmonically as G♯, the leading tone to the tonic, on the downbeat of m. 51). This crescendo curtails itself all the way to triple *piano* without the Picardy third, as if the harper's resurgent outrage had again brought catharsis, as it did in *Wer sich der Einsamkeit ergibt*. Schubert's harper can now gravely accuse the gods of injustice without raising his voice, at peace with himself if not with them. The coda, which restores the Picardy third but omits the crescendo, bears out this impression, but the brief piano postlude reveals the effort of self-denial or of repression that underlies this final calm. The song closes with violently dissonant appoggiaturas that resolve only with the greatest reluctance onto the major triad (ex. 5).

Schubert achieves a less problematical calm in *An die Türen will ich schleichen*, a simple, dignified, wholly untortured song. Marked *Mässig, in gehender Bewegung*, the music envelops its melancholy in an aura of resignation by means of steady quarter-note motion in the accompaniment and a sustained *piano* dynamic that only rarely admits dramatic accents, and those modest ones. In modified strophic form, with a simple melody of markedly narrow compass, the song is a candid evocation of the *Volkston*. The harper of Goethe's lyric sequence reenters the social world as a kind of holy fool who makes others feel fortunate wherever he wanders, and who wanders everywhere. Schubert's harper makes a far fuller reconciliation: he returns as the archaic, anonymous voice of communal experience itself.

To an unfriendly critic, the resignation won by Schubert's harper might seem no more than a rationalization of passivity, his stoicism a thinly veiled moral failure. That view is implicitly Wolf's, whose harper's protest against the gods in *Wer nie sein Brot mit Tränen ass* rises to an operatic triple *forte* over ponderous two-hand chords that compete for audibility even with the baritone's loud upper register. The outcome for Wolf's harper, however, is neither catharsis nor defiant grandeur but paralysis. The burden of his song is not the Promethean power of moral outrage but its Job-like futility.

Wolf approaches *Wer nie sein Brot mit Tränen ass* by way of a bleak, almost featureless setting of *An die Türen will ich schleichen*, which reduces that detachment from pathos characteristic of Goethe's and Schubert's harpers to a frozen insensibility. The first half of *Wer nie sein Brot mit Tränen ass* allows the harper's feelings to reawaken; the second half releases them into uninhibited rage. At Goethe's accusatory, "Ihr himmlischen Mächte," Wolf alludes to the Picardy third with which Schubert sets the same phrase, though Wolf's unexpected major chords are dominants. The prospect of Schubertian restraint, however, is rejected as soon as it arises. Wolf's crescendo of protest begins over a series of rumbling arpeggios and reaches a first climax as the arpeggios give way to chordal attacks, as if the harper were too distraught to command his instrument. (It may not

---

[19] As one who always tries to yield to Freudian temptations, I should point out the classically Oedipal character of cruelly paternal gods who usher one into life and leave one to incur a primal guilt. My sense is that Schubert's song makes more of this latent textual element than Goethe does.

[20] Newman (p. 196) speaks of the "complete obscuring of Goethe's meaning"; Walker (p. 241) suggests that Schubert misunderstood the text and wrote as if "the singer were finding reconciliation to his fate in the knowledge it has brought him of the heavenly powers."

[Example 4: musical notation with text "ü-ber-lasst ihr ihn der Pein, denn al- le Schuld rächt sich auf"]

Example 4

[Example 5: musical notation]

Example 5

[Example 6: musical notation with text "dann ü-ber-lasst ihr ihn der Pein: denn al- le Schuld rächt sich auf Er- den." with harmonic analysis: eb: V$^4_2$ i^6 VI^6 N^6 / f: vii$^5\natural$ vii$^{°7}$ i^6 N^6 V]

Example 6

be fanciful to hear in this a distant echo of Schubert's *Gretchen am Spinnrade*, with its famous suspension of the spinning figure at Gretchen's climactic outburst.) Harshly declaimed, the outcry consummates itself as Schubert's does, with an unexpected, indeed a wrenching, return to the tonic (ex. 6). Unlike Schubert's, however, this tonic finds no cadential confirmation until the last measure of the song. Harmonically enervated, it undercuts the expression of rage that it accompanies.

Then, while the harmony hovers somewhere

in a limbo between iv and V^7, the piano postlude quickly sinks from *ff* to *p* and enters onto a plane of complete immobility. The melodic cadence of the main accompaniment figure begins to stammer; it fails to complete itself three times in the space of two measures. The sudden decrescendo is a recreation of Schubert's gesture of restraint, but in Wolf it becomes a consummate musical image for paralysis, exhaustion, utter dejection. Even the closing cadence, harmonically decisive though it may be, has an alienated sound to it, thanks to the parallel fifths that link it to the bleak close of *Wer sich die Einsamkeit ergibt*.

NUR WER DIE SEHNSUCHT KENNT

Goethe's Mignon is bound to Wilhelm Meister by half filial, half erotic feelings that she is incapable of understanding but is continually expressing. In one of the novel's most startling episodes, she acts out the racking ambivalence and need for repression that Wilhelm elicits from her:

He raised her up, and she fell upon his breast; he pressed towards him, and kissed her. . . . All at once [she] gave a cry, which was accompanied by spasmodic movements of the body. She started up, and immediately fell down before him, as if broken in every joint. . . . All at once she again became quite stiff, like one enduring the sharpest corporeal agony; and soon with a new vehemence all her frame became alive; and she threw herself about his neck, like a bent spring that is closing. . . . Her rigid limbs were again become relaxed; her inmost soul was pouring itself forth; in the wild confusion of the moment, Wilhelm was afraid she would dissolve in his arms.[21]

The barely suppressible violence of Mignon's desires also forms the essential subject of her song, *Nur wer die Sehnsucht kennt*, which she sings in the novel as a duet with the harper:

Nur wer die Sehnsucht kennt,
Weiss, was ich leide!
Allein und abgetrennt
Von aller Freude,
Seh ich ans Firmament
Nach jener Seite.

Ach! der mich liebt und kennt
Ist in der Weite.
Es schwindelt mir, es brennt
Mein Eingeweide.
Nur wer die Sehnsucht kennt,
Weiss, was ich leide!

(Only the one who knows longing knows what I suffer. Alone and cut off from all joy, I gaze at the sky yonder. Ah! he who loves and knows me is far away. It makes me dizzy, it burns my bowels. Only the one who knows longing knows what I suffer.)

The poem pivots on the sudden extravagance of Mignon's rhetoric at "es schwindelt mir, es brennt / Mein Eingeweide." The abrupt rise in intensity corresponds to an abrupt shift of focus from outer to inner reality, from distance and absence to vertigo and a burning in the bowels. Mignon's longing threatens to become insupportable when it "swindles" her thoughts away from the person she longs for and turns them on herself.[22] For both Schubert and Wolf, the main expressive issue in setting *Nur wer die Sehnsucht kennt* is how to realize the rhetorical discontinuity of "Es schwindelt mir, es brennt / Mein Eingeweide" in musical terms. Schubert tried four times in 1815–16 to find a solution, evidently without feeling that he had succeeded; the canonical version of the song, published as op. 62, no. 4 (D. 877), was not composed until 1826.

For most of its course, Schubert's *Nur wer die Sehnsucht kennt* is *sotto voce* music of utter simplicity. The seven measures devoted to a double statement of "Es schwindelt mir, es brennt / Mein Eingeweide," however, are incommensurate with the rest. The voice shifts from melody to declamation and abandons its steady *pianissimo* for a dramatic swell; the gently rocking accompaniment suddenly turns agitated, and the limpid harmony travels ambiguously through a series of diminished-seventh chords before subsiding onto the dominant.[23] Without actually changing tempo, meter, or underlying harmony, Schubert forms a gripping musical image of self-alienation.

---

[21]Goethe, *Wilhelm Meister's Apprenticeship*, trans. Thomas Carlyle (New York, 1962), p. 144.

[22]"Es schwindelt mir": it makes me dizzy. "Schwindeln": to swindle, defraud.
[23]The actual progression is vi–V^7/V–V; the intervening dissonances are constructed on a bass that rises by semitones.

The psychological drama of the song turns on the ability of Schubert's Mignon to make peace with her suffering. As she declaims her climactic phrase for the first time, she yields to a crescendo, only to curtail it as it rises above *forte* at "Eingeweide." Then she repeats her phrase decrescendo with scarcely a pause for breath. In context, this gesture could suggest either self-mastery or exhaustion, an uncertainty that Schubert plays out in harmonic terms (ex. 7). Mignon's second "Eingeweide" comes to rest as the music casts off its mystification and arrives on the dominant. The voice falls on G♯, the third of the dominant chord, in a melodic cadence that is, and is meant to be, remarkably unsatisfying. The unsettled feeling persists for two measures as a terse piano interlude extends the dominant harmony, ending with a fermata on the dominant-seventh chord. In the resolution that follows, the voice both revives the cantabile line of the refrain, "Nur wer die Sehnsucht kennt, / Weiss, was ich leide," and restores simplicity and stability to the harmony. The refrain begins as the voice rises a half-step from the G♯ of "Eingeweide" onto the root of the tonic chord—which is to say, as the voice resolves the G♯ upwards as the leading tone. In dramatic terms, this deferred release of harmonic tension enacts a moment of self-integration. Mignon's pain may not be assuaged—it sounds again through a brief swell on the last "Sehnsucht kennt"—but it can no longer threaten to annihilate her.

Fortunately, Schubert's Mignon was not dealing with Hugo Wolf. The revisionary effort of Wolf's *Nur wer die Sehnsucht kennt* is to abrogate the moment of recovery at the center of Schubert's song. Like Schubert's, Wolf's Mignon declaims her climactic phrase to a crescendo in harmonically unstable surroundings. Wolf's crescendo, however, is completed, not curtailed, and his harmony—a chain of augmented triads that continues almost uninterrupted for eleven measures—is not merely uncertain but genuinely indeterminate. The quiet simplicity that dominates Schubert's song posits a world of common feeling in which Mignon's pain, however fierce and however inward, is anchored. Here the anchor is missing. Everything is edged toward an extreme, even in register; the piano does not descend more than a third below middle C until the closing measures. Tempo, too, is unstable; it changes continuously until the return of the refrain.

Following Schubert, Wolf silences the voice after "Eingeweide," but with a telling difference. Wolf's piano interlude lasts for a full twelve measures in constantly retarding tempo. The passage is marked "allmählich ruhiger werden," but as with the curtailed crescendo in Schubert's setting the effect is ambiguous. The gradually but unevenly ebbing music might suggest a slow recovery of composure in the aftermath of a catharsis, or it might suggest mere enervation, a sinking away into a deathly stupor, as if Wolf's Mignon had been actually consumed, deprived of a voice, by the force of her own longing. The gloomier interpretation owns the margin of preference, not only because the interlude is so drawn out, but because the harmony does not clarify itself as the interlude proceeds. When the chain of augmented triads

Example 7

[Example 8: musical notation with markings "Etwas bewegt", "etwas zurückhaltend", "p", "rit.", "pp", and chord labels Ab⁶, Bb⁷, eb]

Example 8

is broken, the harmony slowly progresses onto a remote dominant-seventh chord that turns out to herald the return of the voice. But the voice does not resolve the dominant seventh: far from it.[24]

What the voice does do is to immobilize the music on the home dominant, where the close comes a few measures later without so much as a half cadence. The dominant: the very sonority that Schubert's Mignon resolves in order to appropriate her desire as a bearable torment.

This dominant ending is not obvious from a casual look at the score, though its debilitating effect is plain enough to the ear. Wolf's song is written with a key signature of G minor, but the one thing it lacks is a G-minor cadence. As ex. 8 shows, the song begins in a tonal fog with an unanchored A♭⁶ chord, then cadences into E♭ minor from B♭⁷. This cadential progression remains the primary point of tonal orientation amid much coloristic sonority until the chain of augmented triads that begins with "Es schwindelt mir" effaces all tonal bearings. When the music eventually closes on D major, the supporting details make it clear that Wolf intends the song as a whole to be heard as a large-scale progression from the submediant to the dominant of G minor. As ex. 9 shows, the closing refrain and the piano postlude rationalize what has been heard earlier. The mysterious A♭⁶ chord is reinterpreted as a Neapolitan sixth; the E♭ minor that pervades the first half of the piece is reprised as E♭ major, the unaltered sixth degree of G minor; and the D-major chords of the postlude appear as extensions of the D⁷ that emerges as the voice brings the refrain to a close.

The effect of this dominant ending is far more frustrating than the abrupt dominant close of *Wer sich die Einsamkeit ergibt*. Supported by its expressive detail—an almost nonexistent melodic cadence in the voice; the long-deferred descent of the piano part into the bass registers—this music bespeaks the disintegration of personality that follows upon a desire that is at once idealized and thwarted. Yet the disintegration is not without a certain seductiveness. The attenuated harmony, long drawn out, evokes a sensuous weariness that is far from the tone of Goethe, but very much that of the Symbolist and Pre-Raphaelite poets who flourished after mid century:

> Stand still, fond fettered wretch! while Memory's art
>   Parades the past before thy face, and lures
>   Thy spirit to her passionate portraitures:
> Till the tempestuous tide-gates flung apart
> Flood with wild will the hollows of thy heart,
>   And thy heart rends thee, and thy body endures.
>   —Dante Gabriel Rossetti, *Parted Love*.[25]

POSTLUDE IN LIEU OF A CONCLUSION

In his *Interpretation of Dreams*, Freud discusses a dream that alludes to Hugo Wolf. The dreamer is identified only as a woman of Freud's acquaintance, but I assume that she was a daughter of Freud's early collaborator, Josef Breuer, some of whose children were Wolf's devoted pupils in the early 1880s. In the dream, a

---

[24] The same discontinuity accompanies an earlier return of the opening at m. 26, the non-resolving dominant seventh being first introduced at m. 21, then prolonged.

[25] Text from *The Pre-Raphaelites and Their Circle*, ed. Cecil B. Lang (Chicago, 1975), p. 103.

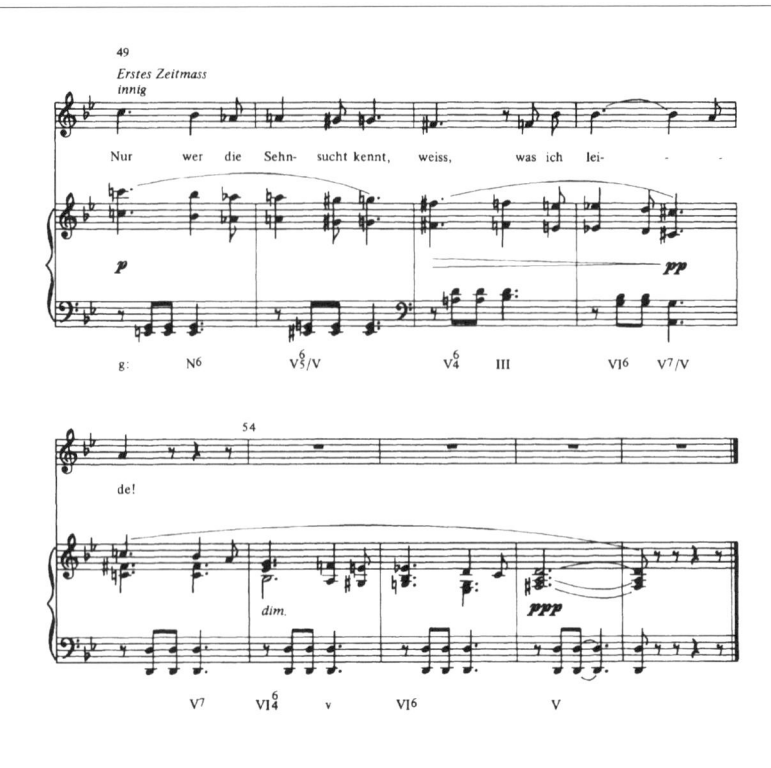

[Example 9: musical score excerpt, "Nur wer die Sehnsucht kennt, weiss, was ich leide!" with harmonic analysis]

Example 9

man with the features of Hans Richter paces back and forth in a violent sweat on the caged-in top of a tower. He is trying to conduct a Wagner opera that has lasted all night. Freud is able to identify the man as Wolf, and he gives a fascinating account of the dream as an expression of the dreamer's predicament.[26] It is also, however, an expression of Wolf's predicament, an astute insight from a pupil who has once loved her teacher. What we have here is a rare opportunity to turn a psychoanalytic dream analysis into music criticism.

The man of the dream is a consummate image for Wolf's harper or Mignon or the persona of dozens of his songs, or, indeed, for Wolf himself. Distraught, harried, a failure on the tower of potency who cannot get the opera done before dawn, a man unable to be himself, to wear his own features, yet someone still trapped by his own identity—the cage that encloses the Wolf: the portrait is recognizable at once. It is a portrait, however, that fits a generation, several generations, and not a man. Wolf recomposed Schubert as he did, not because Wolf's poetic insight was superior—it was not: it was just more articulate—but because he was a man of the late century who had to make music from the top of that tower.

---

[26]Sigmund Freud, *The Interpretation of Dreams*, trans. James Strachey (New York, 1965), pp. 377–79.

CHAPTER 3

Dangerous Liaisons: The Literary Text in Musical Criticism

The field of comparative studies in music and literature is still struggling to be born, or perhaps even to be conceived. The recent interest that musicologists have so strikingly taken in literary criticism is largely methodological, which is perhaps as it should be: the literary field has developed over the past few decades into a methodological gold mine, and the proper object of musical criticism is, after all, music.[1] Extended comparative studies of musical and literary works are still rare; good ones are downright scarce.

Even when a good study does appear, an adequate context for its reception may be lacking. Take the case of "The Double Trajectory: Ambiguity in Brahms and Henry James," by Roland Jordan and Emma Kafalenos (this issue, pp. 129–144). The authors make the intriguing argument that James's story, "Owen Wingrave," and Brahms's Intermezzo, op. 119, no. 1, are alike in their use of systematic ambiguity. Each work is said to project two competing structural patterns throughout, and thus to form a "double trajectory" that allows "a high degree of instability [and density] in a form that still remains closed" (p. 143). What are we to make of this comparison? However intriguing, a resemblance between James and Brahms does not tally conveniently with our customary ways of understanding either man. Perhaps the resemblance is a special case, or perhaps it represents no more than a *jeu d'esprit* on the authors' part.

These uncertainties offer a prime opportunity to weigh the prospects of a musical/literary criticism—something we might call melopoetics. What, if anything, can the tandem reading of musical and literary works have to offer the critical study of music? What methods must we use to carry out such readings credibly? And what standards must a tandem reading meet in order to count as critically adequate? In what follows, I will try to answer these questions, last to first, using "The Double Trajectory" as a test case.[2]

---

[1] On the possibilities opened up for musical criticism and theory by this methodological enrichment, see my forthcoming *Music as Cultural Practice, 1800–1900* (Berkeley and Los Angeles, 1990).

[2] For an overview of melopoetics, see Steven Paul Scher, "Literature and Music," in *Interrelations of Literature*, ed. Jean-Pierre Baricelli and Joseph Gibaldi (New York, 1982), pp. 225–50. Calvin S. Brown's *Music and Literature: A Comparison of the Arts* (1948; rpt. Hanover, N.H., 1988), is useful in some respects but badly dated.

I. Problems of Adequacy

Jordan and Kafalenos succeed in observing a basic standard of comparative criticism that is more often honored in the breach. Their commentary demands serious consideration both as musical criticism and as literary criticism; each half of their analysis can claim to hold up in its own right, apart from the context of the comparison.

This tenability, it is important to add, does not depend on one's agreement with the authors. They would be the first to admit that both "Owen Wingrave" and the Brahms Intermezzo can be read in other terms than theirs. The tenability of their study, indeed, survives even if one disputes some of their cardinal points. Measure 16 of the Brahms, for example, ends with an important F♯-major chord. For Jordan and Kafalenos, the chord forms an *ad hoc* Picardy third that closes out a dominant-minor episode. We might argue, however, that the chord is a real, if reticent, dominant of B minor, especially given the symmetrical spacing of similar dominants in mm. 4 and 8. Similarly, we might argue on the literary side that the authors are subject to the same criticism that James made of George Bernard Shaw: in both of their narrative trajectories for "Owen Wingrave" they simplify the apparently supernatural element of the text, beg too many interpretive questions about the retributive ghost and the white-faced young man who expires in the patriarchal bedroom. Even to make these objections, however, is to enter into dialogue with the authors on terms that they have set successfully. It is not to deny but to reconsider the underemphatic, almost furtive, character of Brahms's dominant, the uncanny ambivalence of James's ending.

In the present context, then, "The Double Trajectory" takes its primary value not from any particular claim that it makes, but from the order of discourse that it establishes. The authors may be contested, but they cannot be dismissed. As a term of comparison—a Horrible Example that will also prove useful later on—consider some remarks from a relatively recent study of the operatic character of Shelley's verse drama, *Prometheus Unbound* (1819). The passage begins with a quotation:

The Earth. Howl, Spirits of the living and the dead,
Your refuge, your defense, lies fallen
and vanquished.

First Echo. Lies fallen and vanquishéd?

Second Echo. Lies fallen and vanquishéd! (II, 185–87).

"Cadencing on the artificially stressed final syllable," we read,

the naturally rising intonation of the first echo's question is answered by the descending scale of the second's confirmatory statement. There is an urge toward symmetry and completion in these lines reminiscent of the balanced phrases of classical sonata form. Later in the act, the Furies' chorus is balanced by a Chorus of Spirits who enter with a decisive triple rhyme, like an opening chord in Beethoven.[3]

Writing of this order invites a quick dismissal: Ah, those decisive opening chords in Beethoven! As in the First Symphony, for instance? A more sober assessment would note that neither Beethoven nor the "descending scale" adds anything substantive to the description of Shelley's text; the terms are simply trotted out to signify the presence of musicality. As for symmetrical phrasing between the echoes, the echo scheme that Shelley uses here is a traditional poetic device; its *locus classicus* appears in Ovid's *Metamorphoses*. The echo scheme does have musical associations, but they are not Classical. Shelley probably never heard of them: echo madrigals were composed during the sixteenth and early seventeenth centuries, and there are numerous echo scenes in seventeenth-century opera.[4]

What are the hallmarks of the order of discourse that Jordan and Kafalenos establish as opposed to its counterpart in the Horrible Example? Jordan and Kafalenos, assenting to a model I proposed in my book *Music and Poetry*, set their agenda with a pair of critical moves. They first remark that "Owen Wingrave" and the Brahms Intermezzo are obviously incommensurate on a semantic level: "the Intermezzo is not a statement on courage and honor"

---

[3] Ronald Tetreault, "Shelley at the Opera," *English Literary History* 48 (1981), 157–58. This essay does provide a useful survey of Shelley's interest in opera, with emphasis on the operas of Mozart. For a more sophisticated treatment of phrase-rhythm in music and literature, see David Michael Hertz, *The Tuning of the Word: The Musico-Literary Poetics of the Symbolist Movement* (Carbondale, Ill., 1987).
[4] My account here is indebted to John Hollander, *The Figure of Echo: A Mode of Allusion in Milton and After* (Berkeley and Los Angeles, 1981), pp. 23–24.

160

(p. 130), nor, one might add, on anything else; it is very absolute music. (This incongruity, however, does not foreclose all semantic issues—issues that will concern us later.) The authors go on to search for analogies based on the combination of structural elements into coherent sequences. To use the language of *Music and Poetry*, they look for a convergence of text and music at this level, the level of "parallel structures on the combinatory axis" ("Double Trajectory," p. 131).

So far, so good. Yet one might say that the Horrible Example, however naively, also looks for combinatory parallels, e.g., between Shelley's echo-scheme and the phrase-structure of the Classical style in music. What *else* are Jordan and Kafalenos doing? The answer may be suggested by what seems initially to be the play impulse, the sheer wit, in the authors' study. For "Owen Wingrave" and the Brahms Intermezzo do not merely fail to resemble each other on a semantic level: they fail to resemble each other on any obvious level at all. A coy Jamesian ghost story and a gently brooding mood-piece by Brahms: what a preposterous pair! The analogy between these works does not merely occupy a combinatory level; it is combinatory on a deep-structural level. It will be necessary to define this level further, but for the moment we can simply stress one of its defining features. A deep structure is a combinatory pattern that may be actualized in forms that do not resemble each other on the surface. Hence the syntagmatically equivalent sentences suggested by Jordan and Kafalenos: "The cat scratches an antique chair" and "The pianist plays a difficult sonata."

The witty preposterousness of bringing together "Owen Wingrave" and the Brahms Intermezzo thus turns out to be a genuine necessity. Jordan and Kafalenos had to frame an argument that would make the lack of any manifest analogy between the two works an affirmative force: a reason to be persuaded by the argument for deep-structural convergence. To achieve this, they had to show in detail that each work actualizes the deep structure in idiosyncratic terms, the terms appropriate to a literary text on the one hand and a musical composition on the other. The structure is the same, but the means of actualizing it are entirely different. Furthermore, the means would be just as different if we were dealing with works somehow similar in mood or genre. This last point may bring us back to our Horrible Example, which is so horrible precisely because it looks for manifest analogies in the absence of deep-structural convergence. The Horrible Example supposes that a sea-horse is a horse.

In general, then, we can posit that tandem readings of literary and musical works must stake their claims on deep-structural convergences *whether or not* manifest analogies are also involved. We can also posit that such convergences may stem from common purposes, effects, or values, but *not* from common techniques. And we should be prepared to be generally cautious about manifest analogies, which must neither be taken as guarantees of structural convergences nor mistaken for structural convergences themselves.

A wariness about analogies is especially necessary when we deal with literature that ostentatiously imitates music, or vice versa. Thomas Mann's novella *Tonio Kröger* uses formulaic repetition at several levels in a way obviously modeled on Wagner's use of Leitmotivs. Given the Wagnerian subtext, it is easy enough to read Mann's tale as an ironic recasting of the libretto of *Die Meistersinger*. Mann's young artist hero finds his vocation but remains an unmarried outcast, a man drawn to Hamlet's Elsinore rather than Hans Sachs's Nuremburg, an Adam with no prospect of "Eva im Paradies." On the terms set by Mann himself, however, the leitmotivic structure of *Tonio Kröger* is not Wagnerian at all. Mann saw Wagner's Leitmotivs as a means of articulating a fusion of psychology and mythology; Wagner's leitmotivic technique establishes him as a precursor of Freud:

> When Siegfried dreams under the linden tree and the mother-idea flows into the erotic; when Mime teaches his pupil the nature of fear, while the orchestra down below darkly and afar off introduces the fire motif: all that is Freud, that is analysis, nothing else—and we recall that Freud ... shows an interest in the mythical, precultural, and primeval which is narrowly associated with the psychological.[5]

Both psychology and the primeval show up in *Tonio Kröger*, but they have little to do with the Leitmotivs of the tale, which are essentially used as tokens of destiny; their recurrence fetters Tonio to the role of the alienated modern

---

[5]"Sufferings and Greatness of Richard Wagner" (1933), from Thomas Mann, *Essays*, trans. H. T. Lowe-Porter (New York, 1957), p. 203.

artist. Mann's leitmotivic technique is not analytic but symbolic; its purpose is to give the text a Wagnerian aura, to appropriate certain values carried by the idea of Wagner. Aside from prestige and authority, what Mann seeks to appropriate here may be a feeling of redemptiveness that his ironic point of view as a narrator forbids him to express directly. "The general tone ... of Wagner's music," he remarks, "is heavy, pessimistic, laden with sluggish yearning, broken in rhythm; it seems to be wrestling up out of darkness and confusion to redemption in the beautiful" ("Sufferings," p. 215).

The example of *Tonio Kröger* suggests that manifest analogies may be quite informative as long as we recognize that they are more closely tied to signification than to structure. Of course, the distinction between signification and structure is not ironclad, but, that understood, it can provide melopoetic criticism with a basic point of departure. When we find a manifest analogy, we should assume that one work is trying to annex certain values associated with another work, or with a class of others. The analogy will become meaningful to the extent that we can interpret the values annexed, their impact on the work that annexes them, and the lack—there generally is one—that motivates the effort of annexation. When we claim to find a deep-structural convergence, we should assume that the convergent works indirectly affirm a common core of values. The deep structure involved is to be understood not only as a vehicle for the expression of these values, but also as one of the means by which the values are produced and put into circulation. The convergence will become meaningful to the extent that we can clarify the interplay between structure and value.

II. Problems of Method

Since our business is with deep structures, we will naturally want to know what kind of structures we are looking for and how to go about finding them. Probably the best answer here is the one that Wittgenstein gave to a classic epistemological question. The question: how do you know if it's raining outside? The answer: go to the window and see.

The structural patterns we have been talking about are notably unsystematic—some might say chimerical. Despite Jordan's and Kafalenos's heuristic use of certain structuralist models, deep structures of this sort cannot be formalized. "Owen Wingrave" and the Brahms Intermezzo do not share anything as rigorous as a grammatical syntagm. From a musical perspective, it may be important to add that they share nothing so rigorous as a Schenkerian middle ground structure, though the *effect* of what they do share is somewhat similar. Deep structures flexible enough to accommodate both literature and music are probably characterized best when they are characterized loosely, whether we are dealing with deep structures in general or some one structure in particular.

In general, then, we are looking for extended qualitative patterns, styles of organizing change, profiles of movement in time. Very often, as I suggested in *Music and Poetry* (p. 24), structures of this type are based on abstract features of temporal progression that can also be strongly invested with emotional energy: too much or too little repetition, blockage or smooth unfolding, clarity or ambiguity of process, and so on. Very often, too, such structures are best understood on the model of J. L. Austin's concept of the performative utterance, i.e., a statement that matters less for what it means than for what it *does* in being uttered.[6] Jordan and Kafalenos, for example, understand the common trajectory of "Owen Wingrave" and the Brahms Intermezzo as a means of breaking a promise. They have in mind a traditional "pact" in which the audience agrees to tolerate local discontinuity in return for the artist's agreement to observe large-scale norms of teleology and causality (pp. 133–34). One might add that both works are conspicuously nonaggressive in their pact-breaking, as if both James and Brahms were trying to persuade, or cajole, or seduce their audiences to embrace an aesthetic in which the acausal and the antiteleological are signs of (higher) truth.

Jordan and Kafalenos also illustrate the conceptual looseness necessary for describing particular deep structures. They give several accounts, from several points of view, of the common trajectory followed by Brahms and

---
[6]See J. L. Austin, *How to Do Things With Words*, ed. J. O. Urmson and Marina Sbisa (Cambridge, Mass., 1962).

James. The last account, and the best, is both linguistically precise and descriptively approximate: "In our two works ... with their 'insistent continuity' ... both trajectories which make up each double trajectory seem simultaneous and unbroken.... Every event [in both the story and the piece] contributes to the ongoing process of both trajectories" (pp. 143–44). This assessment is a general impression that might not, and need not, be supported by every paragraph of the James or every measure of the Brahms. In other contexts, one might want something more; in the present context, more would be less.

A further defining feature of textual/musical deep structures hangs on the question: lyric or narrative? As Jordan and Kafalenos note, my comparative studies in *Music and Poetry* are restricted to compositions and lyric poems. The restriction is based on the recognition of a rhythmic impulse that moves across a plurality of structural levels. Both music and poetry are able to project the periodicity that informs metrical, phrasal, and sectional units across larger structural spans. As the structural span widens, the periodicity loses its strict ordering and evolves into a generalized pattern of continuation.[7] Jordan and Kafalenos, however, suggest that narratological studies have "identified ... combinatory structures in narrative for which parallels can be discerned in music" (p. 132). They thus politely, and correctly, suggest that the restriction to lyric is unnecessary. What we need, accordingly, is a useful distinction between lyric structural rhythms and narrative structural trajectories.

With one caution, the distinction is fairly easy to make on the lyric side. We are looking for patterns of tension against release or blockage, expectation against fulfillment or deferral, and where we find such patterns we also expect to find an underlying principle of repetition. The caution is that these terms are not to be pegged to the manifest features of a work, but to effects of some complexity that cannot be recognized without an effort of interpretation.

As Jordan and Kafalenos point out, the Brahms Intermezzo follows a ternary form in which the middle section, in D major, has a more definite tonal profile than the outer sections, which hover between B minor and D major until the last measure. As it happens, Romantic poetry in English and German uses a similar ternary pattern to structure or formalize the representation of reverie.[8] In the poetic instances, we find a relatively definite and affirmative middle section framed by relatively indefinite and problematical outer sections. As in the Brahms Intermezzo, the middle section is often the longest. More often than not, the middle section involves an effort to overcome a burdensome necessity, to recuperate a loss or limit acknowledged in the outer sections. The middle section, accordingly, often involves imaginary satisfactions that the outer sections interdict.

The paradigmatic instance of this structure in English is probably Keats's "Ode on a Grecian Urn" (1819). For something more economical, we can quote "Nachmittags" (1863), a tiny lyric by Eduard Mörike that distills the reverie-structure to its essence:

Drei Uhr schlägt es im Kloster. Wie klar durch die
    schwülige Stille
  Gleitet herüber zum Waldrande mit Beben der
    Schall,
Wo er lieblich zerfließt, in der Biene Gesumm sich
    mischend,
  Das mich Ruhenden hier unter den Tannen
    umgibt.

(Three o'clock strikes in the cloister. How clear
    through the sultry stillness
  Glides across to the wood's edge, trembling, the
    sound,
Where lovely it dissolves, in the bees' hum mingling
  By which I, at rest here under the firs, am
    surrounded.[9])

For A B A, we can read lines 1, 2–3, and 4. Line 1 hints at but does not name a feeling of oppressiveness as it moves from the tolling of the hour

---

[7] For a full discussion, see *Music and Poetry: The Nineteenth Century and After* (Berkeley and Los Angeles, 1984), pp. 8–15.

[8] For a melopoetic account of Romantic reverie in its unformalized state, see Marshall Brown, "Mozart and After: The Revolution in Musical Consciousness," *Critical Inquiry* 7 (1981), 689–706. Brown's essay closes with some important methodological points.

[9] Eduard Mörike, *Sämmtliche Werke*, ed. H. G. Gopert (Munich, 1954), p. 195. The translation, which is as literal as possible, is mine.

(three o'clock, the ecclesiastical hour of Nones, the hour of Christ's death) through the ascetic precinct of the cloister to the sultry stillness. Lines 2–3 take a detail from this complex, the sound of the bell, and use it to conjure oppressiveness away. The sound moves from center to edge, religion to nature, measured time to the unmeasured hum of the bees. Concurrently, a wave of pleasure and vitality crests and subsides: crests with the syntactic and phrasal arrival at "Schall," subsides in the participial fluidity of "mischend." Line 4, though it does not exactly disenchant what precedes it, is anticlimactic and withdrawn. Grammatically detached, the line hints at but does not name a parallel between the speaker under the firs and the monks under the bell tower, the speaker surrounded by the bees' hum and the monks closed in by the cloister.

The Brahms Intermezzo is a Romantic reverie of the same type as Mörike's lyric, though the music assumes this character with a reticence that, as so often in Brahms, amounts almost to secretiveness. Like the lyric, the Intermezzo frames its transient spell of affirmation with an understated disquiet: an increasingly dissonant texture, a harmony that will not declare itself, but all subdued by consistency, even monotony, of texture. Like the lyric, the Intermezzo presents its middle section as a cresting and subsiding of feeling: here are the only extended crescendos and *forte* dynamics in the piece, separated by an expressive diminuendo that takes off from an *fp* marking in m. 27. And like the lyric, the Intermezzo evolves its middle section by revaluing an element that belongs to the first section: the middle section stabilizes the key of D major, which is the source of ambiguity (against B minor) in the first section, and will be so again in the last. Granted, the Intermezzo does not directly express the interplay of desire and necessity that so frequently shapes the poetic versions of Romantic reverie. Yet the music is strangely hard to describe without borrowing at least a few terms from the lexicon of that very interplay. It may be that a sufficiently well-established structural rhythm is resonant with the meanings typically attached to it, so that we can no longer cleanly separate a structural from a semantic level.

From lyric we must now return to narrative, always a subject of rather daunting complexity. In order to fill out the second half of our lyric/narrative distinction, we need to be clear about just what the word "and" means when we speak of music and narrative. Literary narrative is so closely tied to the social and signifying uses of language that most narrative effects are difficult, if not impossible, to reproduce in untexted music. I noted several of these effects in *Music and Poetry* (p. 10); in a recent issue of this journal, Carolyn Abbate noted several more.[10] Jordan and Kafalenos restrict their narratological borrowings to the level of emplotment, i.e., to the linear ordering of the text, which does not necessarily correspond to the chronological ordering of the tale. In this respect, they share the strategy used in some recent work on music and narrative by Anthony Newcomb.[11] But where Newcomb is mainly interested in the realization of paradigmatic plot patterns, Jordan and Kafalenos concentrate on emplotment as a process. Explicitly with the James, implicitly with the Brahms, their critical approach is guided by a dynamic model of the "minimum complete plot" borrowed from Tzvetan Todorov.

Todorov's model posits a shift from equilibrium through disequilibrium to a new equilibrium. Like most structuralist models, however, this one fails to confront the impact of temporality; it abstracts from the texture and behavior of passing time. This lack is remedied by Frank Kermode, who also tries to model the minimum complete plot. Kermode takes his cue from a ticking clock:

Tick is our word for a physical beginning, *tock* our word for an end. . . . The clock's *tick-tock* I take to be a model of what we call a plot, an organization that humanizes time by giving it form. . . . [Plots] have to defeat the tendency of the interval between *tick* and *tock* to empty itself; to maintain within that interval following *tick* a lively expectation of *tock*, and a sense that, however remote *tock* may be, all that happens happens as if *tock* were certainly following.[12]

---

[10]"What the Sorcerer Said," this journal 12 (1989), 221–30.
[11]"Schumann and Late Eighteenth-Century Narrative Strategies," this journal 11 (1987), 164–74. See also the essay by John Daverio in the same issue, "Schumann's 'Im Legendenton' and Friedrich Schlegel's *Arabesque*," 150–63.
[12]Frank Kermode, *The Sense of an Ending: Studies in the Theory of Fiction* (Oxford, 1967), pp. 44–46.

Kermode's emphasis is on how in-between time, Todorov's period of disequilibrium, becomes meaningful in relation to origins and ends.

Jordan and Kafalenos write more in the spirit of Kermode than of Todorov. One of the cardinal points of their argument, for example, is the claim that James's story and Brahms's piece humanize time in the same way. Both works, they argue, put the perceiver through an "apprenticeship": a process in which "we learn how to perceive . . . as we read and listen" (p. 143). In both cases, moreover, one of the chief things we learn is how to practice what Keats called negative capability: the discipline (and the pleasure) "of being in uncertainties, Mysteries, doubts, without any irritable reaching after fact & reason."[13] One might add that this type of emplotment not only coaxes the perceiver to renounce a craving for answers, but also compels the artist to renounce the mastery or authority that can give answers.

To study a composition in its narrative aspect, then—perhaps in relation to a literary narrative, perhaps not—is to think about musical emplotment: to ask how the music humanizes the all-important interval between *tick* and *tock*. As Kermode's account suggests, this humanizing process is as much a defensive as an affirmative effort, as much an attempt to prevent an emptiness as to provide a fullness. In contrast, to study a composition in its lyric aspect—perhaps in relation to a lyric poem, perhaps not—is to think about conceptual and emotional rhythms: to ask how the music shapes the turns and counterturns of a temporal interval that has been humanized (as it seems) beforehand. This shaping activity, we might surmise, conceals or sublimates the defensiveness that narrative leaves in the open.

III. Problems of Viability

Assuming that an effective melopoetics can be practiced on something like the model suggested here, what is it good for? Why should we learn to practice it? The preceding paragraph already hints at one answer: the literary categories of lyric and narrative offer new and productive terms for thinking about music even in the absence of specific comparisons. The need for such innovations would seem to be clear, even urgent, as formalist models of musical criticism and analysis fall into increasing disfavor, not so much as techniques but as ends in themselves.

The melopoetic methods we have been outlining are particularly useful because they evolve away from an initial separation of semantics and structure. Once identified, melopoetic deep structures continually provoke acts of interpretation. And the structures can also act as "switching stations," so that meanings attached to a text can be tried out in relation to a composition, and vice versa. From a melopoetic standpoint, the distinction between hermeneutics and analysis is a practical convenience, to be dropped unobtrusively in the middle of the critical process.

This interpretive vitality has a broad application. As my examples should suggest, melopoetic deep structures are focal points for cultural values and energies. The proper object of musical criticism may be music, but only if what we mean by "object" is a goal and not a possession. Music is all too easy to treat as an Abstract Entity, something *in* but not *of* culture and history. Perhaps the impulse to idealize music in these terms betrays a need to establish a preserve, a protected area where the compromises and brutalities of the world cannot encroach. Freud once compared our conscious fantasies—daydreams—to preserves like Yellowstone Park; perhaps the compositions we idealize are the national parks of high culture.[14] If so, we might say that the musicological goal of melopoetics is to deidealize music without (entirely) disenchanting it. That goal is pursued by searching out deep structures and asking how they react to, intervene in, try to reinterpret, the

---

[13] Letter to George and Tom Keats, 21/27 December 1817; text from *The Letters of John Keats*, ed. Hyder E. Rollins, 2 vols. (Cambridge, Mass., 1958), I, 191.

[14] "Formulations Regarding the Two Principles in Mental Functioning" (1911), in Freud, *Collected Papers*, vol. VI, *General Psychological Theory*, ed. Philip Rieff (New York, 1963), p. 24n. For a highly pertinent critique of the "national park" mentality in the reception of Beethoven's Ninth Symphony, see Richard Taruskin, "Resisting the Ninth," this journal 12 (1989), 241–56. Leo Treitler's critique of ways of (musical) knowing based on ideals of detachment is equally pertinent; see his *Music and the Historical Imagination* (Cambridge, Mass., 1989), pp. 1–18, 32–36. For further discussion and context, see Joseph Kerman, *Contemplating Music: Challenges to Musicology* (Cambridge, Mass., 1985).

cultural and historical conditions in which they are produced.

With this in mind, consider "Owen Wingrave" and the Brahms Intermezzo one last time. The "double trajectory" in each work endows ambiguity with a special value; James and Brahms, we might say, give ambiguity the structural force usually reserved for clarification. The cultural implications of this gesture are strong and numerous, though my comments on them will necessarily be sketchy. During the second half of the nineteenth century, subjectivity was increasingly associated with error, uncertainty, partiality of perspective. The commanding prestige of "objective" science helped encourage this trend, but I suspect that its main impetus came from the growth of psychiatry, which developed a discourse of mental abnormality based on elaborate classificatory systems. Talk about the mind became talk about delusion and dysfunction. As subjectivity thus fell under ever greater suspicion, its defenders developed a coping strategy. Error, uncertainty, and partiality of perspective were now reinterpreted, celebrated, either as sources of vitality or as the only genuine forms of truth. Robert Browning's *The Ring and the Book* (1868–69), a collection of twelve dramatic monologues in orbit about a Roman murder case, is an ambitious attempt at both kinds of reinterpretation. Nietzsche, too, tries for both, with lapidary intensity rather than volubility, in the fourth book of *The Gay Science* (1882):

Now something that you formerly loved as a truth or probability strikes you as an error; you shed it and fancy that this represents a victory for your reason. But perhaps this error was necessary for you then, when you were still a different person—you are always a different person—as are all your present "truths," being a skin, as it were, that concealed and covered a great deal.... [Thus we find] evidence of vital energies in us that are growing and shedding a skin.[15]

"Owen Wingrave" and the Brahms Intermezzo would seem to form part of a general effort to recuperate the value of subjectivity and to redefine ambiguity not as a deferral of truth but as the truth itself. One reason that "Owen Wingrave" is a ghost story is that late nineteenth-century England experienced a demand for ghosts—real ghosts—that tantalizingly outstripped the supply. For its adherents, the fad for "psychic research," with its seances and table tapping, represented an alternative to the professionalized forms of rationality instituted by the sciences.[16] The Wingrave family ghost, therefore, is to some degree a symbol of James's epistemological attitude.

As to Brahms's attitude, it bears most suggestively on the Intermezzo at the close of the middle section (mm. 33–43). As Jordan and Kafalenos point out (p. 140), this passage is clearly in D major, but the same nine pitch-classes that compose it also compose the ambiguous B minor/D major opening of the piece (mm. 1–8). Brahms thus seems to intimate that D major and B minor are neither the chief structuring forces of the Intermezzo, nor even relative keys, nor even keys at all in the Classical sense. Instead, the two tonalities are alternative realizations of a more primary pitch collection that lacks a traditional identity. This primary collection, however, can only appear with the help of its tonal realizations; it needs them as a ghost needs a table to rap on.

To round off our cultural foray, consider a question of gender. By misogynist tradition, the uncertainty that looms so large in our works by James and Brahms is a weakness characteristic of women's thinking. In some post-Darwinian traditions, this weakness indicates a hereditary or evolutionary inferiority. Accordingly, we might expect works that deliberately seek uncertainty to seek a certain femininity as well. "Owen Wingrave" and the Brahms Intermezzo seem to have done just that.

The opening of James's story presents Owen to us as white-faced, panting, and voluble; contemporary psychiatry listed these attributes prominently among the symptoms of a woman suffering from a hysterical attack. At the close of the story, Owen's death is announced by the cry "of a woman in agonized terror." We eventually discover that the woman is Kate Julian, Owen's fiancee, but the "agonized terror" seems equally to belong to Owen himself. The

---

[15]Friedrich Nietzsche, *The Gay Science*, trans. Walter Kaufmann (New York, 1974), no. 307, pp. 245–46.

[16]See Daniel Cottom, "On the Dignity of Tables," *Critical Inquiry* 14 (1988), 765–83.

"appalling sound" is a displaced form of his (unheard, unuttered) death-cry.

In Brahms's case, it is the entire Intermezzo that seems to be feminized. Clara Schumann, at least, received the piece in these terms. "I almost require a treasure-chest," she wrote to Brahms,

> to keep all the jewels I have received from you. . . . [The Intermezzo in B minor] is a grey pearl. Do you know them? They look as if they were veiled and are very precious (24 June 1893).[17]

Schumann's primary metaphors—jewels, a gray pearl—straightforwardly assign Brahms's piece a feminine value. More telling still is her secondary metaphor of veiling, which not only repeats the gesture of feminization but also identifies the "femininity" of the music with its epistemological values. In this connection, it is also striking that Brahms felt that the Intermezzo should be played as if "one wanted to draw . . . voluptuous joy and comfort out of the [abundant] discords" (to Clara Schumann, May 1893).

To conclude, let me raise again the bluntest of my questions: what is melopoetics good for? If Jordan, Kafalenos, and I have been persuasive, the best answer is the simplest: what it's good for is understanding music. I hope that this statement is unsurprising. Our discussion has focused on the prospects of a comparative discipline, but disciplines are theorized only after they have been practiced awhile. A comparative attitude has always been basic to the best music criticism. What the still-incipient discipline might have to offer is not drastic innovation but greater explicitness, resources of enrichment, wider interpretive adventure.

This last offering is also a demand, and one that deserves to be emphasized. If we want to involve ourselves with the kinds of discourse under review here, we must also be willing to read, in the sense that literary criticism gives to the term. We must, that is, assume an active, value-laden, rhetorically complex role in the production of meaning; we must interpret. This imperative applies with special force when we deal with texted music, the problems of which have been kept under wraps in this essay. In particular, we must not regard texts for musical setting as transparently meaningful statements that the music somehow proceeds to "express." We should be prepared to find that the music tries to annex textual values, or that it "reads" a text with a deep structure that the text itself can be said to conceal or resist. More generally, the imperative to interpret asks us to recognize that all music is in some sense texted music, music allied to the cultural activity of text-production. Where no text is given, our job is to find one, be it a solid "Owen Wingrave" or a typical, composite text that we piece together ourselves.

It remains, of course, an open question whether melopoetics will play an enhanced role in the continuing development of musical criticism. My effort here has been to suggest what such a role would look like, what it would entail. I hope, also, to have conveyed a sense of pleasure in new possibilities: not as something extra, but as a primary motive for critical understanding.

---

[17] *Letters of Clara Schumann and Johannes Brahms, 1853–1896*, ed. Berthold Litzmann, trans. unattributed (1927; rpt. New York, 1973).

CHAPTER 4

Music Criticism and the Postmodernist Turn: In Contrary Motion with Gary Tomlinson

The problem Gary Tomlinson finds with current efforts to frame a postmodernist musicology is a version of the Cubbins Conundrum. The eponymous hero of Dr. Seuss's classic children's story *The Five Hundred Hats of Bartholomew Cubbins* is in serious trouble. After taking off his hat to the king, Bartholomew finds himself ordered by the king to—take off his hat. But no matter how often he does so, another, identical hat, a bedraggled old thing with a lame excuse for a feather, keeps appearing on his head. So, too, the musicological Bartholomew (me, in this case) may try to take off the old hat of modernism with the best of intentions, but no better luck.

Tomlinson spots the Cubbins Conundrum in scholarship that seeks a postmodernist end, a "thick contextualism" in the understanding of cultural phenomena, with modernist means. High on the list of such means is criticism, glossed as "close reading" and associated with "internalism," "aestheticism," "formalism," "transcendentalism," and "westernism." Tomlinson claims that criticism trades in concepts, including "[the] work," "art," "the aesthetic," and "even 'music' itself," that are "darkly tinted for us with modernist ideology" (p. 23). In place of a critical program, he advocates what we might loosely call an ethnographic one, aimed proximately at "describ[ing] a local set of meanings in as full a volume as possible" (p. 22), and ultimately at knowing, in nonappropriative, nondominating ways, the other people, including our own ancestors, "who have made this or that music in the process of making their worlds" (p. 24).

As Tomlinson acknowledges, he and I share in a desire, fast evolving across our discipline, to uncloister music, to understand it as a worldly activity. No one caught up by that desire could fail to find something appealing in the ethnographic program. But the program as Tomlinson formulates it fills me with misgivings.

First, it depends on a hard-and-fast distinction between criticism and ethnography that may be neither necessary, nor desirable, nor even possible: a programmatic phantom. If so, arguments for either program over the other could easily degenerate into sectarian (or worse, careerist) squabbles.

Second, though it might seem hard to quarrel with the ideal of a knowledge free of tendentiousness, scholars do not have the minds of angels; we are driven to knowledge by more things than we know. The very claim to have such an ideal knowledge might be the surest sign that its absence is

26

still the one thing we can be sure of. Even supposing that knowledge and virtue could somehow be reconciled, can we really mistake the prescriptions and proscriptions of any single epistemic program for a panacea that will reconcile them?

Third, even if the break between modernism and postmodernism is radical, something I think likely despite Jürgen Habermas's arguments to the contrary,[1] that does not constitute the postmodern as a moment of absolute novelty, a complete rupture with a failed intellectual past. Ironically, the call for such a rupture is a classically modernist maneuver, epitomized by the memorable slogan from Rimbaud's *A Season in Hell*, "One must be absolutely modern" [Il faut être absolument moderne]. I would say rather that the *post-* in postmodernism designates the moment of disengagement from the very idea of such absolutes, and of the consequent proliferation of intellectual projects that undo what Jean-François Lyotard calls the "grand metanarratives" and Habermas the "unfinished project" of modern, which is to say post-Enlightenment, reason.[2]

Nonetheless, Tomlinson's critique of criticism cannot merely be written off as a caricature, nor his ethnographic program as a blown-up special interest. On the contrary, the program reflects the pressing need to find the apparent collapse of modernism's cognitive paradigms enabling rather than paralyzing. It is important to work out the possibilities and spot the difficulties of doing this. Similarly, the critique can be taken to spell out exactly what is wrong with one familiar mode of modernist criticism, and even exactly what happens when any mode of criticism goes wrong. And that makes it important to counter the underlying, far more drastic claim that no criticism can ever go right. Perhaps Tomlinson has found the right problems but the wrong solutions. Perhaps he has misconstrued the character of criticism and its relation to a possible musical ethnography. Perhaps he has formulated the ethnographic program itself in terms that will quickly prove their own undoing. And perhaps there is no perhaps about it.

Tomlinson's complaint against criticism is that, *in principle*, it passes off personal response as knowledge and blinds itself to the otherness for which it presumes to speak. Criticism inevitably sets a reified object before a solipsistic subject. It inflates the authority of both the critic and the artist and establishes a spurious transparency of communication between them, a relay of (pseudo-)knowledge that also acts as a network of disciplinary and social power. The locus of knowledge is the artwork—in this case the music—in which criticism corrals too much of our attention. Fetishizing the work, criticism withdraws us from the real, scants the weight of history, creates a kind of transcendental museum or mausoleum of canonical masterpieces. The locus of power is the figure (person and trope) of the critic. "Close reading" supposedly proceeds from a discursive position that involves the *a priori* assumption of coercive authority: the (im)posture of mastery, an appropriation by the critic of the composer's voice(s), a falsification of knowledge by the denial of the differences between the knower and the known. Tomlinson, accordingly, asks us to lay down our scores. We must no longer "circle back narrowly to the notes but instead . . . *resolutely historicize musical utterance,* exploding it outwards through an imaginative building of contexts" (p. 22, italics in original).

Tomlinson focuses his objections to criticism on my proposal that we learn "to read as inscribed within the immediacy-effects of music itself the kind of mediating structures usually positioned outside music under the rubric of context."[3] Arguing that any such effort is doomed by the blindness inherent in criticism, which "tends to deal out from the start the most essential and richly problematic historicism of our experiences" (p. 19), Tomlinson in effect asks for the reverse, the dispersal into context of what we usually grasp as the immediacy of music. What he wants, if we take him at his word, is music under erasure: a music so decentered, so bought out or bought off by the entrepreneurial historian's "wealthy . . . concatenation of past traces" (p. 22) that we can no longer claim to know it, or claim it as ours to know. In this dispensation there would be no criticism because there would be nothing to criticize; the death of criticism would follow on the death of what we currently think of as music. For some of us that might seem a steep price to pay.

If Tomlinson's terms of understanding are translated into terms of listening, their relentless negativity becomes obvious—and punishing. What would happen if we gave up listening with the kind of deep engagement, the heightened perception and sense of identification, that both grounds and impels criticism? We might avoid a certain amount of ideological mystification—assuming, that is, that mere exposure to ideologically charged representations renders us helpless against them. (Plato thought so, and said we need guardians.) Meanwhile, the materiality of the music, the dynamic sensuous fullness that arguably offers a major site of resistance to ideological pressures, would be put at risk. Can we really *hear* a music constituted only by its continual flowing outwards into the conduits of world-making? In our unwillingness to fetishize music as an aesthetic object, should we rush to dismantle it into a pure concatenation of signifiers? In pursuit of a credibly modest ethnographic attitude, should we throw the baby out with the bathwater?

If we can avoid an aesthetic ideology only by swapping *musica practica* for a modern-day *musica mundana,* if a postmodernist musicology can develop only as a musicology without music, then our situation is pretty grim. On the one side, participation mystique, ideological muddle, cocksure myths of mastery; on the other, the thickets of thick contextualism,

28

the Pythagorean mysteries of the ethnohistorian supplanting those of the ethnocentric close reader.

Whatever its failings, criticism at least allows more light and air than that. Criticism is the public record of our sustained, thoughtful involvement with some of the music we find moving, enlightening, provoking, oppressive, ambivalent, and more. Talking about music, old or new, whether under the aegis of individuated works, genres, occasions of performance, improvisation, or social ritual, is a means of investing that music with the very cultural value(s) we also want to comprehend through it. Such talk may risk being solipsistic in practice, but in principle, *pace* Tomlinson, it is dialogical. As Mikhail Bakhtin argued tirelessly,

> Any utterance, in addition to its own theme, always responds (in the broad sense of the word) in one form or another to others' utterances which precede it. The speaker is not Adam, and therefore the subject of his speech itself inevitably becomes the arena where his opinions meet those of . . . other viewpoints, world views, trends, theories, and so forth.[4]

If we take *postmodernism* to name an affirmative spirit of diversity, a contestable rather than merely a leveling pluralism, then criticism can serve that spirit best not by falling silent, but by foregrounding its own inescapably dialogical and interdiscursive character. Tomlinson complains that Mozart's music is too much with us, but that Mozart, that "mysterious and elusive subjectivity," has (been) disappeared. Granted, the music is very much with the dwindling "us" who still quixotically harbor a love of "classical" music, but is that really because Mozart criticism has continually falsified and appropriated the composer's "musical utterance?" Or is it because Mozart, through his music, has continually provoked dialogical responses that inevitably refigure both "him," each other, and "us?" We may need to recognize that much of our Mozart-talk has been too introverted and too cozy with an imaginary Mozart, but that is no reason either to dismiss it out of hand or, worse yet, to stop talking.

That brings us to the problem of mastery. There can be no denying that criticism has historically promoted a fantasy of instruction in which the critic poses as the master of truth. Tomlinson's forceful, eloquent warning on this point can be only to the good. Not doing criticism, however, is hardly enough to free one of the mastery pose. Certainly neither Tomlinson in his rhetoric nor his discursive models in theirs are free of it; indeed, Michel Foucault, Clifford Geertz, and Hayden White are old hands at mastery, real master masters. And while Tomlinson's positive program for thickly describing the worldly place of music is not only unobjectionable, but exciting, his use of that program to proscribe thickly describing the place of worldliness in music is a hegemonic gesture, a gesture of mastery, not of distance or reflection. If Tomlinson really wants to avoid establishing "new orthodoxies of postmodern musicology" (p. 18)—a goal hardly anyone would disavow—he has an odd way of going about it.

Not that this is Tomlinson's problem directly, any more than the Cubbins Conundrum is mine. As he rightly says, we are all in this mess together. The problem is that knowledge and power are in it together, too, as Foucault above all has insisted:

> Perhaps . . . we should abandon a whole tradition that allows us to imagine that knowledge can exist only where power relations are suspended and that knowledge can develop only outside its injunctions, its demands, and its interests. . . . We should admit rather that power produces knowledge, . . . that there is no power relation without the correlative constitution of a field of knowledge, nor any knowledge that does not presuppose and constitute at the same time power relations.[5]

Tomlinson is not to be faulted for promoting a certain mode of knowledge, but for imagining that this mode, and this mode only, can transcend power relations. Underlying this imaginary *episteme* is the apparent conviction that power always translates into an abusive or appropriative claim of mastery. The conviction is not to be lightly dismissed, given the frequency with which power has done just that. But power and mastery are not necessarily the same thing; the ability to *pro*pose knowledge is not necessarily the ability to *im*pose it. There should be—must be—ways of keeping them apart.

Certainly it is questionable whether the critic's discursive position automatically, in and of itself, reproduces the mastery scenario. And even where the scenario occurs, it may include the implicit or explicit acknowledgment of its own fictitiousness. Indeed, one type of postmodernist musicology might be conceived precisely as an attempt to engage musical works, genres, and so on dialogically, to write about them either without assuming the pose of mastery or by deliberately assuming it as a rhetorical position, a discursive trope and not a social or institutional force.

Such an attempt requires a rethinking of what it means to say that the critic "speaks for"—that is, has the power to speak for—a composer or a musical community. Tomlinson conceives this speaking-for as inherently appropriative and ventriloquistic: I speak for myself while pretending to speak for the other. But there are other ways to conceive the process, other "speech genres" within which to situate the critical discourse. In

30

speaking of a work by, say, Mozart, I may candidly be speaking for him as an actor speaks for a character in a classic role. I speak for the other precisely in speaking for myself, but always under the possibly resistant impress of the other. Or I may be speaking for Mozart the way a narrator speaks for a character in a novel: again speaking for the other in speaking for the self, but only from a moral or temporal distance that in principle limits my claims to certainty and authority.

Unless I give myself the latitude to speak for the other in some such way, I cannot approach the work (genre, etc.) as an "utterance" at all except as the passive recipient of messages that mean too much or too little. On the one hand I can refer to the most mastery laden concept of all, the paternal word, the authoritative voice of the author. On the other, following Tomlinson, I can depersonalize the utterance altogether, replacing the author with the "metasubjective level of cultural formation . . . beyond the reach of individual subjectivities" (p. 22). That would leave me with a cultural version of the discredited high-structuralist notion that it is language, not the person, which "speaks." Granted, there would be little call to dwell "internally" on utterances not genuinely exchanged between subjects. Such utterances would need thick description to compensate for their wafer thinness. But neutralizing the communicative process does not seem very promising as a means of understanding other people in their world-making.

Tomlinson's will to depersonalization pretty clearly reflects the decentering of the subject that is so prominent a feature of poststructuralist and postmodernist thinking. Even supposing that we can justify the critic's role as dialogical and not ventriloquistic, it is questionable whether we can justify any discursive practice that depends on one unitary, autonomous self speaking for another. Criticism, however, does not require such a dependency. We have already seen that the critic's voice is invested with a certain fictitiousness that can, and perhaps should, be made candid. And the other for whom the critic speaks may be equally provisional, equally embedded in a multiplicity of roles and discourses that no one can hope to master.

For Tomlinson, criticism is simply incapable of these recognitions, as if, paralleling the case with music, the mere representation of "individual, subjective agency" (p. 22) in critical discourse paralyzed our capacities for distance and reflection. Hence Tomlinson would argue that I cannot "close read" music, even for its social character, because in doing so I privilege both the composer as author(ity) over the sociality of musical utterance, and myself as master—a higher author(ity)—over all. We cannot, he argues, challenge "the modernist myths of . . . heroic individualism" (p. 22) in a discourse that perpetuates it. But criticism can do more than merely

31

perpetuate the myths of authorship and authority. Precisely because it is historically and rhetorically engaged with those myths, it can also destabilize them, undo them, and experiment with alternatives. Criticism can interrogate both its own myths and the myths of art. And that is something an ethnographic contextualism cannot do by trying to steer around them.

Suppose we were to rely on Foucault's celebrated demystifying thesis that authorship is something produced in and by discourse rather than by an individual subject? Authorship, by this account, is a function, not an ontological privilege.[6] There is nothing here to derail criticism, but plenty to redirect it. The person who writes (or composes) may at once perform and resist the author-function. And since that function is to personify the conjuncture of discourse and society, the "utterances" produced in its name will everywhere implicate social practices. In that case, I can assuredly make de-authorized social readings of those utterances (say musical ones). Indeed, I can read them prolifically, conceiving their sociality as extending into culture on the one hand and the psyche on the other. Far from privileging me as a master, Tomlinson's "omniscient critic," the presence of such a readable sociality calls me into dialogue with unmasterable realities.

On reflection, then, the opposition between criticism and ethnography proves to be a mirage. Nor is that all. Further reflection will suggest that we cannot even carry out the ethnographic program of thickly contextualizing musical works, styles, or genres without some understanding of their meaningfulness. The knowledge-claims of a dialogical criticism are prerequisite to those of musical ethnography; if either project bans the other, it will suffocate itself.

For if music is really what Tomlinson calls it, "musical utterance," then it must have the speech-act character of utterance.[7] It must, that is, be able to perform or imitate a social action in the act of being uttered. It must further be able to do this in an indefinite number of different circumstances, and must accordingly be subject to a semantic variability that requires it to be interpreted rather than merely decoded. Only through such interpretation, which is to say, through criticism, the putting into discourse of the dynamic interplay of speaker, utterance, and reply that Tomlinson misleadingly calls internalism, can we make knowledge-claims about musical utterance. And if we decline to make those claims in order to avoid the supposed pitfalls of criticism, we will forgo the chance to recognize the various worldly claims that music makes on *us*—and makes precisely through the pleasure that Tomlinson's version of the ethnographic program, in its anti-aesthetic rigor, elides.

In sum, we cannot understand music "in context," thick or otherwise, if we have no means of representing concretely what the music does as utterance. Unquestionably, there are political and moral problems with the aesthetic ideologies that have historically furnished those means, but that is no reason to write off the aesthetic, the valorization of perceptual pleasure as knowledge, *tout court*. One possibility for a postmodernist, which is to say a worldly, aesthetics, is to trace out the interrelations of musical pleasure, musical form, and ideology. Not to pursue that possibility is tantamount to denying—ascetically if not cognitively, but perhaps both—the two cardinal, historically grounded truths that music (or art) is meaningful and that music (or art) gives pleasure.

Tomlinson surely has no wish to make these denials, but his discourse leads implacably in their direction. The reason, I think, is the aversion to old-fashioned subjectivity that everywhere impels his text, and that overlaps imperceptibly into a profound distrust of human agency itself. Schooled in the postmodernist distrust of unitary selfhood and its delusions, Tomlinson's text projects a sense that agency always engrosses too much power, that the subject in action always seeks mastery over something or, worse, someone, as object. Hence his curious assumption that the best means to appreciate someone else's subjectivity is to depreciate one's own. Yet if postmodernism has taught us anything, it is that we do not need to conceive of subjectivity in such Hegelian terms as a force of opposition, inner to outer, private to public, value to fact. We can instead conceive of the subject as a position within a continuous process of communicative exchange, the character of which is simultaneously psychical, social, and cultural. And unless we leave room for this postmodernist subject in the discourses of knowledge, we risk falling back into the worst, most autocratic excesses of instrumental reason.

That is, of course, the last thing Tomlinson wants, but again, his discourse has a will of its own. Despite his sophisticated talk about metasubjectivity and the plural construction of knowledge, Tomlinson's version of musical ethnography is at bottom positivistic. His program appeals to discovery procedures and modes of knowledge uncontaminated by "individual, subjective agency"; it presupposes an oppositional relationship between subjectivity, that is, precisely the partial or localized modes of knowledge that an ethnographic postmodernism is supposed to cultivate, and truth; and it assumes possession of a transparent-enough metalanguage to make good on its epistemic promises.[8] There are no clear means by which to distinguish this program from what Donna Haraway tartly calls the god-trick of modern epistemology.[9] Underneath the invocation of a "collective, kaleidoscopic, and dialogical realm of subjectivities opened out to one another" (p. 23), I sense, with discomfort, a will to truth that is also a will to both intellectual property and purity. Here those metaphors of a historicism "essential" in character and "rich" in problematicity, of "wealthy"

33

concatenations set beyond concepts "darkly tinted" by ideology, make a haunting return. And from these the program reads its proscriptive bias along the ameliorative lines of classic quest romance.

With this turn of argument, I might seem to have thrown Tomlinson's critique back on him in a predictable and somewhat dreary way: You think I'm a crypto-modernist? You're another! But the *tu quoque* game is not the point. Rather, the point is discovering the best means to carry out the overarching musicological project to which we both want to contribute, the understanding of music in its worldliness. From this standpoint the problem with Tomlinson's version of the ethnographic program is that its distrust of subjectivity sets its conceptual mechanism on self-destruct. The knowledge the program seeks is impossible on the terms it sets.

This is clearest, perhaps, in relation to the problem of otherness. I share Tomlinson's desire not to confuse appreciation with appropriation, but I am not ready to identify the necessary limitations of any one person's discourse, his included, with an appropriative solipsism. Unlike Tomlinson, I am not interested in respecting, not to say reverencing, otherness but in deconstructing the opposition of self and other. For that opposition *always* posits a superior self—a master. Tomlinson can judge that a critical reading appropriates the otherness of a Mozart or a Monteverdi or a Leadbelly only if he can claim a sure knowledge of that otherness. But since, by his own account, he can arrive at such knowledge only from a position external to the otherness, the claim to knowledge is both a hermeneutic claim and a claim to mastery. Only if Tomlinson could himself *be* the other could he venture a decisive claim to the knowledge he seeks from the thick context that surrounds the other. But then, since the rest of us remain in a position external to the other, this other Tomlinson would not be able to communicate his claim to us. Of course not: being the other, he would not be empowered to speak for himself, at least to us, and none of us could credibly or transparently speak for him.

At best, I suppose, one might approximate the knowledge Tomlinson seeks by so immersing oneself in the signs of otherness as to identify with it, and then to produce a text that would allow a reader to identify with it. But the text, being a text, would unavoidably be subject to the slippages and metamorphoses of interpretation. And the underlying process of identification would, just as inevitably, lead both the writer and reader into the confusions, alienations, and always questionable jubilances of fantasy, the register of the signifying process that Jacques Lacan calls the Imaginary, and in which desire, not knowledge, is paramount.

Criticism, of course, runs just the same risks, a point that underscores the continuity of criticism and ethnography but also brings us round to the question of conceptual means from a final perspective. How can we

34

write criticism without falling afoul of Tomlinson's critique? From my position as a postmodernist critic, the chief value of Tomlinson's argument is that it forces an explicit answer to that question.

How, then, can one write criticism as an agent, a subject empowered to claim knowledge, rather than as a master, a subject privileged to impose knowledge? Or, failing that, how can one write as a literal agent and only a figurative master? I offered one answer (only one, an instance, not a paradigm) in my reading of Mozart's K. 563. In his essay, Tomlinson declines to consider the content of this reading. He does so pointedly, of course, true to his critique of critical interpretation *as such*, but nonetheless with an indirectness that conceals the problematicity of the gesture. And it is indeed odd, if you consult my piece, to speak of internalism, aestheticism, or mastery in relation to a critical discourse that makes no attempt to account comprehensively for form and structure in K. 563 and that continually refers musical events not only to each other but also to the social construction of the body, to labor, to manners, to heterosexuality and homosociality, to the Rousseauvian concept of civil society, and more. This is certainly not close reading in anything like its original literary sense, which defines the "aesthetic object" as a restricted, semi-sacralized field of inquiry and tries to stay wholly within its borders. The critical effort is manifestly to grant no more than provisional authority to any border, to encourage multiple border crossings, and to efface, in the process, the distinctions between inside and outside, work and frame, text and context. One might even suppose that I was resolutely historicizing the musical utterance, exploding it outwards through an imaginative building of contexts—except that I wasn't interested in exploding anything.

Granted, some of the differentness of K. 563 will necessarily be lost in my discourse. But the loss might have its compensations in insight, and, in any case, if I do not write critically, *all* of the differentness of K. 563 *as* discourse will be lost. There is no musical utterance without an interlocutor; there is no context without a text. Jacques Derrida made this same point with the famous dictum that there is no outside the text. But we should remember that the dictum is credible only because there is no inside the text, either. With luck, each critical effort that puts this recollection into practice will count as a step toward collapsing the ideal(ology) of appropriation, disrupting the trade in authority, mastering the seductions of mastery.

These goals are reachable, if no more than asymtotically, only by writing onward. In other words, the solution to the Cubbins Conundrum is to play it out to the end. When Bartholomew does that, he saves himself, and incidentally triumphs over arbitrary authority, by taking off so many hats that a metamorphosis happens. After 450 doublings, his hats spontaneously begin to blossom; the poor excuse for a phallocratic feather exfoliates into lush ambiguous plumes and gorgeous gems. But Bartholomew, good postmodernist that he is, refuses to fetishize his new headwork. He produces splendid hats at last, but keeps none of them.

NOTES

[1] Jürgen Habermas, *The Philosophical Discourse of Modernity: Twelve Lectures*, trans. Frederick G. Lawrence, Studies in Contemporary German Social Thought (Cambridge: MIT Press, 1987).

[2] Jean-François Lyotard, *The Postmodern Condition: A Report on Knowledge*, trans. Geoff Bennington and Brian Massumi, Theory and History of Literature, 10 (Minneapolis: University of Minnesota Press, 1984); Habermas, *Philosophical Discourse of Modernity*.

[3] "The Musicology of the Future," *repercussions* 1 (1992): 10.

[4] Mikhail Bakhtin, *Speech Genres and Other Later Essays*, ed. Michael Holquist, trans. Vern McGee, University of Texas Press Slavic Series, 8 (Austin: University of Texas Press, 1986), 94.

[5] Michel Foucault, *Discipline and Punish: The Birth of the Prison*, trans. Alan Sheridan (New York: Vintage Books, 1979), 27.

[6] Michel Foucault, "What is an Author," in his *Language, Counter-Memory, Practice: Selected Essays and Interviews*, ed. Donald F. Bouchard, trans. Donald F. Bouchard and Sherry Simon (Ithaca: Cornell University Press, 1977), 113–38.

[7] For a fuller account of the speech-act character of music, see my *Music as Cultural Practice: 1800–1900* (Berkeley: University of California Press, 1990), 6–15. J. L. Austin's term *speech-act* can be taken to indicate both the class of "performative" utterances, those that do something in being said, and the performative dimension (or "illocutionary force") of utterance in general.

[8] Tomlinson is aware of the metalanguage problem, but tries to dispose of it in a single sentence: "In the act of its seeking out its own locale within a plurality of potential meanings, [ethnographic contextualism] will incorporate the very 'rhetorical' and 'subjective' character that Kramer sought in the old haunts of criticism" (p. 22). This statement is problematical at best. The contextualist discourse is said to be both inside its locale (the locale is its own) and outside it (the locale must be sought out). The externality gives the discourse the status of a metalanguage. The internality is somehow supposed to mitigate this status without disrupting it; hence the figure of incorporation. But the mitigation goes too far. On what terms can the discourse incorporate rhetoricity and subjectivity without being constrained and impelled by them?

[9] Donna Haraway, "Situated Knowledges: The Science Question in Feminism and the Privilege of Partial Perspective," in her *Simians, Cyborgs, and Women: The Reinvention of Nature* (New York: Routledge, 1991), 193.

CHAPTER 5

CHARGING THE CANONS

Disciplining Music: Musicology and its Canons. Edited by Katherine Bergeron and Philip V. Bohlman. Chicago, The University of Chicago Press, 1992. xi + 220 pp. ISBN 0 226 04368 1.

THE title of this book is impishly suggestive. It throws off metaphors like scintillas: taming music, regimenting music in barracks and drilling it on parade, punishing music for disobedience, perhaps with a switch, ruler or rod (from the Greek: *kanon*), instructing music in proper conduct, training it in self-denial, constraining music so that it becomes an object of knowledge under systematic scholarly examination, taking music as an object of sadistic pleasure. These figures all endow music with a body, even the scholarly figure, one element of which is the corpus or body of works; the discipline of musicology must produce the body in evidence. Yet the body of music retains something of the pure intractability of music in the air or ear; it is a body felt to be unruly, threatening, a site of pleasure or force in excess. In this symbolic order, musicology arises by taking up the rod (*kanon*), also the reed (*kanna*, Syrinx disciplined as the pipe of Pan), to guide, chastise and conduct this body. And by this means the body becomes 'our' body: initially marked as Other, its unruliness that of a child, woman, savage or beast, it becomes in its disciplined form a thing of beauty and even an incarnation of truth, an icon of the higher existence of Western Man.

No one in *Disciplining Music* tells this just-so story in so many words, although some come close. Disseminated across the volume, the elements of the story wait to be incorporated – disciplined? – into a reading. The discipline narrative, like one of the Blackfoot myths in Bruno Nettl's contribution, emerges as the horizon against which these essays appear. It is possible to leave this horizon largely unremarked while concentrating on the more local issues under discussion: a problem in Schenkerian theory, the status of Miles Davis's fusion music, the reception of Rossini's Neapolitan operas. The editors, however, deploy a frame narrative to force the issue; they discipline the reader.

Bergeron, riffing on the etymology of 'canon' and the concept of the scale, works up to a provocative image: a prison band, tacitly substituting for the symphony orchestra, as the acoustic equivalent of Jeremy Bentham's Panopticon, 'that revolutionary model of eighteenth-century discipline whose primary power, as described by Foucault, lay in the ability to maintain inmates under a constant (and centralized) surveillance' ('Prologue', pp. 3–4). In the orchestral 'Panacouston', each player-inmate performs properly because 'he never knows precisely the moment when the conductor – this master of acoustic surveillance – may be listening to *him*' (p. 4). Bohlman, righting the scale tipped out of tune by Bergeron's in-your-face style, puts on a poker face. In conventional scholarly prose, he identifies the discipline of traditional musicology as an instrument of social repressiveness:

> To the extent that musicologists concerned largely with the traditions of Western art music were content with a singular canon – any singular canon that took a European–American concert tradition as a given – they were excluding musics, peoples, and cultures. They were, in effect, using the process of disciplining to cover up the racism, colonialism, and sexism that underlie many of the singular canons of the West. They bought into these '-isms' just as surely as they coopted an '-ology'. ('Epilogue: Music and Canons', p. 198)

The strategically placed 'in effect' serves notice that the indictment, despite its magnitude, falls well within the bounds of scholarly circumspection.

Those who don't care for this sort of thing, or for the ethos of the discipline narrative in general, may be tempted to dismiss the whole discourse out of hand. Others, more sympathetic, may still find Bergeron's imagery more memorable than convincing and Bohlman's indictment more righteous than right. Nevertheless, the issues engaged here demand to be thought through. It would be foolish to deny that the idealization of centralized authority is endemic to the culture of Western art music, and naive to think that the singular canon of this music, however gratifying it may be to hear, is somehow immune from the ills of Western culture at large. If these issues still need to be forced, then *Disciplining Music* deserves our thanks for forcing them.

Forcing an issue, though, is not the same thing as facing it, and on this score *Disciplining Music* is a disappointment. All the essays in the book are by accomplished scholars, and all are worth reading, but taken together they do little more than parachute musicology into a debate that has itself become virtually canonical in literary and cultural studies and in the highly publicized 'culture wars' over the curricula of American colleges and universities. If only one essay, Richard Cohn's and Douglas Dempster's attempt to rehabilitate the Schenkerian ideal of musical unity, seems to miss the boat entirely, only one essay, Ruth Solie's multifaceted inquiry into the conditions of alternative disciplinary practices as exemplified by Sophie Drinker's *Music and Women*, really completes the voyage it starts. The rest get scuttled somewhere in midcourse, undone by bringing premature or overconfident closure to questions that remain stubbornly open.

Most of the essays proceed on the understanding that canons are the means of discipline. Both as a discursive and a social practice, a discipline, a field of inquiry, centres itself on its canon, from which it constructs both the objects and the methods of knowledge. The canon as such may consist either of a privileged body of texts (works, facts, phenomena) or a set of governing principles; at bottom the two forms are the same because the texts *et al.* are presumed to exemplify the principles. Around this core the discipline generates its own internal canons, again in two forms: both 'classic' texts in the field and the principles exemplified therein.

The contributors to *Disciplining Music* generally look askance at the way this process has worked in traditional musicology. They are rightly critical of the exclusionary, involuted terms on which musicological canons have been formed. The sharpest criticism comes from Gary Tomlinson, who forcefully rejects the 'monological, hegemonic premises that have for so long supported the white, male European canon':

> These premises constitute . . . three closely related strategies that function to distance the value and significance of canonic works from cultural constraints and situational determination. They are aestheticism, the view that the meaning and expression found in artworks are of a different, higher order than those found in other cultural acts; transcendentalism, the view that artistic value and significance can somehow travel with an artwork outside of the specific contexts that determine or redetermine them; and formalism, the view . . . that meaning and value inhere in the internal formal arrangements of the artworks themselves, independent of their contexts. ('Cultural Dialogics and Jazz: A White Musician Signifies', p. 75)

Not everyone in the volume would go this far, or be this sweeping, but the premises Tomlinson identifies have clearly become problematical for most of them.

But not for all. Cohn and Dempster adhere strictly to the premises Tomlinson wants to unstick, and – surprisingly in this setting – give no rationale for their

132

position, let alone do anything to problematize it. The aim of their 'Hierarchical Unity, Plural Unities: Toward a Reconciliation' is to reform the canon of Schenkerian analysis by resolving a contradiction between analytic theory and practice. Although the theory puts a premium on structure (the Ursatz and its prolongation), practice often willy-nilly enhances the role of (especially motivic) design, at times even allowing design elements a share in determining structural descriptions. Cohn and Dempster respond by arguing, with a conceptual apparatus far too elaborate for the purpose, that both structure and design, 'hierarchically generated unity and [surface] richness', should be recognized as independent canons of 'musical and music-analytic value' (p. 178).

Even good friends of undiluted analysis might object that this argument only rephrases the problem as its own solution – declares victory and retreats – and that the implicit equation between musical and music-analytic value, intentional or not, seems a mite imperious. The more pressing question for present purposes is why Cohn and Dempster are so unreflectively bent on patching up the same machinery of old-fashioned canon formation that their colleagues are striving to dismantle. One answer comes forth in a particularly unguarded textual moment:

> [Structural] networks fail to satisfy our critical urge both to acknowledge and to master phenomenal complexity by discovering some underlying structural simplicity. . . . Abandoning the hierarchical home for unconstrained networks threatens theorists with a nomadic life of promiscuous pluralism, indeterminacy, or chaos. (p. 172)

The imaginary scene of music theorists in exile, demoted to the status of the Other by the frustration of their urge to mastery, levelled with Bedouins or archaic hunter-gatherers and beset by an unbridled feminine sexuality associated with the 'phenomenal complexity' – the body – of music: this is not a pretty picture. Faced with rhetoric like this, rhetorics like Bohlman's and Tomlinson's seem calmly factual.

That impression, though, should not be trusted uncritically. The imaginary content of a purple patch may not extend evenly or unproblematically across a larger, more complex field of discourse. Philip Gossett's 'History and Works that Have no History: Reviving Rossini's Neapolitan Operas' forthrightly adheres to formalist-aestheticist principles, but its engagement with them is nuanced, reflective and by no means involuted. Gossett devotes most of his space to showing the social seriousness and aesthetic integrity of the operas referred to in his title. His topical argument is that ottocento opera in general and Rossini's Neapolitan operas in particular have been excluded from the musicological canon only because the discipline has been (and still is) ruled by the 'cultural prejudices' of a 'central Austro-German tradition'. So powerful is this rule that those, like Gossett himself, who

> investigate, respect, and love early Ottocento Italian opera . . . have neglected to subject individual works to the kind of analytic scrutiny we take for granted when the composer's name is Mozart, Weber, or Wagner. . . . Even when we do undertake such studies, we are burdened by doubts concerning the significance of our studies. (p. 109)

This passage describes a kind of colonization of the scholarly psyche. It resonates suggestively with accounts by postcolonial writers of the dilemma they face in trying to work out their own cultural identities with linguistic and educational tools inherited from their former masters. Resisting such conceptual enclosure, Gossett glimpses a new canon in the making. By creating a critical history for works that have been denied one, students of early ottocento opera can not only give it an 'ever-larger role in our conceptual systems', but also contribute to a general re-examination of 'the discourses our discipline employs to study and evaluate the "facts" it enshrines' (p. 113).

As it happens, Gossett's programme runs afoul of a criticism voiced in Don Randel's 'The Canons in the Musicological Toolbox'. Randel uses the treatment of Italian opera to exemplify 'traditional musicology's traditional imperialism', which disregards 'what is most interesting or characteristic' about new bodies of music:

> Musicology has typically added repertories to its domain by a process of colonization that imposes traditional methods on new territories. After years of regarding Italian opera as peripheral, if not frivolous, we discovered that it too has sources and even sketches to study and edit and that it too could be investigated in terms of large-scale formal coherence. (p. 17)

Gossett's reply is tart and to the point:

> In this formulation . . . [approaching] such 'peripheral, if not frivolous' music . . . with techniques derived from 'central, and serious' (that is, German) music fail[s] to address what is 'most interesting or characteristic about it'. This, in *poche parole*, can be translated as meaning that Italian composers, absorbed in their *dolce far niente*, should be allowed to soak in the warm Mediterranean sun and leave canonical matters to their northern brethren. (p. 108)

Although Randel is no happier about Austro-German hegemony than Gossett, his example does seem to reinstate the authority that his essay otherwise questions. Yet Gossett, as he himself recognizes (p. 97), is caught in the same snare. He is, after all, rehabilitating early ottocento opera precisely by showing that it measures up to the 'central, and serious' standards of the Austro-German canon.

Randel's own essay is a synoptic, rough-edged account of the assumptions through which traditional musicology upholds that canon and vice versa. The assumptions at issue – the primacy of notated music, of 'the work itself', of pitch relationships, of art music, Western music, music by men – are designedly familiar. Randel cites them primarily to show how historically contingent they are, and how their contingency makes a disciplinary paradigm shift a necessity. Once the historicity of its traditional canons becomes impossible to ignore, musicology

> must inevitably move in the direction of the listener: away from the process of composition and toward the process of hearing; away from the presumably autonomous text and outward to the network of texts that, acting through a reader or listener, give any one text its meaning. (p. 16)

This is attractive; the reorientation Randel foresees would certainly help to counteract the overvaluation of 'works' in Roland Barthes's sense of commodified texts with fixed meanings.[1]

Nevertheless, there are questions to be asked. It is not clear that problematizing the production of texts necessarily privileges their reception, nor that a generalized intertext 'acts through' reception more intelligibly or more importantly than it does through production, nor whether it makes sense to ascribe agency to such an intertext at all. More disconcerting still is the apparently simple transfer of centralized authority from the composer or 'masterwork' to the

---

[1] Roland Barthes, 'From Work to Text', *The Rustle of Language*, trans. Richard Howard (Berkeley, 1989), 56–64.

134

listener or community of listeners. The recognition of contingency does not lead here to a plural or problematized meaning, but to a single and univocal meaning determined by the agency of the intertext. Difficulties of this sort are hard to avoid; more must be involved in renegotiating a canon than straightforwardly exchanging one set of tools for another.

Bruno Nettl's stance towards traditional musicology is less 'political' than Randel's and (even) more reflective than Gossett's. His 'Mozart and the Ethnographic Study of Western Culture' is a designedly paradoxical text – on the one hand a field study by an 'ethnomusicologist from Mars' charged with describing 'the basics of Western art music culture as manifested by the community of denizens of a fictitious (well, maybe not so fictitious) Music Building' in a North American university (p. 138), on the other hand a rhetorical performance modelled on the form of an eighteenth-century symphony. Foregrounding the uses of mythological narrative, Nettl interweaves the Martian's findings with findings from his own studies of Blackfoot and Persian musical culture. The result is a revealing glimpse of something so exotic, hieratic and ritualistic that it makes the third act of *Parsifal* look like a business meeting: Western art-music culture, defamiliarized.

Among the more striking features of this culture are its reverence for a small group of great masters – a hierarchy of demigods through whose mythified identities musical 'masterworks' are mediated – and the sacramental equation of these masters with their music ('What are we listening to?' 'Mozart.') The 'greatest' (biggest) of the masters' works are reproduced by factory- or army-like ensembles under the absolute control of a central authority figure who (a sacred monster?) is also 'permitted or even expected' to be a cultural outsider, eccentric in manner, dress and conduct (p. 152).

On the basis of these findings, the ethnomusicologist from Mars ponders a contradiction:

> In this system of Western culture that produces wonderful music, what are the principles and values that underlie it and that it expresses? We see intriguing concepts such as genius, discipline, efficiency, . . . the wonders of complexity, the stimulus of innovation, music as a great thing with metaphorical extensions. But, we are forced to suggest, we also see dictatorship, conformity, a rigid class structure, overspecialization, love of mere bigness, and more of that kind. (p. 153)

What are the interrelationships of the West's 'technically and spiritually supreme musical accomplishment' and the 'values of an essentially negative character' that embed it (p. 154)? The Martian is too much on the outside, and his earthling colleague, the imitator of eighteenth-century symphonic form, too much on the inside, to venture an answer. Nettl's modest frankness is admirable when he says, simply, 'I am not sure.' But the question left unanswered is, inescapably, the most compelling that the study of disciplining music needs to address. And in addressing it that study needs to face a daunting challenge. If we no longer find it reasonable to claim that musical accomplishment out-and-out transcends the negativities of its context, then we need to find good new reasons for believing that the technical and spiritual wondrousness of Western art music is anything more than an exploded fiction.

Such reasons might be easier to find if we could forget about supremacy and concentrate on cherishability: if, that is, we could preserve the artistic values of Western art musics while negating the exclusionary principles applied to (and by) them. (My reference to 'artistic' rather than 'aesthetic' values implies the involvement of social and cultural as well as perceptual-hedonic processes.) This classical Hegelian *Aufhebung* might open the way to a non-hierarchical plurality of canons, a kind of polymorphous canon of canons in which no term is securely *dux*, none *comes*. The essays by Bohlman, Tomlinson and Robert Morgan all in some way invoke this pluralization as an ideal. The invocation is an attractive move, if not a surprising one. But it may also, only slightly less than Cohn's and Dempster's dual valorization of structure and design, be a means of declaring victory and retreating.

For Bohlman, the multicanon already exists within ethnomusicology, the model product of a model discipline. His 'Ethnomusicology's Challenge to the Canon; the Canon's Challenge to Ethnomusicology' is, like Nettl's, a paradoxical text, but not exactly by design; it credits ethnomusicology with a vigilantly reflexive and self-critical stance sorely lacking in traditional musicology, but is neither reflexive nor self-critical in its idealization of its own discipline. To the extent that this bias effectively rattles musicology, I am all for it; musicology needs to be shaken up. Bohlman's historical account of ethnomusicology's challenge to 'the very process of canonization, which it believed hammered a wedge between our music and the Other's' (p. 133) is compelling in its own right, and the challenge deserves the praise it receives. But the existence of an 'anticanonic' multicanon says nothing at all about the specific status, value or history of any of the musics of which it consists. This problem is especially acute for the canon of Western art music where individual 'works' do, in fact, exist and have individualized histories. Nor, as Nettl's essay shows, can an ethnomusicological reading of Western art music in particular do more than pose the vexed questions of its status, value and history in provocatively defamiliarized ways. Nor, finally, does the apparent levelling effect of the multicanon automatically deflate Western (or other) claims to supremacy: it is, after all, at least thinkable that some musics, in some senses, are better than others. In short, the multicanon does not solve a problem; it is a problem.

To say as much is also to dissent from Robert Morgan's 'Rethinking Musical Culture: Canonic Reformulations in a Post-Tonal Age'. Much of this essay is devoted to the sophisticated retelling of a familiar story: the demise, with modernism, of common-practice tonality and the emergence of a musical (dis)order in which, as the song says, anything goes. Instead of a new common practice to replace an old one, the 'post-tonal age' offered (and still offers) only a variation on Dostoyevsky's famous formula: if God is dead, all things are permitted. 'With the old grammar gone and no new one to take its place, nothing was either prescribed or forbidden. As if in a single stroke, anything and everything became possible.' Morgan needs no reminding, of course, that tonal music continued to be written, even to thrive. But something had changed forever:

> Once [the] possibilities [of tonality] were widely perceived as exhausted, incapable of further expansion, tonality lost the traditional basis for its expressive force. And without general acceptance, it surrendered perhaps its most essential attribute: its 'universality', its status as a common language. (p. 47)

Morgan thus reads the felt loss of common-practice tonality metaphysically, as a synonym for modern alienation.

Perhaps it is time to start feeling uncomfortable with this undoubtedly powerful story, which, upon reflection, begs all too many questions – not least the question of whether any story focused on the Romantic archetype of a lost centre is still credible. Which was more widespread: the perception that tonality had been exhausted or the judgment that such a perception was illusory? Does the belief that tonality has not been exhausted really constitute its expressive basis, traditional or otherwise? Perhaps tonality during the common-practice period was simply taken for granted, even when called into question. But why should it lose authenticity just because it stops being taken for granted? And does (once) being taken for granted plausibly constitute tonality as a 'common language'

136

with a universal grammar? Might it not make more sense to say that Wolfgang Mozart and The Rolling Stones, Irving Berlin and Franz Liszt, Amy Beach and Louis Armstrong, are not conversing in anything like a common language but speaking in tongues at each other, chatting in Babel, even though all their music is 'tonal'?

At any rate, Morgan sees the outcome of the story, evident now that modernism itself has become 'part of history', as a radical diversification and proliferation of musics, a levelling process no longer controlled by 'an absolute standard of "high" art' (p. 60). He wants to refigure this 'encompassing cultural mix' (the existence of which is not in doubt) as a viable multicanon. The project is spurred by a sense of crisis:

> The loss of a central musical language is merely one symptom . . . [of o]ur fragmented and dissociated manner of life, reflecting the loss of an encompassing social framework capable of ordering and integrating the varied facets of human activity. (p. 58)

This language is eloquent, its appeal palpable, but here again, questions are being begged. It is at least thinkable that Morgan's 'encompassing social framework' never existed in the form he ascribes to it, and that its historical approximations have been at least as oppressive as they have been integrative. And it is at least questionable that artistic practices offer direct, perspicuous reflections of social conditions; their interrelationships may be far more perplexed and mediated.

Suppose, however, that we grant Morgan's assumptions for the sake of argument. We can then follow him in asking, 'How does one orientate oneself in such a free-flowing, unstable environment?' The short answer is: by disciplining it. By demystifying, but not abandoning, canonical standards, we can construct the multicanon as 'a set of multiple canons that, taken individually, are relatively precise in delineation'. Morgan acknowledges that the various subcanons would 'frequently work at cross-purposes', but he also expresses the hope that they would, 'equally frequently, interact in complex and fruitful ways'. 'Ideally, this framework would produce a culture of tolerance and broad understanding, but one in which differences still mattered and standards of excellence still applied' (p. 61).

It is hard to resist the appeal of so civil a culture, and harder still to resist the notion that the postmodern anarchy of musics and cultural practices can somehow become the basis of an ideal polity. But I worry, again, about the questions that are begged when no resistance is offered. At worst, Morgan's call for a 'culture of tolerance' based on the formation of a multicanon has a defensive ring in the face of better disseminated, economically more powerful musics than those housed in the Music Building. At best, his proposal fails to confront (though it does admit) the problems raised by the likelihood of dynamic interplay and conflict among the subcanons, and fails, like Bohlman's, to address the nagging fact that membership in a multicanon does not settle the question of the relative value of the members. What if a scholar of 'classical' music hails a scholar – let alone a practitioner – of American 'popular' music only to be told by the latter that 'classical' music, especially in America, is the plaything of an effete, oppressive and fast-fading cultural elite? What if people devoted to rock, rap or 'world music' feel no need for a multicanon? Who says that they should?

More fundamentally, Morgan's multicanonic ideal, like his history of the posttonal age, reproduces the metaphysical ideal of a common language that supposedly died along with the singular canon. Granted, the ideal replaces a single, global standard of value with something apparently more democratic, a series of local standards. But it does not question the necessary connection between standards and value. Why must plurality, too, be canonical? Why not spare the rod? Would not a local standard, within its own limited sphere, be just as coercive as any global standard it helped render moot? Is it not thinkable that value judgments, which neither can nor should be avoided, might not, or, for social and ethical reasons, should not, derive from an attempt to match an 'is' with an 'ought'? Might not, or should not, the excellence of musics, and of artistic works or practices generally, be negotiated in relation to their historical circumstances and uses, be subject to change and change again, be caught up in conflicting dialogues in which formal execution, expressive content, ideological force and interpretive possibility all have a voice? Must we have canons to have (a) discipline?

Questions of a different order need to be asked of Gary Tomlinson, who himself asks some of the questions I have just posed and whose metacanonical project is far more radical than either Bohlman's or Morgan's. The local topic of Tomlinson's essay is the canonization of jazz, which he (in common with Don Randel) believes to have followed the obnoxious aestheticist-transcendentalist-formalist principles controlling the canonization of Western art music. His case in point is the widespread dismissal of Miles Davis's jazz-rock fusion music of 1969-74 as the sign of a 'fall from grace': unjazzy, corrupt and commercial. Tomlinson's musical concerns, however, subserve a broader concern with what he calls cultural dialogics, the key issues of which are ethical and epistemological. Cultural dialogics is a programme (inspired by Foucault, among others) for decentring knowledge by practising a reflective vigilance against 'monological' claims to universality. Such claims are both false and socially oppressive. Since 'discourses are created and evolve in dialogue with other discourses', every particular discourse must 'retain the memory of its own partiality' by 'maintain[ing] its dialogue with the others at its horizon' (p. 72). Knowledge is not to be constituted as the product of a 'singular, authoritative perception', but as the product of 'parallax'. This term, Tomlinson explains,

> is a metaphor for . . . a way of knowing in which all vantage points yield a real knowledge, partial and different from that offered by any other vantage point, but in which no point yields insight more privileged than that gained from any other. . . . The deepest knowledge will result from the dialogue that involves the largest number of differing vantage points. (p. 74)

Davis's jazz-rock fusion models in music what Tomlinson looks for (and seeks to emulate) in scholarship.

Questions can be raised about whether Tomlinson's own discourse, not heeding its own cautions, falls into the snare of monologically pronouncing on what is and what is not dialogical. As Tomlinson is the first to point out, the snare is endemic; 'monologue can wear the mask of dialogue' (p. 75). But this is itself only a local topic. More important are questions about parallax as a model and ideal, and about Tomlinson's characterization of the aestheticism, transcendentalism and formalism that are its contraries. We may go along with Tomlinson in taking decentred knowledge as an end while still disagreeing with him about means.

The parallactic scheme lays stress on the equality and plenitude of vantage-points. Even, however, if we count as knowledge only what we learn from multiple vantage-points, it does not follow that the constituent vantage-points will be, or need be, equally reliable, informative or perspicuous – unless, of course, we rule in advance that they must be and are. Nor is it clear how conflicts between vantage-points are to be handled. Does, for example, Amiri Baraka's formalist view (later recanted) that Davis's fusion music was merely 'trendy and faddish' represent a parallactic vantage-point or a monological chimera? Nor, finally, is it clear why the sheer multiplicity of vantage-points should produce the deepest knowledge rather than the widest confusion. Less may not be more in the architecture of decentred knowledge, but more can conceivably be less.

138

As to the centralizing principles of aestheticism, transcendentalism and formalism, Tomlinson is surely right that they have been the guiding lights of the Western art-music canon and – in my view, anyway – right that as he describes them they have helped make that canon sclerotic and oppressive. The trouble is that he describes only their strongest and most naive forms. Different descriptions are readily available that would give these principles more credibility as vantage-points and undo, or at least complicate, their apparently rigid monologism. What if we were to rewrite as follows the passage quoted on p. 131 above?

> Aestheticism is the view that the meaning and expression found in artworks are (not 'of a different, higher order than', but) *at least as distinctive and significant as* those found in other cultural acts; transhistoricism (not 'transcendentalism'), the view that *elements of* artistic value and significance (but not always the same elements and not 'artistic value and significance' *tout court*) can somehow travel with an artwork outside of the specific contexts that condition (not 'determine or redetermine') them; and formalism, the view that meaning and value inhere in the internal formal arrangements of the artworks themselves, independent of *as well as in association with* their context of creation and reception.

Even as a postmodernist writer who subscribes to the goals of decentred knowledge, the socio-cultural contextualization of art and the purposeful undisciplining of canons, I have no trouble negotiating with the first two of these positions, minus their '-ismatic' constraints, even if the third still gives me some pause. A canon or multicanon that invoked them, especially if it invoked them among others, would not necessarily be an instrument of strait-jacketed thinking and illegitimate social control.

In general, the attempts in *Disciplining Music* to theorize music's de-, un- or redisciplining reach their limits when they reach for a premature pluralism. The most successful essays in the volume avoid this crux by refracting the general problem of disciplinarity through the thick description of a particular instance, in the process giving full play to the perplexities and ambivalences that attend on the enterprise.

Katherine Bergeron's 'A Lifetime of Chants', an account of how the monks at Solesmes, between 1880 and 1905, won and then lost both material and interpretative control over the body of Gregorian chant, does this only to a limited degree. It tells its tale suggestively, but in too little depth or detail. The topics touched on, among them the disciplinary opposition of 'science' and 'fantasy' and the political impact of what Foucault would call 'technologies', the techniques and procedures used to organize fields of knowledge, are important; they deserve a full-dress treatment.

More detailed and more nuanced is Ruth Solie's 'Sophie Drinker's History', a study of how Drinker's *Music and Women* failed to enter the musicological canon despite being widely noticed when it was published in 1948. Carefully declining to idealize where she esteems, Solie shows how Drinker's text went against virtually every dominant grain of musicological thought, insisting, for instance, on valuing communal music-making over the production of individual masterworks, on recognizing the musico-social problems of women as a class and a caste, and on foregrounding 'the embedding of musical expression within culture' (p. 38). In showing how Drinker, despite her own privileged social position, virtually assured her book of outlaw or outcast(e) status, Solie provocatively raises the question of 'what it would take – how canonic practices and values would have to be different – in order for the participation and experience of women to appear in the history of Western music' (p. 23).

Although studies like Solie's certainly contribute to a theory of disciplinarity, they do not obviate the need for more global approaches. Curiously little progress has been made in this area, even in literary theory, where the whole ruckus over canons and discipline got started.[2] I do not pretend to have a handy remedy for this predicament. I will, though, throw out a pair of suggestions in the hope of advancing the discussion.

First, more attention might be paid to the sheer fictionality of canons, a fictionality which is intriguingly double-edged. On the one hand, canons – and here I specifically mean canons in the arts – dissemble the degree to which they are tendentious, partial and contested. Suitably disguised as the settled truth, they impose constraints on the inherently unruly behaviour of people seeking and finding pleasure. On the other hand, canons provide a stock of communal lore that those same people, not so easily fooled, can negotiate with, ironize and hide behind. Canons make available the risks and pleasures of the non-canonical, to which canonical pleasure itself has underground links. One peculiarity of Western art-music canons is that they manage to leave so little room for such behaviour – although there is, as Joseph Kerman pointed out ten years ago, an impressively wide gap between music as performed and enjoyed (the repertory, shaped by performers) and music as studied (the canon, shaped by scholars).[3] The qualifier entered, musical canons still seem exceptionally rigid; it would be good to know why.

Second, more of an effort might be made to problematize the relationship between artistic canons and (undesirably) dominant ideologies. That relationship is always potentially plural. Although the process of canonization serves, virtually by definition, to advance dominant ideological agendas, it can also serve to retard them. Admittedly, some works, styles and genres of art can and should be read as slavish mystifications of unjust social relationships. More often, though, the arts seem caught up in complex networks of compliance and resistance, discourse and counterdiscourse, credulity and critique, networks full of indeterminacies and points of permanent instability. Nor are even the most slavish cases always monolithic and unselfdivided. Nor, again, are all disciplines mutually congenial; the imposition of one may have as its price or reward the undoing of another. Only by being alert to such possibilities can the study of disciplinary practices become, itself, a discipline in the best sense, capable of being rigorous without being rigid.

But there is no easy recipe for success. Even when we come to understand better how and why canons are formed, the dilemma of what to do with them will remain. The contemporary concept of an artistic canon is inherently oppositional; it suggests that artistic prestige depends on a questionable appropriation of traditional forms of religious and legal authority. To think of artistic canons is, in strict logic, to think ill of them. Yet without some sort of canon, value judgments seem to be relativized into insignificance; it is not just that anything goes, but that nothing matters. Similarly, to think of cherished artistic works or practices as canonical immediately foregrounds what is questionable about them. Yet a refusal, on that account, to cherish some things more than others risks trading a cultural heritage for a laundry list. As I have tried to stress throughout this essay, pluralism, in and of itself, offers at best the illusion, or say the intention, of escaping this impasse. If canons are inherently problematical, then multiplying them only multiplies the problems they pose.

Again, I have no ready solution to offer, only suggestions. What if we were to disengage the notion of a privileged body of works or practices from the notion of a set of guiding principles? What if we abandoned the notion that the body

---

[2] For some exceptions, see Barbara Herrnstein Smith, 'Contingencies of Value', and Charles Altieri, 'An Idea and Ideal of a Literary Canon', *Canons*, ed. Robert von Hallberg, special issue of *Critical Inquiry*, 10 (1983), 1–36 and 37–60 respectively, and John Guillory, 'Canon', *Critical Terms for Literary Study*, ed. Frank Lentricchia and Thomas McLaughlin (Chicago, 1990), 233–49.

[3] 'A Few Canonic Variations', *Canons*, 107–26.

140

must exemplify broadly generalized principles or standards of value? The body, in that case, would be more real than ideal, a repertory rather than a canon. Always evolving, not fixed in canonical marble, repertories could be approached on the understanding that the privileging of artistic works, kinds or practices is a tenable, even indispensable, means of creating cultural continuity, of constituting a history on which cultural meanings may be built. Different 'artefacts', however, would not necessarily enter a repertory for the same reasons, even if the artefacts themselves were similar. And the reasons for worldly success would not necessarily be found among the governing principles ascribed to an artefact, whether by the artefact itself or by commentators involved in its production, reception or disciplining. Tchaikovsky's *Romeo and Juliet* may involve an ambitious reworking of sonata form, but can that really help explain the enormous popularity of this music, and the flexibility that allows it (as my television recently showed) to celebrate not only high Romantic passion but the great taste of Hebrew National hot dogs? On the account I have given, governing principles should be too adventitious to have canonical force. What they can have is persuasive force, illocutionary force, the capacity to spark discussion. Although they would seldom provide the reasons for an artefact's success, they would always, for better or worse, provide a rationale. The principles would not constitute standards of value, but appeals for valuation.

By seconding, countering, revising or devising those appeals as concretely as possible, we might be able to gain some of the ends of pluralism – diversity, tolerance, reflectiveness – without succumbing to its lures. This approach, which requires the use of a historically informed hermeneutics and which emphasizes the moral and social as well as the disciplinary agency of the interpreter, would disenfranchise certain 'monological' positions. Hierarchical distinctions between high and low, self and Other, would no longer be feasible except as historical descriptors. At the same time, this 'heterological' approach would leave open the possibility that some artistic works, practices or types are genuine human achievements, precious in themselves and preferable to others. To pursue that possibility, advocates of particular artefacts would need to create an accessible public discourse in which value and meaning could be clarified and negotiated. For those of us who are advocates of Western art music, with which more people every year seem to be losing touch, the most important work ahead may be just that.

CHAPTER 6

The Strange Case of Beethoven's Coriolan: Romantic Aesthetics, Modern Subjectivity, and the Cult of Shakespeare

Both musical and literary criticism in the nineteenth century were engaged in aggressive projects of canon formation. Although their motives and methods differed in many particulars, the two projects were alike in seeking a centered aesthetic order as a counterweight to the increasingly decentered organization of modern life. To use the language of Max Weber, they sought to make the aesthetic the locus of the charismatic as the social became the locus of the bureaucratic. Given the era's social ideology, this aim required that the aesthetic, always dangerously proximate to the feminine, be a locus of masculine identity as well. The result was a mode of canonization focused more on persons than on texts and centered on the charisma of a single supreme—and supremely virile—figure.[1]

There was never much doubt about the identity of the supreme figure for either music or literature; the archetypal geniuses were going to be Beethoven and Shakespeare. But this selection introduced a slight asymmetry, which gives this article its topic. Because of Shakespeare's chronological priority, Beethoven could best be seen to *equal* Shakespeare if he could be seen to *resemble* Shakespeare. The resemblance, in turn, could best be justified if Beethoven, like so many nineteenth-century composers after him, had written music on Shakespearean topics. But this he perversely declined to do.

Beethoven was an avid reader of Shakespeare, like most German intellectuals of his day, and he did consider writing an opera on *Macbeth*. But the opera remained unwritten, and there is no authorized Shakespearean composition in Beethoven's output. Some musical ideas intended for the *Macbeth* project may have found their way into the eerily atmospheric slow movement of the so-called "Ghost" Trio (op. 70 no. 1), but the link is tenuous at best. The slow movement of the First String Quartet (op. 18 no. 1) is based, by Beethoven's own account, on the tomb scene of *Romeo and Juliet*, but the account emerged in a private conversation, not in the score, and the connection has never become part of the Beethoven legend.[2] Finally, both the "Tempest" and "Appassionata" Piano Sonatas (op. 31 no. 2, and op. 57), according to a remark Beethoven is supposed to have made to Anton Schindler, take Shakespeare's *Tempest* as an underlying "poetic idea," but this allusion has survived mainly as a tantalizing enigma, not as the source of a Shakespearean program.[3]

On this evidence, Beethoven seems to have been willing to endow certain pieces with an underlying poetic idea taken from Shakespeare but not to make the identity of the poetic idea public. Since he was one of the first composers to see himself as a part of a classical canon, and the very first to orient his career around that position, it is possible that he was being prudent or shrewd in this— that he saw the prestige gradient inevitably tilted against him and avoided invoking it. More likely, he was chary of associating his music too closely with any literary text, preferring, where he indicated a poetic idea, to do so in highly generalized terms. To do otherwise would be to risk making the music dependent on literary authority, which would diminish both its claims and the composer's to classical status in their own right. Although the relevant documentation is sparse, it does indicate Beethoven's concern on this front. Writing on the relative powers of poetry and music, he concedes that "the poet's [referential, specifically pictorial] sphere is not so restricted" as the composer's, but at once continues: "On the other hand my sphere extends further into other regions and our empire cannot be so easily reached."[4] Neither the figure of empire nor the implicit figure of quest is entirely casual.

Whatever its motives, Beethoven's distance from Shakespeare could not withstand the interpretive energies of later canonizers. Critics had begun the process of inventing a Shake-toven during the composer's lifetime, calling him the Shakespeare of music and claiming that his works were (or should have been) inspired by Shakespeare's plays.[5] By the 1930s, Arnold Schering had even managed to give Beethoven's unwritten opera an imaginary staging by inferring, on the basis of the music alone, that the "Appassionata" Sonata took *Macbeth* as a program.[6]

The focal point of the Shakespearizing process, however, proved to be Beethoven's concert overture *Coriolan* (in C Minor, op. 62, 1807), a work based not on Shakespeare's play but on a quite different sort of play by Heinrich von Collin. But *Coriolan* was a name to conjure with. Neither E. T. A. Hoffmann nor Richard Wagner nor Donald Tovey would have any truck with Collin; *Coriolan* had to be recognized as Beethoven's Shakespearean overture. Tovey even claimed that Wagner, in his essay on the work, "did well to ignore everything but Shakespeare and Beethoven."[7] What is important about this process is not simply that it happened—Beethoven has had praise enough to bury him—but that it endowed the image of Beethoven with the ideological force otherwise centered on the culturally dominant image of Shakespeare.

The first of three sections to follow offers a sketch—no more, and admittedly too synoptic—of that Shakespearean image. The second section tracks Hoffmann, Wagner, and Tovey as they appropriate the image for Beethoven. This process will involve a much closer attention to the rhetoric of these writers than is customary in musicology and in so doing will also constitute an implicit argument that musical meaning is in part created by the rhetoric of historically resonant critical responses, the textual (re)production of acts of hearing. The third section, following a detour through one more musicological text (by Paul Bekker), asks how far Beethoven himself invited or anticipated the act of hearing *Coriolan* under the aegis of Shakespeare.

1

The effort to establish a secular high culture grounded in literature and the arts has regularly placed Shakespeare, or rather an ideologically loaded image of Shakespeare, in the position of emblematic supremacy.[8] Beginning in England around the turn of the eighteenth century, this process accelerated dramatically around the turn of the nineteenth as part of the discourse of European romanticism, eventually spreading from England and Germany to France, the United States, Russia, and Italy.

The starting point for the construction of the romantic Shakespeare is the idea that Shakespeare's genius comprehends and summarizes the whole human condition. The idea was ubiquitous and produced a consistent family of tropes and topics; my illustrations come largely from two exemplary sources, August Schlegel and Samuel Taylor Coleridge. For Schlegel, Shakespeare "stood like a magician above the world, penetrating with one glance into all the depths, and mysteries, and perplexities of human character."[9] Schlegel's Shakespeare is the master of the human heart . . . plenipotentiary of the whole human race . . . a Prometheus . . . endowing the creatures of his imagination with such self-existent energy, that they afterwards act . . . according to general laws of nature. . . . What each man is, that Shakespeare reveals to us most immediately; he . . . obtains our belief, even for what is singular and deviates from the ordinary course of nature.[10]

Similarly, Coleridge claims that Shakespeare "darts himself forth, and passes into all the forms of human character and passion." His characters are "at once true to nature, and fragments of the divine mind that drew them."[11]

So represented, Shakespeare becomes the paradigm of artistic creativity itself; in the words of a famous *bon mot* by Alexandre Dumas that Hector Berlioz liked to quote, he becomes "the artist who has created the most, next to God."[12] The medium of this quasi-divine creativity, and its object, too, is human character. What makes Shakespeare a Prometheus for Schlegel and "the Spinozistic deity—an omnipresent creativeness" for Coleridge is the power to create human subjects in terms that may simultaneously be true to life (true to nature, "according to general laws") and larger than life (deviating from nature, "fragments of a divine mind"). His characters are rendered in terms that both compel common recognition and impart sublime significance.[13]

This conjunction of creative power and the dramatic realization of character forms an important link between romantic aesthetics and the social process of subject formation. The literary world of the early nineteenth century inherited an image of Shakespeare as the supreme artist of nature, one who mirrored "manners" and "life" with the utmost fidelity. As Alexander Pope put it in 1725, Shakespeare's "Characters are so much Nature herself, that 'tis a sort of injury to call them by so distant a name as Copies of her."[14] The later architects of European romanticism, however, famously rejected the notion of art as the imitation of natural objects; their ideal was a higher-order imitation of natural process. For Coleridge, invoking Spinoza again and closely following Friedrich Schelling, what art should imitate is creative agency, not created form—*natura naturans* rather than *natura naturata*.[15] In Immanuel Kant's version of the same idea, what art imitates is not the aesthetically pleasing forms that nature creates but the freedom by which it creates them.[16] Phenomenal nature was not to be rendered in art but imaginatively transformed by it, and this transformation was understood as an avenue to higher truths.[17] Shakespeare became the foremost exemplar of this process, in which what art "renders" is not the world but the mind's engagement with the world. His works, regarded less as plays to be seen than as texts to be read, became models for the transfiguring expression of internal states in external forms.

This elevating appropriation of the inner through the outer, of the self through representation of (or in) the world, constitutes a leading romantic conception, and ideal, of human subjectivity. Constructed as the virtual origin of that ideal conception, Shakespeare became its most authentic and necessary teacher to modern men and women. To know oneself, one had to know Shakespeare. As Coleridge put it, "In the plays of Shakespeare every man sees himself," or, better, imagines himself in a higher form, like an alpine traveler who catches sight of his shadow in a mist: "a being of gigantic proportions, and of such elevated dignity, that you only know it to be yourself through similarity of action."[18] Similarly, William Hazlitt claimed that Shakespeare "was all that others were, or that they could become. . . . He was like the genius [guiding spirit] of humanity, changing places with all of us at pleasure."[19] So literally did the nineteenth century take statements like these that its "mental science," the forerunner of modern clinical psychology, often had recourse to case studies of Shakespeare's characters—a practice culminating in Freud's reading of Hamlet as the prototype of the modern Oedipus complex and hence of the modern psyche.[20]

The process of finding one's identity through Shakespeare was enhanced by the abundance, especially but not exclusively in England, of edited texts and commentaries. The (in)famous *Family Shakespeare*, edited by Henrietta Bowdler, pruned Shakespeare's texts of everything that might offend middle-class respectability. The plays thus "bowdlerized" were not only defanged but also dehistoricized, rendered "timeless" by being turned into something like Victorian popular fiction. To similar, if less blatant, effect, Shakespeare was the favorite poet of nineteenth-century anthologies, which generally published passages from the plays as separate "poems." Thus decontextualized, the passages were monumentalized for popular consumption, like busts of the great composers. In turn, readers, relieved of the historical presence of Elizabethan drama, could annotate, underline, or dog-ear their own favorite passages at will. A Shakespeare made up of such passages could be infinitely individualized; the monuments could be assembled as the reader liked.

As to Shakespearean commentary, it focused on character with explicitly educative intent. In a century preoccupied with defining separate masculine and feminine spheres, different Shakespeares were parceled out to men (A. C. Bradley's *Shakespearean Tragedy*, initially delivered as lectures to Oxford undergraduates) and women (Mary Cowden Clarke's popular *The Girlhood of Shakespeare's Heroines* and Heinrich Heine's commentary to *Shakespeare's Maidens and Ladies*). The most explicit act of gendered interpellation was probably carried out by Charles and Mary Lamb's highly popular *Tales From Shakespeare,* whose prose retellings of selected plays were aimed primarily at young girls. "Boys," wrote Mary Lamb, "who are usually allowed access to their fathers' libraries at an earlier age than girls," can proceed directly to Shakespeare's "manly text." They should even initiate their sisters by first "explaining . . . such parts [of the Lambs' stories] that are hardest for [the girls] to understand," then by reading aloud from the originals after "carefully selecting what is proper for a young sister's ear."[21]

The twentieth century has continued this nineteenth-century deployment of Shakespeare as a technology of subject production but on rather different terms, most often in relation to a lost sense of romantic collectivity. According to Richard Halperin, twentieth-century Shakespeare criticism is marked by a strong primitivist strain that encourages audience or reader identification with dehistoricized ritual enactments.[22] Somehow or other, Shakespeare is continually being deployed as the paradigm for the subjectivity of his audience.

In this context, the deployment of Shakespeare in music takes on meanings not commonly recognized. When nineteenth-century composers like Berlioz, Verdi, and the young Wagner wrote Shakespearean operas, they were doing more than hitching their would-be canonical wagons to Shakespeare's star; they were also insisting on the universal value of a conspicuously national art form. And when nineteenth-century composers like Liszt, Berlioz, Mendelssohn, Dvořák, Tchaikovsky, and Richard Strauss wrote Shakespearean tone-poems, they were insisting on the power of music, too, to serve as a mirror in which the "depths, and mysteries, and perplexities" of human character would appear in paradigmatic form. The same insistence is the force that propels the critical reception of Beethoven's *Coriolan.*

2

That reception can be said to begin in earnest with E. T. A. Hoffmann's review of 1812. In a long first paragraph, Hoffmann dwells on what he takes to be an incongruity between the music, which is

Shakespearean, and the play it introduces, which is not. Ostensibly, the point is to justify the overture's appropriateness as a prelude despite this incongruity. The deeper work of the paragraph, however, is to transvalue the incongruity and identify the music with the ethos of Shakespearean high tragedy. This is accomplished through a series of rhetorical-conceptual slippages that are allowed, or encouraged, to efface the signifying relationship between the overture and Collin's play. The relevant material requires extended quotation:

> The reviewer must admit . . . that Beethoven's purely romantic genius does not seem to him to be entirely appropriate to Collin's predominantly reflective poetry, and that this composer would seize the soul with his full force and properly arouse it for the scenes that follow [on stage] if he were to write overtures to the tragedies of Shakespeare or Calderon, which express romanticism in the highest sense. The sombre gravity of the present composition, with its awe-inspiring resonances from an unknown spirit-world, foreshadows more than is subsequently fulfilled. One fully believes that the world of spirits ominously announced by subterranean thunder will draw closer in the play, that Hamlet's troubled shadow will steal across the stage, or that the terrible sisters will drag Macbeth down into Orcus. . . . The composition [nevertheless] serves very well to suggest the intended idea, namely that a great and tragic event is to form the content of the ensuing play. Even without having read the playbill nobody can expect anything else. This overture cannot be followed by domestic tragedy but only by high tragedy, in which heroes appear and perish.[23]

There are two layers of slippage in this passage, one involving its argument, the other its imagery. To take the argument first, the conjunction of Beethoven and Shakespeare begins with a judgment about "genius" in the sense of guiding spirit, style, or tone. Beethoven's romantic genius, says Hoffmann, is more appropriate to Shakespeare or Calderon than to Collin. In particular it points beyond language, in which the reflective Collin is encased, to the unknown, hence unverbalizable, spirit world. A paraphrase of this judgment, with examples, then transforms it into an account of audience response. Not only will a competent judge think Shakespeare or Calderon when hearing the overture, but a competent listener will literally expect the stage presence of Hamlet or Macbeth. (Calderon drops quietly out of the picture at this point.) The paragraph closes by mediating between style and response by invoking genre, one function of which is to perform just such mediations. Even lacking the playbill—a hypothetical lack that sends Collin, along with Calderon, into the wings—the listener will recognize a prelude to high rather than domestic tragedy.

And high tragedy is precisely the most prestigious of Shakespearean modes, in Hoffmann's day as in ours, a mode paradigmatically exemplified by the plays to which Hoffmann has earlier alluded, *Hamlet* and *Macbeth*.

This conclusion is resonant with the imagery in Hoffmann's earlier description of audience response, which tacitly replaces Collin's play as the object of response with a play by Shakespeare, namely *Hamlet*. The "subterranean thunder" to which Hoffmann refers can most plausibly be located in the opening passage of the overture, which three times sounds a long, slow, snarling string octave and follows it with a brief outburst for full orchestra, each time with greater dissonance. Hoffmann's association of this passage with the haunted Hamlet and the terrified Macbeth has a general plausibility, but his imagistic detail—a thunderous subterranean message from the spirit world—is more specific and implicitly transforms the passage into incidental music for a pivotal scene in *Hamlet*. (*Macbeth*, as we will see, does not drop out of the picture; it is simply bracketed a while.)

After meeting his father's ghost on the battlements, Hamlet swears Horatio and the watch to silence. When the latter balk at repeating their oath, the voice of the ghost cries out from under the stage; there are four cries, three of them on the single word "swear," and each is followed by an exclamatory outburst from Hamlet, who, although atop a tower, hears this voice in Hoffmann's terms as "subterranean":

> Well said, old mole! Canst work i' th' earth so fast?
> A worthy pioner!
>
> (1.5.162–63)[24]

The resonance with the events of the overture is striking, to say the least.[25]

The close of Hoffmann's paragraph picks up the thread of allusion and knots it tight. As music of high tragedy, the *Coriolan* overture belongs to an ethos in which "heroes appear and perish." This definition of the high-tragic ethos is a generalized paraphrase of Hoffmann's earlier invocation of Hamlet and Macbeth as tragic heroes. Hamlet personifies the hero's appearance, which is to say his becoming manifest as heroic. Or, to be more precise, Hamlet embodies the perplexity and self-alienation of this appearance; it is not his person but his "troubled shadow" that ought to "steal across the stage." The music of the overture embodies the troubles impelling the shadow: the dark demands of the heroic image itself, the shadow (*Schatten*) as silhouette, representation, dumb show; and the looming presence of death, the shadow (*Schatten*) as ghostly shade. Macbeth, for whom "[l]ife's but a walking shadow," concurrently personifies the hero's perishing—not, however, at the hands of his great antagonist Macduff but at those of the "terrible sisters," who are less Shakespeare's witches here than the three Fates. (Hence the odd detail of their dragging Macbeth into Orcus.)

In sum, Hoffmann's Beethoven has distilled into his *Coriolan* overture not only the source of tragedy in *Hamlet* but also the underlying dynamic of high tragedy per se as embodied by both *Hamlet* and *Macbeth*. He has, to go further, even articulated a deeper underlying dynamic defined along the lines of family and gender. The hero appears under the sign of the terrible father and perishes at the will of the terrible mother, of whom the three sisters form a prismatic reflection. Given the overture's compositional rhetoric, which offers an unusually clear demarcation of "masculine" and "feminine" themes, and given the programmatic role of the story of Coriolanus, a hero whose tragic fate is determined by the pleading of *mater* and *matria*, Hoffmann may not be far wrong. It would certainly be foolish to bypass his insight because his critical language is no longer ours.

Something similar might be said for Wagner, although his language is so outrageously florid that the temptation to dismiss it is much stronger. Whereas Hoffmann positions *Coriolan* generically as a Shakespearean tragedy, Wagner gives the overture a specific program derived from Shakespeare's *Coriolanus*. He does so, however, without ever mentioning Shakespeare (let alone Collin) by name. The reader is expected to recognize as a matter of course that the details of the program, at least initially, can refer only to the climactic scene in Shakespeare's *Coriolanus*. For Wagner, as for most readers, this is the scene in which the hero confronts his mother before the gates of Rome and succumbs to her pleas for peace, with fatal consequences to himself.

The reason for withholding Shakespeare's name is not just that in this sort of context Shakespeare's name goes without saying. Wagner's text sets up an allegorical progression from a "universally known" Ur-Coriolanus, to Shakespeare's appropriation of that original in dramatic poetry, to Beethoven's appropriation of the Shakespearean instance in music. Wagner represents the original figure, "universally" known to most classically educated nineteenth-century men from Plutarch's *Lives*, as unconditional and authorless, a mythic embodiment of "untameably forceful" (*unbändig kräftigen*) manhood.

Shakespeare, identified only as "the poet," is said to have drawn his version of this figure amid a "political canvass rich in relationship-laden circumstances"; in Shakespeare, myth is fleshed out to become history. Beethoven, identified as "the tone poet" and "the musician" before being named, seizes only on "one unique scene" in Shakespeare's play, but that "by all means the most decisive scene." In so doing he brings the figure of Coriolanus back to the universality of myth, but on a higher plane than that of the original.[26]

The approach of this "Beethoven" is initially shaped by negation; as a musician, he is said to be "out and out prohibited" from representing political circumstances. His response is to turn prohibition into purification, contingent history into essential meaning. By expressing the emotive content of the climactic scene, he is able to "seize as if at its focal point the purely human emotional content of [Shakespeare's] whole wide-stretching fabric and in the most gripping communication to bring it to purely human feeling again" (115). Beethoven condenses the play into its essential "human" truth, a truth that becomes completely manifest only in this condensation. In the process, the symbolic debt of Beethoven to Shakespeare is canceled. The kernel of Shakespearean power, the gripping rendition of human character, becomes Beethovenian.

For Wagner, this transfer of power becomes manifest both in the immediacy of the music and in the evolution of its program. The beginning of the overture, already singled out by Hoffmann as the generic site of heroic appearance, here becomes the virtual presence of a single heroic character, a heroic individuality. As such, it exceeds anything Shakespeare can offer. Whereas "the poet" must disperse dramatic character across the full length of a play and can crystallize it only in a long-deferred climax, "the musician" can call forth character fully in a single stroke, beginning with totality rather than laboriously totalizing. Thus, according to Wagner, the opening bars "present us immediately with the figure of the *man* himself: enormous force, untameable sense of self, and passionate defiance express themselves as fury, hatred, vengeance, annihilation-seeking spirit" (115). This interpretive move, the reading of the opening characterologically, established a norm of response that remains in effect today. The recognition of narcissistic brutality in the character has largely dropped away, in part no doubt because of Wagner's toxic enthusiasm, but more importantly because modernist hermeneutics have refused to be that specific.

As for the program, it deviates gradually, and in the end widely, from its Shakespearean source. On one level, the rather lurid programmatic vagaries show Wagner's narrative losing control of itself and becoming transparent to the fantasies of its author. The program, indeed, gradually becomes less a recollection of Shakespeare than a prefiguration of Lacan; it culminates in Coriolanus's "anguished voluptuousness" (*schmerzlicher Wollust*) as he reads his death warrant in the gaze of his mother, which has merged with that of the big Other, the "fatherland" for whom she pleads (117).[27] But the solemn, ritualistic closing sentence, set off by spacing and emphasis from the rest of the text—"*Thus Beethoven made poetry of Coriolanus in tones*" (*So dichtete Beethoven in Tönen den Coriolan*) (117)—suggests that the narrative transformation of the program is to be understood as an exact representation of the transformation wrought by the music. It becomes a sign of Beethoven's full appropriation of the inner truth of the climactic scene, a truth that Shakespeare could comprehend only in part.

This appropriation is grounded in both the self-evidence and the content of the truth as Beethoven conveys it. To begin with self-evidence: Wagner proposes a metaphor that effectively transfers the language, and with it the determinate meaning, of Shakespeare's *Coriolanus* to Beethoven's *Coriolan*. "The whole tone-piece," he writes, "could readily pass as the musical accompaniment to a pantomimic performance, in the specific sense that the accompaniment at the same time makes known all the speech perceptible to the ear, the subject matter of which we are constrained to imagine as presented to the eye in the pantomime" (115).[28] Wagner's imaginary pantomime proleptically resembles the situation so often found at or near the end of a narrative film, in which a totalizing image combines with supercharged music. For listeners to *Coriolan*, Coriolanus cannot appear as drama but only as image, while the meaning of the image cannot be grounded in the authority of the poet but only in the imagination, virtually in the guesswork, of the listeners themselves. The effect of the music, in contrast, appears as an effect of language, a transcription or surrogate form of the speech absent from the pantomime, in which the meaning of the drama is condensed and clarified. The musical language becomes full—"all the speech perceptible to the ear"—where the dramatic image becomes empty.

As to content, Wagner, like Hoffmann, grounds it in sexual difference. But whereas Hoffmann merely adumbrates an oedipal subtext for tragic drama in general, and therefore for the overture insofar as it prefigures a tragic drama, Wagner interprets the specific meaning of the overture as an oedipal conflict, and a drastic one. In the shift from implicit to explicit significance, from context to text, from allusion to representation, the terms at issue tend toward overstatement, even caricature. Here, typically for sexual difference, the most aggressive masculinity becomes almost pathetically vulnerable to a feminine pathos that is passive-aggressive to the point of monstrosity. The expression of this extremity testifies for Wagner to Beethoven's grasp of a more-than-Shakespearean truth. The overture raises the dramatic confrontation between Coriolanus and Volumnia to a metaphysical plane when, in another of its acts of condensation, it conflates the figures of Coriolanus's mother, wife, and child into the single, nameless, terrible figure of "the *woman*."[29] The conflict of persons thus becomes a struggle between masculine individuality and femininity as a principle—the eternal feminine.

"The *woman*" who embodies this archetypal femininity, in Lacanian terms the invasive, dispossessing "maternal superego," overwhelms the hero through a combination of her love, her abjection, and her complete incomprehension of his condition.[30] In particular, her love and abjection make her unable to grasp that for the man of untameable force to forgo his vengeance is for him "to cast away his being" (*sein Dasein fahren lassen*). For him to forgo "the annihilation of his father-city," which is to say the annihilation of the nexus linking him to the fatherland through the mother's body, is for him "to annihilate himself" (116). It is the woman's incomprehension that ultimately proves fatal to the hero; unable to make the slightest dent in it, he suddenly "halts in the torturing oscillation" and resolves to make "the offering [oblation, sacrifice] of self" (*Selbtsopfer*, 117).

Wagner's Beethoven accordingly concludes his overture by uniting, or reuniting, two cardinal moments that Shakespeare, as if erroneously, split apart: the hero's surrender to the woman and his resultant death. The overture famously ends with a quiet passage in which the terse, dynamic main motive grows sluggish and dilatory and finally collapses. Three widely spaced pizzicato C's, pianissimo remnants of the sustained fortissimo C's on bowed strings that open the piece, complete the tragic denouement. Presumably with this passage in mind, Wagner writes that "at the feet of the woman who pleaded with him for peace, [the hero], dying, breathes out his last breath" (117).

In framing the "language" for this gynophobic image, Wagner's Beethoven articulates the catastrophe that music, at its origin, arises to prevent. In so doing, he completes his appropriation of the tragedy of Coriolanus by showing that its foundation is neither dramatic nor mythical but musical. Early in his essay, Wagner proposes that we can reasonably conceive "the plastic object of expression of almost all the master's symphonic works as representations of scenes between man and woman" (115). The basis of this conception is that the symphony (in Wagner's account) derives its musical form from the dance, which in turn is the "archetype" of all scenes of sexual difference.

To see where these claims lead, we need to recognize explicitly that the "scenes" Wagner speaks of are just that: not events, but representations of events. The dance ritualizes, and therefore both constrains and interprets, the "real" relations between men and women — relations of desire and dependency that are understood to put masculinity in jeopardy and to find their "sublimest and most disturbing content" in the tragic scene enacted between Coriolanus and "the woman" (115). Symphonic form masters these relations on a higher plane by rarefying — abstracting, sublimating, metaphorizing — the dance as the dance had originally rarefied sexual difference. The distinction of Beethoven's *Coriolan* is that it applies this gesture of mastery to the primal disorder, so to speak the primal scene, over which mastery, through music, is sought. In becoming Shakespearean, or more than Shakespearean, Beethoven becomes the cultural hero who both reveals the foundations of human character and preserves the ever-vulnerable cultural order built on them.

Donald Tovey calls the essay on *Coriolan* "one of [Wagner's] finest and most attractive prose works," and much of his own account consists of variations on Wagnerian themes.[31] Although Tovey's language is almost timorously sober by comparison with Wagner's, his claims are if anything even bolder. The most striking of these takes Wagner's inversion of the Shakespeare-Beethoven hierarchy to its logical, or rather illogical, extreme. Wagner may cancel Beethoven's symbolic debt to Shakespeare, but Tovey does not just cancel it, he reverses it. To conclude his essay, he quotes the passages that begin and end the climactic scene of *Coriolanus* — condensing the scene, as Wagner has Beethoven doing. What the quotations are said to exemplify, however, is not Beethoven's interpretation of Shakespeare's *Coriolanus* but "Shakespeare's analysis of Beethoven's *Coriolan*" (145). As in Wagner, the order of priority depends on inner truth, not on chronology, and the inner truth is more Beethoven's than Shakespeare's. It is only after hearing what Beethoven "says" in the concert room that "readers and listeners may perhaps . . . do the better justice to Shakespeare when they read *Coriolanus*, or at least this scene of the fifth act, at home" (144).

The result, again as in Wagner, is to install a lack in Shakespeare's text that is made good only in Beethoven's music. Wagner's imaginary dumb show produces a *Coriolanus* stripped of language as signifier, leaving behind the Coriolanus story as an underdetermined signified. Tovey's quotations take the more radical step of preserving Shakespeare's signifiers but depriving them of their signified; the text no longer refers to the Coriolanus story at all but to Beethoven's utterance of that story in music, which the text paraphrases. The symbolic value of *Coriolanus* changes abruptly, like that of a supposedly old-master painting that has been deattributed.

It does not matter that Beethoven came to his musical utterance through a reading of Shakespeare that, as Tovey sees it, shaped his reading of a Collin who had also read Shakespeare. Tovey's Beethoven tries to be faithful to Collin and even derives "the vacillating development and the abrupt final collapse of this overture" from Collin's play. Nonetheless, Shakespeare "breaks through like Nature in Beethoven's music" (143). At first glance, that last phrase might suggest that Shakespeare is taking Beethoven as a mouthpiece. A Shakespeare reduced to Nature, however, is no longer an author but a force: impersonal, unhistorical—and mute. When Shakespeare-Nature breaks through in Beethoven's music, it is only, and instantaneously, to become part of Beethoven's music, part of what Beethoven, and Beethoven alone, "says."

At this point it is important to recognize explicitly what our readings of Tovey, Wagner, and Hoffmann do and do not imply. All three authors appropriate Shakespeare on Beethoven's behalf in the service of a certain cultural agenda that Hoffmann helps initiate and Wagner and Tovey jointly carry forward. This agenda, however, enables as much or even more than it slants insight. That the authors have overdetermined motives does not necessarily make them wrong. Hoffmann is surely right to ponder the disparity between Beethoven's style and Collin's; Wagner's programmatic invocation of the climactic scene of *Coriolanus* may be an inspired guess, and one that focuses the sexual politics of the music with great if wrongheaded effectiveness; and Tovey's idea of Beethoven's happy failure to toe Collin's line encapsulates the critical reception of *Coriolan* whether or not it accurately describes the work's production. What Tovey observes, in fact, may be a cultural imperative to recognize a Shakespearean "breakthrough" in this music that neither Beethoven's critics nor perhaps Beethoven himself could escape.

The strength of that imperative can be gauged from its effect on a strenuous effort to defy it. In his *Beethoven* (1911), Paul Bekker declares roundly that "reminiscences of Shakespeare's *Coriolanus* . . . throw no light on [Beethoven's overture]; and for one who has deeply felt and experienced [the] overture they are merely confusing."[32]

270

Bekker describes Collin's play as a "philosophic debate in a stage-setting" and his hero as "a passive, reflective personality." Shakespeare's *Coriolanus*, in contrast, "presents the tragedy of a towering personality which 'drank hatred of mankind from the fullness of love,' but was prevented from giving expression to hate by the persuasion of love" (242). Whereas Shakespeare's hero expiates his guilt by dying a shameful death at the hands of a "petty faction," Collin's avoids incurring guilt by killing himself, nobly acting on the principle that "[m]an as an individual is doomed to utter destruction if he cannot and will not bring his will in accord with the laws governing human society" (242).

Try as he might, however, Bekker cannot conform Beethoven's *Coriolan* to Collin's. His efforts founder on two fronts. First, the sentimental authoritarianism he finds in Collin does not accord well with the received image of Beethoven, or for that matter with Beethoven's music. The result, which I will not pursue in detail, is a reading of the overture as an allegory expressing the destructive will of Collin's hero but not his noble pathos. The overture, indeed, turns out to be more closely related to the *Eroica* Symphony, of which it is "a negative," than to anything in Collin's play.

Second, and more important, the available language for describing Beethoven's music is so rhetorically grounded in the discourse on Shakespeare that it cannot convincingly frame a non-Shakespearean reading. Bekker's critical language thus impels his text to reinstate the very analogies that it seeks to "obviate." Trying to keep (Beethoven's) faith with Collin, Bekker claims that "the philosophic antithesis of aristocratic and social morality, which Collin resolved in a victory for the latter, was transformed by Beethoven into a musical drama of ruthless will-power and emotional feeling" (243). This description, however, associates Beethoven's music more with Shakespeare's version of the story than with Collin's as Bekker construes the two. The "ruthless will power" corresponds better to the "towering personality" of Shakespeare's hero than to the passive reflectiveness of Collin's, and the "emotional feeling" accords better with Shakespeare's conflict of hate and love than with Collin's "philosophic debate" on the limits of free will. Even the phrase "musical drama," innocuous as it may seem, brings the music closer to the "tragedy" of Shakespeare than to the "dramatic monologue" of Collin, which is "no human or personal tragedy."

The most important of these Shakespearean associations is that of the "towering personality." In shifting the grounds of discussion from Collin's *Coriolan* to the *Eroica*, Bekker invokes the towering,

Coriolanean personality of Napoleon. His doing so reanimates the quotation worked into his earlier account of *Coriolanus*: "[one who] drank hatred of mankind from the fullness of love." This line, from Goethe's poem "Harzreise im Winter" (Harz Journey in Winter), is a paradigmatic expression of alienated self-will, the same "will to destruction" that Bekker's Beethoven finds in both Coriolanus and Napoleon. (Musically speaking, the same line alludes to Brahms's *Alto Rhapsody*, a partial setting of "Harzreise" in which a female singer pleads for the alienated hero somewhat as Volumnia pleads with her wayward son.) But if Beethoven's Coriolanus is indeed a towering personality like Napoleon and Goethe's wanderer, then his literary source is not Collin but Shakespeare, and more particularly the romantic Shakespeare who portrays human character under the sign of the sublime.

3

From Tovey's perspective, Bekker's failure to Collinize Beethoven is inevitable and prefigured by Beethoven himself. We are now in a position to ask whether Tovey was right. Beethoven's intentions with regard to Collin remain unknown, but their outcome is clear. His overture, as Hoffmann claimed, is expressively consistent with Collin's play only in evoking the genre of high tragedy. The gap between the overture and the play as renditions of the Coriolanus story is glaring. By juxtaposing terse, dramatic, agitated music to a dilatory, pathetic, ruminative play, Beethoven posed a hermeneutic problem that has largely determined the course of the music's critical reception. The solution, for the authors of that reception, has been obvious (even if, like Bekker, they have thought it a false solution): Beethoven's true orientation was Shakespearean.[33]

The "towering" heroic rhetoric of the overture is consistent with this conclusion, and so is the articulation of the hero's character by means of radical sexual difference—the stark contrast between the aggressively virile first theme group and the lyrical, pleading second theme. (A specifically maternal fantasy may resound in the second theme's texture, which gradually fills out to a tutti of great sensory richness, a musical image of enveloping presence.) This agonic gendering fits in with both the construction of the romantic Shakespeare in general and the text of *Coriolanus* in particular, where it arises not only between Coriolanus and his mother but also between the warring halves of Coriolanus's subjectivity:

272

> *Cor.* Not of a woman's tenderness to be
> Requires nor child's nor woman's face to see.
> I have sat [with my family] too long.
> (5.3.129–31)

Such divided subjectivity itself invokes the romantic Shakespeare, in whose tragic heroes it was thought to be prototypically embodied.

What makes Beethoven's *Coriolan* most Shakespearean by the standards of its own era is, in fact, the impression that is transforming the external conflict between a man and a woman into an internal conflict between masculine and feminine principles, or more precisely between the masculine and feminine elements of a prototypically masculine subjectivity. Wagner's and Tovey's programmatic readings enact a continual, if unacknowledged, slippage between the two perspectives. The overture produces its transformative effect both by its handling of sonata form and, if we accept the programmatic connection, by casting that form as a kind of negative image of the climactic scene of Shakespeare's play.

The "pleading" theme occupies a small and highly consistent place within the overture's sonata form. It occurs twice in full, in the exposition and recapitulation, and once foreshortened, in the coda. In each case it appears abruptly after the merest pretense of transition, interrupts the agitation of the first group, sounds several times in different orchestrations, and disintegrates as a genuine transition leads to an exceptionally violent closing passage. The last and most violent of these closes proves to be self-consuming and devolves into the tragic fadeout. Each phase of this process suggests a greater and more futile masculine effort to resist the internal recognition, which in this case means the fatal triumph, of the feminine element.

The inexorability of that triumph is figured in the recapitulation, which begins by restating the "untameably forceful" introduction and first theme group in severely truncated form but continues by giving the pleading second theme in full. The gesture of truncation makes the heroic masculine principle "small," as if infantilized, in relation to its feminine complement and perhaps suggests that its initial forcefulness is hollow at the core, a disguised lack. Harmonically, the initial materials do not find long-term resolution at this point; they return at the subdominant rather than at the tonic. The second theme, in contrast, resolves strongly, countering the relative major of the exposition with the tonic major. The introduction and first theme are not recapitulated in the tonic minor until late in the coda, and then only in compromised forms, the introduction ebbing in force and the formerly dynamic theme both disintegrated and disintegrating, sounding darkly on the cellos and steadily falling to pieces over a droning bassoon.[34]

Parsed in relation to the quasi-Shakespearean subtext, this tonal scheme means that the heroic first-group material loses the authority of the tonic, while the pleading second theme gains the even greater authority of the tonic major, of which the minor is technically a less stable variant. The subdominant renders the heroic material harmonically "tame" in advance of its being tamed expressively; the tonic major pointedly sounds nowhere but in the second theme. To compound the effect, even the closing passage is recapitulated at the subdominant, a gesture especially striking because the closing passage in the exposition is in the tonic.[35] So contextualized, the necessary long-term "resolution" of the second theme depletes rather than confirms the authority of the primary key. When the second theme itself returns in the coda, it sounds in both the major and minor tonic, the first to reiterate the place and power of the feminine element, the second, ambivalently, to both acknowledge and be tainted by, mourn for and impose, the ensuing masculine tragedy.

The relationship of this sonata scheme to its presumed Shakespearean source is constructively problematical; it produces a hitherto unopened hermeneutic window. Shakespeare's climactic disposition of masculine and feminine voices is close to the opposite of Beethoven's. When Coriolanus and Volumnia meet before the gates of Rome, his voice predominates until he yields to her demand for a hearing. Her voice then takes over with two long eloquent speeches, separated by a few lines from her son (quoted above) as he tries unsuccessfully to tear himself away and followed by his brief speech of surrender, ending with a resigned embrace of death, "But let it come" (5.3.189). An ironic caesura follows as Coriolanus turns to his rival Aufudius and, not so resigned after all, pleads with him in "feminine" style to ratify the surrender.

One way to understand Beethoven's reversal of Shakespeare's emphasis is to hear the overture as a representation not of the external scene but of Coriolanus's tumultuous state of mind as he decides whether or not to heed his mother's appeal. The irruptions of the pleading theme would in that case indicate focal points, shifts of awareness, within the dynamic of the hero's subjectivity. Volumnia's voice would become indistinguishable from Coriolanus's inner hearkening to it. Beethoven suggests as much by his articulation of the pleading theme itself, which unfolds over an agitated accompaniment related, in its note motion, to the agitations of the first theme

274

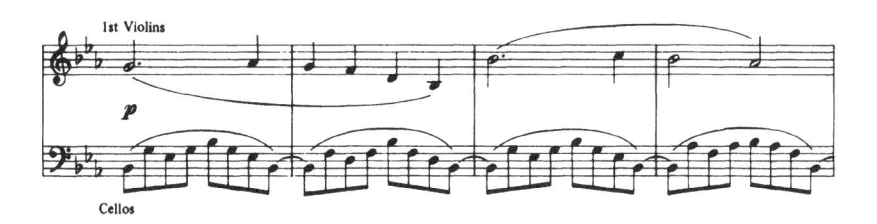

Example 1.

(Ex. 1). Put another way, what the overture produces is not a Coriolanus narrative but a Coriolanean subject-position, the fatality, but also perhaps the redemption, of which lies in its deep identification with "woman's tenderness."[36]

That identification is best articulated by the underlying affinity between the overtly antithetical first and second themes. On the surface, the two project a classic binary opposition of dynamic masculinity, marked by continual intervallic variation of a short primary motive, and static femininity, marked by intervallic fixity in a longer melody. In both the exposition and recapitulation, however, the first theme as a whole undergoes immediate transposition down one scale degree. In the same locales, the second theme as a whole undergoes immediate transposition up one scale degree, a process immediately repeated up a further degree. To be sure, the effect of these transpositions is contrastive: the first theme, shunted off the triad, becomes almost mechanically insistent; the second theme, composing out the lower third of the triad, becomes more fervid, touched with yearning. But the complementary transpositional movement also suggests the deeper identity to which I have alluded: the mechanism of the first theme is the alienated form of the yearning of the second, the yearning of the second the spiritualized form of the mechanism of the first. The binary opposition unravels: not, it must be said, in a deconstructive spirit that affirms the mobility of its terms, but in the spirit of tragic necessity.

Shakespeare, then, may very well break through in Beethoven's overture to *Coriolan*, perhaps by invitation, perhaps by force of culture if not of nature. However tacitly, Beethoven was probably the first to interpret his overture as Shakespearean, the better to claim cultural authority for (his) music as art. If so, he initiated a small but significant subtradition exemplary in its combination of aesthetic canon formation with the strict enforcement of sexual difference and the idealization of charismatic personality. Like the romantic Shakespeare, perhaps even like the historical Shakespeare, he produces the enforcement and the idealization in the name of truth, well aware of their potentially catastrophic consequences but not, for the most part, of their ideological and contingent character.

4. Afterword

These reflections on *Coriolan* raise a pair of broader issues that deserve mention here. The first is the question of where to situate musical meaning, a question particularly vexing to those who think that music's limited referential capacities render all attributions of musical meaning "subjective" in the sense of idiosyncratic. The critical practices of Hoffmann, Wagner, and Tovey all lead to substantive recognitions about both the music of *Coriolan*, considered as meaningful utterance, and the culture shaping and shaped by that utterance. This discovery process occurs despite the fact that the critical texts continually submerge historical specifics, both musical and cultural, under the universalizing rhetoric of idealist aesthetics, and, even more strikingly, despite the fact that the same texts depend on an essentially counterfactual premise.

In other words, the historically specific musical meanings of *Coriolan* emerge from a web of indirect disavowals and virtual fictions. What does the fact that this happens, what does the fact that it *can* happen, imply? Is it exceptional, or just an exceptionally clear case of the unexceptional?

The answer, I think, lies in the recognition that historically specific meaning is never, or at least rarely, transparent or unmystified at the time of its production, a condition that later reflection can improve but not undo. The critical texts here are exemplary in their fertile overcloseness to their subject. These texts appear in their historicity not in the plain sense they might be imagined to make but in the patterns that emerge as they yield to interpretation—an interpretation both historical and theoretical, both informed about earlier discourses and informed by later ones. The historicity of the texts does not ground the interpretation but is constituted by it.

So interpreted, the texts become avenues to musical meaning. But they do not decode or recover a meaning that the music "has" now or "had" then; rather, they supply the discursive framework in which the musical meaning can be, and can have been, produced. In this case, they utilize "Shakespeare" as a cultural trope in which a complex network of sociocultural concerns is condensed, and condensed not only by the critics but also, it seems, by Beethoven, in excess of his explicit intentions toward Collin. Here, too, the meaning involved is historical only insofar as it is produced retrospectively, in a discourse not coincidental with those of the music's original venue.

In sum, the meaning of the music has no fixed locale. It is a complex, uncertainly bounded effect of the interplay, actual and possible, of score, performance, reception, textualization, and further textualization. In that respect, it resembles the meaning of a text—to be cautious, say a literary text, an acknowledged vehicle of multiple and indirect meaning—regardless of its referential paucity. Or, to be less cautious: the mobility of musical meaning renders manifest what from a poststructuralist or postmodernist point of view is the latent mobility of meaning in general.

The second issue is the relation of art and ideology. As I have argued elsewhere, the study of canonicity necessarily focuses on what is most questionable about canonized works or renders questionable much of what has seemed admirable about them, even their very status as "works" of art.[37] Insofar as this skeptical impetus attacks complacency and forces us to take responsibility for our acts of valuation, it is unimpeachably a good thing. Insofar as it prompts mere debunking, or reductions of art to ideological machinery, it is a damaging and self-defeating thing. In recent years we have learned, and rightly, to recognize the questionable side, the ideologically coercive side, of canonical "masterworks." This essay rests squarely on such recognitions in the spheres of sexual and social authority. What we have not yet learned is how to absorb these recognitions into a discourse of valuation, either positive or negative.

Most of us would agree that neither the politics nor the cultural politics of a work—assuming, as I do, that the category of the work is a wonderful invention that ought to be maintained—is a sufficient ground of judgment. At the same time, traditional grounds of "purely aesthetic" judgment that simply ignore political questions—grounds that, I suspect, still form the practical standard for lack of anything better—must now be recognized as equally insufficient.

We are faced, accordingly, with the need to develop a critical language in which political and aesthetic considerations interact so fully as eventually to become indistinguishable. The points at which they do so would presumably be those at which valuations—mixed rather than pure, particular rather than general, and seeking viability rather than authority—would become possible. The development of such a critical discourse will necessarily be the work of many hands.

This essay, fascinated by the ways in which *Coriolan* accumulates and cathartically discharges tragic intensity, but at the cost of accepting a highly questionable mode of hero worship on the very brink of demystifying it, is meant as an opening move.

Notes

1. As understood here, canon formation can neither be reduced to its ideological underpinnings nor disengaged from them; the mixture of motives will vary from case to case. For debates on the issue as it bears on music, see Katherine Bergeron and Philip Bohlman, eds., *Disciplining Music: Musicology and Its Canons* (Chicago: University of Chicago Press, 1992); Sanna Pederson, "On the Task of the Music Historian: The Myth of the Symphony After Beethoven," *Repercussions* 2 (1993); 5–30; Leon Botstein, review of *Disciplining Music*, *Journal of the American Musicological Society* 47 (1994): 340–46; and Lawrence Kramer, "Charging the Canons" (review-essay on *Disciplining Music*), *Journal of the Royal Musical Association* 119 (1994): 130–40. On charisma and bureaucracy, see Max Weber, *The Theory of Social and Economic Organization,* trans. A. M. Henderson and Talcott Parsons (New York: Oxford University Press, 1947), 329–41, 358–72.

2. *Thayer's Life of Beethoven,* ed. Elliott Forbes (Princeton: Princeton University Press, 1967), 261.

3. Anton Schindler, *Beethoven as I Knew Him,* ed. Donald W. MacArdle, trans. Constance S. Jolley (London: Faber and Faber, 1966), 404–5. Schindler also claimed that Beethoven used the term "poetic idea . . . as often as any" (fn. 500).

4. Letter to Wilhelm Gerhard, 15 July 1817, from *Letters of Beethoven,* trans. Emily Anderson, 3 vols. (New York: Norton, 1961), 2:689.

5. The process was advanced enough by 1839 for Robert Schumann to remark on it: "The German forgets in his Beethoven that he has no school of painting; with Beethoven he imagines that he has reversed the fortunes of the battles he lost to Napoleon; he even dares to place him on the same level as Shakespeare." Robert Schumann, *On Music and Musicians,* ed. Konrad Wolff, trans. Paul Rosenfeld (New York: Norton, 1969), 61. See also Robin Wallace, *Beethoven's Critics: Aesthetic Dilemmas and Resolutions During the Composer's Lifetime* (Cambridge: Cambridge University Press, 1986), 27, 30, 121.

6. Arnold Schering, *Beethoven und die Dichtung* (Berlin: Junker & Dunnhaupt, 1936).

7. Donald Francis Tovey, *Essays in Musical Analysis: Symphonies and Other Orchestral Works* (London: Oxford University Press, 1981), 143.

8. This section is greatly indebted to the expert guidance of Nancy S. Leonard, both in conversation and in her "Nineteenth-Century Shakespeare," a program-book essay written for a concert of Shakespeare-inspired compositions given by the American Symphony Orchestra, 26 Sept. 1993. For a detailed history of Shakespeare's reputation, see Gary Taylor, *Reinventing Shakespeare: A Cultural History from the Restoration to the Present* (Oxford: Oxford University Press, 1989).

9. August Wilhelm Schlegel, *A History of Literature,* quoted in *Four Centuries of*

278

Shakespeare Criticism, ed. Frank Kermode (New York: Avon, 1965), 109.

10. August Wilhelm Schlegel, *A Course of Lectures on Dramatic Art and Literature*, trans. John Black (London, 1846), 361-63. The reference to Prometheus actually occurs a paragraph later than the implicitly Promethean sentence with which I have conjoined it. Schlegel subsequently ascribes to Shakespeare a still higher level of characterization in which "most dramatic poets are deficient." Shakespeare "surpasses even himself" by "so combining and contrasting [individual characters] that they serve to bring out each other's peculiarities." Because "a man's true worth" appears only "in his relations to others . . . Shakespeare makes each of his characters the glass in which the others are reflected" (368-69). Dramatic form thus evolves through the articulation of the social matrix in which individual character is always already formed and represented.

11. *Biographia Literaria*, ed. James Engell and Walter Jackson Bate, 2 vols. (Princeton: Routledge and Princeton University Press, 1983), 2:27-28; *Shakespearean Criticism*, ed. T. M. Raysor, 2 vols. (London: Dent, 1960), 2:117.

12. Taylor, 168; translation slightly modified.

13. Coleridge, *Table Talk*, ed. Carl Woodring, 2 vols. (Princeton: Routledge and Princeton University Press, 1990), 1:125. Berlioz goes even further than Schlegel and Coleridge; he blasphemously turns Shakespeare into a superior, dechristianized version of God the Father: "Shakespeare! . . . It is you that are our father, our father in heaven, if there is a heaven. God standing aloof in his infinite unconcern is revolting and absurd. Thou alone for the souls of artists art the living and loving God." *Memoirs of Hector Berlioz*, trans. David Cairns (New York: Knopf, 1969), 462.

14. From the preface to Pope's edition of Shakespeare, in *Literary Criticism of Alexander Pope*, ed. Bertrand A. Goldgar (Lincoln, Nebraska: University of Nebraska Press, 1965), 161.

15. Samuel Taylor Coleridge, "On Poesy or Art" (1818), in *Biographia Literaria*, ed. John Shawcross, 2 vols. (1907; reprint; Folcroft, Pennsylvania, 1969), 2:253-63; the original lecture notes for this essay appear in Coleridge, *Lectures on Literature, 1808-19*, ed. R. A. Foakes, 2 vols. (Princeton: Routledge and Princeton University Press, 1987), 2:217-25. On *natura naturata* and *natura naturans*, Coleridge draws on Friedrich Schelling, *Einleitung zu einem Entwurf eines Systems der Naturphilosophie* (Jena and Leipzig, 1799), 22, who in turn draws on Spinoza's *Ethics*, I, Scholium 29.

16. Immanuel Kant, *Critique of Judgment*, trans. J. Creed Meredith (Oxford: Oxford University Press, 1952), sections 44-45. On the mimetics of freedom in these passages of Kant, see Jacques Derrida, "Economimesis," trans. Richard Klein, *Diacritics* 11 (1981): 8-10.

17. For the classic account, see M. H. Abrams, *The Mirror and the Lamp: Romantic Theory and the Critical Tradition* (New York: Norton, 1953).

18. Coleridge, *Shakespearean Criticism*, 2:125. In a pattern typical of the sublime, the recognition of oneself in heightened form is preceded by a moment of blockage, as indicated by the complete form of the first sentence quoted here: "In the plays of Shakespeare every man sees himself, without knowing that he does so."

19. William Hazlitt, "On Shakespeare and Milton," from *Lectures on the English Poets* (London: Oxford University Press, 1933), 70, 71.

20. On mental science see Ekbert Faas, *Retreat into the Mind: Victorian Poetry and the Rise of Psychiatry* (Princeton: Princeton University Press, 1988). On Hamlet and Oedipus see Sigmund Freud, *The Interpretation of Dreams*, trans. James Strachey (New York: Avon, 1965), 298–300.

21. Charles and Mary Lamb, *Tales from Shakespeare*, 2 vols. (London, 1807), I:vi–vii; see also Taylor, 207.

22. Richard Halperin, "Shakespeare in the Tropics: From High Modernism to New Historicism," *Representations* 45 (1994): 1–25.

23. *E. T. A. Hoffmann's Musical Writings; Kreisleriana, The Poet and the Composer, Music Criticism*, ed. David Charlton, trans. Martyn Clarke (Cambridge: Cambridge University Press, 1989), 287.

24. Text from William Shakespeare, *The Complete Works*, ed. Alfred Harbage et al. (Baltimore: Penguin, 1969). References are to act, scene, and line.

25. Exactly how to assess this resonance is a tricky question. The most attractive possibility, that Hoffmann intuited a subtext followed, consciously or unconsciously, by Beethoven, is also the least likely. A better possibility is that Hoffmann's sense of high tragedy as a genre is consistent with, and subliminally exemplified by, both the passage in *Hamlet* and its apparent counterpart in the overture.

26. My translations from Richard Wagner, "Ouvertüre zu 'Coriolan'," *Richard Wagners Gesammelte Schriften*, 14 vols., ed. Julius Kapp (Leipzig: Hesse und Becker, 1914), 9:114–17. Subsequent citations in text; italics correspond to Wagner's spaced type. The English translation by William Ashton Ellis, in *Richard Wagner's Prose Works*, 5 vols. (1894; reprint, New York: Broude, 1966), 3:225–28, is inexact—a point noted by James Hepokoski, "Masculine/Feminine," *Musical Times* (Aug. 1994): 494–99.

27. Lacan's "big Other" is the symbolic order (or its representative) from which (or whom) the subject seeks recognition and inevitably fails to find it in sufficient measure. "When, in love," writes Lacan, "I solicit a look, what is profoundly unsatisfying and always missing is that—*You never look at me from the place from which I see you. Conversely, what I look at is never what I wish to see.*" Jacques Lacan, *The Four Fundamental Concepts of Psychoanalysis*, ed. Jacques-Alain Miller, trans. Alan Sheridan (New York: Norton, 1981), 103.

28. "Das ganze Tonstück könnte füglich als musikalische Begleitung einer pantomimischen Darstellung selbst gelten, nur in dem Sinne, dass die Begleitung zugleich die ganze dem Gehöre wahrnehmbare Sprache kundgibt, deren Gegenstand wir in der Pantomime uns wiederum als dem Auge vorgeführt denken müssen."

29. "Dicht neben ihm stellt sich nun das *Weib* dar: Mutter, Frau und Kind" (115).

30. The maternal superego enforces obedience by exploiting dependency and fear of loss of love rather than by threatening symbolic castration like its paternal counterpart. For a discussion, see Slavoj Zizek, *Looking Awry: An Introduction to Jacques Lacan Through Popular Culture* (Cambridge, Mass.: MIT Press, 1992), 88–106.

280

31. Tovey, 143. Subsequent citations in text. Later readings along Wagnerian lines include those by Karl Schönewolf, *Beethoven in der Zeitenwende* (Halle: Mitteldeutscher Verlag, 1953), 369–73, and Roger Fiske, *Beethoven's Concertos and Overtures* (Seattle: University of Washington Press, 1970), 55–56.

32. Paul J. Bekker, *Beethoven*, 1911, trans. M. M. Bozman (London: Dent, 1932), 242. Subsequent citations in text.

33. Bekker's approach to *Coriolan* has a significant precursor in that of A. B. Marx, who sees Beethoven's affiliation with Collin as a kind of renunciation. "Had Beethoven," he writes, "annexed [to Collin's] the volume of Shakespeare's, which as is well known he loved very much, his problem would have extended itself beyond what was favorable for the music. He would have had there, raised up before him next to Coriolanus, apart from the bearers of the political action, the high figure of the Roman mother and the purely womanly spouse. On Collin's page the problem simplifies itself." Marx distances the figure of feminine intervention in order to sustain a reading of the overture in which "there is no reconciliation [*Versöhnung*], only rage and destruction." His reading accordingly plays down the role of the second theme. Yet when it comes to a description of that theme, Marx cannot separate it from the Shakespearean image he seeks to disavow: "[Here] the feminine reconciler [*die Versöhnerin*] steps forth, be it the mild Valeria, or the mother, or the pleading, warning voice of the fatherland." My translations from Marx, *Ludwig von Beethoven, Leben und Schaffen*, 2 vols. (1859; reprint, Leipzig: A. Schumann, 1902), 2:51, 52.

34. Hoffmann especially remarks the "hollow" effect of the bassoon "sustaining the fifth above the key-note" (292).

35. In the exposition, the closing passage moves from a pedal on V/V (mm. 78–83) through v (mm. 85, 87) and i (mm. 89, 91) to a tonic pedal (mm. 92–99) overlapping the preparation (mm. 100–101) for the beginning of the development in the dominant minor (m. 102). In the recapitulation, which parallels the exposition closely, the passage moves from a dominant pedal (mm. 206–11) through i (mm. 213, 215) and iv (mm. 217, 219) to a subdominant pedal overlapping the preparation (mm. 228–29) for the beginning of the coda in the tonic minor (m. 230). The appearance of a dominant pedal in the recapitulation heightens the feeling of tonal instability and, given the parallelism between the exposition and recapitulation, renders the ensuing subdominant pedal particularly implacable. The subsequent preparation for the coda is controlled by the dominant, but strong subdominant detail in the foreground upholds the feeling of instability, which thus carries over into the tonic arrival. The integrity of the tonic, like the heroic identity of the overture's protagonist, is torn apart by the force of an inner polarity.

36. In this respect, the overture may help establish the paradigm for program music generally: a paradigm in which, I would argue, the music does not signify or reproduce a narrative but alludes to (or supplements) a narrative through which a subject-position is concretely specified. On music as the supplement of narrative, see my *Classical Music and Postmodern Knowledge* (Berkeley: University of California Press, 1995), 110–19.

37. In "Charging the Canons," 139–40.

CHAPTER 7

The Harem Threshold:
Turkish Music and Greek Love
in Beethoven's "Ode to Joy"

Everyone knows that there is a Turkish march in the finale of Beethoven's Ninth Symphony, but no one seems to think the fact is worthy of much remark. Perhaps this is because the *alla turca* is a sufficiently well-established topic in the idiom of Viennese classicism that it seems to need no explanation, whatever aesthetic problems it may be felt to pose. Or perhaps the Turkish topic creates a certain uneasiness when it comes knocking at the gates of the definitive Viennese masterwork. In any case, the most distinguished recent criticism largely skirts the issue, even though it bears directly on the professed aim of affirming universal brotherhood.[1]

One may have to hark all the way back to 1935 and Donald Tovey to find this Turkish march treated as something remarkable. Tovey, however, shies away from the national character of the passage, preferring instead to understand

---

[1] A few passing references aside, Maynard Solomon, James Webster, and Leo Treitler do not comment directly on the passage; William Kinderman considers it briefly as "the section in B♭ major and $\frac{6}{8}$ meter" forming a "scherzo" (the "Turkish" label shows up only later, also in passing); Martin Cooper cites the lineage of the passage in Haydn, Mozart, and others, but otherwise says only that Beethoven's juxtaposition of it with the immediately preceding image of the Cherub who stands before God "seems almost perverse." (See Solomon, "The Ninth Symphony: A Search for Order," in *Beethoven Essays* [Cambridge, Mass., 1988], pp. 3–32; Webster, "The Form of the Finale in Beethoven's Ninth Symphony," in *Beethoven Forum* 1 [1992], 25–62; Treitler, "History, Criticism, and Beethoven's Ninth Symphony" and "'To Worship That Celestial Sound': Motives for Analysis," in *Music and the Historical Imagination* [Cambridge, Mass., 1989], pp. 19–45, 46–66; Kinderman, *Beethoven* [Berkeley and Los Angeles, 1995], pp. 278–79; Cooper, *Beethoven: The Last Decade* [London, 1970], p. 333.) In his *Beethoven: Symphony No. 9* (Cambridge, 1993), Nicholas Cook counts as a partial exception here, citing the Turkish march as one of a number of "unconsummated symbols" that need to be heard in their troubling strangeness (pp. 92–93), but not even Cook ad-

its bass drum, triangle, and cymbals as an expression of "the Grotesque Ideal . . . a veil covering the terror of things too sublime for human understanding."[2] Although he has suggestive things to say about the relation of this music to images of cosmic space and the memory of Napoleon's armies, what Tovey will resolutely not say is that the vehicle of these suggestions is a representation of what, when the symphony was composed, stood as a non-European, indeed an anti-European, militancy.

Why, then, *is* there a Turkish march in the finale of the Ninth Symphony? One answer may be suggested by Beethoven's unusual, not to say remarkable, treatment of the text. He extracts, arranges, and handles verses from Schiller's "Ode to Joy" in ways that resonate with a narrative paradigm that flourished in the symphony's cultural milieu. The object of this paradigm is world history, which is taken to unfold in large epochal sweeps, the phases of a process by which truth or reason is gradually realized in historical time. Each epoch is characterized broadly by association with an exemplary people and a certain attitude toward existence. Fed by the writings of Lessing and Herder, and common to both the Goethe-Schiller circle and the Jena Romantics, this "universal history," as Hegel called it, focused most often on the relationship between Greek antiquity and German-Christian modernity. Hegel's own version, roughly contemporary with the Ninth Symphony, is more finely grained and also takes non-Western cultures into account.[3]

For Hegel, "Universal History is exclusively occupied with showing how Spirit comes to a recognition and adoption of the Truth" (identified with both Reason and the Idea); it "shows [us] the development of the consciousness of Freedom on the part of Spirit" through a graduated series of "increasingly adequate expressions or manifestations of Freedom, which results from its Idea"; and its objects of knowledge are the characteristic "'National Spirits' of History," each of which functions like a single individual in a long journey that, like the sun itself, takes a westering path from the Orient to Europe. Hegel's solar imagery is of a piece with Beethoven's and Schiller's when they call for a band of brothers to run a victorious course like suns flying through the field of heaven. That call, of course, is the text of the Ninth Symphony's Turkish march. It resonates with Hegel's text not only in deploying a similar image, but also in interpreting the image as one that Spirit has internalized as a principle of action. Hegel's historical process ends when "man has erected a building from his own inner sun," thus completing "the great Day's work of Spirit"; the Beethoven-Schiller brother-band also inspirits itself by absorbing the solar principle, taking action as "gladly as [the] suns fly."[4] (The brother-band, in fact, lives in a wholly figurative, wholly interiorized world: it acts joyously *as a* hero, gladly *as* the suns.) The resemblances here are something between a mere coincidence and the result of a common attitude and a common image-repertoire. They form a kind of symptom marking the possibility that the finale of Beethoven's symphony can be heard to do aesthetically what Hegel's *Lectures on the Philosophy of History* do analytically. The "Ode to Joy," too, may envision a grand progressive synthesis of diverse world-historical Spirits. The process may even involve a westering movement, given the Spirits involved: those of classical Greece, Ottoman Turkey, and German (or Germanized) Christendom.

From the very first, of course, the finale of the Ninth has been heard as an attempt to forge an organic synthesis from a bewildering diversity of materials; as Nicholas Cook observes, the tradition begins with Friedrich Kanne's review of 1824.[5] My point of departure

---

dresses the music's "Turkish" quality as an interpretive issue. Cook also points to a long critical tradition, dating from Friedrich Kanne's review of 1824 (p. 92); Kanne's remarks exemplify the anti-Turkish nervousness mentioned in my text (real Turkish music, he says, is more chaotic than Beethoven's stylization), as Cooper's do its reduction to a self-evident topic.
[2]Donald Francis Tovey, *Essays in Musical Analysis: Symphonies and Other Orchestral Works* (1935; new edn., London, 1981), p. 122.
[3]Georg Wilhelm Friedrich Hegel, [Lectures on] *The Philosophy of History (1822–31)*, trans. J. Sibree (1899; rpt. New York, 1956).

[4]Ibid., pp. 53, 63, 103.
[5]Cook, *Beethoven: Symphony No. 9*, p. 92.

here is the suggestion that Kanne and his successors heard things aright, but that the objects of synthesis are not confined to stylistic gestures, but include the modes of Spirit—in modern terms, of the constructions of subjectivity—that the stylistic gestures implicate.

This is, obviously, a large claim; just how can it be grounded? One answer, as already intimated, may lie in the relationship between text and music. The verses of the "Ode to Joy" devoted to the daughter of Elysium evoke Greek antiquity in several ways beyond the Elysian image; I will turn to these shortly. The verses themselves consist of three stanzas: the initial apostrophe to Joy ("Freude, schöne Götterfunken") and a pair of rhetorical amplifications ("Wem der Grosse Wurf gelungen," "Freude trinken alle Wesen"). Once these three have been combined with the "Ode to Joy" theme and heard in full, the Turkish topic emerges in association with military imagery, the march of the band of hero-brothers to victory. Next, the initial apostrophe to Joy makes the first of what will prove to be a cycle of returns. It is followed by something new and sharply contrastive: the emergence of a Christian topic. Ecclesiastical trombones appear along with the lines "Seid umschlungen, Millionen, / Diesen Kuss der ganzen Welt" [Be embraced, you millions, / By this kiss for the whole world]; the verse thus begun culminates in the image of the heavenly father who dwells beyond the stars, a paternal counterpart to the daughter of Elysium. The contrast between an immediate this-worldly joy and a remote transcendental divinity is very much in keeping with contemporary accounts of the difference between the classical and modern ages; in August Schlegel's typical formulation, "Among the Greeks human nature was in itself all-sufficient . . . and [sought] no higher perfection than that which it could actually attain by the exercise of its own energies," whereas for modern Europeans, above all those of Germanic race, "everything finite and mortal is lost in the contemplation of infinity."[6]

After the Christian verse has been elaborated, the text-music relationship undergoes a striking change. Up to this point, Schiller's verses have been set as wholes, verbally coherent and musically distinct. But beyond this point the verses, or more exactly a pair of them, break down into loosely connected phrases that are combined, repeated, compressed, or distended with scant regard for either verbal coherence or musical distinctness. Initially static and successive, the text-music relationship becomes dynamic and processual; the change suggests that the epochal topics of the finale cannot be reconciled or synthesized merely by being presented, but only by engaging with each other in terms that affect the shape and encroach on the boundaries of each.

In particular, the remainder of the movement freely mixes phrases from the classicizing apostrophe to the daughter of Elysium with phrases from the Christianizing injunction to be embraced by the world-kiss and seek the transcendental father. This Greek-Christian mixture first takes the form of contrapuntal combination in the Allegro energico section following the Christian Maestoso. The disparate fragments of text are here rendered completely indivisible as texture; at no point is either the apostrophe or the injunction heard by itself. It is as if neither made sense without the other, even though, strictly speaking, it is their combination that makes no sense. The

---

[6]August Schlegel, *A Course of Lectures on Dramatic Art and Literature* (1808), trans. John Black (London, 1846), p. 27. At one point, Schlegel's characteristic claim of Germanic pre-eminence (the result of the movement of history northwards, a common alternative to the westering movement noted earlier) takes a form that, insofar as it is itself a common topic or trope, may have particular resonance with the Christian topic of Beethoven's finale. Writing in defense of Gothic architecture ("which ought really to have been termed Old German"), Schlegel claims that "We Northerners are not so easily talked out of the powerful, solemn impressions which seize upon the mind at entering a Gothic cathedral. We feel, on the contrary, a strong desire to investigate and to justify the source of this impression" (p. 24). The movement from awe to active engagement outlined by Schlegel is anticipated in Goethe's account of his own response to the Strasbourg Cathedral ("On German Architecture" [1773], in Johann Wolfgang von Goethe, *Essays on Art and Literature*, ed. John Gearey, trans. Ellen and Ernest H. von Nardoff [Princeton, 1994], p. 6). It also has its parallel in the Ninth Symphony finale as, in succession, the phrases "Seid umschlungen, Millionen" and "Brüder! überm Sternenzelt muss ein lieber Vater wohnen" are heard first in the austere ecclesiastical texture of unison voices and trombones, and then (with textual expansion) in richly textured tutti statements.

Example 1: Beethoven, Symphony No. 9, finale: climax of Allegro energico.

chorus creates an image of complex mutuality by continually passing "Joy" phrases and "Kiss" phrases from one choir to another, the individual choirs sometimes even switching between phrase-types without pause. Punctuating this process throughout are detached shouts of "Freude" and extended outbursts of wordless vocalizing. The surging, full-cry abandon of the music suggests a fusion between a quasi-Dionysian ecstasy and the Christian parallel that the eighteenth century called "Enthusiasm" in the root sense of the Greek *en-theos*, being possessed by a god; the suggestion crystallizes as the Elysian half of the mixture forms a gradual emphasis on the phrase "Wir betreten Feuertrunken, / Himmlische, dein Heiligtum" [We enter fire-intoxicated, heavenly one, your sanctuary], often compressed to a triumphant, appropriative "Wir betreten dein Heiligtum!" The jubilation reaches a grand climax as a melismatic expansion of "dein Heiligtum" combines with "der ganzen Welt," thus envisioning an identity between the two terms in which the fusion pursued by the whole section culminates (see ex. 1).

The section closes immediately thereafter with a solemn, slow-moving, largely quiet restatement of the injunction to seek a transcendental God. A new tempo, Allegro ma non tanto, then takes over, bringing with it an ecstatically jumbled return of the apostrophe to the daughter of Elysium. (Here the emphasis shifts to the second half of the stanza, the part missing in the Allegro energico.) As if working dialectically, this separation of topics leads directly to their reunion in the Prestissimo section that concludes the symphony. Stated once more in succession, divided by just one breathless beat, the Christian and Greek verses unite by sharing the section's headlong tempo, continuous tutti texture, and jubilant noisiness. Their union culminates when, in yet one more dialectical turn, the tempo breaks and the apostrophe to Joy receives its final statement in the Maestoso vein first established by the Christian topic. At this point, everything has been said, and the orchestra rushes to a close.

The Prestissimo, however, also does something else. It brings back the Turkish topic, which has otherwise been sidelined; the orchestral tutti now includes—continuously— the janissary instruments that have been silent since the Turkish march. The section even begins with a variant of the "Joy" phrase for janissary percussion, winds, and brass: pure "Turkish music." The effect is to establish the Prestissimo, and through it the entire finale, as a kind of anthem of universal history: one that, in keeping with the textual emphasis that emerges during the middle of the section, symbolically takes in the whole world. At the same time, however, this is a synthesis in which the classical Greek ethos stands as first among equals. Its priority is established both by the refrain-like returns to the "daughter of Elysium" verse and by the double movement from the

81

Christian to the Greek topic after their contrapuntal fusion in the Allegro energico. Joy's sanctuary always stands as a destination. The finale thus acts as if to satisfy Goethe's famous injunction, "Let everyone be a Greek in his own way, but let him be a Greek!"[7]

Just what, though, does it mean to be Greek in this context, and what do the Turks have to do with it? To sketch an answer, the Turks will have to be sidelined awhile—not, as you see, for the first time—but rest assured: as in the symphony, they will come back at a crucial moment. At stake here is something different from the master narrative outlined by Schiller in his essay "On Naive and Sentimental Poetry" of 1795 and shared, according to Maynard Solomon, by the finale of Beethoven's Ninth.[8] Schiller had proposed a dialectical recovery of the ancient Greek ethos; although humanity could no longer go "back to Arcadia," the artist could lead it "forward to Elysium." Though couched in classical terms, this formula is actually anti-classical, in the sense that it assumes the irremediable loss of the "Arcadian" harmony between nature and humanity supposedly characteristic of the ancient Greeks, even as it looks forward to an "Elysian" overcoming of the modern self-consciousness that imposes the loss. The Elysian imagery of the "Ode to Joy," written some ten years before the essay, suggests a more naive classicism, one less in keeping with Romantic dialectics than with the "Greekomania"—Schiller's own term—that swept through German intellectual life in the second half of the eighteenth century.

German philhellenism, to give it its more dignified name, was in large part inspired by the work of the art historian Johann Joachim Winckelmann. Among its most salient features are a strong focus on visual art, above all on sculpture; the idealization of this art as the embodiment of nobility, simplicity, and grandeur; and a fervent, at least quasi-erotic concentration on the male body and masculine intimacy. Goethe's essay of 1805, "Winckelmann and His Age," links these features, respectively, with the Greeks' love of beauty, especially "the beautiful human being"; their robust concentration on immediate reality in both joy and sorrow; and the need of their "complete personalities" for a friendship in which each man "could perceive himself as a whole only if he was complemented by another."[9] Similarly, the "Greek" verses extracted by Beethoven from the "Ode to Joy" emphasize both plastic form and the joys of brotherhood, qualities that the symphony ties to Grecian grandeur by means of the simple, noble character of the "Ode to Joy" theme that—after much searching—becomes the indelible setting of the verse.

The specifically Hellenic dimension of the Joy verses in the Ninth Symphony finale has not, I think, been much noticed.[10] In representing Joy as a daughter of Elysium in whose shrine and under whose wings all men become brothers, Schiller creates not only a classical personification but also a sculptural image; Joy as goddess belongs to an imaginary group of Greek temple friezes or statues. The image might even be said to suggest an inverted form of the Laocoon group that drew famous essays from Lessing and Goethe; here the sheltering daughter replaces the helpless father and the joyous united brothers replace the agonized divided sons. Joy's wings, in addition, may associate her with Nike, the goddess of Victory, though they may also be a pair of standard-issue allegorical pinions. In combination with the Christian and Turkish topics that it takes as subordinate elements in the "world-historical" synthesis of the movement, the Joy image and the theme associated with it create an effect much like that of the Doric temple facades used for

---

[7]Goethe, "Ancient Versus Modern," in *Essays on Art and Literature*, p. 93.
[8]Solomon, "Beethoven and Schiller," in *Beethoven Essays*, pp. 205–15.

[9]Goethe, "Winckelmann and His Age," *Essays on Art and Literature*, pp. 102–04.
[10]Solomon, however, notes a "speculative" parallel between the finale of the Ninth and the following statement in Schiller's preface to his drama *The Bride of Messina*: "I have blended together the Christian religion and the Pagan mythology, and introduced recollections of Mohammedan superstition" (*Beethoven Essays*, p. 213). Schiller's statement, of course, contains in nuce all three modes of world-historical Spirit, the interrelations of which I seek to trace in this essay.

grand public buildings—university halls, museums, banks—by many nineteenth-century architects. More particularly, the effect might be compared to the one envisioned by Friedrich Gilly's famous proposal of 1797 for a monument in Berlin to King Friedrich II, in which the pure lines of a new Parthenon would crown a rough, massive, eclectic base set at the center of an octagonal promenade.[11] Once again, in the spirit of Goethe's injunction, modern humanity is to realize itself by becoming newly Greek. The unity of humanity is to be retrieved by reimagining the plastic ideal of the Greek world in a modern social and political context.

The means of that retrieval is brotherhood, or so the verses tell us. On closer inspection, however, what does that mean? When "alle Menschen werden Brüder" under the wings of Joy, what form does the redemptive brotherhood take? Are we to imagine that all human beings become coequal partners in a community of joy? Or is it that all males become brothers through the mediation of a Joy that embraces them like a mother—the daughter of Elysium identified as the mother of men through the traditional maternal image of the sheltering wing? Or is it that the band of brothers thus created is redeemed from a certain lack by the intervention of this all-embracing feminine figure, so that the agency of all viable brotherhood is ultimately feminine? This last alternative is not as obvious as the first two, but it is implicit in both the dependency relationship and the strict gender separation depicted in the image. Without Joy's tender magic, those divided by custom ("was die Mode streng geteilt") will never become brothers. This idea may also draw support from an important theoretical argument by Juliet Flower MacCannell, who holds that the liberatory claims of post-Enlightenment brotherhood have a dark, constraining lining. Although the deposed figure of the father-king had been authoritarian, it was also fully humanized; the figure of the brother is more impersonal and anonymous.[12] More an "it" than a "he," the brother always needs supplementation. This is suggested in Beethoven's redaction of Schiller's text not only by the need of the sheltering wing to create the brother-band, but also by the equivocal return of the figure of the father-king in the person of the absent God who dwells beyond the stars.

The Turkish march, however, adds yet a fourth alternative. It suggests that neither a maternal nor a paternal supplement is finally sufficient; there must also be a supplement generated entirely from within the brother-band itself. There is a flat contradiction here that nothing in the symphony will resolve: that the united band of brothers (who are both all men and all humankind) both are and are not dependent on a transcendental agency in the formation of their union. Contradiction or no, the march is notable for being the only extended all-male enclave in the finale. Its verse is addressed solely to the band of brothers; the topic of the verse is military, at least at the figurative level; and the music is, of course, for tenor solo and male chorus. (If Schiller had in some sense sought a corrective to Winckelmann's homoeroticism by centering his "statuary" on a feminine figure, not a male youth, the corrective is uncorrected here—especially by Beethoven's expressive and editorial choices.) But at this point an interesting conundrum arises. Why evoke this band of brothers with music that putatively belongs to the traditional enemy of European, and especially of Viennese, men and their civilization? Why have recourse to the very empire whose possession of modern Greece alienates the ruins of classical culture from the Europe that sees those ruins as one of its chief glories? The reason, presumably, is that the march wants to appropriate something from those whom we might now easily call the oriental Other. But what?

One answer may be suggested by "splitting" the music into two separate aspects, something that I hear it very nearly doing to itself. These two aspects can also be heard to correspond to two different models of manhood current during the early nineteenth century, one rooted in classical Greece, the other in Ottoman Turkey.

The first model involves an ideal of fervent love and loyalty between comrades, which, under the banner of military fellowship, is al-

---

[11] For a reproduction of the design, see Hermann G. Pundt, *Schinkel's Berlin: A Study in Environmental Planning* (Cambridge, Mass., 1972), p. 50; for discussion, pp. 48–52.
[12] Juliet Flower MacCannell, *The Regime of the Brother: After the Patriarchy* (New York, 1991), esp. pp. 1–38.

lowed to assume a nearly explicit erotic quality. The prototype for such manhood was the military pederasty of Sparta, especially as personified by the sacrificial example of Leonidas and his troops at Thermopylae, an association that led Richard Dellamora to name the phenomenon "Dorianism." A Spartan youth, wrote the philologist Carl Ottfried Müller, "wore the military dress which had been given him by his lover [philator], and fought in battle next his lover, inspired with double valour by the gods of war and love."[13] Müller's description of the Dorian ideal was influential in both Germany and England during the nineteenth century, in both civic and erotic venues. It also gave the ideal a sadly nationalist and racialist dimension by stressing the "Aryan" purity of the original Dorians, who had invaded the Peloponnesus from the North at the end of the Mycenaean era. The ideal also finds less tendentious expression in Friedrich Hölderlin's novel of 1797-98, *Hyperion*, in which, for example, the narrator recalls being "unspeakably happy" with his beloved comrade, having "so often sunk into his embraces only to awaken from them with [a] heart [made] invincible," while the comrade confesses to fantasizing that the two of them "would fall together in one battle-torn valley and rest together under one tree." Similarly, Goethe speaks of how classical authors, "with regard to two young men," tend to "inundate us" with accounts of "the bliss of being inseparable, lifelong devotion, or the need to follow the other into death."[14]

The quasi-erotic absorption in loss and death suggested by these extracts is a regular feature of the Dorian ideal, and one that Beethoven may have intimated, at least indirectly, in two of his piano sonatas. In the "Les Adieux" Sonata, op. 81a, the unusual form of the slow movement—a poignant minor-key utterance followed seamlessly by its even more poignant recapitulation in a veiled subdominant—might be taken to express the mournful unity-in-division of the parted friends specified by the music's program. Somewhat less conjectural is the topical affiliation of the funeral march that forms the slow movement of the eponymous "Funeral March" Sonata, op. 26. This march is said to have been written partly in emulation of its precursor in Ferdinando Paër's opera *Achilles*, which Beethoven heard in 1801, the year of the sonata's composition. Paër's march evinces the grief of Achilles for Patroclus; to the extent that Beethoven's march is allusive, its allusiveness would incorporate the feeling-tone typical of the cult of Dorian companionship. This tone can perhaps be heard most clearly in the distraught tritone-related section—on D minor in the key of A♭ minor—that moves from *pianissimo* resignation to *fortissimo* lament amid the otherwise ceremonial tread of the march (see ex. 2).[15] It's important to note, however, that Paër's Achilles is a romantic as well as a Dorian lover, as are both Hölderlin's Hyperion and the members of Beethoven's and Schiller's brotherband, who hope both to become "the friend of a friend" and to win "a lovely woman." Although there is often tension between the terms, there is no flat either/or of homo- and heterosexual love in this cultural framework.[16]

The second pertinent model of manhood involves controlled brutality and what Hegel called fanaticism, the superlative degree of single-mindedness. In general, this is the manhood of the Other, powerful, ruthless, and fierce; it is a kind of concentrated dangerousness viewed with an unstable mixture of envy, awe, and revulsion. For Hegel, this "abstract and therefore all-encompassing enthusiasm—restrained by nothing, finding its limits nowhere, and absolutely indifferent to all beside," is the principle of Spirit in the "Mahometan East," especially in the epoch of the Persian Caliphate. "It is the essence of fanaticism," he writes,

---

[13]Richard Dellamora, *Apocalyptic Overtures: Sexual Politics and the Sense of an Ending* (New Brunswick, 1994), pp. 43–64; quotation from Müller, p. 47.
[14]Friedrich Hölderlin, *Hyperion; or, The Hermit in Greece*, trans. Willard R. Trask (New York, 1965), p. 48; Goethe, "Winckelmann and His Age," in *Essays on Art and Literature*, p. 103.

[15]This sonata has bearings on the *Eroica* Symphony as well as the Ninth; for discussion, see my "*Eroica*-traces: Beethoven and Revolutionary Narrative" in *Musik/Revolution: Festschrift für Georg Knepler zum 90. Geburtstag*, ed. Hanns-Werner Heister (Hamburg, 1997), II, 35–48.
[16]For further discussion of this complex topic, see the essays collected in *Outing Goethe and His Age*, ed. Alice A. Kuzniar (Stanford, 1996).

Example 2: Beethoven, "Funeral March" Sonata: movt. III, mm. 15–22.

"to bear only a desolating destructive relationship to the concrete; but that of Mahometanism was, at the same time, capable of the greatest elevation . . . free of all petty interests, and united with all the virtues that appertain to magnanimity and valor."[17] In the modern era, the East has degenerated in the grip of "hideous passions" and the "grossest vice," but what remains of the fanatical spirit, although "cooled down," is lodged firmly in the janissaries of the Ottoman Turks. From the mid-eighteenth century on, the most typical embodiments of this type of manhood are probably a pair of "Oriental" types, the despotic Pasha and the brigand chief. Examples might run from Mozart's Bassa Selim and Byron's Hassan (from *The Giaour*) who, unlike Selim, really does kill the hero's beloved, to Tolstoy's Haji Murad and nineteenth-century media constructions of real-life figures like the Mahdi, the Islamic leader who played Crazy Horse to General Gordon's Custer in the Sudan in 1885. Both Byron's *Don Juan*, however, and Beethoven's and Kotzebue's *The Ruins of Athens* offer revealing alternatives.

When Byron's hero, dressed as a girl, comes to the threshold of a Turkish harem, he encounters a massive portal guarded by a pair of grotesque dwarfs:

> Two little dwarfs, the least you could suppose,
>   Were sate, like ugly imps, as if allied
> In mockery to the enormous gate which rose
>   O'er them in almost pyramidic pride;
> The gate so splendid was in all its *features*,
> You never thought about these little creatures,
>
> Until you nearly trod on them, and then
>   You started back in horror to survey
> The wondrous hideousness of these small men,
>   Whose color was not black, nor white, nor grey,
> But an extraneous mixture, which no pen
>   Can trace, although perhaps the pencil may;
> They were mis-shapen pigmies, deaf and dumb—
> Monsters, who cost a no less monstrous sum.[18]

These "small men" exist for two purposes: to murder any bigger ones who happen to trespass into the harem, and to open the gate for authorized women and eunuchs, which they alone are strong enough to do. Endowed with "little looks" said to be both poisonous and fascinating, the dwarfs represent masculine danger at

---

[17]Hegel, *The Philosophy of History*, pp. 359, 358.

[18]Text from Byron, *Don Juan*, ed. Leslie Marchand (Boston, 1958), V, lxxvii–lxxviii.

85

its most concentrated. Misshapen, deaf, mute, and minuscule, they manufacture extreme potency out of extreme lack. In context, they can be taken to represent the masculine essence that Byron's Juan progressively misplaces as he assumes the identity of the harem girl "Juana." In the dwarfs, that essence appears in its raw form, that of the homunculus, the "little man" traditionally thought to be carried by seminal fluid—but the homunculus as toxin. (Slavoj Žižek might see the dwarfs as little pieces of the Lacanian Real, the obscene substance of pleasure or desire that cannot be symbolized and appears only as a blot or deformation in ordinary reality. Hence their indescribability and their racial indeterminacy in a text where race is everywhere marked.[19]) In this guise the dwarfs also suggest an imperviousness to castration, a topic certainly on Juan's mind and one much joked about in a canto devoted to cross-dressing and presided over by a eunuch. That the priceless little creatures form an inseparable pair is a none-too-subtle clue to their identity.

Byron's dwarfs have less grotesque but equally potent brethren in *The Ruins of Athens*, the dramatic spectacle by Kotzebue with music by Beethoven written in 1811 as part of the inaugural of a new theater in Pesth. Like Hölderlin's *Hyperion*, *The Ruins* proposes that the classical Greek spirit must be revived by cultural, not military, means. Awakening from a millennium of sleep, Kotzebue's Minerva despairs at the wreck of Turkish-occupied Athens and chooses to migrate to central Europe, which will thenceforth become the new Greece. One source of Minerva's despair is the formidable power of Islamic "fanaticism," represented by Kotzebue in a chorus of dervishes that Beethoven amalgamated into a march of janissaries. Accompanied by "all available noise-making instruments such as castanets, bells, etc.," continuous triplet motion in the upper strings depicts a dervishlike whirling while aggressive march rhythms in the brass invoke martial force. (Hegel notwithstanding, it would be some time yet before the image of Saracen invincibility gave way to that of Ottoman Turkey as "the sick man of Europe.")

Like Byron's dwarfs, Beethoven's warrior-dervishes produce extreme potency from extreme lack—a lack, in this case, with a series of specifically musical definitions. First, the dervish chorus has not even the most elemental harmony; its tenors and basses sing in a strident, unbroken unison, often abetted by doubling from cellos and basses. Second, the E-minor music of the chorus is almost wholly unrelieved by the major mode, leaving the minor to assume a relentless, motoric, "fanatical" character. Finally, and most importantly, the chorus contains not a single V–I cadence; cadences are replaced by movement from the tonic (minor) six-four to the five-three, a gesture given a sense of resoluteness, if not of resolution, by emphatic semitone motion to the melodic fifth degree just prior to each cadential substitute (see ex. 3). The dervishes thus lay claim to an anti-European musical space and hold it with defiant tenacity.

The male chorus and solo tenor of the Ninth Symphony's Turkish march are at one level the very antithesis of these militant dervishes, but at another level their heirs. As is probably evident by now, I have been leading up to the conclusion that the symphony's march is an amalgam of Dorian and "oriental" elements. On the Dorian side, the march is set in a jaunty $\frac{6}{8}$ meter rather than a militant $\frac{2}{4}$ and its format—the tenor first apostrophizing the chorus, then engaging in dialogue with it—emphasizes the process of bonding at the heart of the brother-band. The vocal style is lyrical, florid, even at times effusive; it projects a heroism grounded as much in ardor as in strength—"the bliss of being inseparable, lifelong devotion, or the need to follow the other into death." On the oriental side, of course, there is the punctuation of the march by the janissary triad of bass drum, cymbal, and triangle. This "noise-making" is continuous throughout, even "fanatical" in its insistence on a single rhythmic figure. (When the same sonority returns in the closing Prestissimo, it is rhythmically quite varied, as if integrated with the other musical elements at a "higher" level.) The Turkish rhythm section is also, however, self-con-

---

[19] See Slavoj Žižek, *Looking Awry: An Introduction to Jacques Lacan Through Popular Culture* (Cambridge, Mass., 1991), pp. 1–47.

Example 3: Beethoven, *The Ruins of Athens:* Chorus of Dervishes, mm. 65–72.

sciously symbolic, three times changing its rhythmic profile to form a "cadence" emphasizing the phrase "wie ein Held zum Siegen."

As the march proceeds, the lyrical and militant elements exert a variable pressure on each other, depending in part on how the interplay of their fervid melody and tireless jangle is heard at any given moment. The Dorian band seeks to supplement its dream of victory with a certain "barbarian" invincibility that, in turn, seeks to sublimate its single-minded force in the ethical beauty of the Dorian ideal. One might paraphrase the conjunction of these elements by saying that the lyrical march of the European hero-band is pictured as unfolding (as having to unfold) against a non-European horizon that may be subordinated but may not be simply transcended or erased. The synchronic relation of Dorian idealism and janissary vitality is also a diachronic relation that traces, and in tracing preserves, the shape of historical progress. The measure of that progress may perhaps be taken by the music that follows the march: the orchestral double fugue marked *sempre fortissimo,* its form symbolizing the acme of European musical intellect, its pacing and texture evoking a dynamism of spirit that nothing can withstand. The fugue seems to signify both the fruits of the victory to be won and the means by which to win it.

The topical mixture of Dorian and janissary masculinities in the Turkish march is consistent with the synthesizing, "world-historical" impulses of the Ninth Symphony, but it can-

87

Example 3 *(continued)*

not entirely be explained by them. If I am right in suggesting that philhellenism is one of the initiating impulses of the finale, then the logic that impels the march might run something like this. The impulse to "be Greek" could not easily be separated in Beethoven's milieu from the Dorian ideal, but the ideal brought with it at least two difficulties. One was its eroticism, which could only be sanctioned by disengaging it from modern morality, as Müller, for example, explicitly sought to do. Goethe had done exactly the same thing in "Winckelmann and His Age" when confronting what we would call Winckelmann's homosexuality. Beethoven might accordingly have been trying to desexualize the Dorian topic by combining it with janissary music, which, like Byron's dwarfs, never ventures beyond the harem threshold. At the same time, he might also have been trying to temper any feeling of effeminacy that might attach to the Dorian ethos. Hölderlin does something similar when he transfers Hyperion's love from a youth to a maiden, the Platonically named Diotima, who teaches him—in vain, as it turns out—the true meaning of his desire to restore the ruins of Athens.[20]

[20]The complex issue of Dorian effeminacy is strikingly illustrated by a painting I encountered shortly after completing this paper. The Nationalgalerie der Romantik in Schloss Charlottenburg, Berlin, houses a copy (dated 1836) of a panoramic "historical" canvas by the architect Karl Friedrich Schinkel depicting the world of ancient Greece. In the foreground, scantily clad or naked men labor at building a temple; in the middleground, heavily armored

The second difficulty with Dorianism is its association with sacrificial death. Schiller's and Beethoven's military image of the transcendental achievement of the brother-band is, on the contrary, an affirmation of life. By overlaying his Dorian music with a janissary sheen, Beethoven may have been trying at a symbolic level to reverse the fate of Leonidas and his comrades. (Here again there is an analogy to Hyperion, who is destined to live and who, for that reason, is explicitly denied a Thermopylae of his own.[21]) Perhaps Beethoven needs to intimate a Dorian vitalism because he is worried, however unwillingly, by the lifeless impersonality that may threaten the ideal of brotherhood from within; the very verses he sets, joining the hero's career with the preordained movements of the cosmos, are inflected by that threat. Or perhaps, with greater confidence, he wants to suggest that the spirit of classical Greece can be reborn in central Europe despite the oppressive rule of modern Greece by the Turks. Whatever the reasons, he seeks to secure the triumph of European values by mending a defect in European masculinity. He guarantees the invincibility of European brotherhood by endowing the brother-band with a measured, medicinal dose of concentrated danger, the masculinity of the Turkish Other.

Furthermore, like Byron with his dwarfs, Beethoven at one point lets that dose of masculinity appear in its own right as a "wondrous hideousness" deforming the texture of normal experience. The music involved is that of the notorious introduction to the Turkish march, a series of grunting noises produced by combining the bassoons and contrabassoon in abyssal octaves with strokes on the bass drum. The sound is half guttural, half visceral, a travesty of the body as a source of vocalization. Given its ultrabass quality, it may even suggest an obscene, abjected piece of the male voice, perhaps of the very baritone that ushers voice as such into the symphony. (When the baritone, after singing mainly in his upper register, ends the opening solo on a pair of low As, a visceral-guttural tone almost always intrudes.) This obnoxious sound forms the nucleus of the march. It is absorbed into the purely "Turkish" first episode for percussion, winds, and brass, and, though the contrabassoon breaks off when the vocal part begins, it returns under the voices in the concluding passage. The sound thus acts as a kernel of radical otherness underlying not only the Dorian efflorescence but even the Turkish jangle, in which, again like Byron's dwarfs, it figures as a presence both integral and alien.

This otherness also has an important harmonic dimension that deserves at least passing mention. The march forms the first point of large-scale harmonic contrast in the finale, a shift to the flat submediant. The initial grunting noises announce that shift, but the sonority is so bizarre that the structural value of its pitches is rendered dubious—or at least so defamiliarized that the chromatic third-relation assumes a quality of incalculable remoteness. If, as is sometimes suggested, the harmony here suggests something like the second group of a sonata form, the sonority simultaneously implies the impossibility of any such thing.

I do not, of course, want to pretend that this passage in any aspect is the little treasure that holds the key to the "Ode to Joy." It is merely symptomatic of something—but nonetheless, of something important. The radical or, so to speak, Real otherness embedded in this music tellingly exceeds the more manageable orientalizing otherness of the Turkish topic, although the latter is far from being a simple device of cultural imperialism. Once recognized, once localized, this more difficult otherness becomes traceable in vital places elsewhere, both as actual sonority and as a more general alienating effect—one might almost say alienation-effect. The most notable sonorous trace undoubtedly comes in the final Maestoso statement by the chorus, where the key phrase "Freude, schöne Götterfunken" receives heavy

---

troops march off to war. To the viewer's left, two men in the foreground watch the departing troops, the arm of one around the other's shoulders. At the foreground center, a naked man lounges in a posture usually reserved for female nudes in modern European painting; another, also in a stereoptypically feminine posture, stands nearby, twisting himself around to gaze at the lounger. There are no actual women anywhere in the scene.

[21]"If only [there were] . . . a Thermopylae where I could honorably let it bleed to death, all the lonely love [for Greece] for which I never find a use!" (Hyperion, p. 161).

janissary reinforcement, the drums and cymbals pounding and triangles trilling on every beat at the *fortissimo* peak. More generally, there are the leaps of logic that seem almost a "structural" principle in this movement, such as the bizarre juxtaposition of the cherub passage, march, and fugue, or the ending of the choral part with the repetition of an epithet, "Götterfunken," that has received little emphasis in the body of the movement.

These features of the music may help throw new light on what has become perhaps the major cultural issue surrounding it. Late-twentieth-century sensibility has often tended to prefer what might be called, following Richard Taruskin, a "resisted" Ninth, a work that to some degree distances itself from its own affirmative message.[22] The preference, as Taruskin suggests, stems from a perception that the idealistic frenzy of the finale is dangerously close to the fanaticism it seeks to subsume, even bordering on totalitarian irrationalism. To some degree, however, the presence of an ironic or skeptical distance in the finale is part of the problem, not the solution. The Romantic utopianism voiced by the "Ode to Joy" is arguably self-resisting as a matter of genre, its idealism engaged on principle with "something evermore about to be."[23] Critics or performers who demonstrate that resistance are advancing the music's own project. They offer a valuable corrective to the idolatry (and its obverse, the derision) that the finale of the Ninth has sometimes elicited, but the result is still to legitimate the work, to reaffirm its monumental status, by identifying its aesthetic interest with a desired social attitude. Perhaps what is needed here is a measured resistance to the very dialectic of resistance and assent. By opening itself to a radical otherness, and by locating that otherness at the nexus of masculine identity and the westering movement of universal history, the finale of the Ninth exposes the raw nerves of the utopian project, the uneasy ground on which the "inner sun" must build a subjectivity at a particular moment of history. Perhaps this music endures—and endure it does, despite being oversold, overplayed, debased, and clichéd—because, although the moment has passed, the sexual and cultural grounds of engagement remain, uneasy as ever, if not more than ever.

---

[22]Richard Taruskin, "Resisting the Ninth," this journal 12 (1989), 241–56.

[23]The quotation is from William Wordsworth, *The Prelude* (1805), VI, 542; on the self-resisting character of Romantic utopianism, see my "Beethoven's Two-Movement Piano Sonatas and the Utopia of Romantic Esthetics" in *Music as Cultural Practice, 1800–1900* (Berkeley and Los Angeles, 1990), pp. 21–71.

CHAPTER 8

Primitive Encounters: Beethoven's "Tempest" Sonata,

Musical Meaning, and Enlightenment Anthropology

Prologue: Signifying Littorally

Most of Beethoven's piano sonatas are as highly individualized as his symphonies and quartets, but many of them also bear strong family resemblances to each other. These pieces are alike enough to form coherent groups, or series of studies akin to those produced by a painter who keeps returning to the same subject until its visual possibilities have been exhausted.

One such series is formed by the Piano Sonatas, ops. 54, 78, 90, and 111, each of which consists of two highly contrastive movements in the major and minor modes of the same key. As I have shown elsewhere, the second movement in each of these pieces forces the perception of a lack in the first and seeks to supply what was missing. Another series is formed by the two Sonatas "Quasi una fantasia" (op. 27) and their close companion, the "Funeral March" Sonata (op. 26). All of these pieces deform a standard multimovement design by altering the sequence and/or the proportions of the movements. The effect is to raise acutely a question that habitually goes unasked, the question of just what it means to say that one movement "goes with another." Finally—and here the door to this essay swings open—there is a series of four minor-key sonatas: op. 10, no. 1, and op. 13, the "Pathétique," both in C minor; op. 31, no. 2, in D minor, the "Tempest"; and op. 57 in F minor, the "Appassionata."[1]

A shorter form of this essay was presented in New York at Carnegie Hall during a March 1996 symposium on the Beethoven piano sonatas organized by Glenn Stanley.

1. For discussions, respectively, of the series of two-movement sonatas and multimovement design in the "Funeral March" Sonata, see my *Music as Cultural Practice: 1800–1900* (Berkeley and

32

The D- and F-Minor Sonatas have long been linked by a dubious anecdote that gives the D-Minor its nickname. The anecdote is reported by the notoriously unreliable Anton Schindler, who claims that he asked Beethoven about the "poetic idea" underlying these pieces after hearing Carl Czerny perform the two of them together. Beethoven is supposed to have replied, "Just read Shakespeare's *Tempest*."[2] Its authenticity aside, this remark left at least one of Beethoven's most important nineteenth-century critics dissatisfied; the two sonatas, snorted A. B. Marx, have as little in common with *The Tempest* as they do with each other.[3] The sonatas, however, actually have a great deal in common, not only with each other but also with the two earlier sonatas just mentioned. Each of them follows a three-movement fast-slow-fast design with the finale as well as the first movement in the minor. What's more, each piece does so in the same way, by framing a tranquil, inward-looking slow movement with outer movements of nearly continuous agitation.

The question I wish to raise here is how to understand this design. What prompts it? What does it seek to do? This is a question, not of how to describe the music, but of what the music means; that is to say, the question is concerned with form and technique only insofar as it is also concerned with culture and history. The question is accordingly one of interpretation, which is to say that it necessarily has more than one answer, as will become evident even as I pursue the one answer most compelling to me. This answer, in brief, is that the design is prompted by the same concept of human nature that underlies one of the leading intellectual projects of the Enlightenment, the project of speculative anthropology or "universal history." This project seeks to represent the emergence of the human being, called "Man," from a primitive state of nature into the state of civil society. The sonatas, in what might be dubbed Beethoven's "tempest series," do something very similar. I will try to make good on this understanding by means of a case study of one exemplary sonata from the series, the eponymous "Tempest" Sonata, with occasional reference to the others, particularly the "Appassionata."

First, however, a pair of preliminary clarifications may be in order. The kind of interpretation to be pursued here stems from the desire of a critical or postmodernist musicology to overcome the traditional opposition of musical and extramusical meaning. One consequence is that the traditional technique of referring

---

Los Angeles: U California P, 1990), pp.21–71, and idem, "*Eroica*-traces: Beethoven and Revolutionary Narrative," in *Musik und Revolution,* ed. Hanns-Werner Heister (Hamburg: von Bockel, 1996).

2. Schindler-MacArdle, p.406.

3. A. B. Marx, *Ludwig van Beethoven: Leben und Schaffen,* 2 vols. (1859; rpt. Hildesheim: Georg Olms, 1979), II, 38.

33 *Primitive Encounters*

"extramusically" to some external narrative, scene, or concept ceases to operate, except in the rare cases—intermittent even in programmatic works—when the music is explicitly imitative. (In those cases, moreover, what is important is no longer the object imitated but the rhetorical act of imitation.) Schemes of external reference are generally quite poor in meaning, and their poverty has often been taken as proof that true musical meaning lies in "the music itself." All it really proves, however, is that one type of interpretation is unsatisfactory; others may have better luck. Nothing in what follows, therefore, should be understood to suggest that the "Tempest" Sonata or any of the others tells a story, paints a picture, or transcribes an anthropological theory. What the music does, instead, is to exemplify the kinds of human subjectivity, and the kinds of communicative situation, that make it possible for certain types of stories to be told, certain types of pictures to be painted, certain types of theory to be formulated. Music shares this exemplifying function with other forms of communication, narrative and painting among them, from which it differs in degree of referential power.[4]

As to the second clarification, the objection is sometimes raised that attempts to explore musical meaning rely illegitimately on formalist techniques of description and analysis aimed primarily at "the music itself."[5] The assumption seems to be that it is incumbent on critical musicology to invent new techniques of its own. Why this should be so is unclear, unless one also assumes that new musical knowledge is simply identical with new types of description and analysis—which, I should say, is pretty much the assumption that defines formalism. No one, however, disputes that existing formalist procedures do a very good job of description and analysis. That being the case, there is no reason not to use them, although not necessarily on their own terms or by their own standards of completeness. The point is not to make surprising discoveries in the sphere of technique, or to be responsible to prescriptive notions of structural integrity, but to propose credible ways of hearing and understanding what is most characteristic, most unmistakable, about the music under scrutiny. If that project leads into subtler territory, including new technical territory, so much the better; but if it doesn't, we are none the worse. It should not be ground for objection, therefore, that what follows is not ambitious about technique, but only about meaning.

4. For fuller consideration of the issues raised in this paragraph, see my *Classical Music and Postmodern Knowledge* (Berkeley and Los Angeles: U California P, 1995), pp.1–32.

5. For examples, see V. Kofi Agawu, "Analyzing Music under the New Musicological Regime," *Music Theory On-Line* 2:4 (1996), p.12; and Pieter van den Toorn, *Music, Politics, and the Academy* (Berkeley and Los Angeles: U California P, 1995), p.36.

34

Whethering the Storm

With the D-Minor Sonata, a good way to start thinking about meaning is to regard the first movement with a certain studied naiveté. The movement is one of those traditionally described as "agitated" and "stormy"; the terms are so plainly suitable as to suggest that the sonata has kept its nickname mainly because the word *tempest* is accidentally descriptive. But what do such descriptions really tell us? At one level, to call music like the first movement of this sonata "stormy" is to excuse oneself from thinking about its expressivity; the term is more or less vacuous, both a dead metaphor and a cliché. I would like to raise the possibility, though, that in this case the cliché contains, sedimented within it, traces of a lost network of meanings. The stormy movements in Beethoven's "Tempest" and "Appassionata" Sonatas, it turns out, elicited images or narratives of literal tempests from some of their early critics. Although they were ultimately more concerned with questions of controlled fantasy than with representation, both A. B. Marx and Wilhelm von Lenz heard stormy weather in the "Appassionata" (in the first and last movements respectively), and so did Czerny, who also described the first movement of the "Tempest" Sonata in terms suggestive of a genre painting of a storm.[6] It would seem that when Donald F. Tovey later wrote dismissively of the distance between the "tragic power" of this movement and "mere foul weather" he was being ahistorical.[7] Something more than meteorology was involved in the iconography of tempests current through the mid-nineteenth century; Hegel certainly thought as much when he suggested that the possibility of storms at sea formed the measure by which Man first achieved a practical relationship with the infinite.[8] Regardless of either Shakespeare or Schindler, it is worth asking where, in the "Tempest" Sonata, a tempest is brewing.

This, it turns out, is not a simple question. It is tied up with larger questions of meaning in music, even of meaning in general, and will require some patience in the unraveling. In this particular case, the most rewarding way to frame an answer may be in terms of the classical division of the sign into a material manifestation, or signifier, and a concept, or signified. The ideal scene of communication is sometimes held to be one in which signifiers lead immediately and unambiguously

---

6. Wilhelm von Lenz, *Kritischer Katalog sämtlicher Werke Ludwig van Beethovens mit Analysen derselben*, 4 vols. (Hamburg: Hoffmann and Campe, 1860), III, 4–5; Marx, *Beethoven*, II, 36–39.

7. Donald Francis Tovey, *A Companion to Beethoven's Pianoforte Sonatas* (London: Royal School of Music, 1931), p. 121.

8. G. W. F. Hegel, *The Philosophy of History*, trans. J. Sibree (1899; rpt. New York: Dover Books, 1956), pp. 90–91.

35 *Primitive Encounters*

to their signifieds. In other words, the communicative ideal is to unite expression and understanding. This ideal may or may not be genuinely desirable, but, even if it is, it is rarely realized. The relationship between signifiers and signifieds is not tight but loose. Signifiers change or exchange their signifieds more or less constantly; signifieds are continually transcribed as new signifiers, which at once enter the process of exchange; and, most importantly for present purposes, signifiers can operate meaningfully in the absence of determinate signifieds, and indeed in the absence of any signifieds at all. It is possible to have meaningfulness without meaning.[9]

For example, since storms are at issue, consider the sentence "I have forgotten my umbrella." As Jacques Derrida has remarked, this unremarkable sentence, isolated and in quotation marks, was found among Nietzsche's unpublished papers. Without knowing the context in which Nietzsche wrote or copied the sentence, or how he planned to use it, one cannot know what the sentence was supposed to mean. It might have meant virtually anything—or nothing, or only a little, or again it might only have pretended to mean something. The knowledge of umbrellas and the tendency to forget them is of no help here. The sentence might have been meant figuratively, or symbolically, or ironically, or merely phonetically, or in any number of other ways. Moreover—and this is the cardinal point—finding a context for the sentence *would not change* this semantic variability. Even supposing that Nietzsche wanted to mean something, and that we could know what this was, we can never rule out the possibility that his meaning was no more than partial and unstable. The meaning may only have represented a temporary limit placed on an intention to mean—Derrida speaks of a "will to mean"—that is constantly, and of necessity, self-divided and pluralistic.[10]

What can be said of the D-Minor Sonata from this perspective? Well, the first

---

9. On signification without signifieds, a process he calls *signifiance*, with particular reference to music, see Roland Barthes's brief comments in "Rasch," from his *The Responsibility of Forms: Critical Essays on Music, Art, and Representations* (Berkeley and Los Angeles: U California P, 1991), pp.308–12. The relationship between signifier and signified is classically understood to be arbitrary, but this arbitrariness obtains only at the level of system, not that of discourse. For discussion, see Paul Ricoeur, "Structure, Word, Event," in *The Conflict of Interpretations*, ed. Don Hyde (Evanston: U Illinois P, 1974), pp.79–98.

10. Jacques Derrida, *Spurs: Nietzsche's Styles/Eperons: Les Styles de Nietzsche*, trans. Barbara Harlow (Chicago: U Chicago P, 1979), pp.123–35. My text specifically paraphrases statements on pp.125–27, 132–33, the latter of which merits quotation: "Si Nietzsche avait voulu dire quelque chose, ne serait-ce pas cette limite de la volonté de dire, comme effet d'une volonté de puissance nécessairement différentielle, donc toujours divisée, pliée, multipliée." (If Nietzsche had wanted to say something,

36

movement is obviously pretty stormy, but it does not posit a storm as a signified. We might be happy enough to accept such a signified if offered, but none is. This absence, moreover, is not simply a matter of negation. It is not only that there is no authentic title to designate a representation, or that the movement does not sound even remotely like the storm music in the Pastoral Symphony.[11] The absence is asserted as a positive value. The movement takes great pains to insist on its unmimetic character by insisting, instead, on its preoccupation with a purely formal problem—by insisting, indeed, as Carl Dahlhaus has suggested, on its preoccupation with the problem of form.[12] The result is a persistent tension between expression and form, the expression being clear but indeterminate, the form determinate but unclear.

As both Dahlhaus and Janet Schmalfeldt have argued, the main constituents of this first movement are subject to disconcerting changes in formal function.[13] The movement opens with a passage (mm.1–21) that sounds introductory or improvisatory but turns out to be the first group of a sonata exposition. Although it contains some tonic-defining features, the passage is primarily oriented toward the dominant, especially in its cadenzalike close (mm.13–20), which builds to a powerful cadence. This cadence (m.21) introduces a vehement theme that, in contrast to the foregoing, sounds the way a first theme "ought" to. But although this is indeed the first theme in the sense of being the first discrete melody heard, complete with a pair of contrastive two-measure phrases on the tonic balanced by a parallel pair on the dominant, it is not a first theme in a formal sense. Structurally, if not expressively, it turns out to be a transitional idea. The theme constitutes the largest single item in the exposition (mm.21–40), and it completely engrosses the first half of the development (mm.99–118), but does not appear at all in the recapitulation. What does appear, although with telling distortions, is the quasi-"introduction."

---

might it not be just that limit of the will to mean, necessarily differential like the effect of a will to power, thus always divided, folded, multiplied [my trans.].)

11. Or, *pace* Owen Jander, popular late-eighteenth-century storm music, including Beethoven's own belated contribution in the genre in the *Prometheus* ballet. See below, p.43.

12. Carl Dahlhaus, *Ludwig van Beethoven: Approaches to His Music*, trans. Mary Whittall (Oxford: Oxford UP, 1993), pp.116–18, 169–71.

13. Janet Schmalfeldt, "Form as the Process of Becoming: The Beethoven-Hegelian Tradition and the 'Tempest' Sonata," *Beethoven Forum* 4 (1995), 37–71. My treatment of form and its significance in this movement differs from both Dahlhaus's and Schmalfeldt's in ways small and large, but it is obviously indebted to them. The large difference (discussed below, pp.60–65) is that I resist assimilating the discontinuities of the music to the reconciling model of dialectic. My thanks go to Professor Schmalfeldt for providing me with a copy of her paper in advance of publication.

37 *Primitive Encounters*

The movement, in sum, is alive with formal ambiguity. Its sonata form, however, does not arise from a resolution of this ambiguity in favor of a familiar scheme. Instead, the form consists in the activity of producing the ambiguity with no certain means of resolving it. The presence of the problem does not necessarily mandate a solution.

As with the other first movements in the tempest series, what is most striking about this movement is precisely the combination of such a high-profile formal problem with vehemence of motion, feeling, and harmony.[14] The vehemence cries out for explanation, but the tensions accruing to the formal problem are not in themselves sufficient to provide one. At the same time, the formal problem invites us to find a cause for it in the vehemence, but the cause will remain merely quantitative—the higher the intensity, the greater the deformation—unless we can say what the vehemence signifies, which is just what can't be said. At the level of the signified, these pieces are not narrative or pictorial, but enigmatic.

Their enigmatic character, moreover, is the primary basis on which they and cognate pieces stake a historically resonant claim to have meaning. For Dahlhaus, this claim seeks to raise music to the level of "art in the strong sense," to give it a symbolic authority like that of a literary or philosophical text.[15] I would suggest that the claim is above all a claim of depth, of meaning possessed as something profound, interior, and complex, the product of a "will to mean" of the sort described by Derrida. A. B. Marx sensed as much in relation to the "Appassionata," saying of the piece that it was "probably a dream from the underworld" in which the "fearful spirit" was "submerged," and adding: "Who can interpret the dark story? Perhaps not even Beethoven himself."[16] As will be seen, the specific character of the claim to depth links the music that makes it to the thematics of speculative anthropology.

The first movement of the D-Minor Sonata is more concerned with its own meaningfulness, one might even say more conscious of it, than any other member of the tempest series, even the "Appassionata." It is, so to speak, deeply concerned with depth, and it makes that concern manifest by staging or symbolizing its own

---

14. The problems grow progressively more difficult. Opus 10, no.1, makes much of the characteristic question of whether the second half of the exposition, in the relative major, should be recapitulated in the tonic major or minor. Opus 13 equivocates about the identity of its second theme (for discussion, see Dahlhaus, *Ludwig van Beethoven,* pp.104–05). Opus 57 features a nonrepeated exposition ending in the minor of the relative major, and a recapitulation that merges *in extenso* with a dominant pedal.

15. Dahlhaus, *Nineteenth-Century Music,* trans. J. Bradford Robinson (Berkeley and Los Angeles: U California P, 1989), pp.10–11.

16. Marx, *Beethoven,* II, 29.

Example 1: "Tempest" Sonata, beginning.

39 *Primitive Encounters*

standing as an enigma. The symbolization, indeed, is the very first thing to occur in the movement, and it recurs at both the subsequent turning points, the beginning of the development and that of the recapitulation. The sonata opens with a soft, dark, closely spaced arpeggio, marked Largo, that ripples up from the low bass and slows further in the middle register to enunciate a dominant sixth chord, which lingers under a fermata. A brighter, highly agitated Allegro passage, like a fragment of a fantasy, follows without transition and ends, again without transition, in a one-measure Adagio. The Adagio introduces the root-position dominant, which, like the earlier sixth chord, lingers under a fermata. Another slow arpeggio follows, again lingers, and again triggers an Allegro, this one at first resuming the previous fantasy but then shifting in midcourse to resemble a fragmentary cadenza elaborating on the cadential six-four. This double juxtaposition (shown in ex.1) turns out to be the "first group" of the sonata form in the absence of any "proper" group and especially of any "proper" first theme. In its heterogeneity, its pregnant pauses, its preoccupation with the dominant, and above all in its contrast of depth and height, stillness and motion, the arpeggio-Allegro juxtaposition posits itself as profoundly meaningful, but there is no way of knowing what it means. As with an oracle, whose words also rise from a depth, one can only guess.

But we were looking for a tempest. If there is one, and it is not in the signified, then it must be in the signifier. It must be, not in what the music "says," but in the way the music sounds. The tempest brews in the force of an adjective; the music is tempestuous. Instead of signifying a tempest, such music signifies in the manner of a tempest; it engages in signification as a tempest might. A signifying tempest, however, is not a natural phenomenon but a cultural formation, even when it is made of wind and water. It is something observed from a certain perspective, or something described, imagined, or fantasized. The tempests in Beethoven's sonatas, together with all other such "adjectival" forms, operate on the margins of a general, culturally conditioned signifying practice.

Czerny's remarks on the first movement of the D-Minor Sonata and the finale of the "Appassionata" bear directly on this point. Czerny, indeed, who is reliable on such matters, and who studied both sonatas with Beethoven, indirectly lends some credence to Schindler's anecdote, at least as regards tempests if not Shakespeare's *Tempest*.[17] Czerny says that the last ten measures of the D-minor movement are to

---

17. Carl Czerny, *On the Proper Performance of All Beethoven's Works for the Piano,* trans. unattributed, ed. Paul Badura-Skoda (Vienna: Universal, 1970). Given Czerny's comments, it is possible—and pleasurable—to imagine that the reported conversation between Beethoven and Schindler went something like this: S. Such wonderful sonatas. What could be the poetic idea underlying them?

be played "with the pedal, and the bass like distant thunder, and *rallentando.*" He describes the movement as a whole with three epithets: "tragic," "romantic," and "picturesque."[18] The last of these is particularly suggestive, especially when combined with the implications of misfortune and passion carried by the first two. As an aesthetic category, the picturesque indicates qualities of ruggedness, fragmentation, and ruin.[19] It ordinarily implies a certain contemplative detachment as well, which in this case would be overridden by the tragic and romantic elements. As for the finale of the "Appassionata," Czerny says explicitly that "Beethoven . . . perhaps imagined to himself the waves of the sea in a stormy night, while cries of distress are heard from afar:—such an image may always furnish the player with a suitable idea for the proper performance of this great musical picture."[20] Both this remark and those on the D-minor movement are careful to avoid assigning the music a signified. They focus, instead, on how proper performance can fully realize the qualities of the musical signifier.

Beethoven's tempestuous movements, then, involve the presence of tempestlike signifiers in the absence of determinate signifieds. (This is not, of course, to deny that there may also be other credible ways of characterizing the same signifiers.) It might be tempting to consider this "broken" signification as a good example of the way in which even the most suggestive music transcends definite meaning, and thereby affirms what is unique to it as music. There is, however, nothing unique in the situation at all. Literary texts and paintings offer up indeterminate signifiers all the time, and so do more recent forms like photographs and films. When such signifiers are at their most portentous, we commonly name them symbols. When Lord Byron describes a nocturnal storm breaking over an alpine lake and calls on the night to let him be "A sharer in thy fierce and far delight,— / A portion of the tempest and of thee," his tempest is no more transparent, no more yoked to a

---

B. Well, they're pretty stormy, you know. S. Ah! You mean as in Shakespeare's *Tempest?* B. Maybe. I guess so.

In the unlikely event that Schindler was telling the truth, it may be worth noting in light of what follows that *The Tempest* was often read in the early nineteenth century as an allegory of control over the elements, especially over the primitive passions embodied by Caliban. August Schlegel gave this reading canonical status in his famous "Vienna lectures" of 1808. See Schlegel, *On Dramatic Art and Literature,* trans. John Black, lecture 24 (London: Henry G. Bohn, 1846), pp.394–96.

18. Czerny, *Proper Performance,* p.43. Czerny's statement refers to "this sonata," but the context makes clear that the reference is to the first movement only.

19. The category emerged toward the end of the eighteenth century to supplement the distinction between the sublime and the beautiful. See Samuel Holt Monk, *The Sublime: A Study of Critical Theories in XVIII-Century England* (1935; rpt. Ann Arbor, Mich.: U Michigan P, 1960), pp.157–59.

20. Czerny, *Proper Performance,* p.50 (trans. slightly modified).

41 *Primitive Encounters*

predetermined signified, than Beethoven's tempestuous music.[21] In less emphatic settings, indeterminate signifiers simply—or not so simply—make up the network of nodes and cruxes that characteristically galvanize interpretation.

It would be reasonable, then, to expect tempestuous music like the first movement of the D-Minor Sonata to behave much as other tempest signifiers do. We would expect it to gravitate to one or more definite, topical fields of communicative action: to follow characteristic patterns, to form characteristic associations with other signifiers, and to serve characteristic ends. At the same time, we would also expect the music to add something of its own to the mixture: partly because we want it to, partly because semantic variability is inescapable.

Weather Rapport

In Beethoven's time, at least three topical fields were particularly hospitable to tempests, along with cognate blasts, tumults, and pandemoniums. These were the fields of emotional turmoil, revolutionary violence, and the return of Man to a state of nature. Needless to say, the three continually overlap, as they do, for example, in Shelley's poem "Ode to the West Wind" and in Théodore Géricault's painting "The Raft of the Medusa," both completed in 1819. Shelley's invocation casts the tempestuous wind as both nature gone wild and a "Wild Spirit"; it involves extreme despair and hope, revolutionary prophecy, and the "sore need" of a man devoid of resources. Géricault's raft, shown on a heaving sea under darkening clouds, bears bodies living and dead in postures of extreme hope and despair, in the aftermath of both shipwreck and mutiny, in the sore need of men devoid of resources. Such overlapping significations drew particular urgency from memories of the French Revolution, the violence of which was often understood as a return to a state of nature from which Europe as a whole had never fully recovered. In their very different ways, both Hegel, in *The Phenomenology of Mind,* and Dickens, in *A Tale of Two Cities,* represent the worst excesses of the Revolution as a Hobbesian war of all against all in which the founding principle of civil society, namely mutual human sympathy and recognition, has completely collapsed. Dickens describes the mob storming the Bastille as "a sea of black and threatening waters, and of destructive upheaving of wave against wave, whose depths were yet unfathomed and whose forces were yet unknown. The remorseless sea of turbulently swaying shapes, voices of vengeance, and faces hardened in the furnaces of suffering until

---

21. Byron, *Childe Harold's Pilgrimage,* III.93.3–4. Text from the Oxford UP Standard Authors edition of *The Works of Lord Byron, Poetry,* ed. E. H. Coleridge, rev. John D. Jump (Oxford: Oxford UP, 1970).

the touch of pity could make no mark on them."[22] Hegel's treatment of such "tumult" is more far-reaching; it posits the "absolute freedom" of revolutionary terror as the very nadir of universal history. The principle of terror produces an atomized chaos indistinguishable from the state of nature: "It cannot arrive at any positive work, either at the universal works of language or reality, or the laws and universal establishment of *conscious* freedom, or the deeds and works of *volitional* freedom. . . . There remains to it only *negative action;* it is nothing but the *frenzy/Fury* of disappearance."[23] Like Shelley, who identifies the west wind with the streaming hair of a Maenad, Hegel merges a wild whirl of negations with the image of a goddess of vengeance.

The revolutionary topic may often be taken as an unspoken subtext to other uses of tempest signifiers, including those in our Beethoven sonatas. Marx, outdoing Czerny, calls the finale of the "Appassionata" "a night of tempest, without rest, with no recovery imminent, like the night in which Lear yielded his tormented, venerable head to the wind and the pelting of the torrent."[24] Similarly, Beethoven's nineteenth-century biographer Ludwig Nohl speaks of an "agitation churned up from the deep" that arises in the "Pathétique," achieves a more "spiritual" expression in the "Tempest," and culminates in the "Appassionata" with the "passionate outpouring" of the composer's "painfully agitated, almost *grollenden*—thundering or grudge-bearing—inner self." Nohl, or something in his will to mean, finds an antisocial rumbling at the core of Beethoven's subjectivity; Marx, invoking the most illustrious depiction of a state of nature available to him, centers on the figure of a deposed king.[25]

At a level closer to text than subtext, Marx's vivid invocation of Lear as a spectacle, seen with sympathetic intimacy, alludes to a situation that was fundamental to speculative anthropology. This is the primitive encounter, the face-to-face meeting

---

22. Charles Dickens, *A Tale of Two Cities* (New York: Barnes and Noble, 1993), chap.21, p.216.

23. "[Es] zu kein positive Werke, weder zu allgemeinem Werken der Sprache noch der Wirklichkeit, weder zu Gesetzen und allgemeinem Einrichtungem der *bewussten,* noch zu Taten und Werken der *wollenden* Freiheit kommen kann. . . . [Es] bleibt ihr [absolute Freiheit] nur das *negative Tun;* sie ist nur die *Furie* des Verschwindens" (Hegel, *Phänomenology des Geistes,* in *Werke in zwanzig Bänden,* ed. Eva Moldenhauer and Karl Markus Michel [Frankfurt am Main: Suhrkamp, 1970], III, 434, 435–36 [my trans.]). For the double meaning of "Furie," see Grimm's *Deustches Worterbuch,* IV, 749–50.

24. Marx, *Beethoven,* II, 36.

25. Ludwig Nohl, *Beethoven's Leben,* 3 vols. (Leipzig: Ambrose Abel, 1864–67), II, 171. Nohl also includes the "concentrated heartfelt suffering" of the "Moonlight" Sonata in his sequence. Thomas Sipe has discussed the Shakespearean associations of these passages from Marx and Nohl in "Beethoven, Shakespeare, and the 'Appassionata'," *Beethoven Forum* 4 (1995), 73–96.

43   *Primitive Encounters*

of a civilized person with someone closer to a state of nature—either a cultural primitive or a victim of misfortune or disaster.[26] Such meetings were felt to recreate the primeval conditions under which the unformed human being, lacking all practical and intellectual resources, could begin to become Man. (In many versions, these conditions even had a precise—and tempestuous—date; universal history was supposed to have begun after the Flood, when humanity was stripped of the resources God had given it through Adam.[27]) Primitive encounters were accordingly taken as the "experimental" basis of the anthropological project. Their more popular function, however, was to circulate a value-laden image in which human suffering is relieved and sublimated by civilized benevolence.

The primitive encounter had a typical structure that is best illustrated by example. According to Owen Jander, the "Tempest" Sonata incorporates many of the imitative techniques of popular late-eighteenth-century storm music and raises them to the level of art. Jander further suggests that Beethoven may have been influenced by a popular French painter of tempest scenes, Joseph Vernet (1714–89), engravings of whose works were regularly on view in Vienna at the shop of Beethoven's publisher Artaria.[28] Although I differ from Jander in not construing the tempestuousness of the D-Minor Sonata as mimetic, I find his recourse to Vernet highly suggestive. Plate 1 shows one of Vernet's best-known paintings, *Tempest by Moonlight* (*La Tempête au claire de lune*). Much of this work is occupied with depicting a standard form of what Kant called the mathematical sublime, a natural phenomenon of overwhelming magnitude from which the mind recoils into a sense of its own even greater magnitude as spirit, that which transcends nature.[29] A small corner of the painting, however, offers a contrast. Here a concentrated patch of moonlight opens a little pocket or reserve in which the sublime yields to one of its regular alternatives in eighteenth-century aesthetics, namely the pathetic. The pathetic (the expression of "moving," "touching," or "affecting" feelings) has

26. I take the term "primitive encounter" from Alan Bewell, *Wordsworth and the Enlightenment: Nature, Man, and Society in the Experimental Poetry* (New Haven: Yale UP, 1989), pp.71–108.

27. For example, see Étienne de Condillac, *Essay on the Origin of Human Knowledge*, trans. Thomas Nugent (1756; rpt. Gainsville: U Florida P, 1971), p.169; and Jean-Jacques Rousseau, *Essay on the Origin of Language*, in *The First and Second Discourses and Essay on the Origin of Languages*, trans. Victor Gourevitch (New York: Harper and Row, 1990), p.264.

28. Owen Jander, "Genius in the Arena of Charlatanry: The First Movement of Beethoven's 'Tempest' Sonata in Cultural Context," in *Musica Franca: Essays in Honor of Frank D'Accone* (Stuyvesant, N.Y.: Pendragon, 1996), pp.585–630. My thanks to Professor Jander for allowing me to read the manuscript of this article, and for providing slides of Vernet's *Tempest by Moonlight*.

29. Immanuel Kant, "Analytic of the Sublime," *Critique of Judgment*, trans. James Creed Meredith, 2 vols. (Oxford: Oxford UP, 1952), pars.23–29.

44

Plate 1: Joseph Vernet, *Tempest by Moonlight* [*Storm in the Moonlight*], engraving by Jean Jacques Flipart (1771). Courtesy of the Fogg Art Museum, Harvard University Art Museums. Gift of William Gray from the collection of Francis Calley Gray.

a tangled mutual history with the sublime that resists easy summary; suffice it to say here that the most intense forms of the pathetic tended to be understood as a kind of second-order sublime, while the "softer" forms were referred to the quite different category of sensibility, the coalescence of aesthetic and compassionate responsiveness.[30]

30. There has been no systematic study of the interrelations of the sublime and the pathetic since those that thread Monk's classic study, *The Sublime*. A good example of the pathetic as a second-order sublime is offered by the Kantian aesthetic theorist Christian Friedrich Michaelis, who distinguishes between the objectively sublime, that which is unconditional and arouses sublime emotions, and the pathetically sublime, which is contingent on the objective sublime and is moving or stirring. Only the objective sublime invokes the infinite; it resembles epic poetry (the highest poetic genre) where the pathetically sublime resembles the lyric. See Michaelis, "The Beautiful and the Sublime in Music," *Berlinische musikalische Zeitung* 1 (1805): 179, rpt. in *Music and Aesthetics in the Eighteenth*

45 *Primitive Encounters*

Plate 2: Detail from Joseph Vernet, *Tempest by Moonlight* [*Storm in the Moonlight*], engraving by Jean Jacques Flipart (1771). Courtesy of the Fogg Art Museum, Harvard University Art Museums. Gift of William Gray from the collection of Francis Calley Gray.

As plate 2 shows, the reserve in Vernet's painting is primarily of the "sensibility" type. It is above all a place where human sympathy and the state of nature meet. Its most distinct, best illuminated figure is the one who most visibly suffers: a woman, half-crumpled, who is supported by two companions with tender solicitude. The seminakedness of this figure is a signifier of her reduction to a primitive state, as is the tepeelike shelter that stands behind her; the faux tepee is there because speculative anthropologists considered the so-called North American Indians to

---

and Early Nineteenth Centuries, ed. and trans. Peter le Huray and James Day (Cambridge: Cambridge UP, 1988), p.202. See also Monk's discussion of John Dennis's theorization of the sublime a century earlier, *The Sublime,* pp.45–54.

be exemplary primitives.[31] The sympathy of the companions provides the means by which the state of nature is transcended, allowing the three figures to form the symbolic kernel of civil society, which is thus preserved from the tempest that threatens it.

The iconography of this painting reproduces the underlying structure of primitive encounter as it is formulated in one of the most influential books of the eighteenth century, Étienne de Condillac's *Essay on the Origin of Human Knowledge* (1746).[32] In Condillac's staging of the archetypal encounter, the sublime of the state of nature yields to the pathetic of the reserve when a person who does not suffer comes on one who does. The unafflicted person opens the reserve by shifting attention from the sufferer's frenzied, uncoordinated cries and gesticulations to an object that makes sense of them. The object in turn becomes a vehicle of identification between the afflicted and the unafflicted parties. It should be noted that the masculine pronouns in Condillac's description are not gender-specific.[33]

> He who suffered, by being deprived of an object which his wants had rendered necessary to him, did not confine himself to cries or sounds only; he used some endeavours to obtain it, he moved his head, his arms, and every part of his body. The other, struck with this sight, fixed his eye on the same object, and perceiving some inward emotions which he was not yet able to account for, he suffered in seeing his companion suffer. From that very instant he felt himself inclined to relieve him, and he followed this impression to the utmost of his power.[34]

By this account, sympathy with suffering is the origin of both human subjectivity and social bonding. On the one hand, sympathy advances the unafflicted person beyond mere sentience by introducing him to the perception of inward

---

31. Bewell, *Wordsworth and the Enlightenment*, pp.20–24.

32. As we will see, Condillac formulated this structure—the coupling of sublime and reserve—mainly as a device for theorizing the relationship of language and thought; his treatment of the topic produced extensive discussion in both France and Germany during the second half of the century, peaking in the 1790s. The structure itself may be realized in numerous ways; the sublime, for instance, may either be embodied in the object of sympathy (the case in Condillac himself) or in the landscape (the case in Vernet).

33. This is not to say that the scene of compassion raises no gender issues; as I have just noted, Vernet's *Tempest by Moonlight* is quite gender-specific, or at least seems to be at first glance. The exemplary primitives of Condillac himself are "two children, one male and one female, who wandered about in the deserts" after the flood (*Essay*, p.169). I shall return to issues of gender below, pp.56–57.

34. Condillac, *Essay*, p.172. See also Bewell, *Wordsworth and the Enlightenment*, pp.75–76.

47 *Primitive Encounters*

emotions; on the other hand, it gives him the impulse to offer relief to one who is now a "companion." Again, on the one hand, sympathy produces subjectivity by taking the other into the self: "he suffered in seeing his companion suffer." On the other hand, it produces sociability by infusing the recognition of likeness—"he fixed his eye on the same object"—with sensibility. The archetypal experience of sympathy becomes the first primitive encounter precisely because, by the time it is over, one of its participants is no longer wholly primitive.

Condillac's model is also important for its association of primary subjectivity with the dimension of depth. The original subject of sympathy is already a divided subject, confronted not simply by an inwardness, but by an inwardness he cannot fathom. The inward emotions induced by sympathy draw a boundary within the subject between immediate self-understanding and a self-understanding that must be deferred, between surface impulse and underlying motive. Unlike his friend Rousseau, Condillac does not postulate a primary, unreflective sympathy—Rousseau calls it pity—in the state of nature itself.[35] Condillac's version of sympathy departs from the state of nature by producing, rather than presupposing, the deeply interior capacity of one person to recognize another as a subject. The medium of this production is the complexity and self-divisibility of subjectivity itself, as prompted, in the first instance, by an imitative response to the sight of suffering. For Rousseau, and subsequently for Kant, the same divisibility would be prompted much later when civil law or duty replaced natural impulse as the ground of action.[36]

The association of spectacle, sympathy, and depth, together with the logic of sublime and reserve, installs the subjectivity of primitive encounter as one of the horizons of meaning for Beethoven's "tempestuous" sonatas. Wherever the sonatas assert their enigmatic combination of vehemence and formal indeterminacy, they invite the listener (at least a listener willing to defer decisions about musical form or structure) to assume a subject position resembling that of Condillac's unafflicted

---

35. Rousseau, *Second Discourse: On the Origins and Foundation of Inequality among Men*, pt. 1, pars. 35–38; Gourevitch trans., pp. 160–63. Rousseau, however, regards primary pity as no more than a virtuality, which must be awakened reflectively by imagination. (For discussion, see Derrida, *Of Grammatology*, trans. Gayatri Chakravorty Spivak [Baltimore: Johns Hopkins UP, 1976], pp. 181–88.) Even for Rousseau, the *subject* of pity (as opposed to presubjective man in the state of nature) is necessarily divided.

36. Rousseau, "On the Civil State," bk. 1, chap. 8, *The Social Contract*, trans. Donald A. Cress (Indianapolis: Hackett, 1983), pp. 26–27; Kant, "Conjectural Beginnings of Human History," in *Kant on History*, trans. Lewis White Beck, Robert E. Anchor, and Emil L. Fackenheim (New York: Bobbs-Merrill, 1957), pp. 53–68.

man. They present the subject holding that position with the musical equivalent of being struck by a sight, as if the perceptual accent in Condillac's primal scene of sympathy had shifted from gesture to cry. The result would be a kind of urgent, baffled fascination; to borrow some terms from Christian Friedrich Michaelis's article of 1805 on the musical sublime, this aspect of the sonatas would exemplify the mode of sublimity in which "innumerable impressions succeed each other too rapidly and the mind [is] too abruptly hurled into the thundering torrent of sounds."[37] The gap between the music's perceptual intensity and its formal integrity would not so much signify the state of nature as threaten to reproduce it. The danger to the listener's civilized subjectivity is a real one; as Schiller put it, "Even the most ethical music, by reason of its matter, has a closer affinity with the senses"—the correlative of "mere Nature" in Schiller's thought—"than true aesthetic feeling allows."[38]

Such a musical projection of what one might call the regressive sublime sets up the precondition for reenacting the sympathetic response that is also the founding experience of depth, but it does not yet produce these effects. Both the fully realized sense of enigma and the direction of the listener's sympathy toward another subject require the reflective distance made available by the reserve. In terms of Condillac's primal scene of sympathy, the tempestuous sublimity of the music acts as if to suspend the listener between the protosympathetic fascination with natural affliction, as embodied in the striking presence of the sufferer's frantic, uncoordinated, bodily motions, with their accompanying cries, and the moment of intersubjective recognition in which the two subjects become companions. In his tale "Automata" (1814), E. T. A. Hoffmann invokes a similar nexus of tempestuous music, sympathy, and subjective depth. Through a fictional spokesman, he speculates on the construction of a musical instrument that will mediate between certain primitive natural sounds that induce "painful compassion and profound terror" by imitating "the sounds of human sorrow and suffering," and the realization on "familiar instruments" of "the music which dwells within us [as the counterpart]

---

37. Michaelis, "The Beautiful and the Sublime in Music," *Music and Aesthetics,* p.203.

38. Friedrich Schiller, *On the Aesthetic Education of Man,* trans. Reginald Snell (New York: Ungar, 1954), letter 22, p.105. Schiller's scruples can be said to put in question Michaelis's assumption that the musical sublime is unproblematically edifying. Michaelis, however, is at least willing to leave open the gap between sense and form. As Dahlhaus has observed (*Ludwig van Beethoven,* pp.67–76, 131–34), musical aesthetics in and around Beethoven's lifetime was very concerned with the affirmation of form amid apparent disorder; I would suggest that this concern is fringed with a genuine anxiety about music as a danger. For a theoretical account of this topic, see my *Classical Music and Postmodern Knowledge,* pp.33–66.

of that which lies buried in nature as a profound mystery." His solution is a kind of sublime Aeolian harp, a "storm harp . . . made of thick cords of wire, which are stretched out at considerable distances . . . in the open country, and give forth great, powerful chords when the wind smites them."[39] In the storm harp, nature and civilization, indeed nature and technology, combine to produce the regressive sublime in the form of a tempest sonata.

How does one move from being "struck" by perceptual intensity into the intersubjective depth of the reserve? How does one cut into the tumult of the sublime with the involution of the pathetic? Before venturing an answer, I must put into place one more element of primitive encounter.

As Condillac describes it, the first primitive encounter precedes the development of language. (In the *Essay on the Origin of Human Knowledge,* Derrida notes, "anguish and terror are the double root of language."[40]) Subsequent repetitions of the same scene, however, gradually teach the subject to recognize bodily gestures, "the cries of the passions," and eventually arbitrary speech sounds as calls for sympathy. As a result, the reserve of the pathetic may come to be occupied by responses in kind, above all by vocal expressions of sympathy. Such expressions may take the form of either speech or song. According to Rousseau, these two acts of voice were originally identical.[41] Both are grounded in the flow of vocal inflection, which developed independently of the production of meaning. Even after the demands of civil society have separated speech from song, the affective power of pure inflection is still capable of restoring their lost unity. The medium of this restoration is once again sympathy, the original matrix in which voice became expressive:

> By imitating the inflections of the voice, melody expresses plaints, cries of suffering or of joy, threats, moans. . . . [Its] sounds act on us not only as sounds but as signs of our affections, our sentiments. . . . As soon as vocal signs strike your ear, they herald a being like yourself; they are, so to speak, the organs of the soul, and if they also depict solitude, they tell you that you are not alone in it. Birds whistle, man alone sings; and it is not possible to hear a song or a symphony without immediately telling oneself: another being endowed with sense is present.[42]

39. *Best Tales of Hoffmann,* ed. E. F. Bleiler (New York: Dover, 1967), pp.97–98 (trans. slightly modified).
40. Derrida, *Grammatology,* p.278.
41. Rousseau, *Essay on the Origin of Languages,* chap.12; Gourevitch trans., p.276.
42. Ibid., chap.14; p.282; chap.15, p.283; chap.16, p.287. Rousseau's text involves two complexities that my account ignores: an ambiguous use of the term "vocal signs" to refer to both natural

50

Melody arises by reenacting natural vocalizations—cries, moans, plaints—as social signs. Fundamentally imitative in character, it expresses not the subject's own unique state of mind but rather the relationship between one subject and another. All melody simultaneously signifies both a feeling and the bond of fellowship that makes the feeling meaningful. Melody thus recapitulates the birth of articulate sympathy that is supposedly produced through incremental repetitions of Condillac's primitive encounter. This recapitulation, in fact, is a double one. Melody is both an act of sympathetic imitation by the music maker and a stimulus to sympathetic identification by the listener. It is both a response to an appeal and an appeal for response.

Thus, in Hoffmann's "Automata" the speculative fantasy of the storm harp is interrupted by the unexpected sound of a singing voice, in particular "a profoundly sorrowful melody sung by a female voice" heard at a distance. Only with the intervention of this voice do intersubjective recognition and the full intuition of mystery establish themselves. A little girl, previously unnoticed, announces that her sister is singing; the "marvelous tones" of the singer's voice "float in the air like the breath of a zephyr"—the counterpart in the reserve of the sublime storm wind—and invite contemplation of the "world beyond the skies."[43]

Something very similar happens in Beethoven's tempest sonatas. The full humanization of sympathy in these pieces involves the reproduction of the complete primal scene of sympathy; with varying degrees of emphasis and complexity, all four sonatas can be heard to open up one or two small sympathetic reserves within a prevailing tempestuousness. All these reserves involve an allusion to a vocal sign of sympathy, in most cases to a sorrowful voice that is either of indeterminate gender (op.10, no.1) or feminine (the "Pathétique" and "Tempest"). This process, it is important to add, does not follow the kind of progressive sequence evident in Condillac and Hoffmann; the music shares in the logic of primitive encounter, but not in its narrative format.

In op.10, no.1, the reserve does not appear until a few measures before the end of the finale, when, after a slackening of the furious Prestissimo tempo (mm.106–11), a sighing figure introduces a dissonant pause (m.112; see ex.2a). At this point, foreshadowing the beginning of the "Tempest" Sonata, a mysterious arpeggio rises from the depths of the bass and lingers under a brief Adagio. The arpeggiated chord is doubly alienated, doubly the intimation of a depth too unaccountable to leave

---

and imitative utterances, and the melodic imitation of the inflections underlying language as well as of prelinguistic vocalization.

43. *Best Tales of Hoffmann*, pp.99, 100.

51 *Primitive Encounters*

more than a faint trace on the music. The chord is a dissonance within a dissonance, a diminished seventh produced by altering the chord under the preceding sigh. Played very softly, it turns into what seems like a far-distant echo of that sigh. For a lingering moment, the music is suspended in a classic trope of lament, that of the voice whose plaint is answered only by the echo of its own plaintiveness. The tessitura of the sigh makes it accessible to virtually any voice, perhaps underscoring the universality of the appeal for response and recognition. The Prestissimo resumes by stenciling over the intruding arpeggio with an arpeggio in the tonic, a gesture that does not quite cancel out the feeling of intrusion.[44]

In the first movement of the "Pathétique," longer, more exigent reserves appear when fragments of the Grave introduction recur before both the development and the coda. The introduction itself can be thought of as a combination of toccatalike passagework (mm. 4, 9–10) and ariosolike melody (mm. 1–3, 5–8). The passagework varies, in the spirit of an improvisation, while the melody, an elaborated sob figure, is repeated at successively higher pitch levels until the full compass of the soprano voice has been spanned (mm. 1–7). The process is imbued with an archaic feeling, thanks to persistent dotted rhythms that, at this tempo, are reminiscent of a French overture. When the reserves appear, they progressively undo the original toccata-arioso combination, shutting toccatalike passagework into the agitated main body of the movement and keeping the arioso for themselves.

More exactly, the reserves *retrieve* the arioso, the elements of which persist disfigured amid the prevailing agitation. The locus of this persistence is nothing less than the first theme of the sonata form, which acquires its substance by appropriating the series of rising pitch levels that has been traversed by the arioso.[45] The theme both negates the vocal appeal and contains it in embryo. In turn, the first reserve reappropriates the arioso and affirms the power of a vocal utterance to hold a place apart within the music. The second reserve both ratifies the first and takes a further step. In both mm. 1–3 of the introduction and the first reserve, the arioso arises out of a clamorous, quasi-orchestral downbeat. The second reserve eliminates the downbeat and passes the doleful remainder of the arioso through the gamut of all

---

44. This kind of "failure" has wider implications, which will emerge in subsequent discussion. The situation in op. 10, no. 1, also has a suggestive harmonic dimension. The tonic arpeggio and the i–V–i progression that it initiates can be heard as an unconvincing attempt to reinterpret the chord of the first sigh; what was very clearly V7/II♭ is declared to have been a German sixth. The echo, in effect, is subjected to a willed forgetting by denying the harmony from which it evolved.

45. The arioso traces an ascent from c^1 to f^1 to c^2 on the downbeats of mm. 1–3; the first theme traces the same ascent in mm. 11–13 via a similar melodic path. In the remainder of its first half, the theme more loosely compresses the remaining ascent of the arioso from c^1 (m. 3) to c^3 (m. 7).

52 Example 2:
   a. Sonata in C Minor, op. 10, no. 1, finale: the reserve.

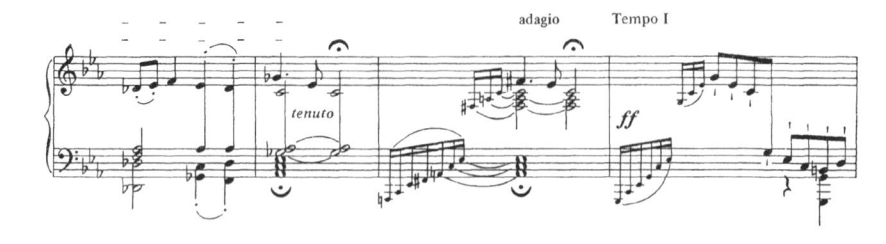

Example 2:
b. "Pathétique" Sonata,
movt. I: the reserves.

53   *Primitive Encounters*

Example 2: b. *continued*

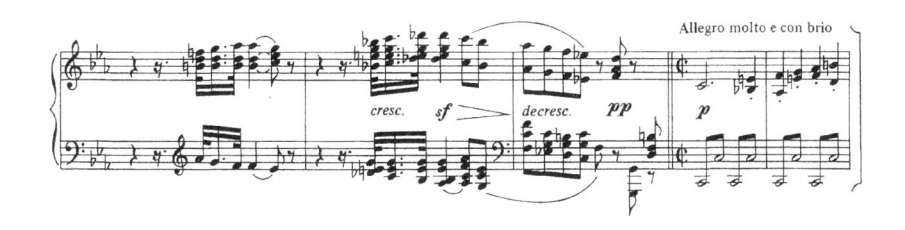

Example 2:
c. "Appassionata" Sonata, movt. I: the reserve.

three possible diminished-seventh chords (ex.2b). In tones of intensified weakness and lament, voice returns at last in something like pure form. Its return, however, occurs just in time to be silenced by the restatement of the first theme that serves as a terse, explosive coda. This act of silencing occurs just as the arioso edges past the vocal limit symbolized by high C. The same limit, suggesting a kind of border between reserve and sublime, is also marked in the introduction; after passing it (m.7), the arioso sounds only in compressed and distorted form, and without its characteristic sob.

The situation in the "Appassionata" is less clear-cut; the sonata's reputation for exceptional intensity rests on a sense that the tempestuousness of its outer movements is unremitting. It is possible, however, to single out the second theme of the opening Allegro assai, which is the only melody of any warmth in the movement and the only major-mode subject in the exposition. Just before the coda, there is a kind of interior dialogue: the famous semitonal bass motive reminiscent of the Fifth Symphony is intoned, diminuendo and ritardando, under a distorted ascending form of itself, ending under a fermata marked Adagio (ex.2c; the passage is prefigured in the exposition [mm.12–13] and recapitulation [mm.147–48] but completed only here). What follows, in the fastest tempo of the movement, is an extra recapitulation of the second theme in the tonic minor: in effect a withdrawal of the only affirmative element the music has allowed. The withdrawal also constitutes an implicit negation of voice, because at the new tempo whatever may have been songlike in the melody is stripped away. This loss is already implicit in the dialogue passage, which is vocal in its dialogical form but not in its style; the passage suggests an interior resistance to the final negation, a desire to defer the inevitable that registers in both the distorted self-echoing and the slowing of the tempo.[46]

That leaves the "Tempest" Sonata, the first movement of which harbors the most explicit, most voicelike, and also the "deepest" of Beethoven's (sym)pathetic reserves. In the exposition, the first arpeggio-Allegro juxtaposition, mentioned above, places the arpeggio on the dominant, A major. The second shifts the arpeggio to C major, the lowered third degree of the dominant (see ex.1). This chromatic

---

46. The inclusion of the second theme in the reserve here, although the only thing of its kind in the tempest series, suggests that the relation between reserve and sublime can be understood as a kind of perspective distortion of the normal, contrastive use of the second theme in sonata form. The disproportion between reserve and sublime elements turns an element of structure into a force of destructuration. Similarly, the structure of primitive encounter is always shocking; it uncovers and reenacts the traumatic underpinnings of normal subjectivity. My attention was turned to this issue at the Carnegie Hall Beethoven Symposium by a question from Walter Frisch.

55 *Primitive Encounters*

third relation produces a tension between C♯ and C♮. In relation to the tonalities on A, these tones mark the difference between the major mode, which is qualified to serve as a functional dominant, and the minor mode, which in 1802 is generally disqualified. This tension is subsequently projected on a larger scale when the secondary tonality of the movement turns out to be the dominant minor rather than the customary relative major. In the recapitulation, the arpeggios return with their original harmonies, but their juxtaposition to the Allegros is interrupted by a pair of unaccompanied recitatives. The first interruption proves temporary; the deferred Allegro follows it. The second, however, is permanent; it is followed by a brand new transitional passage that eventually leads, not to the missing Allegro, but to the recapitulation of the second subject in the tonic minor. In this case, the voice that calls for sympathy is all but audible, and its pathos trespasses the boundary of the reserve set out for it—trespasses, as will be shown, by giving the tension between C♯ and C♮ an enigmatic turn of the screw.

Rich in sobbing half steps, played softly with the pedal down throughout, the recitatives, according to Czerny, sound like voices "complaining at a distance."[47] They are by far the most intrusive, as well as the most explicitly vocal, reserves in the "tempest" series. The recurring fragments in the first movement of the "Pathétique" are disruptive, but they are also cyclical—symbolic returns to the origin of the movement. The "pathetic" elements in the first movement of the "Appassionata," such as they are, are downright organic. Even the intrusive arpeggio in op.10, no.1, ends in an echo. But the recitatives of the "Tempest" return to nothing and intermesh with nothing. They have no referent within the work; they come from somewhere else.

At one level, of course, their source is *opera seria,* a locale notable for being about as far from a state of nature as it is possible to get.[48] At another level, though, the recitatives sound, not like allusions to operatic voice, but, as Czerny says, like voices at a distance. They are literally in-vocations, voicings, tropes of voice in the indeterminate mixture of speech and song that Rousseau places at the origin of both music and language, and that recitative may be taken to replicate. At this level, the recitatives come from a fathomless, locationless depth of subjectivity whose mark on the work is not a trace but a disfigurement. At best, one might try to

---

47. Czerny, *Proper Performance*, p.43.

48. To the extent that opera is invoked here, it seems to represent a coincidence of culture and affectivity; in real *opera seria,* the relationship of these terms is fraught with problems. For discussion, see Martha Feldman, "Magic Mirrors and the *Seria* Stage: Thoughts Toward a Ritual View," JAMS 48 (1995), 423–84.

ground the recitatives by saying that they are latently invoked by the arpeggios at the start of the movement. As Schmalfeldt has suggested, these rolled sixth chords have some affinity with the harpsichordist's improvised introduction to a recitative.[49] But since what follow these operatic allusions are *not* recitatives, but something like a fantasy-fragment and a cadenza, the arpeggios do not ground the recitatives at all—at least not until the recapitulation. The recitatives are thus both grounded and ungrounded, both "in" the movement and not in it at the same time.

To take this recognition further: the recitatives are instances of what Kant called the *parergon,* from Greek, *par ergon,* "outside the work." The parergon is nominally an extra, something added to the work from outside, like a picture frame or colonnade. In a close reading of the relevant passages of Kant's *Critique of Judgment,* however, Derrida has shown that the parergon typically exceeds its status as an extra and is characterized by precisely the copresence of belonging and nonbelonging that is exhibited by Beethoven's recitatives. The parergon, Derrida continues, is the trace of a loss or lack in the work "itself."[50]

In the case of the "Tempest" Sonata, it is not hard to identify that lack. The recitatives make it audible, even palpable, as the pedal envelops them in overtones: what is lacking is the rich, vibratory, sensitive self-division of voice itself. In the context of primitive encounter, to lack voice is to lack the medium in which the human subject, the subject of sympathy, comes both to express itself and, more, to become conscious of itself as sensibility and fellow-feeling. The state of nature in the sublime of the "Tempest" Sonata is the positive negation of the human subject in this sense. Given the vocal range in which the recitatives lie, one might even suggest that the subject negated is not only that of Enlightenment Man, but also of the woman that the concept of Man, and the discourse of primitive encounter, typically denies full recognition. The sonata may be enfranchising that feminine voice in terms consistent with those of Rousseau, for whom pity always speaks in a "gentle voice" that is ultimately maternal.[51] To some degree, both during and

---

49. Schmalfeldt, "Process of Becoming," p.58.

50. Kant, "Analytic of the Beautiful," *Critique of Judgment,* pars.13, 14, 24; Derrida, "The Parergon," in *The Truth in Painting,* trans. Geoff Bennington and Ian McCloud (Chicago: U Chicago P, 1987), pp.52–67. Derrida discusses Kant's use of the Greek term to gloss the German *Zieraten* (adornment, embellishment) and refers further to the treatment of the parergon in a note Kant added to the second edition of *Religion within the Limits of Reason Alone.* Richard Littlefield has recently utilized the Derridean concept of the parergon in a reading of musical silence; see his "The Silence of the Frames," *Music Theory On-Line* 2:1 (1996).

51. Rousseau, *Second Discourse,* pt.1, par.38; Gourevitch trans., p.162. Another important instance of the maternal association (perhaps one derived from Rousseau) occurs toward the end of Coleridge's

57 *Primitive Encounters*

after the eighteenth century, suffering is understood to feminize the subject that it also humanizes.

This effect can be found at an allegorical level in the reserve of Vernet's *Tempest by Moonlight*. In part, the formation of the reserve around a passive, bare-breasted woman eroticizes the scene of sympathy, producing a typical and deeply problematic fusion of male benevolence and pleasure. Even more, however, the reserve fulfills a cultural mandate by providing a feminine term of reference (the woman is the only one in the painting) for the experience of sympathy itself. Those who attend suffering become Man by resembling women; even rough sailors respond with feminine tenderness. Beethoven's recitatives act in much the same way, inserting themselves in the sympathy-forged chain of response and appeal that Rousseau postulates for melody. They both express a deep solicitude and summon the listener to respond solicitously.

The recitatives recall the missing subject of sympathy, in the sense of both remembering it and calling it back, by holding open the space in which it can be heard. The effect of the recitatives is to suspend what counts as the natural impetus of dissonance resolution, an impetus that the arpeggio-Allegro passages seek, on the contrary, to enhance. While the suspension lasts, voice may be recalled, even if only at a distance, disembodied into its instrumental substitute. The reference point for this process is the most "natural" of dissonant junctures, the hinge between dominant and tonic. The arpeggio-Allegro passages at the beginning of the sonata play evasively on and around dominant sonorities for fully nineteen measures. When a clearly precadential dominant finally arrives in m.20, it is full of pent-up demand, and the perfect authentic cadence that hinges on it, the cadence that introduces the "false" first theme, satisfies that demand with a commensurate violence (see ex. 1). With the recapitulation, however, demand is inhibited virtually at its source, as the first recitative grafts itself onto the close of the first arpeggio. The melody of this recitative enunciates the dominant (V^6_5, ruefully extending the arpeggio's V^6), but in terms that denature the dominant function. With the advent of voice, harmony becomes incidental to melody; housed in the pedal blur, the recitative takes plaintive harmonic dissonance as its *métier* and replaces harmonic

---

ode, "Dejection" (1802): "[It is] a little child / Upon a lonesome wild, / Not far from home, but she hath lost her way: and now moans low in bitter grief and fear, / And now screams loud, and hopes to make her mother hear" (121–25). Here the sympathetic-imitative movement of the verse, corresponding to the poem's own description of the lost-girl narrative as "A tale of less affright / and tempered with delight" (118–19), supplies the maternal solicitude for which the lost girl seeks. Text from Samuel Taylor Coleridge, *Poems*, ed. John Beer (London: Dent, 1963).

58

resolution by the melodic resolution of nonharmonic tones, always by expressive half step (see ex.3). Perhaps, though, "resolution" is the wrong word here, since the recitative also ends on a nonharmonic tone. Perhaps the chordal framework is only a vehicle by which the voice, as plaint, as call for sympathy, makes itself heard as an essential dissonance.[52]

The second recitative would seem to bear out these possibilities. The dissonance here is extreme, involving three distinct layers of unstable sonority, yet it is completely without violence or urgency. The first layer is supplied by the dominant, which remains unresolved after the deferred recapitulation of the Allegro that goes with the first arpeggio. The second layer is supplied by the second arpeggio, with its sixth chord on C, the chromatically lowered third degree of the preceding dominant. And the third layer is supplied by the second recitative itself, not only in its enveloping pedal blur, but also in its melodic line (see ex.3). Unlike the first recitative, the second emphasizes, not the resolution of nonharmonic tones, but their production, starting with D♭, about as rueful a tone as the ambit of C major affords. With this tone, plaintiveness touches the outer or lower limit of intelligible subjectivity, the boundary beyond which, one can only surmise, suffering would undo its former work and return the subject to the state of nature. The D♭ marks the point at which the missing subject of sympathy finds itself most fully recalled, invested with both the greatest sensibility and, in every sense, the greatest resonance.

The liminal quality of this D♭ is reinforced by its enharmonic identity with C♯, the signature tone of the dominant. In the second recitative, this identity becomes a difference. As the putative equivalent of C♯, the D♭ imports the latent conflict between C♯ and C♮, dominant and nondominant, into the harmonic field of C♮ itself. In so doing, the D♭ prefigures the resolution of the conflict, which necessarily favors the dominant and therefore the C♯. As something that is *not* C♯, however, the D♭ sets the conflict at a distance; as enharmonic *difference,* it draws a boundary that keeps the conflict outside the sympathetic reserve. The D♭ draws its distinctive identity from its position a diminished seventh above the bass and a minor ninth above the root of the C-major sixth chord onto which it grafts itself. The effect,

52. At the Carnegie Hall Symposium, both Carl Schachter and William Rothstein suggested to me that the closing tones of the recitatives could be taken to imply harmonic resolutions. In accepting this suggestion, I would emphasize that the resolutions are precisely *implied,* that is, potential rather than actual. In relation to the A six-three and C six-three chords of the arpeggios, the sound of which still lingers faintly in their respective pedal blurs, the tones remain dissonant. One might even suggest that the sonorities produced in the passages, consistent with their abyssal origin, constitute challenges to the very notion of a resolution, implied or otherwise.

59   *Primitive Encounters*

Example 3: "Tempest" Sonata, movt. I: the recitatives and subsequent transition.

60

as well as the purpose of the second recitative, is to affirm voice against nature by upholding the identity of this D♭ as against C♯. As long as the D♭ is different, in quality if not in sound, from C♯, the progress of the conflict will be balked, the natural hinge of dominant and tonic will be denatured, and the essential dissonance of voice will be sustained as something that does not want "resolution"—only sympathy.

Example 4: "Tempest" Sonata, movt.I: sketch of recapitulation, mm.158–71.

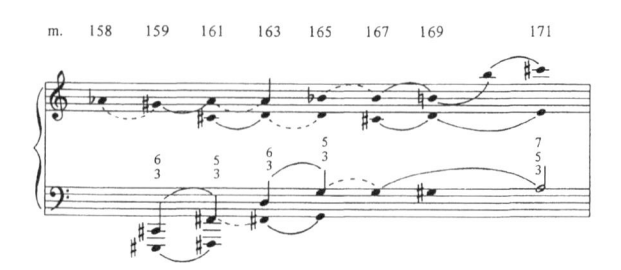

One purpose of the transitional passage that follows the second recitative in lieu of the exposition's "cadenza" is to reclaim the identity of C♯. The recitative, like its predecessor, ends on a nonharmonic tone, A♭. The transitional passage begins by converting this tone enharmonically to G♯ as the fifth degree of a soft, staccato series of C♯-minor sixth chords. The passage ends by dramatically attacking a high C♯, now the third of a dominant-seventh chord, to introduce the recapitulation of the second theme. In between, there unfolds a sequential logic that, as ex.4 shows, takes the initial C♯ chords as the point of origin for the reattainment of the dominant. The vindication of C♯ could scarcely be more forceful, and the passage that carries it out could scarcely be more turbulent. Nevertheless, the impress of the nonpareil D♭, the continued resonance of the now silenced reserve, can still be felt via the absence of the "false" first theme. Lacking its introductory "cadenza," the melodic C♯s of which would not be sufficient to reaffirm the tone, this theme has had to be sacrificed. Understood in these terms, the absence of the theme from the recapitulation is not simply a question of formal ambiguity, of a preference for process over scheme, but a question of the incalculable effects that the reserve may have on the whole, the pathetic on the sublime, voice on nature.

Climates of Thought

This question, moreover, may not be confinable to one place. The relationship between the recitatives of the "Tempest" Sonata and the first movement "proper" may be reenacted on a larger scale between the slow movement of the work and

61 *Primitive Encounters*

its outer movements. The same may also be true in varying degrees of the other sonatas in the series, which, as noted earlier, also enclose a reflective, major-key slow movement with agitated minor-key fast ones. The circularity of this three-part design invites us to raise the question in dialectical terms: To what extent do the finales of these works reconcile or synthesize the contradictions between the first two movements? In a sense, a similar question has been raised here already. Both Dahlhaus and Schmalfeldt describe the formal processes in the first movement of the "Tempest" Sonata as dialectical, Dahlhaus referring primarily to sonata form and Schmalfeldt to deep structure. Neither writer, however, considers the possibility that the contradictions in this music may resist the synthesizing, idealizing force of dialectic, which, after all, identifies contradiction at one level only to abolish it on a higher one. Even to speak of contradiction here tacitly rules out the recognition of some more intractable form of difference.

My account of reserve and totality in the first movement of the "Tempest" and associated sonatas is meant to give this other differential possibility full play. It situates the music in a symbolic network or economy in which aesthetic, moral, cultural, and psychological terms are continually exchanged and intermingled. To the extent that the multimovement design is understood as dialectical, however, the activity of the first movements must be understood as subject (resistantly or not) to a higher-order resituation in a more stable, more reified framework.

Each of the four "tempestuous" sonatas broaches this possibility differently. The "Pathétique" seems to reach eagerly, even anxiously, for dialectical integration. Its rondo finale segregates an impetuous main theme from episodes of a more convivial liveliness; the display of balance, of conspicuous normality, is successful only because its sheer energy masks its impulse toward retrenchment. In contrast, the finale of op. 10, no. 1, can be taken as an equivocal rejection of dialectic. Its Prestissimo pace and compressed sonata form—there is next to no development, so that the movement becomes a travesty of the nondeveloping sonata form of the cantabile slow movement—seem to invest in energy rather than order, exacerbation rather than integration. Nonetheless, this finale does contain an important, if fleeting, reserve, the dissonant arpeggio noted earlier, which in context may seem to echo the mitigations of the slow movement. And the finale ends with a modal mixture, a C tonality with E♮ (for I) and A♭ (for iv and vii°), that conjoins, although without quite integrating, harmonic acerbity and its mitigation.

With the "Appassionata," the case is entirely unequivocal; as the reception tradition has agreed from the outset, the finale is merciless. Its rejection of dialectic is both clear and brutal. It arises, indeed, from an act of rejection, an interrupted cadence that denies closure to the contemplative slow movement. Converting the

62

dissonant interruption to a *grollend* roiling in the deep bass, the finale surges forth and never once looks back. To be more exact, its only backward glance is hostile. As I have suggested elsewhere, the sonata form of the finale grossly travesties that of the first movement. The first movement omits the repeat of the exposition and becomes a quasi-strophic cycle, passing through four parallel but varied sections consisting of the exposition, development, recapitulation, and coda. The finale repeats the development and recapitulation instead of the exposition and becomes a kind of rondo-without-variation (A B A B A), a form that, combined with an overinsistent, low-contrast texture, sounds like a *moto perpetuo* in overdrive. For 1804, this is the ultimate in exacerbation. In order to break the cycle of repetitions and veer into a coda, the movement even seems to require a violent wrenching, an ungrounded passage (mm. 308–24) that is both furious and banal, "the musical equivalent of banging one's fist on the table to shut someone up."[53]

The "Tempest" Sonata, characteristically, is more problematic than any of the others in its relationship to dialectic. In the general mood and character of its successive movements, the sonata does give a dialectical appearance. The Adagio introduces an island of calm that remains undisturbed even when the main theme comes to be enveloped by swirls of rapid figuration, echoes of the first movement's tempestuousness (mm. 50–58). The finale recasts that tempestuousness as unbroken impetuous motion, reviving the energy of the first movement but not its violence. Similarly, the Adagio begins a process of formal rectification that the finale will complete. The Adagio opposes an unproblematical nondeveloping sonata form to the "processual" form of the first movement, but also incorporates a processuality of its own in the recapitulation of the first theme, which introduces the aforementioned rapid figuration. The finale reverts to the standard developmental sonata form that the first movement had precluded, but imbues that form in toto with a stabilized, no longer ambiguous version of the first movement's processuality. The finale's form is filled out by a richly variegated *moto perpetuo* texture, fluid where that of the "Appassionata" would prove to be rigid, and continuously sustained except during statements of the second theme group. The finale makes process a quality of form where the first movement had made form a quality of process. Or, to make the same point in the discourse of speculative anthropology, the finale grounds subjective interiority in the Rousseauian-Kantian rule of principle where the first movement had grounded it in the Condillacian fellowship of sympathy.

Attended to more closely, however, this dialectical appearance proves to be just

---

53. From my *Music and Poetry: The Nineteenth Century and After* (Berkeley and Los Angeles: U California P, 1984), p.49; for sonata form in the "Appassionata," see pp.35–38, 46–47.

63   *Primitive Encounters*

that: a semblance, meant to be heard, certainly, but also meant to be heard through, much as one hears one layer of sound through the veil of another. Many of the basic gestural and melodic elements of the Adagio and finale of the "Tempest" Sonata draw allusively on the first movement. The source of the allusions, however, is not the first movement proper, the tempestuous whole that seems to ground the multimovement dialectic. Instead, the source is a discontinuous fragment, the ensemble of Adagio and Largo passages that stand partly outside the whole or form its margins. In effect, the source is an extended form of the reserve. What sounds through the semblance of dialectic is a continual emanation of the music from the depths of the reserve, the inner folds of the parergon. The reserve, moreover, is the original site of sounding- or hearing-through itself, the locale where the recitatives have sounded through the veil of the pedal blur. *In* the sonata without being *of* it, the reserve is nonetheless the sonata's origin.

The Adagio announces this state of affairs by beginning with a gesture that is both an allusion to the margins of the first movement and an exemplary parergon in its own right: a slow, dark arpeggio rippling up from the deep bass, which, once heard, will never be heard again. The movement offers an unusual combination of epigrammatic and lyric expression in its first and second themes, respectively, almost as if it were conjoining speech and song, which is to say, replicating the conjuncture that typically marks the transition from primitive encounter to civil society. Both themes give prominence to a double-dotted rhythm previously heard only in the first-movement recitatives; the first theme also picks up a turn found only in the one-measure Adagio by which the first movement curtails its initial Largo-Allegro pairing.[54] The two themes are also exemplary instances of listening-through. Portions of the first typically occur as a middle or lower voice, and this theme passes behind a veil of rapid note motion during its recapitulation. The second theme is distinguished by an active inner voice, the effect of which is not so much contrapuntal as bidimensional; instead of subject and countersubject, there is a theme unfolded on two levels at once (see ex. 5). Finally, both themes segue into transitional passages punctuated by an ominous drumbeatlike figure, a short octave tremolo heard primarily in the deep bass with occasional echoes in the high treble. This figure has multiple sources in the first movement: the second recitative, the all-important D♭ of which is articulated as a falling octave; the arpeggios, which span an octave between the upper note of their rolled portion and the completion of their slower, written-out portion; and the "false" first theme, which spans a

---

54. Schmalfeldt ("Process of Becoming," pp. 64–66) observes a similar turn articulated at a higher structural level in mm. 3–6, 55–57.

Example 5: "Tempest" Sonata, movt.II: the second theme.

rising octave. This last source itself derives from the arpeggios, but it has enough independent presence to trouble slightly the apparently definite boundary between dialectical semblance and the activity of hearing-through.

The finale's method of drawing on the reserve of the first movement is more diffuse than that of the Adagio, but by the same token more pervasive. The finale of the Seventh Symphony may or may not be what Wagner famously called it, the apotheosis of the dance, but the finale of the "Tempest" Sonata is undoubtedly the apotheosis of the arpeggio, even if its 3/8 time also renders it light on its feet. The movement is a virtual prelude or étude in arpeggios dressed up as a sonata form. Virtually all of it unfolds within what one might call the sonata's arpeggio-space, the portion of the first movement's expanded reserve that borders on both the depth of the recitatives and the breadth of the tempestuous whole. Even the exception, the second group, is linked to this space by continuous note motion in the value of the arpeggios. In addition, the octave/drumbeat figure also reappears here, sounding through the continuous texture both in the articulation of some of

65 *Primitive Encounters*

the arpeggios and as a thematic element, part of the second group's closing theme. At the level of dialectical semblance, the finale can be said to bring discipline to the unruly motion of the first movement, to exchange a tempest for the dance—or, following Czerny's account of the origin of this movement, for the gallop of a passing horseman, bound for the unknown.[55] At the level of hearing-through, however, the finale differs *from* the first movement by inhabiting the difference *within* the first movement, which is the very difference in which the sympathetic subject of the Enlightenment finds its identity.

Beethoven's tempestuous sonatas, and above all the "Tempest" Sonata itself, participate in the cultural work of establishing the legitimacy of that subject, a project still very much unfinished in the first years of the nineteenth century—as it remains in the last years of the twentieth. The posing of this legitimation as a question, the question of how to ground the human subject in its own interiority rather than in a centralized external authority, is one of the defining conditions of modernity.[56] The rise of aesthetics as a discipline in the early eighteenth century was in part an attempt to answer that question by affirming the social value of organized perception, and of its disruption at the limit of the sublime. The Beethoven sonatas studied here mark an early and exemplary break with this tradition, which nonetheless forms their indispensable context. The sonatas stake their construction of subjectivity not on the edifying perception of a musical object, but on the listening subject's sympathetic capacity to recognize another subject in the course of perceiving that object. The result is a fellowship of voice, depth, mystery, and the sharing of signification. This relationship—an imaginary one, to be sure, and fraught with problems of gender and social position—legitimizes the subjective interior by identifying it with the social bond, and vice versa. By the mid-nineteenth century, this kind of subjective fellowship would become independent of sympathy and assume, more and more readily, a destructive character. What begins in the eighteenth century as sensibility ends in the nineteenth as psychopathology. The ethos of these Beethoven sonatas stands precariously in between, at a moment when eighteenth-century ideals of sympathy could still anchor a far more complex subjectivity than the eighteenth century ever envisioned.

---

55. Czerny, *Proper Performance*, p.44.
56. For a history of the legitimation crisis of modern subjectivity since the seventeenth century, see Anthony J. Cascardi, *The Subject of Modernity* (Cambridge: Cambridge UP, 1992).

CHAPTER 9

Tolstoy's Beethoven, Beethoven's Tolstoy: The *Kreutzer* Sonata

Adapted from *After the Lovedeath: Sexual Violence and the Making of Culture* (Berkeley: University of California Press, 1998), passim.

Leo Tolstoy's infamous story "The Kreutzer Sonata" is the tale of a self-loathing husband, one Pozdnyshev, who murders his wife for her infidelity. Whether the infidelity occurs in a literal sense is moot, and really does not matter. The sexual performance is supposedly brought to light by a musical performance but actually consists in that musical performance itself. The music is Beethoven's "Kreutzer" Sonata, as played, with a passion too great for its salon-like occasion, by the wife at the piano and the down-at-heels son of a bankrupt landowner at the violin. Pozdnyshev sees this violinist, Trukhachevski, as a monstrosity not because he, Trukhachevski, desires Pozdnyshev's wife but because he resembles her. In Trukhachevski a cultural secret that must be kept at any cost, the inevitable presence of a certain "feminine" dependency and receptivity within the structure of masculine identity, ceases to be a secret; it becomes transparent, even blatant.

Is Tolstoy just using and abusing Beethoven here? Is he dragooning a great and independent work of music into the service of his own or his culture's anxieties over se and gender? ("I can detect no sex in the Kreutzer," wrote E. M. Forster—who could, however, detect it in the *Appassionata*—"nor have I come across anyone who could, except Tolstoy."[128]) Or has Tolstoy discerned some genuine possibilities of meaning in the music and chosen to realize them with ruthless honesty? Is he perhaps right to treat the "Kreutzer" Sonata as a nerve-center of social energies even if his particular understanding of them is idiosyncratic? And just how idiosyncratic (not to say perverse, and in some ways he *is* perverse) is that understanding? Is Tolstoy a necessarily flawed model for how to do critical musicology, or for how not to?

To propose some answers, we need both to read the text and listen to the music, both together and apart.

Punta d' arco. Pozdnyshev's murder of his wife is an impromptu ritual meant to re-conceal what the music has revealed, the feminine flaw within the diamond of masculinity. To make it so, the details of the murder, which are particularly brutal, fall into a symbolic pattern. Pozdnyshev's dagger encounters a resistant substance—both his wife's corset "and something else"—before plunging into "something soft"; the murder is initially a kind of rape. But the result is the production of a striking bloodstain, marked both as the immediate gush of blood from under the corset and, later, as a black stain spread over the wife's discarded dress. The eroticized murder produces the traditional sign of the virtuous wife's deflowering.

The resistant "something else" acts as a surrogate hymen; the murder re-enacts the original sexual act by which the husband, with or without his wife's consent, ratifies his manhood by legitimately shedding her blood.

'*Any man has to, wants to, needs to . . .*' In relation to his wife, as he tells us repeatedly, Tolstoy's Pozdnyshev acts like all men of his social class, the landed gentry. In relation to women in general, haunted by "woman, every woman, woman's nudity" (366) he acts like all men: "nine-tenths, if not more, not of our class only but of all classes, even the peasants" (367). He is an absolutely typical figure; his individuality seems to consist of nothing but the excessiveness of his typicality, even when his typical rage at his wife vents itself in her murder.

Yet this absolutely typical man has become something absolutely exceptional. Remorse over the murder has transformed him into an uncanny figure. He has become a charismatic stranger on a train, Coleridge's Ancient Mariner as a chain-smoking modern neurotic, complete with a vocal tic, a strange tale to tell, and glittering eyes that rivet the listener-victim to the telling. The listener, who serves as a frame narrator for "The Kreutzer Sonata," is a fellow-passenger on a railway journey who makes several failed attempts to engage Pozdnyshev in conversation. In the end, as with the Ancient Mariner, the initiative comes from the side of remorse and the uncanny. Compare:

> We heard, behind me, a sound like that of a broken laugh or sob; and on turning round we saw my neighbor, the lonely gray-haired man with the glittering eyes, who had approached unnoticed during our conversation. . . . He stood with his arms on the back of the seat, evidently much agitated; his face was red and a muscle twitched in his cheek.
>
> [To the frame narrator:] 'Would you like me to tell you [alone] how . . . love led to what happened to me?'. . .
> I repeated that I wished it very much. He paused, rubbed his face with his hands, and began:
> 'If I am to tell it, I must tell everything from the beginning.' ("Kreutzer," 360, 364)

> It is an Ancient Mariner,
> And he stoppeth one of three.
> 'By thy long gray beard and glittering eye
> Now wherefore stopp'st thou me?' . . .
>
> He holds him with his skinny hand,
> 'There was a ship,' quoth he. . . .
>
> The Wedding-Guest sat on a stone:
> He cannot chuse but hear.
> And thus spake on that ancient man,
> That bright-eyed Mariner. ("Rime of the Ancient Mariner," ll. 1–4, 8–10, 16–20)

Other figures of nineteenth-century masculine iconography also lurk in Pozdnyshev's shadow. There is the Flying Dutchman, the Wandering Jew, the Byronic hero: each one a personification of the utter insider's dread and desire of being utterly on the outside.

The value of such a figure is supposed to lie in his no longer being the man he was. Pozdnyshev narrates the story of his sexual violence, which is the story of his typicality, precisely when he is no longer typical, after he has undergone the "spiritual conversion" that (again like the Ancient Mariner's) makes him a spellbinding storyteller. Yet he still loves and compassionates the man he was; his narrative shows it at every turn. Distanced from his former self in principle, he is in practice constantly intimate with it. He identifies with it as a reader does with a character, or as the frame narrator identifies with him. When Pozdnyshev narrates the events surrounding his wife's murder, the gripping immediacy of his tale invites the frame narrator—invites us—to abandon all sense of critical distance. Male or female, with or without our consent, we are drawn into imagining the killing from the killer's point of view. We are seduced by the Pozdnyshev-character's theatrical-aesthetic pleasure in acting the role of murderer, and by his erotic-narcissistic pleasure in making the role a reality. It is no wonder that the frame narrator ends the story with an expression of sympathy for Pozdnyshev, not for his victim:

> I touched him with my hand. He uncovered his face, and I could not see if he had been asleep.
> 'Good-bye,' I said, holding out my hand. He gave me his and smiled slightly, but so piteously that I felt ready to weep.
> 'Yes, forgive me . . .' he said, repeating the same words which which he had concluded his story. (428)

Sadder but wiser, the frame-narrator gives the grieving killer a token of forgiveness that is also a token of affection. Unless we're careful, we readers, we will let him do it as our surrogate.

(Coup de) Grace Notes. Why did Tolstoy seize in particular on Beethoven's "Kreutzer" Sonata? Perhaps because it embodied a contradiction for him. Its genre, the duo for violin and piano, had not yet been fully professionalized in the 1890s. In genre, the piece is still salon music. But its substance, or rather the substance of the first movement, is nothing of the kind. Just listen to the extravagance of this music, the emotional abundance of its Baroque introduction, the passionate, utterly relentless dynamism of the main sonata form! When I teach the Tolstoy story with the sonata, even students who know nothing of classical music are dazzled by these things. Tolstoy is dead right to stress the music's explosive incongruity: the way its importation of formal monumentality and emotional ferocity into the salon medium suggests the workings of an incommensurable force, something presocialized and unsocializable, that threatens to erupt amid polite conversation, and, more dangerously, to erupt there from within.

From the traditional perspective of the musicologist, this suggestion of uncanny power can be sublimated—sublimated all too easily, so that it disappears or, failing that, becomes merely "subjective"—into the effect of aesthetic success. Thus Charles Rosen writes that the first movement of the "Kreutzer" Sonata is "unequalled in formal clarity, grandeur, and dramatic force by anything Beethoven had yet written" (399). But Tolstoy is deaf to such sublimation, and rightly so. Even though what he makes of what he hears is repugnant, he is right to hear critical and even destructive energy in this music. He is right to hear this energy exposing and attacking a social order built around a dissembled commerce in male desires and female bodies: "How can that first Presto be played in a drawing room among ladies in low-necked dresses? To hear that played, to clap a little, and then to eat ices and talk of the latest scandal?" (411).

Fascinatin' Rhythm. Pozdnyshev loathes Trukhachevski at first sight, yet he seemingly can't get enough of the man. He virtually seduces this object of loathing, not only by his own smarmy politesse, but more importantly by making bait of his wife, dangling her before the violinist's roving eye—and hand: virtually pimping for her, as Richard Leppert observes (171). It is as if Pozdnyshev were compelled to make the archetypal Other Man appear in person, perhaps in order to master him, perhaps in order to woo him. (Leppert notes the strong current of unacknowledged homoeroticism in Pozdnyshev's fascination [169–70]. We might even say that Pozdnyshev asks music to awaken his wife's desire for Trukhachevski in order to keep his own desire dormant.) Trukhachevski is not merely encountered; he is conjured up. "If he hadn't appeared," says Pozdnyshev, "there would have been someone else. If the occasion had not been jealousy it would have been something else."

But the outcome of this conjuration is infuriating. This other man, this archetypal Oedipal rival, carries his masculinity only in hiding, as if concealed in his violin case. He is no commanding masterly presence but just a "not-bad-looking" cad; he does not look manly in the least. In fact he looks just like a woman:

> With moist almond-shaped eyes, red smiling lips, a small waxed moustache, hair done in the latest fashion, and an insipidly pretty face, he was what women call "not bad looking." His figure was weak though not misshapen, and he had a specially developed posterior, like a woman's, or such as the Hottentots are said to have. They too are reported to be musical. (397–98)

Trukhachevski's red lips and bulging bottom suggest that masculine desire, the result of unstinted participation in the sexual marketplace, is in and of itself feminizing within the nineteenth-century bourgeois order. The man who successfully becomes the subject of desire finds himself prompted to identify with the object of desire, and thus paradoxically defaces himself as a masculine subject. Worse yet, the character of this identification suggests that masculine desire by its very nature includes the feminine desire to be desired, to relate to the object of desire not as a proprietor but, uncertainly and ambivalently, as both proprietor and property. Hence on the one hand Trukhachevski's effort to look attractive, which Pozdnyshev sees as fey primping: the French fashions, the waxed mustaches, the au courant hairdo. Hence, too, on the other hand, Pozdnyshev's impotent fury at these details, combined with his fetishistic fascination by them. ("Though I did not realize it, I observed everything connected with him with extraordinary fascination." [405])

The ultimate medium of this fascination is music, in particular first movement of the "Kreutzer" Sonata. The music evokes in Pozdnyshev the same combination of desire, identification, and repulsion at both that the sleazy-charming musician does. It draws him out of himself in two illegitimate pieces, one that desires his wife as Trukhachevski does, and one that desires Trukhachevski as his wife does.

In this connection it is particularly striking that Pozdnyshev initially fails to recognize the Gordian knot of being and wanting that Beethoven's Presto arouses in him. He makes this recognition only in retrospect, several nights later. Awakening suddenly in the middle of the night, he recalls that, after the Beethoven, his wife and Trukhachevski had played something extra: a nameless little piece "impassioned to the point of obscenity" (414), presumably something like ordinary sentimental salon music, something that at the time "[made not] a one-hundredth part of the impression the first piece had" (412).

Only through this little extra piece does the element of phallic display in the Beethoven, and its effect of virtual adultery, become manifest. Pozdnyshev's initial failure to recognize that display has been spurred by his unwilling susceptibility to it. The Beethoven has produced in him an unknown, unknowable, but "very joyous" state of mind, replete with "new feelings, new possibilities, of which [he] had till then been unaware" (411). He embraces this new condition with a "feminine" combination of yielding and avidity. In so doing, however, he also builds up a desperate need to reject the music, to expel it, which later appears as an expression of visceral disgust: "Ugh! Ugh! it is a terrible thing, that sonata. And especially that part" (410). What Pozdnyshev hears in the Beethoven, what he has turned procurer in order to hear in it, is a movement of transcendence, a breakthrough into a spirituality quite inconsistent with the lust, decolletage, and triviality of the drawing room. Yet it is only in the drawing room that the breakthrough can occur; the sign of the breakthrough is, precisely, a transfigured drawing room: "All these same people, including my wife and [Trukhachevski,] appeared in a new light" (412). Pozdnyshev's rage and resentment may thus come from his unwelcome understanding that this visionary experience of his can be generated only through the sleazy, illicit medium of music, the medium, above all, of the feminine, the feminized, and the feminizing body. In killing his wife, he is killing that body, above all killing it in himself. Hence, perhaps, a telling later image: dying, his wife lies on his side of the bed.

Mincing along. His side, because listening to the opening Presto of the Kreutzer has unmanned him, or rather reveals to him that he has always already been unmanned by the very condition he calls his masculinity.

Perhaps one should say that the music *out*-mans him, thrusts him into the feminine posture that he cannot acknowledge as his own.

Certainly this music seems to present itself as virile from tip to toe. Even the contrast between first and second themes, which is often glossed as a masculine-feminine opposition, can sound brusquely pro forma here, with the chorale-like second theme serving merely as a parenthesis, a voice from outside that highlights, by deferring, a continuation of the first theme and its headlong energy. The movement as a whole is borne on and born of the masculine body, emblematized at the outset by the rich strenuousness of the violin's double stops and propelled dynamically in the main sonata sections by intense, repercussive, muscular melodic figuration. Donald Tovey called this movement "a magnificent piece of Homeric fighting" (68), and rightly so; it belongs to the closed virile world of Achilles and Patroclus, or the equally virile German-Classical world of Winckelmann (ideal grace, the sculptural, the broad, clear sonata form) and Hölderlin (the rhetorical force, the expressive intensity, the uncontainable passion). "Homeric fighting" also suggests what is most admirable about the movement, what keeps its masculine ethos from lapsing into mere anti-feminine belligerence. Its antagonists are neither intimate nor social but existential; its violence is abstract and depersonalized, meant to inscribe its energies, in the manner of Homeric similes, the wider circle of destinies—mythic for Homer, historical for Beethoven.

Pozdnyshev lives in a smaller world, which is another thing the first movement tells him. But he is able to exercise his resentment at that fact by admiring the first movement even while hating it, then despising the second movement for being the sort of thing he ought to like, and perhaps secretly does.

Tolstoy hears this as a "beautiful, but common and unoriginal, andante with trite variations" (412). But is Beethoven really returning to the salon here? Charles Rosen thinks so; he, too, describes this "beautiful" slow movement as "elegant, brilliant, ornamental, and a little precious," and adds that it belongs to a "totally different style" than the first movement (399). And it is true that the slow movement begins by parading its good behavior, cultivating a genuine but deliberately stilted beauty. It even seems to be seeking a lulling monotony. The theme and first three variations follow the most redundant of classical melodic patterns, the somewhat old-fashioned "rounded binary," A A B A B A, this one drawn out even further by making the B strains 11 bars long rather than the more customary 8. Both strains of the theme are heard first on piano, thereafter on violin, but this modicum of internal dynamism is lost in the variations, where each strain has only a single form, repeated literally.

All of this studied formality, however, is scheduled to vaporize in the last variation. Here literal repetition ceases as each strain adds something new in texture and melody; the music dissolves in rapid ornamentation, it assumes a fantastic delicacy and inventiveness, exfoliating into a poignant sense of radiance, of a lost innocence recaptured, in the instruments' bright upper registers. The ensuing coda, long enough to stand in for a fifth variation, is quasi-improvisatory and expressively diverse, suggesting a subjective mobility to which the last variation has found the gateway. These transformations are what Tolstoy cannot hear, and what it is important for him not to hear. For to hear them without the distance supplied by a judicious formalism would be to hear like a Trukhachevski: and what one would hear, and what would draw one fatally, like a Siren song, is the pure indeterminacy both of the object and the subject of desire.

The calm of the second movement ought to be the reward for the storm of the first—what could be simpler and less objectionable than that aesthetic formula?—but this is a reward that Pozdnyshev, and perhaps not he alone, feels bound to refuse. That volatizing and transfiguration of ornament in the last variation, that un-harried pleasure in the field of the treble, the high voices of both instruments blissfully intertwining but without erotic friction; the erasure of surplus repetition and stilted-static texture in both the variation and the coda, their increasingly "free" forms full of dynamism without pressure—all this is too open to be borne, too unguarded, too careless of difference. It must be silenced in the very act of being heard. Tolstoy could hear, could let himself hear, only convention in this movement. He could be attracted by the Homeric masculinity of the first movement even as he felt it to impose the composer's all-powerful phallic will on him and thus even as he dreaded and abjected this imposition in the person of Trukhachevski. But what could be dreaded or abjected here?

The answer, perhaps Beethoven's own answer, was: everything—the whole second movement, and, for good measure, the whole sonata. For Beethoven, one part of Beethoven, must have felt as Tolstoy did and decided to hear only convention in his middle movement. That might explain why he followed it with a flashy, even a trashy, piece of virtuoso superficiality, a brilliant tarantella written originally for another piece, thoroughly effective, thoroughly superficial, thoroughly—shall we say?—cynical. By this means he can repress the uncertainties that the second movement retrospectively reveals in the Homeric ethos of the first. As he would later do in the "Appassionata" Sonata, he had written a two-part form, supplanting violence by bliss, that could not stand as such. Convention required a third movement, partly just in order to deny legitimacy to such a two-part design and its vision of transcendental pleasure. (Beethoven finally revoked the convention in his final piano sonata, Op. 111.) So Beethoven condemned his own deviancy by writing a swaggering miles gloriosus of a finale. He "corrected" his errant departure from the heroic standard by reinvoking that standard parodistically: in other words, the first time as tragedy, the second as farce.

The Pobble that has No Toes. Tolstoy's wife-murderer frets about doing the deed in his stocking feet. The omission of shoes renders him undignified, somehow unmanly: for this man, any absence can become a castration.

In this case the missing item is both a fetish, a nice firm extension of the body to replace the absent phallus, and a bit of body armor, a safeguard for a tender part; Pozdnyshev's wife has, after all, stepped on his toes. On the one hand, or rather foot, the man's shoe capitalizes on the value of a more popular fetish, the woman's shoe, while sidestepping the debasement that the woman's shoe imposes. On the other, the shoe identifies comfort and protection with the tread of the solid middle-class householder, the sort of man who does not parade (or sneak) around in his socks and who could hardly be missing the phallus in the first place.

No wonder, then, that Pozdnyshev cannot feel quite right about killing his wife without wearing his shoes. But on the reading just given, the shoe-logic, already cobbled together for two left feet, continues to trip over itself. In the first place, if Pozdnyshev could wear his shoes he would have no need to kill his wife. In the second place, the absence of his shoes means that he must kill her. In the third place, the murder, given this absence, will not be quite satisfactory. A murderer in his stocking feet is not really a murderer, even though his victim is really dead.

Hence Pozdnyshev, as always sharing the fate of Coleridge's Ancient Mariner and the glittering eyes that betoken it, is compelled to tell his story over again to strangers—presumably neither for the first time nor the last. As it happens, his murderous intention crystallized on a train journey, so the story of his crime must be narrated—over and over?—on a train journey. Each re-narration constitutes an attempt to get the murder right; but it always goes wrong. Sexual violence always "comes short" of its goal, reinscribes the castration it spectacularly denies, requires its own repetition at another time, in another place, on another woman's body.

Consider in this light what the second movement of Beethoven's "Kreutzer" Sonata may have to say about the first? Is the first theme of the latter fiercely insistent? The middle movement parodies this insistence in the pat insistence of its own A sections, heard four times each through variation 3. Does the first movement's first theme aggressively hammer out repeated notes? The middle movement parodies this aggression with punctilious repeated-note figures in variations 1 and 2. Is the first movement's minor mode riddled with turbulence? The minore variation 3 is almost languorous. The middle movement becomes transfigurative precisely when it reaches an expressive plane that has no parallel in the movement before. The virile stance of the first movement is thus revealed as rooted in a denial of vulnerability (obedience to the rule of the salon, a feminine and feminizing rule) as much as in the affirmation of Homeric fighting strength. In Tolstoyan terms, the first movement's heroism is revealed in retrospect to be less like that of Achilles than like that of Count Vronsky, Anna Karenina's tin-soldier lover. Such heroism is a false front that never stops looking good but that always somehow betrays itself at second glance.

Counterparts. But there is always a third glance. In Beethoven's sonata, the exaggerated masculinity of the first movement and the exaggerated femininity of the first several variations of the second movement melt away into something else, something mixed, not to be named this or that. Yet for this to happen the extremes must be fully unfolded, and not merely pro forma: they must be arresting, each in its kind, the first movement domineering in its relentless passion, the early variations (even the lyric minore) alienating in their frigid beauty. The point is not to deny the appeal of the extremes (which after all are what pass for normal) but to transform both it and them.

—*Obsequies*. Pozdnyshev feels a certain obligation to visit his wife's deathbed. "[I] immediately decided that I must go to her. Probably it is always done, when a husband has killed his wife, as I had—he must certainly go to her" (426). Expecting to personify manly dignity in a scene culled from popular melodrama, and once more remembering his stocking feet, he puts on bedroom slippers as the tokens of bourgeois normality and goes to her. But his wife spoils the scene. She reproaches him and denies him custody of the children and, worse than with her speech, undermines his position with her silence: "Of what was to me the most important matter, her guilt, her faithlessness, she seemed to consider it beneath her to speak" (427).

Worse, perhaps, she forgets to put on her makeup. "What struck me first and most of all," Pozdnyshev tells us, "was her swollen and bruised face, blue on part of the nose and under the eyes. This was the result of the blow with my elbow when she tried to hold me back. There was nothing beautiful about her, but something repulsive" (426–27). The point of sexual violence is to punish the victim for vacating the feminine position that ratifies (that masks the dissimulation of) the aggressor's masculine position and at the same time to return the victim to the place she has vacated. But the results of sexual violence unfit her to occupy that place: she becomes repulsive. The marks of violence (on the body, as here, or in behavior—the wince, the cringe, the will to placate) become alienating to the man who has inflicted them; they render the woman even more problematical than she was before. Such marks act as signs of their victim's deviation, reminders that she has slipped her place, that her place may be slipped at will, and that when she slips out of this place the man must slip into it. At the same time, the marks block the man's sexual desire by depriving it of its object; literally or figuratively, the violated woman defaces this desire instead of embodying it. The marks of sexual violence thus make further violence all but inevitable. This is so regardless of the guilt they may also induce in the man (they even induce guilt in Pozdnyshev). If Pozdnyshev had not killed his wife he would have battered her again. And again.

Just Married. Pozdnyshev, to put it mildly, is turned off by the sex on his honeymoon. He explains his loathing with a pair of loathsome analogies:

[It was like a time in Paris] when I went to take in the sights, and, noticing a bearded woman and a fishtailed dog on a sign-board, I entered the show. It turned out to be nothing but a man in a woman's low-necked dress, and a dog done up in walrus skin and swimming in a bathtub. . . .

It was something like what I felt when I learned to smoke—when I felt nauseated and the saliva gathered in my mouth and I swallowed it and pretended that it was very pleasant.

(410, translation slightly modified.)

Sex in marriage is something that, when you take it in, either takes you in, like a sideshow, or makes you want to get it out, like smoky spittle. Of course it's not supposed to be like that. What could be the problem?

In sex the man is familiarly supposed to "possess" the woman, a possession redoubled in the married man's proprietary right over his wife's body. (These metaphors have gone underground since the nineteenth century, but no one should underestimate their persistence, both covert and overt.) What Pozdnyshev discovers on his honeymoon is that sex is a failure at upholding the sense of possession and, more, that its pleasure consists in this failure. Sex continually subverts the sexual difference it is supposed to confirm. Like music, it makes a man feel what he keeps telling himself he doesn't really feel, meaning rather that he is not supposed to feel it. Pozdnyshev does not enter the show in spite of its freakish attractions, but because of them.

But why just these attractions?

The bearded lady and the cross-dressed man, one and the same, raise one and the same question: phallus, phallus, who's got the phallus? Desiring one's wife is like desiring the bearded lady: well, then, does one desire the lady or the beard, and, if the latter, does that mean one has no beard? Desiring the bearded lady is desiring the cross-dressed man: well, then, is femininity merely a screen for the phallus, and, if so, does that mean one lacks the phallus and desires only to "possess" (but how? and how in a woman?) the man who possesses it?

For those who subscribe to it, the sex mandated by such questions is a sideshow monstrosity. Its masculine position is like that of a dog cased in a walrus skin and a bathtub, the phallus lost or absorbed in the dark sheath and wetness of the feminine. For the man who insists that sex involve the phallus (as distinguished from his penis), it would be better to hold back the emissions of his body and merely pretend to enjoy himself: but this, or so he thinks, he cannot do: there is no holding back and therefore, or so he thinks, no distance, no space of theatricality, no pretense. Sex, including the pleasure of sex, is always to some degree disgusting for the man whose masculine position is supposed to be exclusively phallic. Such a man mistreats women because they make him want to puke up the femininity he has always had to swallow.

—"*Isolde sinks, as if transfigured . . .*" Pozdynshev gradually discovers that what he has heard in the first movement of the "Kreutzer" Sonata, as played by his wife and Trukachevski, is a lovedeath. The lovemaking that he sees through, or in, their playing becomes something terrible, something more than mere adultery, precisely insofar as its association with the music promotes it to a lovedeath, a synchrony of passions in which the performers' normal, social identities disappear, leaving them exhausted and transfigured. "I had never seen my wife as she was that evening[—t]hose shining eyes, that severe, significant expression while she played, and her melting languor and feeble, pathetic, and blissful smile after they had finished" (412).

But why a lovedeath? Why, for that matter, is the lovedeath the nineteenth century's favorite fictional moment? Perhaps it is because, in the lovedeath, the actors die so that the spectator might live. Their death absorbs, and turns to bliss, the guilt that the spectator feels for desiring what they do. The imaginary bodies of the actors are consumed by their bliss but leave the bliss behind, make it available to the spectator who is dying to have it and only now can have it without dying. Only the spectator can both experience and survive the lovedeath. Only the spectator can both "have" the pleasure like a woman (the imaginary experience) and "know" it like a man (the survival). The spectator is thus thrown out of position, thrown beyond positionality itself, and the throw feels indescribably good. In free fall, the spectator is identified neither with the punitive law that demands the death in love nor the obedient receptivity that welcomes love as death. There is no position from which to experience the lovedeath; in that sense it is not experienced at all: it just is. Hence Pozdnyshev's strange joy at the performance of the "Kreutzer" Sonata, the joy of being and having he knows not what—"That's how it is—not at all as I used to think and live, but that way" (411). Hence the enormous melodic sequence, an impassioned phrase rising in two crescendos through the whole gamut of semitones, by which Isolde's Transfiguration arches to the climatic peak from which it falls, lingeringly falls, and dies away. Hence the tears, sobs, vertigoes, catches and losses of breath that even today spectators bring to their lovedeaths.

Tuning up. The violinist Trukhachevski plays on the strings of Pozdynshev's wife, which is to say on her nervous system, the exquisite excitability of which had been for a century or more the nexus of music and hysteria. In her own playing the wife redoubles on the piano strings this fiddling on her nerves, the fibers of her being, the web of sexuality in which her husband is ensnared. (Compare T. S. Eliot: "A woman drew her long black hair our tight / And fiddled whisper music on those strings.") Pozdnyshev is perfectly right to see the performance of the "Kreutzer" Sonata as an act of adultery. This sonata is a sexual appliance. Its performance is a sexual act that sexualizes—or rather re-sexualizes—all the apparently less dangerous music in its vicinity. In its sensory fullness, emotional violence and intricate, passionate intertwining of instrumental voices, the "Kreutzer" Sonata breaks the bounds of genteel piano performance proper to women. Once that happens, nothing is safe. Nothing can keep the simple little piece played later, the little extra piece that forces the fatal outcome, from revealing itself to be what all music seeks to become, a thinly veiled erotic abyss.

Music is the speech of the female body, and it must be fetishized, handed a prosthetic phallus, before men can tolerate it. Anything with a point will serve; Pozdnyshev finds that the handiest fetish is a knife. (Understandable, says the court: not guilty.) Later on his language, an oral performance replacing the manual one, replaces the knife. If only the wife had not been tempted to play this "Kreutzer" Sonata, or better yet, had not been able to play it! The nineteenth-century piano is given to Woman as a vehicle for the sublimation of her sexuality, which in turn is the vehicle by which her family is ritually unified. A good bourgeois wife is always also a musician—but a bad one.

The Soundtrack of the Sirens. Does that mean a good musician must be a bad wife? The myth of the sirens says so, but everybody knows how easy it is to defeat a siren: you just stuff your ears. (Pozdnyshev must have known that, too, yet he refused to let his wife cancel her performance. Foolish man, he wanted to hear that legendary song.) But nothing, of course, is quite that simple. Count on Franz Kafka, a man much bothered by sirens, to grasp the fact. In his parable "The Silence of the Sirens," Kafka explains that the sirens are most dangerous not when they sing, but when they don't. They did not, for example, sing for Ulysses; he just thought they did. Kafka's Ulysses, unlike Homer's Odysseus, stuffs his own ears with wax, not those of his crew; he triumphs in the false belief that he has been deaf to a song that was never sung. (Probably he knew, says Kafka, that the sirens' song could easily penetrate the wax; he was simply so charmed by his own cleverness that he forgot it.) The triumph of this Ulysses is merely a fantasy. The trouble is, merely this fantasy is a triumph. The sirens themselves are seduced by it; they want to "hold as long as they [can] the radiance that fell from Ulysses' great eyes" (431). You can defeat a siren by being narcissistic. Just assume, on no ground whatever, that she must want to sing to you—you above all.

—*Cyanosis*. When Pozdnyshev feels repelled by the unattractiveness of his wife on her deathbed, what else is he feeling? Surprise, for one thing: dead and dying women were notoriously seductive for nineteenth-century men. The bodies of such women, imaginary ones anyway, were felt to combine the pliancy of flesh with the perfection of sculpture, making the death of women at once a form of art and a form of sex.

The source of this necro-voyeurism is less the desire for complete feminine passivity than it is the wish to be absolved of responsibility toward women as human beings. "It is not I," says the necro-voyeur, "who petrifies this woman into a mere object of visual pleasure; it is Death."

With Pozdnyshev the formula is reversed. "I, Death," he says, "enflesh this object of visual pleasure into a mere woman." Pozdnyshev at one level kills his wife in order to be repelled rather than aroused by her. Repulsion secures the masculine position that desire has always subverted. Repelled, Pozdnyshev can be feminized by neither the desire he feels in himself nor the desire he projects into other men and feels as jealousy. What he sees at the deathbed is thus "first and most of all" the disfiguration that marks his imperviousness to desire. In an earlier spate of rage, he has hurled a paperweight at his wife and dashed an inkwell to the floor; now it is as if her face were a paper blotched by ink, a parody of a legal document attesting to his mastery: "What struck me first and most of all was her bruised and swollen face, blue on part of the nose and under the eyes."

Only by her coffin, three days later, does Pozdnyshev feel remorse at the sight of his wife's face, now no longer described as marked by his hand. Where the bruise on a dying face was the sign of his mastery, the lividity on a dead one is the sign of his guilt; repetrified, it petrifies. Yet even here the effect is not debasing but exalting: Pozdnyshev undergoes a "spiritual conversion" and becomes the archetypal masculine figure we have seen him to be, the Wandering Jew-Flying Dutchman-Ancient Mariner with hypnotically glittering eyes who goes about the world seeking forgiveness by telling his story, and who, failing to find what he seeks—because no amount of forgiveness could ever satisfy him—greedily sucks in perpetual clouds of cigarette smoke as a substitute.

"*It glides quickly in through my ears . . .*" What more must Tolstoy be hearing in the Presto of Beethoven's "Kreutzer" Sonata? Beyond all the passion and impetuosity on the surface, might it be the visceral effect of instrumental writing that summons up and magnifies the raw physicality of making music, above all in an urgent mutual rhythm that punctuates the score with accentual thrusts, the full weight of the players' bodies repeatedly borne down on the bodies of their instruments in unison or alternation? This would involve a degree of intimate, deeply attentive interplay that exceeds anything a Pozdnyshev, or perhaps a Tolstoy, could ever share with his wife. It does not matter that this Presto sounds nothing at all like conventional "love music"; there is a palpable erotic script in its duo writing.

In Beethoven's day, with the performers presumptively male, it is a homoerotic script, something like a celebration of passionate friendship that at its height becomes indistinguishable from passion itself. The Presto searches for the outer boundaries of masculine partnership and leaves the players or listeners to say whether those boundaries have been crossed. By Tolstoy's day, with the piano anchoring the bourgeois drawing room, the erotic script is that of heterosexual seduction. The family piano, installed as a site where women give pleasure by acting out the constraints on their sexuality, constantly threatens to become the site where women take so much pleasure that their sexuality erupts. (The danger is especially great between teacher and student, professional and amateur; see Leppert for the full story.) Pozdnyshev even sees the piano as a sexual appliance, which Trukhachevski does little more than, so to speak, turn on:

> The door to the dancing room is shut but I hear the sound of a rhythmic arpeggio and his and her voices. . . . I quickly opened the door. He was sitting at the piano playing those arpeggios with his large white upturned fingers. She was standing in the curve of the piano, bending over some open music. . . . She did not start or move but only blushed. (405)

It is as if the bending body of the woman harmonized with, blended itself into, the curve of the piano and the rhythm of the arpeggios. The sexual machine is the female body itself.

What Tolstoy hears in the Presto of the "Kreutzer" Sonata is the terrifying converse of this disclosure, the uncanny animation of the piano as a female body, fully human in its endless vibration and expressive force. The instrument sounds as through a gap in a piece of clothing that we agree not to notice as we keep surreptitiously gazing over or through it. ("How can that first Presto be played in a drawing-room among ladies in low-necked dresses?") The body of the music is the body he wants, not to "possess," but to inhabit. He wants it to be his body, oblivious of the fact that it already is, or would be if only he would let it. When the music carries him away, takes him beyond himself, he is enabled to yield to this truth without speaking it, to enjoy it without knowing it. That's why listening makes him so extraordinarily happy, and why, on later reflection, it disgusts him so much: exactly the same process that he goes through with sex. "Music," says Pozdnyshev (we have heard it before) "carries me immediately and directly into the mental condition [of the man] who composed it. My soul merges with his and together with him I pass from one condition to another" (411). In the immediacy of listening, music is blissful submission, erotic merging with a superior soul; afterwards, on reflection, it is debasement. Pozdnyshev describes this debasement as a forgetting of his "true position," and so it is, but not in the sense he means. The forgetting coincides with, and covers up, the acting-out of the truth of his true position. The truth is that what he thinks of as the masculine position differs from what he calls the feminine only in being hysterical about its own femininity.

Tolstoy, hearing through Pozdnyshev, thus incidentally discovers one of the main purposes of listening to music with nothing else in mind, one of the distinctive aesthetic practices of modernity. The otherwise oblivious listener wants to obey the music, even to be loved by the music for obeying it, but does not want to want this. Listening works, accordingly, by turning something voluntary, a desire to obey, into something involuntary, a commotion of feeling and sensation that the music is felt to impose. The listener cannot be responsible for what cannot be helped.

Gimme Shelter. One thing that Tolstoy does *not* hear in the Presto of the "Kreutzer" is the movement's lyrical second theme. Earlier I treated this theme as a mere parenthesis in a sea of virility. Now it is time to listen again, recognizing that a parenthesis, too, can make a difference. It may even expand, if only as a nimbus, to envelop the whole that contains it.

The contrast between the Presto's first and second themes conforms closely to the classic format for movements of its sonata-allegro type as described, or prescribed, by the nineteenth-century German musicologist A. B. Marx:

> The first theme is the one determined at the outset, that is, with a primary freshness and energy—consequently that which is energetically, emphatically, absolutely shaped . . . the dominating and determining feature. On the other hand, the second theme . . . is the [idea] created afterward, serving as a contrast, dependent on and determined by the former—consequently, and according to its nature necessarily, the milder [idea], one more supple than emphatically shaped, as if it were feminine to that preceding masculine. In just this sense each of the two themes is different, and only with one another [do they constitute something] higher, more perfect. (Die Lehre, 221).

Marx's emphasis is not on masculine dominance, but on the complementarity of the genders, musical and otherwise, each of which is imperfect until the two join to form a balanced whole. But complementarity of this sort has historically served as a deceptive, often self-deceptive, ideal, the good face put on a hierarchical order. The point has been theorized for music by Susan McClary, who in effect identifies the feminine in music as expressive dissonance, as that which demands resolution. In sonata forms like this one, the complementary themes are harmonically unequal. The first sounds in the music's primary key; the second is introduced in a secondary key and later resolved to the primary one, its feminine waywardness ultimately subdued to masculine order.

In the "Kreutzer" Presto, the second theme observes this policy in relation to the movement as a whole, but at the same time it fosters a countervailing mutuality within itself. "Feminine" in relation to the first theme, the second theme is itself subdivided into masculine and feminine segments. The masculine, which sounds first, is in the major and presents a chorale texture in the piano with the "voices" in tenor-bass registers. The feminine follows in the minor with the voices of its parallel chorale texture in the alto-soprano registers. The masculine segment is longer, the feminine more expressive.

This internal disposition of the second theme both puts into question the hierarchical order of the movement as a whole—the "feminine" term of which turns out to be two-thirds masculine in itself—and also creates a musical image of nonhierarchical reciprocity. This is best heard at the moment of overall long-term resolution, when the second theme returns in the primary key. At this point the gendered voicing of the piano's chorales intensify, the first segment's voices sounding deeper than before, the second segment's higher. The result is a resonant space of mutuality in which the formative processes of the entire movement momentarily crystallize.

This mutuality ripples throughout the entire movement. On its original appearance, the "feminine" segment of the second theme appears in the dominant minor after the "masculine" segment has introduced the dominant; the feminine segment thus presents itself as the single most unstable element in the movement's thematic makeup. This instability is mirrored in the segment's own half tranquil, half rueful expressivity. On its recapitulation, however, the feminine segment sounds in the tonic minor after the masculine segment has returned in the tonic major. As it happens, though, the movement as a whole is "in" the tonic minor, not the major; structurally, the feminine segment thus forms the single most stable element in the movement's thematic makeup. In thus reversing its former identity, the segment also re-enacts and consolidates the relationship between the slow introduction of the movement, which is in the major, and the minor-mode movement proper. (This major-to-minor direction is distinctly unusual in music of the classical period.) Thus the masculinity of the movement overall arises only within a feminine frame that sets the boundaries of stability and instability.

At the same time, however, the music's masculine energy carries it outside this frame into outlying harmonic regions as the movement takes its course. And in the recapitulation of the second theme, the masculine segment has greater melodic stability than the feminine because in the masculine the melodic line of the chorale is shared by the violin and piano for the first and only time. In the special interlude created by the second theme, then, masculine and feminine energies are genuinely interdependent. Neither is complete without the other and neither can claim priority over the other, be it structural, expressive, or ideological. The second theme may form only a subordinate episode from one standpoint; from another it is an episode of magic.

"Impassioned to the point of obscenity..." Why does Tolstoy need the trashy little piece, by who knows what composer, that is the real agent of seduction in "The Kreutzer Sonata"? Probably because he needs to be able to despise the music that has wrought such havoc, and therefore needs something feminine. The "Kreutzer" Sonata itself is too overbearingly virile; even its "trite" second movement is too potent. No one feminizes Beethoven. (No one except Beethoven: but by tacit consensus this has gone unheard.) An overwrought salon piece for violin and piano is the perfect object of contempt. Although for many years it was considered indecent for women to play the instrument, the violin in the nineteenth century, in a certain strain of throbbing lyricism, often represented feminine gracefulness, sentiment, or sensibility. Famous and once-famous examples include the "Scheherazade" theme from Rimsky-Korsakov's tone poem, the "Meditation" from Massenet's opera *Thais*, and Ernst's "Elegy" ("On the loss of a dear object"), which is also on the program at Pozdnyshev's salon.

Even more to the point here, the violin in this vein could also suggest feminine desire, especially in figurative association with the female voice. In some cases such violin-voices were romantically coupled with masculine counterparts on cello: in the Romance movement of Schumann's Fourth Symphony (oboe and cellos in the outer sections, solo violin in the middle section, the whole suggesting a portrait of the marriage of Robert and Clara Schumann in a work originally called the "Clara" Symphony); the Romance "Vois sous l'archet fremissant" [See beneath the quivering bow] from Offenbach's opera *Tales of Hoffmann* (solo cello and solo violin in lyric alternation, the voice that of a soprano in a trousers role); and the Nocturne of Borodin's Second String Quartet (solo cello and violin interchanging a melting melody at the emotional heart of a work dedicated to the composer's wife and written to commemorate the idyllic period of their first meeting). The feminine desire of the violin-voice is certainly at stake when Tolstoy's trashy piece is played by the effeminate Trukhachevski on behalf of Pozdnyshev's all too feminine wife. "I remember," says the husband, "her weak, piteous, and beatific smile as she wiped the perspiration from her flushed face when I came up to the piano" afterward (414).

The significance of these violin-voices appears, as if at a single bow-stroke, in "Councillor Krespel; or The Cremona Violin," the story by E. T. A. Hoffmann that became the basis for the "Antonia" act in *Tales of Hoffmann*. Hoffmann's Antonia explicitly identifies her singing voice with the sound of a unique violin played by her father. The identification is a symbolic means of constraining her sexuality within the quasi-incestuous field of the father-daughter bond; when the father, in a dream or vision, sees and hears Antonia singing, what he observes is a lovedeath in which the intertwining of the violin-voice and piano assumes a patently sexual character:

> He heard Antonia's voice singing softly and delicately until it grew into a shattering fortissimo . . . . . He saw B. and Antonia embracing and gazing at each other rapturously. The notes of the song continued and the accompaniment of the piano continued, although Antonia was not visibly singing nor B. playing. (146)

The outcome of this passion is Antonia's actual death, narratively from the consumption-like disease that gives her voice its magic, but symbolically from the excess of her sexual pleasure, or perhaps of his. In the father's fantasy, the climactic strain of the violin-voice is the daughter's orgasmic cry, which is a cry of separation from him that she is not permitted to survive. (She is not permitted to survive it even if, in fantasy, the lover is a cloak for the father himself.) The version by Offenbach and his librettist Jules Barbier adds a necromantic meta-father, the evil Dr. Miracle, who denies Antonia to her actual father just as the father would deny her to her suitor. The result is a haunting image of the infinite regress of masculine authority. In the opera, Miracle orchestrates Antonia's fatal vocal ecstasy by visibly playing on a solo violin that we do not hear except insofar as it "sounds" imaginarily in Antonia's voice.

Hoffman's and Offenbach-Barbier's scenes form the extreme horizon of Tolstoy's. Unlike Antonia, Pozdnyshev's wife (by this time it should be obvious that we never learn her name) survives her violinistic orgasm very nicely. Indeed, she thrives on it, it would never even occur to her to die of an orgasm, vocal or otherwise, which is one reason why her husband has to kill her.

Tolstoy's scene, in turn, forms a horizon for the lyrical effusions by solo violin I mentioned above, many of which are still popular, and more as well, from Beethoven's two Romances for violin and orchestra to the from-the-heart passages of Richard Rodney Bennett's symphonic arrangement of Jerome Kern's "Smoke Gets in Your Eyes." The quality of these pieces is unmistakable, a strange fusion of the bourgeois ideal of emotionally saturated femininity with a sexual overflow that the ideal seeks constantly to reabsorb. One might even suggest that the officially great solo violin concertos of the core repertoire, running from Beethoven to, say, Sibelius, are mainly concerned with assimilating the feminine vocality and sensitivity of the expressive solo violin to a masculine ideal. By integrating fervent lyricism and soloistic display into a large-scale sonata-based structure, the concertos create a fantasy space in which the risk of castration does not exist. The voice of the era's violin concerto is that of a man of sensibility who is nonetheless truly manly. As McClary says, the formal ideals of this musical tradition regularly depend on, and articulate, mastery over feminine expressivity.

Too much mastery, though, is as bad as too little. As Beethoven, for one, found out, it can lead the ear astray as well as a siren. Tolstoy probably did not know it, but Beethoven's "Kreutzer" Sonata has its own sort of connection to the sentimental passion of the fatal little piece, although the sonata does not contain anything of the sort itself. Recall that the finale was taken over from another work. The first two movements of this earlier piece, the Sonata in A (Op. 30, no. 1), are sweetly lyrical, especially the second movement, Adagio molto espressivo, the melodies of which seek precisely the hyper-feminine lyricism that crosses into the zone of the female voice. This is true above all of the main theme, which, however, is a little nervous about its own emotional luxuriance; the theme is punctuated by curiously square and formal cadences, as if continually to give feminine fantasy an antidote of masculine self-control. The original finale, which we hear now in the "Kreutzer," is aggressive, percussive, and propulsive; its effect on the Sixth Sonata would be to disown the feminine fantasy with shocking roughness. Beethoven accordingly replaced it with a lyrical, rather subdued set of variations that, depending on how we are disposed to hear it, lets the fantasy stand or gives it a gentle corrective dose of formality and constraint.

The joke is that, transferred to the "Kreutzer," the original finale of the Sixth Sonata lacks enough weight to integrate the very large, highly contrastive movements that precede it. Its manliness sounds like bravado. This revelation of masculinity as lack sets up an impulse toward femininity as surplus, or so we might conclude from Tolstoy. After the "Kreutzer," one simply has to hear a little piece impassioned to the point of obscenity in order to release the eroticism that the great piece leaves pent up.

Postscript quasi Postlude. A too-impassioned sequel: it would not be unfair to apply that description to "The Kreutzer Sonata" itself. And the sequel has a sequel—impassioned, one might say, to the point of obscenity.

In 1923, Leos Janacek wrote a string quartet later published as no. 1 and entitled "After Tolstoy's Kreutzer Sonata." The third of four movements begins with a canon between violin and cello, another instance of the love-duet trope noted earlier, this one lyrical but edgy, as if voiced between Pozdnyshev's wife and her imaginary lover. The first part of this canon invokes Beethoven's "Kreutzer" Sonata as well as Tolstoy's. It is modeled on the ambiguously gendered second theme of the opening Presto, but it lacks (is meant to lack) the transformative power of its model and it meets with a harsher fate. On each of its several statements, the canon meets with a brutal interruption. Eventually the melody loses its canonic partner, becoming the voice of solitary desire, and the rhythm of melody and interruption becomes the essential business of the movement.

According to Janacek, the quartet as a whole depicts "an unfortunate woman, suffering, beaten, ill-used, just as Tolstoy describes in his 'Kreutzer Sonata.'" Yet this compassionate, quite un-Tolstoyan portrayal may also harbor an all too Tolstoyan ambivalence about feminine desire and anti-feminine violence. The quartet was avowedly written out of Janacek's hopeless love for Kamila Stosslova, a married woman thirty-eight years his junior. The erotic lyricism and brutal interruptions of the "Beethoven" canon openly represent the composer's own desire and frustration over an infidelity that (most likely like that of Pozdnyshev's wife) took place only in music.

References

For more on Kafka and the Sirens, see my "'Longindyingcall': Of Music, Modernity, and the Sirens,' reprinted in this volume from *Music and the Sirens*, ed. Linda Austern and Inna Naroditskaya (Bloomington, Indiana: Indiana University Press, 2006), 194–215. For an account of Tolstoy's other "intermedial" treatment of a Beethoven work, the "Moonlight" Sonata, in the story "Family Happiness," see my *Musical Meaning: Toward a Critical History* (Berkeley: University of California Press, 2001), 33–45.

Samuel Taylor Coleridge. *Poems*, ed. John Beer. London: Dent, 1974.
T. S. Eliot. *Collected Poems: 1909–1962*. New York: Harcourt, Brace, and World, 1963.
E. T. A. Hoffmann. *Tales*, ed. and trans, Leonard J. Kent and Elizabeth C. Knight. Chicago: University of Chicago Press, 1969.
E. M. Forster. "On Not Listening to Music." In Forster, *Two Cheers for Democracy*. New York: Harcourt Brace Jovanovich, 1951.
Franz Kafka. Complete *Stories*, ed. Nahum Glatzer. New York: Schocken, 1971.
Richard Leppert. *The Sight of Sound: Music, Representation, and the History of the Body*. Berkeley: University of California Press, 1993.
A. B. Marx. *Die Lehre von der musikalische Komposition*, 2nd. edn. Leipzig: 1845.
Susan McClary. *Feminine Endings: Music, Gender and Sexuality*. Minneapolis: University of Minnesota Press, 1991.
Charles Rosen. *The Classical Style: Haydn, Mozart, Beethoven*. New York: Viking, 1971.
Leo Tolstoy, "The Kreutzer Sonata," trans. Louise and Aylmer Maude, in *Great Short Works of Tolstoy*. New York: Harper and Row, 1967.

CHAPTER 10

Like Falling Leaves
The Erotics of Mourning in
Four *Drum-Taps* Settings

Walt Whitman regarded *Drum-Taps* (1865), his cycle of Civil War poems, as the fulcrum of his life's work, even declaring it superior to the first three editions of *Leaves of Grass* (1855, 1856, and 1860). "Although I had made a start before," he wrote, "[it was] only from the occurrence of the Secession War, and what it show'd me as by flashes of lightning, with the emotional depths it sounded and arous'd . . . [that] the final reasons-for-being of an autochthonic and passionate song definitely came forth."[1] The book was successful with mainstream nineteenth-century reviewers as *Leaves of Grass* had not been, but twentieth-century literary critics, intent on celebrating what the nineteenth-century mainstream had deplored and deploring what it had celebrated, proved relatively indifferent. The cornerstones of the twentieth-century Whitman canon would be "Song of Myself," "Out of the Cradle Endlessly Rocking," and "When Lilacs Last in the Dooryard Bloom'd," the latter more often regarded as heir to a line of English elegies including Milton's "Lycidas" and Shelley's "Adonais" than as a text of the American Civil War. In the last years of the century, the "Calamus" poems also came to the fore because of their open homoeroticism—a topic pertinent to *Drum-Taps* as well—but this welcome development was shaded by a certain irony, since the kind of homoeroticism celebrated in these poems was to a large extent a part, though a forgotten part, of the nineteenth-century mainstream.[2]

Whitman's musical reception followed a different course. The poet's primary musical persona has not been the inspired roughneck who gallivants through "Song of Myself" with a "barbaric yawp" but the modernist mystic who chants credos of oceanic union with the nation and the cosmos in the postbellum editions of *Leaves of Grass*. This version of Whitman rationalizes and renders programmatic his raw pleasure in human diversity, in material and bodily existence, and in all the minute particulars of American

152

experience—a pleasure rampant in the first three editions of the book but already subject to a certain discipline by the second. Whitman himself was well aware of the temporizing process, which he would ground in the revelation about his own purposes granted him by his war experience. The successive editions of *Leaves of Grass* (which include *Drum-Taps* after 1867) do not so much renege on the intuitions of the first one as buffer it, enveloping it in tissues of explanation. sublimation, and ideology. The resulting image of Whitman as sage, the substance of what David Reynolds calls the Whitman Myth, is the one inherited by most twentieth-century composers, who, in contrast to the literary critics of the age, sought more to perpetuate the myth than to circumvent it.[3]

This is the image promulgated in the century's first decade by Ralph Vaughan Williams's settings for voices and orchestra, the grave "Toward the Unknown Region" (1907) and the grandiose "A Sea Symphony" (1910). In its climactic passages, the symphony's finale explicitly gives Whitman's primary image of modern spiritual and material adventure, his dialogue with his own soul, a traditional mythographic form. Impassioned dialogues for solo baritone and soprano realize the trope of hierogamy, the mystic, divine, or cosmic marriage, in terms reminiscent of the duets in some of Bach's cantatas between Jesus and the soul. Frederick Delius's slightly earlier "Sea Drift" (1903), though drawing its text from "Out of the Cradle," realizes the same large prophetic stance in more sensuous, more frankly eroticized terms. The Whitman of these works is something like the formative spirit of the new century, paradoxically both forward-looking and steeped in archaic images of the soul's journey; as the London *Times* reviewer put it after the premiere of "A Sea Symphony," in language sounding oddly like D. H. Lawrence: "In both [poet and composer] there is the distaste for the old-fashioned forms, both are striving for the newer poetic life."[4] The same persona in its wartime guise, chastened but undaunted, is still discernible in Paul Hindemith's midcentury setting of the "Lilacs" Requiem (1946), as it is, to a lesser degree, in the ritualistic gravity that threads the poem itself.

The persona of *Drum-Taps,* a lover of union, a seeker of reconciliation, a mourner over a fragmented community symbolized traumatically by the fragmented bodies of its young men, has figured importantly in this tradition almost from its inception. Yet here, too, a certain irony shades the historical development. The majority of *Drum-Taps* settings have been expressions of antiwar sentiment; *Drum-Taps* itself is nothing of the sort. As John Adams observes in reference to his setting of a long excerpt from "The Wound-Dresser," Whitman's war poetry is

> remarkably honest in that it expresses not just the horror and degradation of war but also the thrill of battle and the almost manic exhilaration of one caught up in a righteous cause. Whitman hated war—this war of all wars—

but he was no pacifist. Like his idol, Lincoln, he never ceased to believe in
the Union's cause and the dreadful necessity of victory.[5]

Yet there is more at stake even than this. For Whitman, the fratricidal character of the Civil War demanded a special, personal, intimate reckoning with its dead. As his poems delineate them, these war dead belong to a sacrificial process that is, paradoxically, both a bringer of absolute loss and yet regenerative. To borrow a suggestive turn of phrase from Robert Pogue Harrison, the force of regeneration gives the absoluteness of the loss its absolution:

> *Over the carnage rose prophetic a voice,*
> *Be not dishearten'd, affection shall solve the problems of freedom yet,*
> *Those who love each other shall become invincible,*
> *They shall yet make Columbia victorious. . . .*
>
> *One from Massachusetts shall be a Missourian's comrade,*
> *From Maine and from hot Carolina, and another an Oregonese, shall be*
>   *friends triune,*
> *More precious to each other than all the riches of the earth.*
>   ("Over the Carnage," 1–4, 9–11)[6]

Grief for the fraternal dead becomes the medium of possibility for a renewal of fraternal love.

For the leading composers drawn to Whitman's Civil War writings, however, among them Vaughan Williams, Ned Rorem, and Adams, whose settings (together with one of my own) form the focal points of this essay, no absolution is possible. The mourner of the dead can do no more than bear them witness in the hope that such deaths as theirs may not be repeated in the future. This act of witness, however, depends on an intimacy between the living and the dead or dying that is, indeed, projected in Whitman's poems, derived in part from a culture of such intimacy endemic to the Civil War and in part from Whitman's own gift—plain enough in the lines just quoted from "Over the Carnage"—for intense, homoerotically inflected compassion. Whitman and the modernist composers who set him simply draw different conclusions from the premise of this intimacy. But even in Whitman the moment of intimacy tends toward a self-sufficiency in which the question of being "for" or "against" the war, any war, temporarily makes no sense. Although the moment of loving fraternal care does not "transcend" the carnage of war—what could?—it briefly transforms the space around the body for which the battle is over, the body wounded or dead, into a kind of transient haven.

In "Vigil Strange I Kept on the Field One Night," a soldier returns to the spot on the battlefield where his comrade has fallen. He sits by the body all night long, gazing intently at the dead man's face: "long, long I gazed, / Then

154

on the earth partially reclining sat by your side leaning my chin in my hands, / Passing sweet hours, immortal and mystic hours with you dearest comrade" (11–13). The survivor's love literally takes the form of witnessing, of testifying by his vigil that his comrade has been; this alone makes it possible to bury the dead, which the survivor does at dawn. The act of witness is (fictitiously) repeated by the poem, which also is a form of testimony; and this, too, is in a sense necessary, because it allows the strange pleasure, the "sweetness," of the "mystic hours" to find intelligible form in the chanting rhythms of the verse, through which the poem becomes a kind of secular liturgy for the vigil. So powerful is the bond thus expressed that it easily encompasses strangers, even enemies. The survivor and fallen soldier in "Strange Vigil" are father and son, at least figuratively. In "The Wound-Dresser," based on Whitman's experience as a nurse during the war, a mere glance is enough: "One turns to me his appealing eyes—poor boy! I never knew you, / Yet I think I could not refuse this moment to die for you, if that would save you" (37–38). There is no saving the boy, but the appeal in his eyes is returned, and the double meaning of "appealing" strangely vindicated. Finally, in "Reconciliation," the speaker extends the moment of fraternal care to the body of a Confederate soldier, whose coffin he approaches with slow-motion tenderness: "I look where he lies white-faced and still in the coffin—I draw near, / Bend down and touch lightly with my lips the white face in the coffin" (5–6). Again the gaze engages; again the reiterative rhythm implies both ritual and sweetness.

What all this means musically is a tendency that cuts across the boundaries of style, generation, intention, and influence: a tendency to convey the epiphanic moment of fraternal intimacy by adding or singling out a unique expressive thread amid the musical texture. This "thread" may be vocal or instrumental, drawn from within or added from without; its defining trait is its singularity, a literal or figurative uniqueness that allows it to bear witness to the unique pain or death it compassionates or mourns. My guess is that this tendency implies a recognition, however tacit, of the culture of fraternal intimacy fostered by the Civil War, and that this recognition is in turn based on the persistence of a trope for fallen soldiers with a lineage that goes back to classical Greece. Before I turn to the music, both the culture and the trope require some comment.

America in the nineteenth century was freer than it would be in the twentieth in giving physical and affectionate expression to close bonds between men. As David Reynolds has noted, however, before the Civil War these expressions were both tendered in private and privately recorded in diaries and letters. The war made them public. In venues ranging from press dispatches to popular poetry to political oratory, the wounds or deaths of soldiers assumed sacrificial, redemptive value in imaginary scenes of comradely intimacy.[7] But sometimes the scenes were real, acted out in the hospitals and on the battlefields; the press simply helped conventionalize a widely improvised social script. If the script seems "sentimental" by later standards ("youths . . . pure as the mothers who bore them, and beautiful as their sisters in their homes") that may be because the carnage it had to contend with was unprecedented. Reynolds suggests that the shift to public intimacy involved a displacement of family bonds: "It was normal for a soldier to assume the role of parent, sibling, or spouse for a dying comrade. Since actual family members were rarely present to witness a soldier's death, fellow soldiers or other kindly disposed people filled familial roles, even to the point of expressing deep affection" (428). Another possibility is that by enveloping the soldiers' suffering and death in tender care and "feminine" delicacy, it was possible to assimilate both the physical brutality and fratricidal trauma of the war to the nineteenth-century ideal of the good death—pious, sententious, moving, and exemplary (terms invoked here with no pejorative cast). For reasons like these, Whitman found that the war vindicated his own belief in the sanctity of same-sex love, though he was painfully aware of the cost.[8]

The trope of mortal intimacy involves the paradox that soldiers who die in battle die, so to speak, in two registers: they are one of many, a nameless multitude of bodies on the field, and they are one only, unique beings who have borne a name. Robert Pogue Harrison traces the history of this idea from *The Iliad* ("As is the generation of leaves, so is that of humanity" [6.146]; the one lost in the many) to the Vietnam Veterans Memorial Wall, where "it is the individual who shines in and through the generic multitude of names" (each of the many is one).[9] Whitman's realizations of this trope conjoin the one and the many in terms that Harrison traces to a passage (transmitted from Homer through Virgil) in Dante's *Inferno:* the dead wait to be ferried across the river Acheron "As, in the autumn, leaves detach themselves, / First one and then the other" (3.112–13). Harrison calls attention to Dante's individuation of the falling leaves (182), but this is an individuation of a special kind: each of the many leaves (souls) is one, but none is singular enough to bear a name. In *Drum-Taps* likewise, the fallen soldiers with whom Whitman bonds are all singled out of the many, but none bears a name: each one, in that sense, is any or every one.

"As Toilsome I Wander'd Virginia's Woods" gives this version of the trope in its full traditional form:

> *As toilsome I wander'd Virginia's woods,*
> *To the music of the rustling leaves kick'd by my feet,*
> *I mark'd at the foot of a tree the grave of a soldier;*
> *Mortally wounded he and buried on the retreat, (easily all I could*
> * understand,)*
> *The halt of a mid-day hour when up! no time to lose—yet this sign left,*
> *On a tablet scrawl'd and nail'd on the tree by the grave:*
> Bold, cautious, true, and my loving comrade. (1–6)

156

The intimate bond is double here, performed by the survivor who made the inscription and repeated by his poet-successor who immediately forms an instinctive grasp of the whole situation. The poet comes on the grave amid the symbolic array of fallen leaves, to find among this many the one "leaf" nailed back to a tree, as if restored to its place of crucifixial honor. What he finds is a token of comradely intimacy that, he goes on to say, keeps coming back to him in later years as an involuntary memory. But what he does not find is the identity of the lost comrade; he finds, indeed, the positive form of that identity's loss.

This is the form of the trope that I think I hear in the settings by Vaughan Williams, Rorem, and Adams, and that I think I wrote—without conscious design—in my own settings. I turn to those settings now.

Ralph Vaughan Williams's cantata *Dona Nobis Pacem* was composed in 1936 as an explicit plea to the European powers to avert the war then looming. According to Ursula Vaughan Williams, the music was a response to the "dark picture" formed as Mussolini and especially Hitler declared their intentions, including the first signs of what would become the Holocaust: "The Nazis were dividing the world between Aryans and Jews in hysterical discrimination against some of their greatest citizens. . . . People in every walk of life were suddenly dispossessed."[10] The cantata embeds a miniature Whitman cycle on poems from *Drum-Taps* within a larger whole based on liturgical and prophetic texts. This cantata within a cantata consists of two large-scale movements, "Beat, Beat Drums" and "Dirge for Two Veterans," surrounding a gently elegiac and much briefer centerpiece, "Reconciliation." The first number emits a feverish war cry, a blindly enthusiastic *Carthago delenda est;* the third enacts a public ceremony recognizing the tragic folly of that cry. Both of them can be said to outdo their texts in extremity—and the texts are extreme enough. Only the central song bears some trace of the hope that peace, however unlikely, is possible.

The hope takes root in the mortal intimacy between the poem's speaker and his dead enemy:

> *Word over all, beautiful as the sky,*
> *Beautiful that war and all its deeds of carnage must in time be utterly lost,*
> *That the hands of the sisters Death and Night incessantly softly wash*
>   *again, and ever again, this soil'd world;*
> *For my enemy is dead, a man divine as myself is dead,*
> *I look where he lies white-faced and still in the coffin—I draw near,*
> *Bend down and lightly touch with my lips the white face in the coffin.*
>   ("Reconciliation," complete)

The text of "Reconciliation" turns on a version of the commemorative paradox of the one and the many. The speaker sees the other man's death as a violation of the divine principle incarnate in each of them and on that basis finds

Like Falling Leaves 157

beautiful the oblivion that must eventually overtake them both. The deed of carnage can be cleansed only by being lost without a trace. Yet this embrace of oblivion immediately prompts a memorial act, and one that is perpetuated for future remembrance by the poem. Though transitory in itself, the look that bears witness to the loss of the other becomes fixed in the image of the white face with which the poem ends. The light touch of the speaker's transient kiss becomes permanent and marmoreal as the word—not just the word "Reconciliation" but the word in general—indeed becomes that which is over all. The purely contingent encounter between a living and a dead man thus becomes an ideal encounter between all the living and all the dead.

The music seems to recognize this paradox but to reverse its emphasis. For Vaughan Williams, the speaker's intimacy with the dead man isolates the pair of them in a singularity corresponding to the fragility of the hope that their encounter upholds. This singularity crystallizes in the setting of the poem's second half, which is embedded as a unique event within a cycle of quasi-strophic repetitions.

The cyclical process begins with an orchestral introduction distinguished by a lyrical violin solo; the isolated instrumental "voice" helps individualize the intimacy of mortal encounter and prefigures the solo human voice soon to enunciate it. The introduction ends with a melodic phrase that will form the setting for "this soil'd world," the words that close the poem's first half and become something like the motto of the setting. A solo baritone then enters with the first strophe, singing a cantabile line extending from "Word over all" to "this soil'd world." This strophe is immediately reprised (with variations) by the chorus, with the women's voices leading the men's. The full significance of this texture will not emerge until later, but its immediate effect is to enhance the sense of isolation in what follows. The solo baritone now returns to sing the text of the mortal encounter, the poem's second half. He does so in parlando style, and in the virtual absence of orchestral melody. The texture is unlike anything else in the setting, which it as much interrupts as completes; it quietly challenges the comforting lyricism that surrounds it.

When the lyricism returns, it is subtly eroded, haunted by the baritone's absence—he does not sing again—and in need of supplementation. The introduction is the first thing to come back, this time with the solo violin in a less "speaking" role—another departing voice. This is followed by a reprise of the first strophe in its choral version, now adorned with a melismatic halo of high-register women's voices. Given the text, the choral sonority may seem to realize something implicit in it earlier, a transference of the healing work of the hands of the sisters death and night into the female voices of the chorus. But the work breaks down before it can be completed. Just before the expected "this soil'd world," the chorus breaks off, to be supplemented by a solo soprano singing "dona nobis pacem" to a cadential phrase. The chorus follows with the deferred "this soil'd world," expanding on the melodic

158

motto, but then breaks down again. The soprano returns twice more with "dona nobis pacem," the second time ending on a stark, unaccompanied dissonance. Reconciliation remains unachieved as snare drums and tympani intervene with a march figure that leads directly into the ensuing "Dirge."

A word remains to be said about the replacement of the baritone's voice by the soprano's, which is a multivalent gesture. It simultaneously suggests that some external, perhaps sacramental force is required to plead effectively for peace; doubly enhances the once-only solitude of the baritone and his terrible intimacy with a silenced enemy and comrade; subtly diminishes that intimacy by detracting from its intensity of same-sex feeling; and shifts the accent of "dona nobis pacem" from inner to outer peace by merging the liturgical phrase into the ancient trope of the woman who mourns a fallen warrior.

Ned Rorem's *War Scenes* (1971) sets five prose sketches selectively drawn from Whitman's Civil War diaries; the texts give a misleading impression of senseless slaughter unmitigated by the idea of sacrifice so important to Whitman and his contemporaries. Rorem's context, however, is not the Civil War but the war in Vietnam, another conflict of North and South in which the vital interests of America were supposed to be at stake—this time falsely, says the irony formed by conflating the two wars. The cycle expresses the feeling, widespread in the late 1960s and early 1970s, that Vietnam had travestied the idea of sacrifice; the young men sent to this war were butchered in a bad cause, and some had become butchers in their turn. The first song, "A Night Battle," begins with the horrified exclamation, "What scene is this?—is this indeed *humanity*—these butchers' shambles?" The fifth song ends with a vision of "the whole land, North and South," as "one vast hospital," leading to the admonishment: "Think how much, and of importance, will be, has already been, buried in the grave." There is no hint of idealization, let alone redemption, anywhere in the cycle. Yet there is one song, "Specimen Case," that does revert to Whitman's ethos of sacrifice and to its correlative, the sentimental-erotic trope of mortal intimacy. The song is too brief and comes too early—it's the second of the five—to counteract the dominant tone of grim and grisly reckoning. But for that very reason it testifies to the strength of the trope it bears, which is not so much rejected by the cycle as embedded in it in a solitary space apart. Though the sounds involved are very different, in "Specimen Case" Rorem draws close to Oliver Stone's Whitmanesque use of Samuel Barber's *Adagio for Strings* as the theme music for his Vietnam War movie *Platoon*. The movie shrouds its savage action in the sensuously melancholy music; the song shrouds its fallen soldier in an atmosphere of dignified tenderness. The three motives of mortal intimacy—the intimacy itself with its eroticized compassion, the act of bearing witness, and the evocation of singularity—are all present in concentrated form.

The text of "Specimen Case" seems chosen for those motives; except for the prose form, it could well be a lyric from *Drum-Taps:*

Like Falling Leaves 159

> Poor youth, so handsome, athletic, with profuse shining hair. One time as I sat looking at him while he lay asleep, he suddenly, without the least start, awaken'd, opened his eyes, gave me a long steady look, turning his face very slightly to gaze easier, one long, clear, silent look, a slight sigh, then turn'd back and went into his doze again. Little he knew, poor deathstricken boy, the heart of the stranger that hover'd near.[11]

Rorem mirrors the single action of the poem, the arrival and departure of the mutual look, with a long, slowly mounting crescendo that peaks just past the midpoint of the song and ebbs steadily away to the close, with a slight rising of voice at a late moment, as if the vocal persona were reluctant to let the moment go. The process is lucidly framed by cadential passages and, on that foundation, punctuated by two unique events that encapsulate the once-only moment of mortal intimacy between the wounded soldier and his nurse-comrade.

The more dramatic of these events is the *fortissimo* peak of the long crescendo, which initiates the setting of "one long, clear silent look." The moment is melodically as well as dynamically unique: "long" is set to the highest notes reached by the voice, which has been climbing slowly but steadily to this point from a low initial tessitura and will steadily descend thereafter in conjunction with the dynamics (with the same little "bump" near the close). The first high note is attacked via an octave leap, by far the widest vocal interval in the song. Thus singled out, the high note lingers, becomes long itself (the longest sung so far) before dissolving into a melisma, as if both to extend the moment of looking and to enact its dissolution, which inevitably comes too soon. The transparent literalness of the tone-painting adds to the tone of pathos, suggesting less the commemorative power than the futility of the symbolic gesture. The full phrase from "long" to "look," implacably descending by step against melismatic resistance, seconds this impression, musically acting out the loss of the look while verbally announcing its advent.

Less immediately striking, but in the end even more significant, is the setting of "awaken'd" about a third of the way through the song. The wounded man's awakening both makes possible the intimacy to follow and contains it in embryo; the sign of wakefulness and the means by which the caretaker's loving look becomes mutual are one and the same, the opening of the soldier's eyes. The voice intones "awaken'd" just as the dynamic level changes for the first time (from *p* to *mp*) and the piano first releases the soft pedal, which has been in use from the outset. "Awaken'd" also coincides with the song's only genuine cadence, or at least the closest thing to one on offer. Written with a key signature of B♭ minor, "Specimen Case" anchors its harmony in deep-bass oscillations between the tones of the tonic and dominant; these frame the piece, the central portion of which uses harmony more coloristically than structurally. (The way the harmony undulates between relatively stable boundaries perhaps suggests the fluid, ambiguous space of

160

romantic compassion.) Dominant harmony, however, never appears directly. Tonic chords, which arise throughout at critical junctures, are at best approached via dominant substitutes consisting of a dissonant collection over the dominant bass note. The final bass oscillation supplies a partial exception to this rule, telescoping a progression from a dominant-minor chord with added sixth to a tonic seventh. The only full exception occurs at "awaken'd," which moves from a pure dominant six-five—albeit a dominant-minor six-five—to a cadential tonic triad. The triad, moreover, in a kind of modal exchange with its dominant, is in the tonic *major,* imparting to the moment of awakening a sense of brightness and relief with no parallel anywhere in the song, a condition it shares with the tonic-major harmony.

This condition is the more poignant for being fleeting; a tonic-minor inflection supervenes the moment the word "awaken'd" has been uttered. Like the song itself in relation to the cycle, the cadence on "awaken'd" is premature, and too brief to offset the grave realities that envelop it. But like the song, it records a moment of witness anyway, investing the moment with a singularity meant to stand as a memorial sign like the frozen kiss of "Reconciliation" or the scrawled epitaph in "As Toilsome I Wander'd Virginia's Woods." It is no accident that the voice's cadential B♭ begins the rise in tessitura that ends with the climatic setting of "one long, clear silent look."

Unlike most of the *Drum-Taps* poems on the subject, "The Wound-Dresser" does not deal with one particular moment of mortal intimacy but with a proliferating series of them, each singled out by one or two vivid physical details that stick in the speaker's mind. The poem is framed as a recollection in old age; John Adams's 1989 setting of it for baritone and orchestra omits the prefatory verses, beginning in medias res amid the full immediacy of tending the wounded: "Bearing the bandages, water and sponge, / Straight and swift to my wounded I go." Only at the end does the setting reveal that what has seemed so fully present is actually a distant memory: "Thus in silence in dreams' projections, / Returning, resuming, I thread my way through the hospitals." The moment of recognition is doubly marked: in the text by a play on words, whereby the phrase "I sit by the restless all the dark night" refers to both the imaginary act of keeping vigil and its symbolic repetition in the speaker's dreams; and in the music by a grand pause, a commemorative moment of silence in which the reality of absence is concentrated.

Adams individualizes the moments quilted into the fabric of memory by breaking the text up into discrete segments and assigning each one its own distinctive orchestral texture, passing from one patch to another without transition. Or, to change the metaphor with Sarah Cahill, "the instrumental character changes ... almost like panels of a painted screen."[12] These scene changes, however, occur within a context of overall continuity, even homogeneity, of texture, something created by an emphasis on rich, deliberate string sonority (Barber's *Adagio for Strings* again hovers near as a model)

Like Falling Leaves

and a kind of continuo on synthesizer. Though fervent, the piece is restrained, indifferent to strong contrasts and grand climaxes; as Adams says of Whitman's poem, "it is . . . free of any kind of hyperbole or amplified emotion . . . a statement about human compassion of the kind that is acted out on a daily basis, quietly and unobtrusively and unselfishly and unfailingly." (On this reading, the statement—both poem and music—widens its scope beyond the war dead to include all the mortally ill, from Adams's own father, a victim of Alzheimer's disease, to the recent generations of those suffering from AIDS.) As the music, too, goes about its work unobtrusively, the character of that work unobtrusively clarifies itself. When the scenes described are acknowledged as memories, the memories, though involuntary, do not appear as traumatic flashbacks: on the contrary, they are strangely consoling, virtual presences to which the speaker gladly and continuously submits. The sequence of distinct patches or panels of memory thus gradually evolves into a single enveloping act of mortal intimacy that is both immediate and commemorative.

Like both Vaughan Williams and Rorem, however, Adams also seeks to separate out a singularity of moment or voice—in this case one of each—in which to embody the core paradox of mortal intimacy, the combination of anonymous universality and absolute particularity. As in *Dona Nobis Pacem,* the voice belongs to a solo instrument playing a lyrical monologue, but with a reversal of symbolic values. Vaughan Williams's violin prefigures the solo human voices, baritone and soprano, the moral or spiritual force of which is immanent and clear. When the baritone first sings "this soil'd world" he identifies the truth at which the violin could only hint. Adams's solo, which passes back and forth between violin and trumpet, is transcendental and mysterious, a "higher" voice of which the baritone solo is only an earthbound realization. This impression can be grounded in both the doubleness of the instrumental solo or solos and their relationship to the baritone line. The violin and trumpet (actually two trumpets, a full-sized and a piccolo instrument) draw on their traditional associations to project the complementary halves of the soldiers' identity, ideally conceived. The violin (which shows a strong affinity for its highest registers) suggests the sensitive, spiritual, "feminine" persona revealed in the young men's keen suffering and the caretaker's compassionate response. The trumpet suggests the warrior persona, but one made remote and elegiac by the disfiguring or fatal wounds that the men have borne away from the battlefield. The two instruments never play at the same time, suggesting the ideal character of the unity they each represent in part. Each takes its turn in a process that surrounds and pervades the voice with an independent melodic line more continuous and more expressively marked than the voice's own. Only at the end, after a second grand pause, does the voice so to speak inherit the full expressive capacity of the solo instruments. There, virtually the only moving thing in a soft and static expanse of sound, the voice gives

162

cantabile utterance to the poem's concluding fusion of eros and compassion: "(Many a soldier's loving arms about this neck have cross'd and rested, / Many a soldier's kiss dwells on these bearded lips)."

This final moment has its own kind of singularity, but the song's center of uniqueness lies elsewhere. With one exception, the segments of Adams's "Wound-Dresser" set Whitman's text without repetition or alteration.[13] The exception occurs at the midpoint of the song when the baritone apostrophizes death, pleading for it to come quickly to those who need it as a deliverance. Here the words "In mercy come quickly" are repeated with the phrases reversed, creating a rhetorical chiasmus: "In mercy come quickly, come quickly in mercy." The vocal line echoes this formation with unusual literalness. The settings of "come quickly" are almost identical; the second "in mercy" reaches for the first but cannot quite grasp it (the mercy slips away). Enclosed at the core of the song, therefore, lies an image of further enclosure, a still deeper core marking the most intimate, least guarded point of contact between the wound-dresser and his dearest charges, those he remembers best because he could help them least.

The texts to my "Three Poems of Walt Whitman" (1984)[14] all deal with music as a form of social energy; their order in the song cycle—"I Hear America Singing" "Dirge for Two Veterans," and "That Music Always Round Me"—is meant to suggest Whitman's preferred postbellum narrative of national unity, traumatic disruption, and the search for recovery, although the framing poems were actually written in the same antebellum year, 1860. "I Hear America Singing" is a utopian text in the spirit of the first edition of *Leaves of Grass*. It depicts a nation of artisans and manual workers united in unalienated labor; the custom of singing at work becomes both a literal sign of contented activity and a new version of the traditional metaphor of social harmony. "Dirge for Two Veterans" abrogates that metaphor as the Civil War has abrogated its world—or its fiction of one. The heavy, formulaic sounds of a military funeral replace spontaneous singing; the music, meant to ease trauma with ritual, instead becomes traumatic itself as it nears the speaker in a steady crescendo. "That Music Always Round Me" recovers the image of social harmony in a new form, but a subtly diminished one. The image is that of a mixed chorus and orchestra, but the ensemble is purely figurative; its music is "unceasing, unbeginning," an ideal sound rather than a real one, utterly remote from the homely realism of "I Hear America Singing." The poem was originally one of the "Calamus" group, suggesting that its musical ideal has an amatory basis; Whitman eventually moved it to the mystical later cluster, "Whispers of Heavenly Death," so my own anachronistic use of it can lean on his. Positioned as the last song, the poem suggests a consoling dream, the tentative beginning of recovery rather than its assured end.

The setting of "I Hear America Singing" (CD track 18) employs a "panel" technique much like Adams's in "The Wound-Dresser." The accompaniment shifts from texture to texture as the scene shifts from one group of workers to another; there also are three "panels" of tempo, each quicker than the last. The piano has spacious opening gestures and an increasingly rich part to suggest the feeling of a broad canvass; vocal climaxes on the open vowels of the poem's last line, "Singing with open mouths their strong melodious songs," seek to convey an utter lack of limitation or inhibition. (There is also a counterelegiac stress on the workers' uniqueness, conveyed by a climax and textual repetition on "none other"—changed, for the vowel, from Whitman's "none else"—in the line "Each singing what belongs to him or her and to none [other]." The effect is anticipated by a repetition of "each singing.") The music proceeds with a lyrical vigor that seems heedless, or wills to be heedless, of the catastrophe to come. By contrast, "That Music Always Round Me" (CD track 20) cannot escape the memory of catastrophe recorded in the preceding "Dirge," even though the music recalls it in no specific way. More homogeneous in texture than "I Hear America Singing," "That Music" seeks to combine rich piano sonorities with a liquid vocal line. It aims at a tranquility that persists even at the most excited moments. But the song carries its lyricism with obvious vulnerability, as if a single wrong note, a single thought, could silence it. The real silence, though, lies in the central song, which, like so many other *Drum-Taps* settings, turns on the trope of mortal intimacy.

My main "expressive intention" in setting "Dirge for Two Veterans" was to avoid imitating the sounds of trumpets and drums; Vaughan Williams's use of the actual instruments was a negative model. What I wanted to depict was not the funeral music, but the act of hearing it. This was to be a difficult act; the poetic speaker was to be so burdened with grief as almost to lose sight of the men being mourned. The external sounds, particularly the drum sounds, were to be persistent but muffled, only occasionally breaking through to a real hearing. I imagined the voice as striving to surpass and finally to silence these aftersounds of war, eventually passing beyond them to a fuller acknowledgment of the fallen soldiers.

That acknowledgment takes the form—it just seemed right it should—of an isolated intimate moment, a singularity that, as a trope, is not singular at all, but communal. As the song draws to a close, the voice and piano separate antiphonically, each making a series of stark, simple statements in the silence of the other. Freed from its bond to the piano, which here "speaks" for the world of history and ritual memory, the voice is free to speak with the dead. Four times, each longer than the last, it addresses them *pianissimo* in a field of silence. Its final statement ("My heart gives you love"), after a premonitory swell on "heart," closes—and closes the vocal line—with a long crescendo and decrescendo, *pp* to *ff* and back, on a single note intoning "love." After a short pause, the piano follows this anguished-ecstatic cry with a short coda, perhaps—though this is by no means certain—with the significance of its characteristic gestures altered by what the voice has gone through.

164

It seems appropriate to end this volume by discussing my own Whitman songs because they reflect the same long-standing fascination with Whitman, and affection for him, that prompted me to undertake the volume in the first place. What I hope to have suggested both as editor and contributor is that Whitman's role in the shaping of modern memory has a musical dimension that deserves serious attention. What America means—"America" being the ideal, ideological, Adamic name given to itself by the United States—has always been in part a question of what Whitman means, of what it means to have given Whitman the place he claimed as a canonical modern figure. To understand that fully, it's necessary to understand how modern musicians, both Americans and others, have heard Whitman hear America singing.

Notes

1. "A Backward Glance O'er Travel'd Roads" (postscript to the 1889 edition of *Leaves of Grass*), text from *Leaves of Grass,* Norton Critical Edition, ed. Sculley Bradley and Harold W. Blodgett (New York: Norton, 1973), pp. 567–68.

2. On the mainstream type of male homoeroticism in the nineteenth century, with specific reference to Whitman, see David S. Reynolds, *Walt Whitman's America: A Cultural Biography* (New York: Knopf, 1995), pp. 391–403.

3. Reynolds, *Walt Whitman's America,* pp. 451–63.

4. Quoted in Michael Kennedy, *The Works of Ralph Vaughan Williams* (London: Oxford University Press, 1964), pp. 98–99.

5. "Note by the Composer," prefatory to the score of *The Wound-Dresser* (New York: Hendon Music/Boosey and Hawkes, 1989).

6. This and all subsequent quotations of Whitman's poetry are from the Norton Critical Edition of *Leaves of Grass* (n. 1). For Harrison, see below, n. 9.

7. Reynolds, *Walt Whitman's America,* pp. 426–31.

8. This trope was confined neither to America nor to the Civil War, as the following passage from Émile Zola's novel of the Franco-Prussian War, *The Debacle* (trans. L. W. Tancock [1892; Harmondworth: Penguin Classics, 1972]), illustrates: "Maurice let himself be carried away like a child. No woman's arms had ever held him as close and warm as this. In the collapse of everything, in this utter misery, with death staring him in the face, it was an ineffable comfort to feel another person loving him and looking after him.... Was this not the brotherhood of the earliest days of the world, friendship before there was any culture or class, the friendship of two men united and become as one in their common need? ... And so friendship became a kind of broadening out for both of them: they might not kiss, but they touched each other's very souls, the one was part of the other ... the two of them making a single being in pity and suffering" (pp. 136–37). From the perspective shown here, the boundary between comradeship, eroticism, and compassion becomes impossible to draw, perhaps even senseless to imagine. On the reservation implied by "they might not kiss," and its paradoxically liberating effect on same-sex love in the nineteenth

Like Falling Leaves

century, together with other reflections on music and sexuality with particular reference to Whitman, see my *After the Lovedeath: Sexual Violence and the Making of Culture* (Berkeley and Los Angeles: University of California Press, 1997).

9. Robert Pogue Harrison, "The Names of the Dead," *Critical Inquiry* 24 (1997), 176–90; quotation, 189.

10. Ursula Vaughan Williams, *R. V. W: A Biography of Ralph Vaughan Williams* (London: Oxford University Press, 1964), p. 209.

11. Text from "Some Specimen Cases," *Specimen Days,* in *The Works of Walt Whitman, Deathbed Edition in Two Volumes,* vol. II: *Collected Prose* (New York: Funk and Wagnalls, 1969), p. 32. Ironically, given the paradoxes of naming discussed in this essay, Rorem does not record the name of the soldier described in this passage: Thomas Haley.

12. Note to a recording of *The Wound-Dresser* (#9-79218-4) by the Orchestra of St. Luke's, conducted by the composer with Sanford Sylvan, baritone (New York: Elektra Nonesuch, 1989).

13. I am setting aside a single repetition of "life" in the phrase "life struggles hard," which occurs just before the truly exceptional segment, to which it acts as a prompt.

14. A score of this song cycle, though unpublished, can be found in the Music Research Collection of the New York Public Library, under the longer original title "'That Music Always Round Me': Three Poems by Walt Whitman."

CHAPTER 11

Chopin at the Funeral: Episodes in the History of Modern Death

Chopin's B♭-minor Funeral March first accompanied a real funeral procession on 30 October 1849, when Chopin himself was buried. Orchestrated for the occasion by Henri Reber, the march set the pace as Chopin's coffin was borne along the aisle of the Church of the Madeleine in Paris. The subsequent cortège maintained a solemn silence during its three-mile passage through the streets to the Père Lachaise cemetery. Almost a century and a quarter later, on 25 November 1963, the same music, now arranged for military band, helped usher the body of John F. Kennedy through the streets of Washington, D.C., to Arlington National Cemetery. My own memory of the occasion, if it can be trusted, includes the televised sight of a somber Charles de Gaulle following Kennedy's horse-drawn hearse to the time of Chopin's music.

The continuity between these two events testifies to the consistency with which this music has been received. Virtually since it was written in 1837, the Chopin Funeral March has been Western music's foremost expression of public mourning. Often taken as a threnody for Chopin's Poland, it has served in general to express collective grief for fallen heroes or other exemplary, larger-than-life figures. Chopin's early biographer Moritz Karasowski said that it expresses "the pain and grief of an entire nation," and figures as diverse as Franz Liszt, Duke Ellington, and Orson Welles all heard it in similar terms.[1] In a

---

A shorter version of this paper was presented at the symposium "Chopin 1849/1999—Aspekte der Rezeptions- und Interpretationsgeschichte," organized by Andreas Ballstaedt and Volker Kalisch at the Robert-Schumann Hochschule, Düsseldorf, 6–8 December, 1999.

1. Moritz [Maurycy] Karasowski, *Friedrich Chopin: Sein Leben, seine Werke, und seine Briefe* (Dresden: F. Ries Verlag, 1877), quoted in James Huneker, *Chopin: The Man and His Music* (1900; reprint, New York: Scribners, 1927), 298. Liszt's contribution is discussed briefly in the text of the present essay. Ellington quoted the Funeral March to conclude his *Black and Tan Fantasy* in 1927. In *Black and Tan*, a short film he made in 1929, the heroine martyrs herself for music, dancing herself to death so that the band (which backs her) can get its big break. On her deathbed, she asks to hear the *Black and Tan Fantasy*; the quotation from Chopin sounds just as she dies. (For more on Ellington and Chopin see Mark Tucker, *Ellington: The Early Years* [Urbana: University of Illinois Press, 1991], 242–48; and David Metzer, "Shadow Play: The Spiritual in Duke Ellington's 'Black and Tan Fantasy,'" *Black Music Research Journal* 17 [1997]:

parallel popular tradition, the march becomes an expression of mock solemnity. As a child in the 1950s I could hear it used that way in cartoons at the movies and even on the playground at school. Most Americans of a certain age will remember hearing it chanted to the phrase "Pray for the dead and the dead will pray for you," especially around Halloween. The travesty and solemnity merged unintentionally in the Soviet Union, where arrangements of the march were used so regularly to bury state officials—the model was Stalin—that radio broadcasts of the original music had to be banned, lest people think someone important had died.[2]

These traditions are wholly independent of the Piano Sonata in B♭ Minor, Op. 35, in which the Funeral March was incorporated in 1839. Within just a few weeks of Chopin's death, the march was published separately from the sonata; by the end of the century, it had become the object of hundreds of transcriptions.[3] In 1852, an extended interpretation by Liszt or his partner and ghostwriter Carolyne Wittgenstein brushed the sonata aside and dwelt on the sublime power of the march both to mourn and to assuage "great losses," as well as to voice "the full solemnity and heart-rending grief of a nation."[4] By 1900, James Huneker could state as a truism that "the march, when isolated, has a much more profound effect than in its normal sequence."[5] My aim in what follows is to treat that effect historically, which, it turns out, is also to fragment and multiply it: to trace the process by which the march assumes multiple meanings in relation to the social history of death. The results will suggest that the dominant tradition of reception is to some degree based on a lapse of cultural memory. This is not to say that the tradition is "wrong" in any crude sense; it could not have lasted so long if it were. But the social and symbolic practices by which the dead were disposed of and commemorated form a prime hermeneutic window that deserves to be opened. When the music is inserted into its first cultural context, the management of death in Chopin's Paris, the Funeral March pulls away from the two leading features of its traditional reception: its restriction to great men or lost generations, and its restriction to a purely civic conception of death.[6]

137–58.) Welles quoted the Funeral March in his 1941 film *Citizen Kane*, which begins with Kane's death. As lights in Times Square flash the news, the famous theme is briefly heard on the soundtrack. The quotation is ironic: since Kane is a failed hero, he receives only a fragment of the march.

2. Reported by Irena Poniatowska at "Chopin 1849/1999."

3. Regarding the hundreds of transcriptions, see Maciej Golab, "Chopinsche Transkriptionen aus dem 19. Jahrhundert. Versuch einer Systematik," presented at "Chopin 1849/1999"; Jozef M. Chominski and Teresa Dalila Turlo, *Katalog Dziel Fryderyka Chopina* (Krakow: Polskie Wydawn. Muzyczne, 1990), 384–88.

4. Franz Liszt, *Frédéric Chopin*, trans. Edward N. Waters (New York: The Free Press of Glencoe, 1963), 37–39.

5. Huneker, *Chopin*, 298–99.

6. The word *men* in the foregoing sentence is to be taken literally: the recipients of great funerals in the nineteenth century were virtually always male. The mortuary context, of course, is not the only one pertinent to Chopin's Funeral March; for a comprehensive account of the

Modern Death and the Crisis of Symbolization

The contextual story begins in the 1790s, a decade in France when even death became a victim of the Terror. Among the early outcomes of the Revolution was a removal of death from the province of the church and even from the realm of the human. Religious services were abolished, tombs were destroyed, and the dead were unceremoniously carted to mass graves, where their naked bodies were dumped with no family members in attendance.[7] All this was normal practice; it was not reserved for victims of political violence. Burial lost its status as a mourning ritual and became primarily a technique of waste disposal. The state concerned itself with persons only insofar as they were citizens; the dead, being citizens no longer, were no longer persons. As individuals, they could safely be erased from history. The only exceptions were state-anointed heroes, a small group that included Voltaire, Marat, and Mirabeau; these men received spectacular public funerals, as extreme in their ceremony as ordinary burial had become for lack of it.[8]

Aside from state policy, the sources of the general debasement of death included the recognition that French burial grounds had long since become a serious danger to public health. Overcrowded churchyards and shallow graves led to foul odors, polluted wells, and the threat of contagion.[9] In Paris during the Terror, the machinery of death on a large scale made the problem so bad that the city itself seemed to become a necropolis; the tumbrils on which the bodies of the guillotined were borne to festering mass graves drew trails of blood on the streets.[10] As a result, public policy both before and after 1789 sought to separate the living from the dead. Churchyards were closed to further burials, and cemeteries were established by decree on the outskirts of towns and cities. On winter nights in Paris between 1785 and 1792, the bones

---

movement's genesis and significance, see Jeffrey Kallberg, "Chopin's March, Chopin's Death," forthcoming in *19th-Century Music* 25 (2001).

7. Johannes Willms, *Paris, Capital of Europe: From the Revolution to the Belle Epoque*, trans. Eveline L. Kanes (New York: Holmes and Meier, 1997), 113.

8. Michel Ragon, *The Space of Death: A Study of Funerary Architecture, Decoration, and Urbanism*, trans. Alan Sheridan (Charlottesville: University Press of Virginia, 1983), 215–36.

9. Philippe Ariès, *The Hour of Our Death*, trans. Helen Weaver (New York: Alfred A. Knopf, 1981), 479–96.

10. Willms, *Paris, Capital of Europe*, 77–79. Something similar happened again during the cholera epidemic of the early 1830s, when Paris became a necropolis in which the symbolization of death often took the form of unintended travesty (see Willms, *Paris, Capital of Europe*, 208–12; and Karlheinz Stierle, *Der Mythos der Paris: Zeichen und Bewusstsein der Stadt* [Munich: Carl Hensler Verlag, 1993], 314–19). Heinrich Heine remarks on the transportation of coffins in taxis and the conversion of furniture vans to "buses of the dead" (*Totenomnibusse;* quoted in Stierle, *Der Mythos der Paris*, 317). The perception that "the world of the dead parodies the world of modern life" (Stierle, *Der Mythos der Paris*, 318) may also be connected to the Parisian dance crazes that followed both the Terror and the epidemic: they were literally movements of recovery, retrospective conversions of meaningless death into a danse macabre that could at once be reversed into a dance of life.

of over two million persons, some of them buried since the seventh century, were transferred into a network of abandoned quarries, which thus became the city's famous catacombs.[11] By the end of the century, the state recognized that it had blundered, and badly. Death had been isolated in a purely civic setting where no adequate means could be found to deal with it. In 1799, the administrator of the Department of the Seine, Citizen Cambry, was asked to inspect the cemeteries of Paris. His conclusion: "No other people, no other age, shows man after his death in such a cruel state of abandonment."[12] In 1801, the minister of the interior, Lucien Bonaparte, ordered a public competition to generate ideas for reform.[13] Something had to be done.

That something turned out to be the creation of new symbolic institutions, particularly in Paris, that could help reintegrate death into the national culture. At one level, this turn to the symbolic was a simple process of restitution. Symbolization itself was newly recognized as necessary to the social management of death, and the state provided new symbols to replace those that the First Republic had abolished. The process began in 1801 when the prefect of the Seine, Citizen Frochot, issued a decree regulating funerals in Paris. "Burial institutions," he wrote in the preamble, "are of the utmost importance to mankind." The Revolution had gone too far when it abolished them in the name of equality. "Public opinion, which is equivalent to a moral attitude, condemns the austerity of contemporary graves. It is proper for the capital of the Republic to lend dignity to burials by its example."[14] According to the new rules, everyone, rich or poor, was entitled to a shroud and a permanent coffin, and funeral cortèges had to proceed through the streets at a walking pace led by a horse-drawn hearse. Later initiatives would establish new cemeteries (1804) and require that all bodies once more be taken to the church unless there were written orders to the contrary (1811).[15] The provision of new symbols, however, raised more questions than it answered about the three-way relationship of death, the symbolic, and the organization of society. Some useful perspectives on these questions can be derived from the concept of a general symbolic order, which requires a short discussion.

The idea of the symbolic order was developed in the 1950s as part of Jacques Lacan's structuralist rereading of Freud. Almost worn out by English-speaking literary critics from the 1960s through the 1980s, it was renovated more or less single-handedly by Slavoj Žižek during the 1990s. Lacan argues that human beings become subjects only by taking their place in a preexisting network of symbolizing systems, of which language is the prime example. This network is not merely something available to the subject, like a tool kit, but an

11. Ragon, *The Space of Death*, 57–64, 200–202.
12. Ariès, *The Hour of Our Death*, 504.
13. Willms, *Paris, Capital of Europe*, 113; Ragon, *The Space of Death*, 237–54; Ariès, *The Hour of Our Death*, 506–13.
14. Willms, *Paris, Capital of Europe*, 113.
15. Ariès, *The Hour of Our Death*, 516–17, 519.

order imposed on the subject that both supports and delimits the possibilities of action, knowledge, and feeling. Žižek has repeatedly sought to transfer this idea from the universalizing sphere of psychoanalytic theory to the world of historical realities. He has usually done so without explaining just how it can be done. What his practice suggests, however, is that the symbolic order is itself continually being symbolized, and that these symbolizations endow it with a perceptible character and agency of its own relative to particular historical circumstances. The symbolic order becomes effective, is indeed constituted, only by playing specific parts in contingent human dramas, often in personified forms that justify its alternative name, "the big Other." Put another way, the symbolic order is the continually reinvented figure by which we both acknowledge and produce the need for symbolization. When I speak of the symbolic in what follows, the reference is to the historically sensitive concept whose genesis has just been described with brutal brevity: a concept drawn from Lacan, but not a "Lacanian" concept, or something meant to yield a "Lacanian" interpretation.

One way to redescribe the debasement of death during the French First Republic is to say that for a short time death fell wholesale out of the symbolic order, which means that it also fell wholesale out of the sphere of subjectivity. More than simply lacking symbolization, or being a prohibited object of symbolization, death became unsymbolizable and therefore impossible to cope with. The result was a gap in the bond between state and citizen that continually made itself manifest in the material unpleasantness of death and burial, especially during the Terror, a situation that could not be rectified by exceptional state funerals or occasional festivals devoted to the dead en masse. What was needed, as the state recognized in the first years of the nineteenth century, was sweeping reform. Religious practices would have to be restored, funerary customs reinvented, and new means of commemoration established. The state would have to forge a new culture of death with multiple links to everyday life.

That culture developed on the basis of three great public institutions, each of which reestablished a place for death in the symbolic order. The three were the catacombs, visited after 1800 and formally opened to the public in 1809; the Paris Morgue, where bodies were put on public display after 1804; and the modern cemetery—what Michel Ragon calls the cemetery as museum—which after a decree issued by Frochot in 1804 begins to construct a scene of pastoral consolation to replace the gloom and decay associated with the traditional churchyard.[16] Each of these institutions represented a symbolizing tendency rather than an airtight system, but each had its own distinctive logic, its own characteristic pattern of trope, topic, and representation. To anticipate briefly, catacomb logic was based on the epitaph, morgue logic on narrative,

---

16. Willms, *Paris, Capital of Europe*, 115; Ragon, *The Space of Death*, 89–107; Ariès, *The Hour of Our Death*, 516–31. Although Frochot's decree got it started, the cemetery-museum did not truly begin to flourish until after the Restoration.

102

and cemetery logic on the monument. At the same time, these three logics were linked by an element of reflectiveness grounded in the recent past. Following a traumatic period in which death counted as that which empties out the symbolic order, the new logics of death tended to stage as a dialectic the historical sequence of the loss and recovery of symbolic value.

Each of these logics persisted into the 1830s and beyond, and each can be said to have left an imprint on Chopin's Funeral March, albeit one that faded with changing times. There is, however, no question of Chopin intending to make encoded or esoteric references to these logics, and no question, apart from the depiction of a funeral, of any programmatic meaning. What I hope to suggest is that the formal and expressive qualities of the march can be heard to perform the same kinds of symbolic action that typically appeared at the catacombs, the Morgue, and the nineteenth-century cemetery. These actions are not necessarily consistent with one another; within each separate logic, the most obvious and familiar features of the music take on different meanings as one or another feature of the culture of death presses in on them. In moving from one logic to another, we will regularly meet with the changing faces of three musical elements in particular: the dark, heavy ostinato that accompanies the march theme without interruption or variation; the marked contrast between the sections of the complete Funeral March (uppercase), a ternary form in which the somber B♭-minor march (lowercase) frames a sentimental character piece (the trio) in the relative major; and the highly cyclical and symmetrical organization of the march.

Catacomb Logic

Although they originated as a public heath measure, the catacombs of Paris quickly became a popular tourist attraction after they were opened to the public as part of Frochot's campaign to humanize death in the capital. In 1810 Frochot had them restored and enlarged. A later prefect, the comte de Rambuteau, closed them on grounds of unseemliness in 1833, two years after Chopin's arrival in the city, but they were reopened in 1859 and in 1861 became the object of a famous series of photographs by Nadar (Félix Tournachon).[17] Nadar's images highlight the paradox at the heart of this modern underworld, which turns on the dialectic of de- and re-symbolization. The catacombs are literally gigantic heaps of bones, over six feet high and in places more than a hundred feet across.[18] In this respect they are aptly described by Christopher Prendergast as "random, gratuitous, and absurd."[19] Yet the bone-heaps are also inlaid with rows, series, and patterns of skulls and crossed tibias

---

17. Christopher Prendergast, *Paris and the Nineteenth Century* (Oxford: Basil Blackwell, 1992), 80–81 and plates 11–13.
18. Ragon, *The Space of Death*, 63–64.
19. Prendergast, *Paris and the Nineteenth Century*, 80.

set forth with geometrical precision (Fig. 1). Gratuitous disorder is punctuated by rigid order; the mass of bones is both utterly meaningless and the most ancient of symbolic forms, the *memento mori*. The iconography here belongs to the Christian tradition of *vanitas* painting, but the underlying logic is that of the classical epitaph, which issues to the living a reminder of mortality from the world of the dead. The catacombs unequivocally embody that other world, as both their design and the inscription at their threshold declare. A stairway and shaft lead underground from the street; at the bottom, the ossuary opens under a stone lintel engraved with a line from the poet Jacques Delille: "Stop: this is the empire of death."[20] In the nineteenth century a book stood on this threshold in which visitors could write (and read) appropriate reflections, the entries of a communal epitaph.[21]

The extreme contrast between the march and the trio of Chopin's Funeral March can be heard to suggest a similar division of worlds. The two sections have always been judged to be incompatible.[22] Their bad fit is partly generic, a clash between solemn ritual and sentimental sociability, between the coffin as a focal point and the salon or parlor piano. The genre of the trio is hard to pin down. The piece has qualities suggestive of both the piano nocturne and, as Jeffrey Kallberg has shown, the *preghiera* (prayer) of Italian opera, but it cannot definitely be identified with either. Although calling the section a prayer might seem to make more programmatic sense, the appearance is deceptive. The texture of the music is decidedly pianistic—it is, unmistakably, a simplified (etiolated? grief-stricken?) version of nocturne texture—which imparts a character of distance to the *preghiera* association. If a prayer, this is a piano paraphrase of one in the spirit of a nocturne. The generic hybridity creates an aporetic knot in which the public, performative space of opera; the private, introspective place of the parlor; and the intermediate space of the salon all interweave without any one of them becoming a stabilizing point of reference. Perhaps the best way to sum up is to say that the trio is neither a nocturne nor a prayer with the same certainty that the music that frames it is a funeral march, and that this relative indeterminacy (deliberate or not) must be reckoned with as one reckons with the piece.

However the generic differences between the march and the trio are interpreted, the music seems to exaggerate them into a chasm. The insistent gloom of the march seems to disconnect it from the world of the living; the studied sweetness of the trio seems to deny or overidealize its connection to the world

---

20. Ragon, *The Space of Death*, 63.
21. Prendergast, *Paris and the Nineteenth Century*, 80.
22. For a summary of the critical literature on the B♭-Minor Sonata see Jim Samson, *The Music of Chopin* (London: Routledge and Kegan Paul, 1985), 129–33. For recent commentary on the trio, see esp. Jim Samson, *Chopin* (Oxford: Oxford University Press, 1996), 211; and Wayne C. Petty, "Chopin and the Ghost of Beethoven," *19th-Century Music* 22 (1999): 281–99. Petty's discussion of the equivocal character of the trio is pertinent to my own, though the two do not always agree.

104

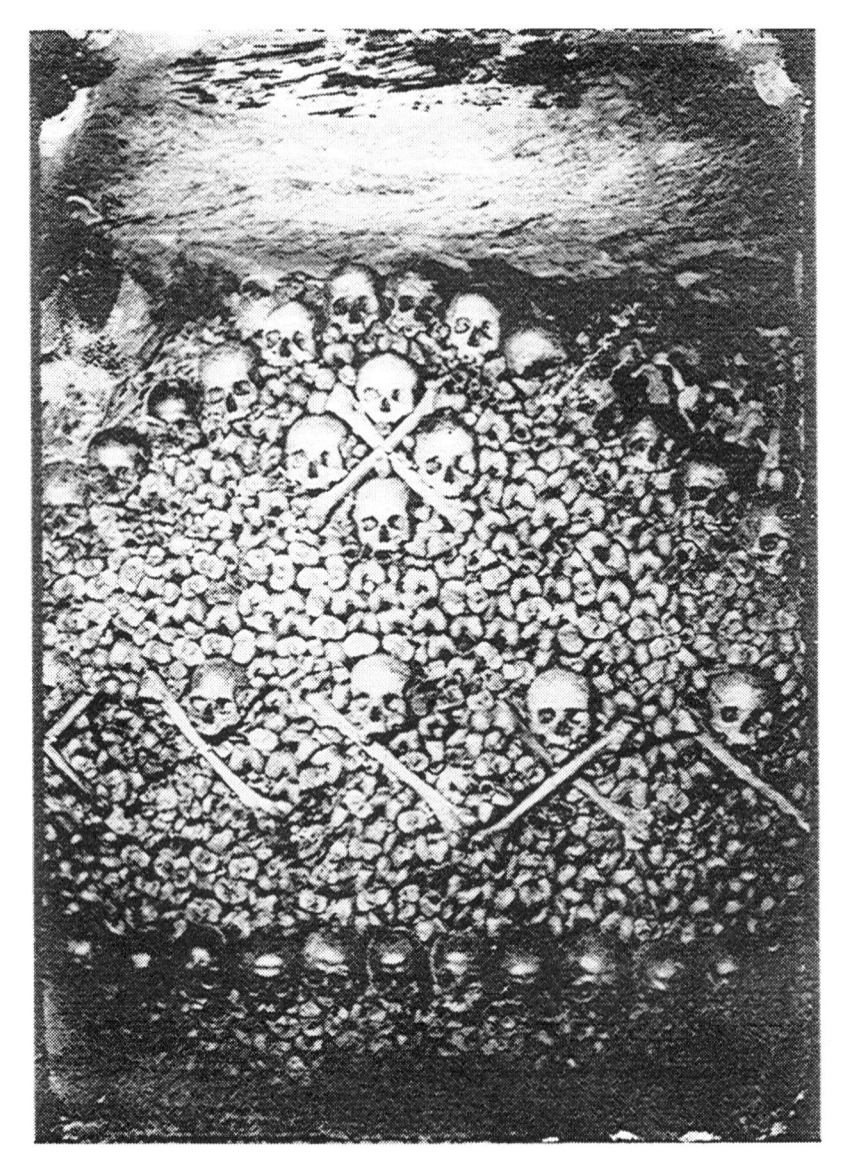

Figure 1 Nadar, "Paris, catacombs: façade avec ornamentation de tibias et de crânes." Collection Médiathèque du Patrimoine, Archive photographique, (c) Centre des monuments nationaux, Paris.

of the dead. As in the catacombs, the question thus posed is how to turn the conjunction between the two worlds into a communication.

Clues to a historically resonant answer can be drawn from the recollections of Wilhelm von Lenz, who heard Chopin himself play this music:

> What Chopin made [of this Trio] is indescribable. Only Rubini sang like that, and even then only exceptionally ("il mio sasso" in [Bellini's] *Il Pirata;* "fra poco" in [Donizetti's] *Lucia*). It is very easy to make the Trio the most vulgar thing in the world [*den vülgarsten Dinge(n) von der Welt*], very hard to raise its cajolery of the ear [*Ohrschmeichelei*] to the level of sorrow in the poetry of the Funeral March. But it [the Trio] depends on that, and never in Chopin's interpretation did the euphemism of the Trio appear to me as a dualism to the main portion, however people want to reproach the Trio [*wie man dem Trio vorwerfen will*]. This is where you learn whether the pianist performing is also a poet or merely a pianist; whether he can tell a story [*fabulieren*] or merely play the piano.[23]

Lenz chose his operatic examples with care; both of them involve a tomb visited by night. Their allusive presence can be taken as the index of a certain mortuary logic to Lenz's remarks: catacomb logic, to be exact.

The linchpin of this logic is the epitaph. As a *memento mori*, the epitaph traditionally threatened to trivialize the world of the living. Its purpose, often explicit, was to stop passersby in their tracks. Literally petrified, figuratively spoken by the dead, it was credited with an uncanny power to admonish even when meant to console. Paradoxically, what averts this power is the literary form of the epitaph itself, which contains the dangerous message of the dead within the symbolic order. It is on this basis that the Greek epitaph became the prototype of lyric poetry in the Western world.[24] For Lenz, Chopin's Funeral

---

23. Wilhelm von Lenz, "Übersichtliche Beurtheilung der Pianoforte-Compositionen von Chopin, als Prodromus eines kritischen Katalog seiner sämtliche Werke," *Neue Berliner Musikzeitung* 37 (1877): 289; translation mine, with thanks to Andreas Ballstaedt for tracking down the original German. Cited in Petty, "Chopin and the Ghost of Beethoven," 295; and Kallberg, "Chopin's March," which details the generic implications of Lenz's reference to Giovanni Battista Rubini's performances of arias by Bellini and Donizetti.

24. It might be safer to say "one of the prototypes," but the epitaph, represented primarily by the examples collected in *The Greek Anthology* (trans. W. R. Paton, 5 vols. [New York: G. P. Putnam, 1917–20]), can be said to contain both idyll and elegy, the two primary lyric forms, *in nuce*. Some of the epitaphs themselves celebrate the power of the symbolic, represented by the works or words of the dead; others register despair or issue admonitions, for example, "I, Dionysius, lie here, sixty years old. I am of Tarsus; I never married, and wish my father hadn't" (2:169) or "I am dead, but wait for you, and you, too, shall wait for another. Hades receives all mortals alike" (2:185). Either way, the epitaphic form, in which disembodied speech intrudes on the course of ordinary life, is decisive both as problem and as solution. Similarly, in Nicolas Poussin's famous painting *The Arcadian Shepherds* (ca. 1638–40), paralysis overtakes the figures named in the title when they find a tombstone inscribed with the phrase "Et in Arcadia Ego" ("I, too, am in Arcadia"), but the very scene of discovery becomes an Arcadian trope. On this general question see Geoffrey Hartman, "Wordsworth, Inscriptions, and Romantic Nature Poetry," in his *Beyond Formalism: Literary Essays, 1958–1970* (New Haven: Yale University Press, 1970), 206–30.

106

March poses the threat of trivialization without the advance assurance of symbolic containment. Only a performance of the trio that rises to the status of symbolic action can avert the loss of meaning. By bringing the insinuating "cajolery of the ear" to the march's "level of sorrow," the performance acquires the commemorative power of a poem or a story; it acts like a musical epitaph. The process of symbolization takes over from its form the work of protecting the living from the petrifying speech of the dead.[25]

Another thing the Funeral March shares with the catacombs is the use of "geometrical" design to impose symbolic meaning on the world of the dead. The march is exceptionally rigid in its structure; it consists of an unbroken series of two-measure phrases that are symmetrically arranged like the tiles of a mosaic. But the mosaic seems to move: although each phrase is melodically closed, each is also harmonically open, so that the momentum of the music—its funereal tread—seems inexorable.

In form, the march is a not-quite-standard binary (Ex. 1). Its first half, amid considerable repetition of melodic units, evolves continuously as the tessitura of the music rises. Its second half consists of two eight-measure periods; the second of these is a written-out repeat of the first. The dynamism of the first half is narrowed—perhaps appeased, perhaps quashed—by the stasis of the second. The first half concentrates relentlessly on statements of the funeral march theme, set off by outbursts of a grief-laden descending-tetrachord figure; the second half is devoted to counterstatements that close with the theme. The cyclical movement of the theme's return, however, cuts across the sectional division. The spacing of the returns is strictly symmetrical in both halves and is organized so that the design of the first half is reduplicated at the level of the march as a whole.

The first half subdivides unevenly into a longer first statement of the theme (mm. 1–6) and two shorter restatements linked by repetitions of the tetrachord figure; the pattern is ABABA, evenly spaced in two-measure units after the thrice-two measures of the first A. This pattern is continuously supported by the ostinato accompaniment, which invites one to regard the whole section as an extended statement of the theme, a higher-level A. If we do so, then the remainder of the march fills out another ABABA pattern, where B is the counterstatement and A the combination of the march and ostinato, with the units again evenly spaced (thrice-two measures for B; two for A) after the longer first A. The effect of this "fearful symmetry" is closely akin to that of the skull-and-crossbones ornamentation in the catacombs. The quasi-geometrical

---

25. The trio thus stands on a threshold where it must either succumb to or assume an uncanny, quasi-epitaphic force. Lenz presupposes that the march sections are immune to inexpressive performance, as if their symbolic value were already inscribed in them by virtue of being linked with mortality: all the risk falls on the side of life. It is worth noting that Lenz often used storytelling as a metaphor for expressive performance (just as jazz musicians did later), thus suggesting that his concept of expressivity hinges precisely on bridging the gap between a presymbolic form (the musical score) and symbolic agency.

Example 1 Chopin, Funeral March from the Sonata in B♭ Minor, Op. 35, first statement, complete

Example 1 continued

structure both acknowledges and defies the "random, gratuitous, and absurd" character of death by asserting the excess rigidity of its own form as a measure of symbolic law. This assertion translates into a sensory, almost visceral, effect in the rigid tread of the ostinato bass, whose succession of identical half-measure phrases carries symmetry to its farthest extreme. At every level, the regularity of form merges into the discipline of ritual.

Morgue Logic

Unlike the catacombs, which drew on the mortuary practices of both ancient Rome and Baroque Europe, the Paris Morgue was a uniquely modern phenomenon, and a phenomenally successful one. Between 1804 and 1907 (when its doors were closed to the public) the Morgue was one of the chief attractions of the capital. Free of charge and open seven days a week from dawn till dusk, it sometimes drew as many as forty thousand visitors in a day. Practically all the guidebooks listed it; Thomas Cook's famous tours included it; and Parisians from every social class flocked to it, some of them, according to Émile Zola, making daily rounds. The Morgue was popularly referred to as "Le Musée de la Mort," and by the latter part of the century its building—the second of two to house the Morgue—was surrounded by street vendors hawking oranges, cookies, and coconut slices.[26]

Officially, the purpose of the Morgue was to house unidentified corpses in the hope—obviously a slim one—that they might be recognized. What visitors saw there, behind a glass screen, were naked bodies in various stages of decomposition, laid out on slabs. It seems safe to say that what drew most people to this spectacle was some combination of thirst for sensation and prurient curiosity. People came to the Morgue as they would later read tabloid newspapers. Once on the scene, however, many did participate in a certain process of identification, speculation, and description. The Morgue, too, had its logic. The dialectic between the corpse as meaningless waste and the corpse as person played itself out there in the most graphic of terms. It was even inscribed in the external design of the first Morgue. The original building was a featureless oblong, built in 1568 as a slaughterhouse; when it became the Morgue in 1804, it was given the façade of a Doric temple (Fig. 2). The clash between the heaviness of the building and the lightness of the pilasters formed a sharp though probably unwitting image of the clash housed inside between meaningless and meaningful death, decomposing matter and symbolic aspiration.

The logic of that clash was narrative. The glass screen dividing the corpse from the spectator was obviously there for hygienic reasons, but it also acted like a photographic border or the screen-space for a projected image—a magic lantern still in the nineteenth century, a moving picture in the twentieth.[27] By framing the spectacle, the screen turned the corpse into a narrative image, but only a nascent one; the spectator had to supply the narrative. In the language of Roland Barthes's classic study *S/Z*, the Morgue display invoked the hermeneutic code, the formal means "by which an enigma can be distinguished, suggested, formulated, held in suspense, and finally disclosed."[28]

According to both Robert Browning and Émile Zola, the role of the spectator was to solve the enigma. In his poem "Apparent Failure" (1863), Browning recalls his own visit to the Morgue in 1856. Behind the "screen of glass, we're thankful for," he observes the bodies of three men, all suicides, that seem to be making an explicit appeal for symbolic restitution: "Each on

---

26. See Vanessa R. Schwartz, "Cinematic Spectatorship Before the Apparatus: The Public Taste for Reality in *Fin-de-Siècle* Paris," in *Cinema and the Invention of Modern Life*, ed. Leo Charney and Vanessa R. Schwartz (Berkeley and Los Angeles: University of California Press, 1995), 297–319, esp. 298–304; and Anne Higonnet, Margaret Higonnet, and Patrice Higonnet, "Façades: Walter Benjamin's Paris," *Critical Inquiry* 10 (1984): 391–419, esp. 408–14. The New Morgue opened in 1868.

27. Schwartz suggests that the closing of the Morgue in 1907 coincided with the rise of the movies as an alternative spectacle ("Cinematic Spectatorship").

28. Roland Barthes, *S/Z*, trans. Richard Miller (New York: Hill and Wang, 1974), 18–19. "These terms," Barthes adds, "will not always occur, they will often be repeated; they will not appear in any fixed order."

Figure 2 Augustus Charles Pugin, *La Morgue, Quai Notre Dame*; engraved by C. Heath for Pugin, *Paris, Its Environs Displayed in a Series of Two Hundred Picturesque Views* (London: Jennings and Chaplin, 1831). Reprinted courtesy of the Department of Painting and Graphic Arts, Houghton Library of the Harvard College Library, Typ 805.31.7155 vol 1.

his copper couch, they lay / Fronting me, waiting to be owned," that is, to be acknowledged, to be given their own, so that they can posthumously be assured that "their sin's atoned."[29] Browning obliges by constructing a speculative narrative for each of the three and connecting it to particular features of their bodies:

> And this—why, he was red in vain,
>   Or black,—poor fellow that is blue!
> What fancy was it turned your brain?
>   Oh, women were the prize for you!
> Money gets women, cards and dice
>   Get money, and ill-luck gets just
> The copper couch and one clear nice
>   Cool squirt of water o'er your bust,
> The right thing to extinguish lust!
>
>   (46–54)

Similarly, a character in Zola's novel *Thérèse Raquin* (1868) has reason to visit the Morgue repeatedly. While there, he, too, reads narrative histories from bodily details, which render legible both the social status of the corpse and the cause of death. A young woman appears as "a buxom working-class girl"; a dark stripe around her throat "like a necklace of shadow" reveals that she has hanged herself for unrequited love. A badly decomposed drowned man (drowned, in fact, by the spectator himself) seems "skinny and miserable.... You could have guessed that he was a twelve-hundred-franc employee ... brought up by his mother on herb-tea."[30] Zola's text starkly juxtaposes the Morgue's repugnant physical details and the symbolizing processes that link them to both the histories of the dead and the fantasies of the living.

The mood of the Chopin Funeral March shares something of the morbidity of the Morgue for many listeners; Robert Schumann famously called the gloom of its outer sections "repellent."[31] What really links this music to the Morgue, however, is not a shared mood but a shared logic. Much as the Morgue's glass screen rivets the eye of the spectator—the term *morgue* itself originally meant both a proud stare and the observation hold of a prison—the thudding basso ostinato of the march sections rivets the ear. With the music as

---

29. Lines 25–26; text from *The Shorter Poems of Robert Browning*, ed. William Clyde Devane (New York: Appleton-Century-Crofts, 1934), 252. The autobiographical reference comes in the poem itself, which refers to the speaker's visit to Paris "seven years since" the time of writing, thus placing it at the time of Browning's own visit. In detail (especially the absence of female bodies) the account is probably fictionalized.

30. From chapter 13 of Émile Zola, *Thérèse Raquin*, trans. Leonard Tancock (London: Penguin Books, 1962), 107–13.

31. Robert Schumann, *On Music and Musicians*, ed. Konrad Wolff, trans. Paul Rosenfeld (New York: W. W. Norton, 1969), 142. Chopin's own view of the march may have been (or become) similar; see Kallberg's discussion of a letter in which the composer purportedly recalls an experience of uncanny dread while performing the march late in his life ("Chopin's March").

112

with the Morgue, the aim is to exert a fascination that is hermeneutically active, one that distinguishes or formulates an enigma and holds it in suspense. The listener must know how to hear a story, not just someone playing the piano.

As this paraphrase of Lenz suggests, the place of the "hermeneutic code" in the Funeral March is the startling contrast between the march and the trio. From this standpoint, the risk of trivialization posed by the trio is a positive technique of symbolization, a cultural trope, regardless of whether it is by some standards an aesthetic fault. As in the Morgue, what matters most is not the answer to the enigma but the effect of finding an answer. By combining the extremes of somberness and sentiment, the music poses a question to which any answer, regardless of its content, reaffirms the place of death in the symbolic order. This indifference to content is the heart of morgue logic. It does not matter that Browning's speaker devises the story of a gambler, among others, only that he devises a story that elicits both irony and sympathy. It does not matter that Frederick Niecks in 1888 finds the trio "a rapturous gaze into the beatific regions of a beyond" whereas Louis Ehlert in 1872 objects to the impropriety of its showing "white lingerie" too soon after wearing "black crepe."[32] Niecks taps into a standard sentimental narrative of consolation, and Ehlert into a social practice that imparts dignity and social meaning to death. Their particular views are not ends, but means.

The morgue logic of the Funeral March also extends to the cyclical organization of the march, where the recurrences of the theme can be heard to play out a dialectic between the capture and loss of death to the symbolic order. This process is literally a matter of being "on the one hand" and "on the other." For Liszt/Wittgenstein, Huneker, and others, the basso ostinato in the left hand imitates the tolling of a passing bell and therefore symbolizes the solemnity and inevitability of death. The symbolic tie is reinforced by the fact that the ostinato also gives the walking pace of the imaginary procession. But the incessant repetition of the bass figure steadily strips it of its symbolic value, much as constant chanting will reduce a word or short phrase to phonetic babble. The ostinato gradually becomes mere sound; what one hears is less the figure itself, as something meaningful, than the meaninglessness of its interminable repetition. This effect, of course, depends on more than repetition alone; otherwise it would be true of ostinatos in general. The repetition here has qualities that render it both irrational and obtrusive. The irrationality lies with the harmony; the ostinato oscillates between the root-position tonic triad —always lacking its third when the theme sounds at pitch—and an unstable third-related chord (VI_4^6) that cries out for some sort of explicit reinterpretation and never gets one. In effect, the ostinato makes less sense the more it is heard. The obtrusiveness lies with the resistance of the ostinato figure to being integrated into the musical texture. Its sonority is too weighty and its profile—

---

32. Niecks and Ehlert both quoted in Huneker, *Chopin*, 298.

the oscillation of just two chords—is too sharp. The ostinato is not just something one can hear, but something one can't stop hearing.

Quite unlike its accompaniment, the right-hand melody begins in a sort of limbo. The theme (mm. 3–4) is a miniature ABA structure dominated by dotted rhythms. The outer segments consist of four repetitions of a single note, the keynote B♭; the interior is a stepwise descent toward this note from the D♭ a minor third higher. The march begins with a two-measure introduction that anticipates the theme by twice stating a slightly elongated form of the repeating-note first segment. As a result, the melodic line remains fixated on the one note until the last beat of the third measure. Until the line departs from this dead level, the structural value of the repeated note is merely potential, and the melodic shape of the theme is nil. The turn to and from D♭ reverses the situation. When the B♭s return they assume the meaning they previously lacked; they form the goal of melodic motion through the lower third of the tonic triad. At this point the entire theme moves sequentially from B♭ to D♭ (mm. 5–6), which confirms the access of meaning by reaching up to F, thus filling out the space of the full tonic triad. Melodic descents through the tones of this triad echo twice thereafter in the descending-tetrachord passages of the first half of the march (mm. 7–8, 11–12; the tetrachord figure, spanning B♭–F, is followed by a descending skip to D♭), and twice again in the bass line of the second half after deep, grumbling trills have prepared for the return of the theme (mm. 20–21, 28–29). Every time it returns in either half, the theme reenacts the process of its own becoming meaningful, though the reenactment admits of a certain dialectical tension because the confirmatory D♭ sequence is never repeated.

In sum, the left-hand part of the march begins with a meaning that it steadily loses, while the right-hand part begins by lacking a meaning that it steadily gains. These two processes cannot be reconciled, but they cannot be separated, either. The music gives their conjunction a precise expressive location in the interval B♭–D♭, which is not only the fulcrum of the right-hand process but also the interval through which the basso ostinato oscillates. With each return of the theme, the right hand clarifies the melodic meaning of the interval while the left hand holds in suspense the enigma of its harmonic underpinning. The same interval, incidentally, separates the keys of the march and the trio.

Cemetery Logic

The Parisian cemetery, which essentially reached its modern form by 1830, evolved as the polar opposite of the Morgue. Visitors went to the Morgue for a "realistic" view of the horror of death, though with the proviso that the very conditions of viewing made that horror manageable. Visitors went to the cemetery to receive consolation from its presentation of death as a bringer of peace, though only after it had become a place that people visited rather than avoided. Where the old churchyard shrouded itself inhospitably in a morbid—morguelike?—gloom, the modern cemetery combined the functions of a park and a museum, uniting the literary and pictorial traditions of pastoral with commemorative stonework. The Morgue was a show; the cemetery, an environment. Beneath this contrast, however, both the Morgue and the cemetery were concerned with the uniqueness of the person, each in its own way seeking to forestall the obliteration of personal identity. The difference is that cemetery logic casts its work of preservation as reverent and uplifting—edifying both figuratively and literally. Its symbolic device is not just a transient, ad hoc narrative but a pair of durable material symbols: the burial plot and the funeral monument.

After 1804, the reforms initiated by Frochot secured the right of every person to an individual grave that could, if desired, be decorated with a monument. Within a few years, this would become the rule throughout France, but in Paris, and Paris alone, the rule had a catch to it. The system of individual burials in the capital did not involve the elimination of mass graves, only the requirement that coffins be laid side by side rather than stacked up. Throughout the nineteenth century and into the twentieth, the coffins of the poor were laid down in trenches, *les fosses communes,* in rows of forty or fifty. After five years any monuments were removed, a layer of earth was added, and a new trench was installed over the old one. For those who could afford it, an individual grave could be leased for five or ten years, after which the site could be cleared and the ground reused.[33] The price of living in "the capital of the nineteenth century" was thus a kind of second death that assured the loss of identity a few years after the loss of life. The only way to escape this fate was to buy the plot of ground where one was buried, an option also made available by Frochot in 1804. Originally, one could buy a grave only at Père Lachaise, which over the next two decades became the model for the modern cemetery-museum.

The idea caught on slowly at first, but its growth was exponential. Between 1805 and 1807 only fifteen graves were sold; by 1815, the number had risen to 530; by 1835, over 11,000 plots had been bought and equipped with headstones, tombs, or mortuary sculpture.[34] Aside from inscribing the names

---

33. Ariès, *The Hour of Our Death,* 516–18; Willms, *Paris, Capital of Europe,* 114–15. Frochot originally meant to ensure individual graves for all, but the plan was later abandoned on economic grounds. In 1911, according to the contemporary (eleventh) edition of the *Encyclopedia Britannica* (5:660), the cost of a five-year concession was 20 francs; of a ten-year concession, 50 francs. Ariès notes that by the end of the nineteenth century, "the five-year grants and the free trenches were pushed back and reduced to a minimum, and perpetual grants, instead of remaining an exception to the rule, were extended to persons in modest circumstances" (*The Hour of Our Death,* 517).

34. These figures are derived from a report by Rambuteau cited in Willms, *Paris, Capital of Europe,* 115. Ariès gives higher figures for tombstones installed, which nonetheless show the same growth curve (*The Hour of Our Death,* 518).

of the dead, many of these monuments bore epitaphs identifying the deceased as a virtuous person and beloved family member. With men, professional accomplishments might also be commemorated.[35] Sculptured figures added "beatific" sentiment and attested to the worthiness of a good and useful life. Nothing could have been further from the revolutionary practice of debasing both death and the dead.

But none of it was free. Frochot had emphasized the state's responsibility to support the burial of the poor "as an obligation and a sign of communal respect,"[36] but the bourgeois state that would triumph in the July Revolution of 1830 was more concerned to reproduce in the world of the dead its hegemony over the world of the living. In 1800, a private monopoly offered four classes of funeral in Paris; in 1806, in the name of reform, the state established a price structure and fixed the division of funerals by social class; by 1859, nine classes of funeral were available, ranging in cost from fifteen francs to slightly over four thousand.[37] The power to preserve one's identity in death was a class prerogative, the mark of belonging to the aristocracy or haute bourgeoisie. The majority had to settle for the five- or ten-year fiction of a resting place in the cemetery-museum—not a monument but a short-term facsimile of one, a second-order symbol of a symbol. Yet even the facsimile had real meaning; no one who could afford it would do without one. The point is famously illustrated at the end of Balzac's novel *Le Père Goriot* (1834) when the protagonist, Rastignac, defiantly buys a five-year concession at Père Lachaise for the destitute old man whose well-to-do children have rejected him. The novel concludes with Rastignac vowing to conquer Parisian high society as he gazes at the lights of the city from the highest point of the cemetery that so accurately mirrors its social order.

Which brings us back to Chopin's Funeral March, a work whose cemetery logic clearly invokes the most privileged classes of burial. The march evokes a funeral procession whose final destination is surely a permanent plot in the modern cemetery, and more particularly in Père Lachaise, as Chopin's own funeral would illustrate. The solemnity of the march implicitly celebrates the self-representation of a whole social world, an image of cultivation, distinction, and personal attachment in which Chopin was pleased and grateful to share. In saying this, however, my point is not to chastise either Chopin or his milieu for being undemocratic or ideologically blind, but to help locate a key moment in the social history of modern death, a moment that would eventually generalize far beyond the social world of its origin. One might say that this is

---

35. Ariès, *The Hour of Our Death*, 524–31.
36. Quoted in Willms, *Paris, Capital of Europe*, 113.
37. Ariès, *The Hour of Our Death*, 519; Michelle Perrot and Anne Martin-Fugier, "Private Spaces," in *From the Fires of Revolution to the Great War*, ed. Michelle Perrot, trans. Arthur Goldhammer, vol. 4 of *A History of Private Life*, ed. Philippe Ariès and Georges Duby (Cambridge: Belknap Press of Harvard University Press, 1990), 333: "The various classes of funeral differed as to the quality of casket, flowers, and so on as well as the solemnity of the service."

the moment when death becomes privatized: when its reincorporation into the symbolic order takes the form of a monument to the individual's private life.

Like its cousins of the catacombs and Morgue, the cemetery logic in Chopin's Funeral March shows itself most obviously in the contrast between sections. The simple, heart-on-sleeve trio connects the solemnity of the march to the pastoral quiet of the modern cemetery. Its potentially "beatific" quality offers the same sort of consoling imagery as funerary sculptures of angels, the idealized dead at peace, or genre scenes like the Arcadian grove or edifying deathbed. Its appeal to sentiment may evoke the refinement of feeling, often measured by decorous tears, considered proper to the graveside, as in the somewhat ironic case of Rastignac, who sheds "the last tears of his youth ... wrung from the pious emotions of a pure heart" while gazing on the tomb of Goriot. The trio also has links to what Philippe Ariès identifies as the cult of the beautiful death, in which the language of sentiment was applied to the process of dying, not least by the dying themselves. As one young woman confided to her diary in 1832, "Death is always mingled with poetry and love, because it leads to the realization of both."[38] At the same time, the "feminine" sensitivity of the trio, echoed in Ehlert's remark about white lingerie and reinforced by the feminine associations of the nocturne, might be taken to suggest that the peace evoked in this music is allied not only to the pastoral space of the cemetery but also to the cultivation of psychological inwardness. Women like our diarist would be likely to seek consoling symbols in what they regarded as the depths of the self because, as of 1837, they were normally confined to the house immediately after a death and were not allowed to attend funerals.[39]

More subtly and pervasively, the cemetery logic of Chopin's Funeral March is realized by what the music is not. Regardless of its later reception, the march does not depict the grand public funeral of a larger-than-life, state-anointed hero or martyr. It is, instead, the anthem of important private death. Of course, there is no proving such a negative, but the music seems to invite this one by the contrasts it maintains to its acknowledged model, the Funeral March of Beethoven's Piano Sonata in A♭, Op. 26.[40] The sonata was one of Chopin's favorite teaching pieces, and his performance of its last two move-

---

38. Alexandrine la Ferronays, quoted in Ariès, *The Hour of Our Death*, 415.

39. Ariès, *The Hour of Our Death*, 419–20, 431–32; Perrot, *From the Fires of Revolution*, 333–34. On the feminine associations of the nocturne, see Jeffrey Kallberg, "The Harmony of the Tea-Table: Gender and Ideology in the Piano Nocturne," in *Chopin at the Boundaries* (Cambridge: Harvard University Press, 1996), 30–61.

40. Will Crutchfield has recently suggested a second model, the funeral march in the gallows scene of Rossini's *La gazza ladra* ("Chopin, the Day After the Opera," *The New York Times*, 30 June 1999, sec. AR, pp. 21–22). The suggestion is persuasive, although Crutchfield's description of Chopin's "overall scheme" (with "the somber march heard twice in a horrific crescendo" around a lyrical interlude) is inaccurate. The likelihood of multiple models bears on the vexed

ments, as recollected by one of his pupils, seems to have sounded like a virtual (and ideal) performance of the corresponding movements of his own sonata:

> He played that *Marche Funèbre* of Beethoven's with a grand, orchestral, powerfully dramatic effect, yet with a sort of restrained emotion which was indescribable. Lastly he rushed through the final movement with faultless precision and extraordinary delicacy—not a single note lost, and with marvelous precision and alternations of light and shade.[41]

The sequence of movements in Beethoven, Funeral March and moto perpetuo, predicts the sequence in Chopin. But Chopin brings it off with a difference.

Beethoven's movement is explicitly titled "Funeral March on the Death of a Hero," and its rhetoric is military throughout. Its march is studded with drumbeat figures, "trombone" proclamations, and cymbal crashes; its trio is a tone-painting of a trumpet and drum salute, perhaps including punctuation by gunfire. Sectional contrast is minimal, where in Chopin it is maximal. In Chopin's Paris, this is the kind of music that would be composed for a state funeral, the kind that Hector Berlioz did compose in 1840 for the Funeral March of his "Symphonie funèbre et triomphale," a work commissioned to accompany the bodies of fifty heroes of the Revolution of 1830 on their transfer to a monument (the July Column) newly erected in the Place Bastille. Chopin's march does not so much avoid this sort of military rhetoric—that would scarcely have been possible—as render it distant, equivocal, polyvalent. The military topics seem to have been subtilized to let the essence of a funeral march be heard. The ostinato is a good example: part drumbeat, part tolling bell (invoking the solemnity of the church, not the state, even though the music is not liturgical), and part pure piano sonority.

Piano sonority plays a key role in this process; Chopin, unlike Beethoven, italicizes his medium. The climactic gestures in both halves of the march involve a turn to self-consciously pianistic devices: plangent octaves and arpeggios to enhance the descending-tetrachord figure of the first half (mm. 11–12, followed by the march theme in octaves), and massive two-hand octaves to

---

question of musical influence and its supposed anxieties. Unlike Wayne Petty ("Chopin and the Ghost of Beethoven"), I do not hear Beethoven's role in the Opus 35 sonata as evidence of a private, Oedipalized struggle over originality à la Harold Bloom, but as the mark of a complex social embeddedness that incorporates a plurality of contexts and persons and that both enables and restricts Chopin's musical utterance. There is little evidence that Chopin was anxious about his originality in relation to Beethoven or anyone else; as Rose Subotnik has pointed out, the utter individuality of Chopin's music was the first thing everyone recognized about it. For the basics of Bloom's theory, see his *Anxiety of Influence* (New York: Oxford University Press, 1973); for Subotnik, see "On Grounding Chopin" in her *Developing Variations: Style and Ideology in Western Music* (Minneapolis: University of Minnesota Press, 1991), 141–65.

41. From a letter (in English) to J. C. Hadden, 27 March 1903; quoted in George R. Marek and Maria Gordon-Smith, *Chopin* (New York: Harper and Row, 1978), 87.

introduce the counterstatement of the second half, which also culminates in a right-hand arpeggio spanning a tenth (mm. 15–18, 23–26). The result is the assimilation of the music to the idiom—and implicitly to the world—of the home, the salon, and the concert stage. The heroic genre remains, but its venue changes. The music is no longer addressed to a generalized citizen-subject but to (and perhaps by) a mourner who must confront the reality, gravity, and majesty of death.

In this context, military topics lose much of their imitative value and become means of symbolization. Such as they are, they arise in the second half of the march as part of a process of privatization and internalization, rather than throughout (as in Beethoven) as part of a depiction of a public event. In particular, the counterstatement begins, as Kallberg observes, like "a transmutation of the fanfare from the standard-issue funeral march,"[42] but ends by veiling itself in the distance of a further, more internalized symbolization. The rising quasi-fanfare figure, proclaimed crescendo in both hands, yields to a falling and fading mirror image for left-hand middle voices under static right-hand chords (mm. 15–16, 23–24). Heard again at a greater remove, in the right hand alone, the rising figure ends with its big arpeggio and collapses into deep-bass trills that prepare the return of the march theme (mm. 17–20, 25–28). Taken straight from Beethoven, these trills represent drumrolls that Chopin declined to silence; they mark the limit of the march's transmutation of its genre. But as the link between the steadily transmuting fanfare and the march theme, the trills can be heard to continue the work of transmutation. Where Beethoven's drumrolls are primarily mimetic, Chopin's are primarily metaphorical. Military or not, they underwrite the social claim of the march that the highest, most sublime expression of mourning does not require a hero for its object.

In this connection the virtually unrelieved gloom of the music is a virtue, almost a consolation, because it asserts the supreme gravity of personal loss. This is another point of contrast with Beethoven: where Beethoven's melodic line is redemptive, Chopin's is entropic. The difference is a simple matter of up and down.

Beethoven's march theme gradually traces an ascent from deep voices within the thick, shrouded texture to the light of the upper voice (Ex. 2). The rise in voice-position also involves a clarifying rise in register. This process occupies the quasi-expositional and developmental spaces of the march, and it is reaffirmed by both the subsequent return of the theme and the ensuing codetta, especially when the latter expands into a full coda to round off the Funeral March as a whole. The codetta (mm. 26–30, 64–67) also executes a shift in emphasis to the march theme's rising countermelody—something Chopin's march conspicuously lacks—which mounts resolutely from bass to treble in three sequential strides (Ex. 3). In the coda (mm. 68–74) the

---

42. Kallberg, personal communication—one of several to which this essay is deeply indebted.

Example 2 Beethoven, Funeral March from the Sonata in A♭, Op. 26, mm. 10–19

melodic line elaborates on the theme's dotted rhythms to achieve an unwonted suppleness and also to find its registral peak, while the march rhythm gradually dissipates in the bass. Gloom gives way to the *gravitas* of sublimation.

Chopin's theme embarks on a similar journey only to reverse its course. Introduced and recalled in a lower register, the theme appears an octave higher to end the first half of the march (mm. 13–14). When, however, it returns twice more in the second half, the theme appears in the original low register (mm. 21–22, 29–30), the second time to bring the march—and later the whole movement—to a strangely unceremonious close, more curtailment than ending. This registral parabola (another instance of rigid symmetry) is only the widest realization of a gesture that pervades the march: an abrupt rise and inexorable fall in register. The descending-tetrachord figures of the first half initially jump to the B♭s an octave above those of the theme, to which they fall back before the whole process is repeated another octave higher; in the second half the unchecked scalar ascents of the "fanfare" figures come to grief against the more halting descents that balance and cancel them out; and the thematic reprises of the second half arrive on the heels of dramatic two-hand drops in register marked especially by the descending pairs of trills in the bass. This literal depression or dejection in register, focused on returns of the

120

Example 3 Beethoven, Funeral March from the Sonata in A♭, Op. 26, conclusion

theme, gives iconic form to the sense of desolation so widely felt to pervade the piece. From there it is only a small step to the potential nihilism that hovers over the sonata's ominous moto perpetuo finale—a nihilism intimated in Chopin's own trivializing description of the finale as merely peevish: "the left hand and the right hand grumble in unison after the march."[43]

The negativity of the Funeral March, however, is not an enticement to accept meaninglessness but an incitement to change the grounds of meaning. In transmuting the military topic, the march also seeks to subvert it, creating a tone of negation that cannot be overcome by an appeal to greatness, heroism, or the ideal of sacrifice but requires instead the private consolations of the trio. It is in this context that Chopin's internalized fanfare and solemn trills are (they hope, or claim) no longer military, but rather evidence of the displace-

---

43. From a letter to Julian Fontana, 8 August 1839; translation modified from *Selected Correspondence of Fryderyk Chopin*, ed. and trans. Arthur Hedley (London: Heinemann, 1962), 181. My thanks to Jeffrey Kallberg and Barbara Milewski for help with Chopin's verb, "ogadac," which has roughly the force of "kvetching" or "bitching"—the kind of word, I'm told, that would describe what two old farm crones do over the kitchen table. Hedley's rendering, "gossip," is inaccurate.

ment of heroism from the soldier to the exemplary citizen who has now come to stand for the human being.[44]

This symbolic identity may have weathered away for the very same reason it arose: a change in the social history of death. All of the "logics" I have described here assume that death is a constant presence in everyday life. But one of the fundamental aims of the modern era was precisely to immunize everyday life from death. As mortality rates from illness declined and life expectancy increased, as sanitation improved and sickness and death came to seem unsanitary, as care of the dying passed from the hands of families to those of doctors, death was increasingly asked to occupy a place apart—though of course it did not always comply. The modern cemetery, which initially provoked resistance because of its distance from people's homes, literally put the separate sphere of death on the map. According to Ariès, the final phase in constructing what he calls the invisible death was the transfer of the deathbed from the home to the hospital, a process that began in earnest around 1930.[45]

Just by chance, but a suggestive one, 1930 was the year in which Sergei Rachmaninoff made what is probably the most famous of all recordings of the Chopin B♭-Minor Sonata. (A set of the 78-RPM platters sat atop a battered old manually operated Victrola in my grandmother's basement; the family had no interest in "classical" music.) This recording makes a striking expressive change in the Funeral March. Ignoring Chopin's dynamics, Rachmaninoff plays the first statement of the march with a steady buildup from *pianissimo* to *fortissimo*, then reverses the pattern for the second statement. He thus projects the impression of a funeral cortège that slowly approaches from a distance and slowly moves away. The idea of performing the piece this way was not new; it originated in the nineteenth century with Anton Rubinstein and was picked up earlier in the twentieth by Ferrucio Bussoni.[46] But it was through Rachmaninoff's recording that the idea had real impact. One reason why, no doubt, was the combination of sound-recording technology and sheer pianistic skill, but another may have been the close fit between this realization of the music and the modern culture of death. This is not at all to say that the performance was illegitimate, regardless of its indifference to printed indications. On the contrary, the performance allowed the music to do just what it had always done: to reaffirm the place of death in the symbolic order. The terms of this reaffirmation were simply those that felt right for the way of death that was then emerging as the norm.

---

44. On the identification of the exemplary (usually bourgeois) citizen as the model human being during this period, see Jürgen Habermas, *The Structural Transformation of the Public Sphere: An Inquiry into a Category of Bourgeois Society,* trans. Thomas Burger with Frederick Lawrence (Cambridge, Mass.: MIT Press, 1989), 27–51.

45. Ariès, *The Hour of Our Death,* 559–601.

46. Alan Walker, "Chopin and Musical Structure," in *The Chopin Companion: Profiles of the Man and Musician,* ed. Alan Walker (New York: W. W. Norton, 1973), 246.

122

Rachmaninoff's performance changes the presumptive character of both the music and the listener. Chopin's dynamics, like Beethoven's, are emotive, especially perhaps in the first six measures of the march, which are played *piano* on the first statement and crescendo (starting from *piano*) on the second; a controlled solemnity yields to a swell of grief. Rachmaninoff's dynamics are purely an acoustic fiction. The march is objectified by them, even theatricalized; the listener is reduced from an empathetic subject absorbed in a funeral to an abstract point of perspective from which a funeral is observed. Both changes project the sense of distance and impersonality appropriate to the invisible death. At the same time, however, the dark solemnity of the music continues to function symbolically and invests these potentially frigid qualities with a humanizing warmth. The result is a kind of alienated mournfulness: Rachmaninoff's performance is anything but unemotional, but its emotions have no concrete subjective location. Traditionally "heartfelt" expression is relegated to the trio, which even so becomes in this context a kind of nonevent, a purely formal point of division between crescendo and decrescendo. Although the trio does preserve a trace of the subjectivity expunged from the march, its interruption of the otherwise continuous crescendo-decrescendo process literally makes its sentiment extraneous.

Meanwhile, the programmatic side of the performance realigns the march with the death of heroes and the state funeral: the observer remains stationary while the cortège passes with solemn music. Insofar as the march thus assumes some of the military character that Chopin tried to strip away, it suggests a nostalgic reference to an ideal of sacrificial death that World War I had made profoundly questionable. The moral distance at one with modern death overlaps with a temporal distance at odds with modern experience. Real state uses of this music can be said to suffer from the same nostalgia. At the Kennedy funeral, for example, Chopin's march joined other nineteenth-century pieces to form a symbolic bulwark against the trauma of a seemingly senseless assassination. The music helped turn back the clock: as a pair of gray horses drew a caisson bearing the president's coffin, and a riderless black horse, caparisoned with boots turned backwards, brought up the rear, Kennedy's death was made meaningful by being restaged as Lincoln's.[47]

The Kennedy funeral was the last event of its kind that I can recall in the United States, and it may be that the world in which Chopin's Funeral March can do any form of cultural work has become a thing of the past. For perhaps a hundred and fifty years, and for a wider than usual public, this music acted as a

---

47. William Manchester, *The Death of a President, November 20–November 25, 1963* (New York: Harper and Row, 1967), 489. Manchester singles out Chopin's march for special mention: "The hushed crowds and the music. The melodies were very different. The Marines struck up 'Holy, Holy, Holy' and 'The Vanished Army,' and the other service bands played 'Onward Christian Soldiers,' 'Vigor in Arduis,' the funeral marches of Beethoven, R. B. Hall, and Chopin—the most famous of them all and the most dolorous—and, at the end, the redemptive 'America the Beautiful'" (p. 578).

kind of shibboleth. Even more than the Funeral March of Beethoven's *Eroica* Symphony, it provided a seemingly universal signifier of death, the very repetition of which came to act as a reassurance that death could be brought under ritual control. It is doubtful whether any music could do that today, let alone a piece of "classical" music. Chopin's theme can still boast of name-brand recognition, but his Funeral March is now most often met with only as a famous movement in a familiar sonata, something perilously close to absolute music. Such changes are usually impossible to reverse and pointless to bemoan. The thing to do with them is write their history, some fragment of which I have attempted here.

Works Cited

Ariès, Philippe. *The Hour of Our Death*. Translated by Helen Weaver. New York: Alfred A. Knopf, 1981.
Barthes, Roland. *S/Z*. Translated by Richard Miller. New York: Hill and Wang, 1974.
Bloom, Harold. *The Anxiety of Influence*. New York: Oxford University Press, 1973.
Browning, Robert. *The Shorter Poems of Robert Browning*. Edited by William Clyde Devane. New York: Appleton-Century-Crofts, 1934.
Chominski, Jozef M., and Teresa Dalila Turlo. *Katalog Dziel Fryderyka Chopina*. Krakow: Polskie Wydawn. Muzyczne, 1990.
Chopin, Fryderyk. *Selected Correspondence of Fryderyk Chopin*. Edited and translated by Arthur Hedley. London: Heinemann, 1962.
Crutchfield, Will. "Chopin, the Day After the Opera." *The New York Times*, 30 June 1999, sec. AR, pp. 21–22.
Golab, Maciej. "Chopinsche Transkriptionen aus dem 19. Jahrhundert. Veruch einer Systematik." Paper presented at the symposium "Chopin 1849/1999—Aspekte der Rezeptions- und Interpretationsgeschichte," Robert-Schumann Hochschule, Düsseldorf, 6–8 December 1999.
Habermas, Jürgen. *The Structural Transformation of the Public Sphere: An Inquiry into a Category of Bourgeois Society*. Translated by Thomas Burger with Frederick Lawrence. Cambridge, Mass.: MIT Press, 1989.
Hartman, Geoffrey. *Beyond Formalism: Literary Essays, 1958–1970*. New Haven: Yale University Press, 1970.
Higonnet, Anne, Margaret Higonnet, and Patrice Higonnet. "Façades: Walter Benjamin's Paris." *Critical Inquiry* 10 (1984): 391–419.
Huneker, James. *Chopin: The Man and His Music*. 1900. Reprint, New York: Scribners, 1927.
Kallberg, Jeffrey. *Chopin at the Boundaries*. Cambridge: Harvard University Press, 1996.
———. "Chopin's March, Chopin's Death." *19th-Century Music* 25 (2001), forthcoming.
Karasowski, Moritz [Maurycy]. *Friedrich Chopin: Sein Leben, seine Werke, und seine Briefe*. Dresden: F. Ries Verlag, 1877.
Lenz, Wilhelm von. "Übersichtliche Beurtheilung der Pianoforte-Compositionen von Chopin, als Prodromus eines kritischen Katalog seiner sämtliche Werke." *Neue Berliner Musikzeitung* 37 (1877): 289–92.

Liszt, Franz. *Frédéric Chopin*. Translated by Edward N. Waters. New York: The Free Press of Glencoe, 1963.

Manchester, William. *The Death of a President, November 20–November 25, 1963*. New York: Harper and Row, 1967.

Marek, George R., and Maria Gordon-Smith. *Chopin*. New York: Harper and Row, 1978.

Metzer, David. "Shadow Play: The Spiritual in Duke Ellington's 'Black and Tan Fantasy.'" *Black Music Research Journal* 17 (1997): 137–58.

Paton, W. R., [ed.] *The Greek Anthology*. Translated by W. R. Paton. 5 vols. New York: G. P. Putnam, 1917–20.

Perrot, Michelle, ed. *From the Fires of Revolution to the Great War*. Translated by Arthur Goldhammer. Vol. 4 of *A History of Private Life*, edited by Philippe Ariès and Georges Duby. Cambridge: Belknap Press of Harvard University Press, 1990.

Petty, Wayne C. "Chopin and the Ghost of Beethoven." *19th-Century Music* 22 (1999): 281–99.

Prendergast, Christopher. *Paris and the Nineteenth Century*. Oxford: Basil Blackwell, 1992.

Ragon, Michel. *The Space of Death: A Study of Funerary Architecture, Decoration, and Urbanism*. Translated by Alan Sheridan. Charlottesville: University Press of Virginia, 1983.

Samson, Jim. *Chopin*. Oxford: Oxford University Press, 1996.

———. *The Music of Chopin*. London: Routledge and Kegan Paul, 1985.

Schumann, Robert. *On Music and Musicians*. Edited by Konrad Wolff. Translated by Paul Rosenfeld. New York: W. W. Norton, 1969.

Schwartz, Vanessa R. "Cinematic Spectatorship Before the Apparatus: The Public Taste for Reality in *Fin-de-Siècle* Paris." In *Cinema and the Invention of Modern Life*, edited by Leo Charney and Vanessa R. Schwartz, 297–319. Berkeley and Los Angeles: University of California Press, 1995.

Stierle, Karlheinz. *Der Mythos der Paris: Zeichen und Bewusstsein der Stadt*. Munich: Carl Hensler Verlag, 1993.

Subotnik, Rose R. *Developing Variations: Style and Ideology in Western Music*. Minneapolis: University of Minnesota Press, 1991.

Tucker, Mark. *Ellington: The Early Years*. Urbana: University of Illinois Press, 1991.

Walker, Alan. "Chopin and Musical Structure." In *The Chopin Companion: Profiles of the Man and Musician*, edited by Alan Walker, 227–57. New York: W. W. Norton, 1973.

Willms, Johannes. *Paris, Capital of Europe: From the Revolution to the Belle Epoque*. Translated by Eveline L. Kanes. New York: Holmes and Meier, 1997.

Zola, Émile. *Thérèse Raquin*. Translated by Leonard Tancock. London: Penguin Books, 1962.

Abstract

This essay seeks to shed fresh light on Chopin's all-too-famous Funeral March by exploring its relationship to the social history of death. Virtually from the day of its publication, the march has had a career independent of the Piano Sonata in B♭ Minor, Op. 35, into which Chopin inserted it. It quickly became Western music's paramount anthem of public mourning, a role it played at funerals from Chopin's own to John F. Kennedy's. This civic character, however, at best represents only a fraction of the music's cultural resonance. By consulting the first context of the march, the treatment of death and burial in Chopin's Paris, it becomes possible to tell a different and a richer story. Responding to a historical crisis bequeathed by the French Revolution, France during the first half of the nineteenth century was engaged in renovating the culture of death literally from the ground up—and down. Three major institutions emerged in the capital to carry on this work, each with its own distinctive set of customs and symbolic practices: the catacombs of Paris, the Paris Morgue, and the modern cemetery, the prototype for which was Père Lachaise. Each of the three can be said to have left a mark on Chopin's Funeral March; deciphering those marks is the project of this essay.

CHAPTER 12

Recognizing Schubert: Musical Subjectivity, Cultural Change, and Jane Campion's *The Portrait of a Lady*

When classical music is used on a movie soundtrack, it is a safe bet that most members of the audience will neither be able to identify it nor, as they say, identify with it. Even at its most expressive or impassioned, classical music today carries a distinct charge of historical distance for most listeners. The cultural marginality responsible for this distance may be cause for regret, but the distance itself should not be. A sense of its positive value is one of the underpinnings of this paper. The question I want to ask is, What happens when a film made in the 1990s, based on a novel written in the 1870s, uses music composed in the 1820s to negotiate historically specific spaces of social, personal, and sexual desire? What does happen will prove not only to remap those spaces but also—in its own good time—to register recent cultural tendencies that go well beyond the immediate topics broached by the names of Campion, James, and Schubert.

The role of music in this process is more prominent than usual, or at least than usually acknowledged, in Campion's film. But that role is also indicative—not only of the semantic power of music in cinema, so often underestimated, but also of the logic by which this power operates. The operation involves far more than the mere appropriation of music in a cinematic context. It depends on the unfolding, within the film, of cultural meanings and resonances that—in an intelligible sense—have always already belonged to the music even if they have not previously been actualized.

Title Sequence
Henry James's *Portrait of a Lady* is the story of Isabel Archer, an American girl with a hunger for life in James's special sense of that word. *Life* means

the pursuit of happiness regardless of conventional but powerfully internalized moral precepts. It means a scorning of prudence or timidity and an "'intensely determined'" embrace of "'the usual chances and dangers . . . what most people know and suffer.'"[1] As so often in James, it also means transplantation from America to Europe, where American innocence is severely tried. Isabel ventures from Albany to London, and from London to Florence and Rome, in the belief that it is not her "fate" to "give up" her chances at life. Her doing so marks her as a modern woman in the later nineteenth century. Late in the twentieth, Jane Campion's film version of James's novel would take that modernity as its mainspring.

The film opens with a miniature music video showing the young women of today dreaming and dancing alone or posing together. The screenplay speaks of "a series of portraits—not stills but living, breathing young women . . . innocent and dogmatic, spontaneous, full of theories, with delicate, desultory, flamelike spirits, facing their destinies."[2] The camera, though, cannot quite cross the gap between inanimate stills and "flamelike" animation. All but one of the images—a brief flicker of living flame—are in marmoreal black and white. The camera repeatedly draws close to the figures it captures, as if seeking to embrace or understand them, but they seem indifferent to it. Their very contemporaneity, the unclosed, barely opened shape of their stories, seems to be making them inscrutable.

In the same vein, the women also seem deaf to the music on the soundtrack; one even sways to her own music on a portable CD player with headphones. The soundtrack music is dreamy and lyrical; its texture—a Dorian melody on recorder against pastoral strings—invokes an earlier time, a gesture reinforced by the black-and-white photography. All in all, the video creates a cinematic time warp in which the present appears with the distance of the past. And the past reciprocates; it ends the video and begins the diegesis by assuming the immediacy of the present. The film's title appears written on a pointing hand, an archaic type of sign vivified by a switch to

---

1. Henry James, *Portrait of a Lady*, ed. Robert D. Bamberg, 2d ed. (New York, 1995), p. 119; hereafter abbreviated *PL*.
2. Laura Jones, *The Portrait of a Lady: Screenplay Based on the Novel by Henry James* (New York, 1996), p. 1; hereafter abbreviated *PLS*. James's novel, serialized in 1880 and published in 1881, is set in the preceding decade. Jones takes the phrase about the "desultory, flamelike" spirit of the girls in the video from James's description of Isabel early in the novel. The screenplay is not always as pertinent to the film as it is here; Campion departs from it frequently.

color and one that will recur, in marble, at a key moment. What the hand points to is Isabel's face, which becomes the magnet for a long, intimate, color close-up. "We have settled," says the screenplay, "in intimate detail on [her] face.... She could be today's girl, but she happens to live in 1870" (*PLS*, p. 1). The story comes to life from this moment of face-to-face intimacy, which will be renewed and deepened throughout the film.

Modern as she is, though, Isabel is still a nineteenth-century woman, which means that her proper fate, whatever it is, presupposes that she will marry. This is a fate she would like to give up—she turns down two good proposals before she can afford to—but one that catches up with her from within. Isabel is free to pursue life only because she inherits a large fortune, secretly shunted her way by its original heir, her cousin Ralph Touchett. Ralph and Isabel are obviously soul mates, but their relationship founders on Ralph's health; he is a consumptive, doomed to die young and thus, both assume, doomed to love Isabel vicariously. Though he secures her freedom with a vague, generous air of infinite possibility, the point of that freedom reduces to the fact that she can marry anyone else she chooses—and James's point in chronicling her freedom is that she unaccountably chooses to marry an icy narcissist, a man who enmeshes her in a moral and psychological prison from which there is no escape.

A key role in this story is played by the mysterious Madame Merle, a pawn—revealed too late—of Gilbert Osmond, Isabel's husband, as well as his former lover and the mother of his daughter, Pansy. The meeting of these two women forms a key scene early in the novel. Strange to tell, the person who introduces them is Franz Schubert:

> The lady at the piano played remarkably well. She was playing something of Schubert's—Isabel knew not what, but recognized Schubert—and she touched the piano with a discretion of her own. It showed skill, it showed feeling; Isabel sat down noiselessly on the nearest chair and waited till the end of the piece. When it finished she felt a strong desire to thank the player and rose from her seat to do so .... "That's very beautiful, and your playing makes it more beautiful still," said Isabel with all the young radiance with which she usually uttered a truthful rapture. [*PL*, p. 151]

Schubert disappears from the novel after this, but his bit part in the scene is important. His music is the medium for the state of entrancement that prefigures Madame Merle's "momentous influence" (*PL*, p. 151). Just what music doesn't matter; it is the ineffable and familiar Schubert style that inveigles Isabel into an emotional intimacy measured both by her noiseless sitting down and her voluble getting up. James's text clearly assumes that

Schubert in The Portrait of a Lady

the reader shares Isabel's cultural lore as common property. It assumes an image of Schubert as the composer of a very beautiful but somewhat enervating music, a music both prized and mistrusted for eliciting gushes of emotion.[3]

An image of Schubert also plays a role, and an expanded one, in Campion's film, but both the image and the role it plays are very different. Campion's Schubert is a tormented outsider, a figure for what Isabel, against all expectation, turns out to be. This Schubert, this musical double for Isabel Archer, evolves out of the dialogue with which the scene in the novel continues. Isabel is referring to her dying uncle: "'I should think that to hear such lovely music as that would really make him feel better.' The lady smiled and discriminated. 'I'm afraid there are moments in life when even Schubert has nothing to say to us'" (*PL*, p. 151). James's irony here goes mainly to Isabel's naivete, her failure to divine the disenchantment hidden beneath the musical and social surface. Thanks to Schubert's slightly overripe beauty, Isabel mistakes a common blackbird—*le merle*—for a nightingale. Campion goes further. She takes Madame Merle's pronouncement as a kind of witch's spell or hypnotic suggestion and shapes the film's narrative around it through the medium of the soundtrack, into which Schubert increasingly steps as a haunting presence. As the failure of Isabel's marriage drives her to despair, Schubert will indeed have "nothing to say" to her, but he will have a great deal to say *for* her, and about her, in her place. At the turning point in her crisis, when she wins an equivocal moral victory at the cost of continued misery, Schubert will once again speak "to" her through the medium of memory, albeit a deeply internalized and perhaps unconscious memory.

The film thus constitutes itself musically as a tragic history of modern feminine desire. Along the way, it reconfigures the interrelations of music, desire, and the film image. The Schubertian soundtrack mostly follows the standard protocol that subordinates music to the image, but its internal consistency is so fully developed, as if to excess, that the soundtrack also becomes a nearly independent narrative in which the meaning and even the outcome of Isabel's story exceed the terms of their nominal presentation. That excess provides the site on which the film negotiates the historical import of the narrative "portraits" that form its different time lines: of Isabel, of Schubert, and of "today's girl" who may know little of either. My aim

---

3. The image James invokes is retrospective, already formed in 1880 but inserted when *Portrait* was revised in 1908, by which time the image—the "Victorian" Schubert—had become a fixture. James's revision is discussed below. On the history of Schubert's nineteenth-century image, see David Gramit, "Constructing a Victorian Schubert," *Nineteenth-Century Music* 17, no. 1 (1993): 65–78.

here is to trace this process by commenting, in turn, on the film version of the scene at the piano, its narrative aftereffects, and the relationship of both to the changing image of Schubert, which, I will suggest, is a symptom of a changing culture.

Turn: Schubert, Woman to Woman

The event of first meeting Madame Merle acts on Isabel like the process usually called ideological interpellation; it inserts her into a script written by others while she perceives herself as acting on her own feelings and exercising her will. Her "strong desire to thank the player" interprets the effect of being controlled as an expression of her autonomy. The concept of interpellation has traveled considerably beyond the Marxist context in which Louis Althusser introduced it in 1970, but the scene by which he illustrated it remains paradigmatic. By answering an address or summons, what Althusser calls a "hail," I assume a certain subjective character tacitly prescribed by the summons; when, says Althusser, a policeman or someone else on the street says, "'Hey, you there!'" my unreflective turning around in response installs me in a preordained subject-position. "By this mere ... physical conversion, [the hailed individual] becomes a *subject*. Why? Because he has recognized that the hail was 'really' addressed to him, and that 'it was *really him*' who was hailed."[4]

In a critique of Althusser, Judith Butler suggests that the limitations of his model can be made apparent by taking as essential the details that it presents as merely illustrative. One consequence might be to undercut the assumption that the subject-position involved must be fully or automatically accepted; I might pause before turning to answer the hail or contrive to put on a false front, especially when not actually confronted with the law in person. Butler, however, focuses on other details, in particular the voice and the turn, which, she says, are neither necessary to accomplish the effect of interpellation nor necessarily able to accomplish it. My obedient turn assumes that the voice I hear possesses a secular authority equivalent to that of the divine voice addressing Moses or Peter—both examples offered by Althusser. But as Butler notes, "Human speech rarely mimics that divine effect except ... [when] backed by state authority, that of a judge, the immigration authority, or the police, and even then there does sometimes exist discourse to refute that power."[5] Besides, one can also be interpellated in absentia, in the third person, often with an even more compelling effect.

---

4. Louis Althusser, "Ideology and Ideological State Apparatuses (Notes towards an Investigation)" (1970), in *Mapping Ideology*, ed. Slavoj Žižek (London, 1994), p. 131.

5. Judith Butler, *Excitable Speech: A Politics of the Performative* (New York, 1997), p. 32.

30   *Schubert in* The Portrait of a Lady

For example, let's add, by music, with its legendary power to speak to a listener as if to someone really and especially addressed. James's interpellative scene is one of a rich series, from E. T. A. Hoffmann to Proust, Tolstoy to Salman Rushdie. From roughly Schubert's time to ours, music has been culturally constructed so that, subsuming or displacing the human voice, it can mimic divine authority without help from the police.

As filmed by Campion, the meeting of Isabel and Madame Merle proves the point, inverting the subject's turn and displacing the speaking voice towards music as a higher, more numinous source. Campion's Isabel (Nicole Kidman) is not merely controlled by the playing of Madame Merle (Barbara Hershey); she is mesmerized by it, almost made its puppet. When her presence causes an interruption, she gropes for the nearest chair as if her nerves had come unstrung and haltingly asks to hear more. Madame Merle, meanwhile, with her back to her listener, has not seemed to be addressing Isabel at all. The authoritative voice that puts one woman under the other's spell is entirely Schubert's, figuratively or incorporeally present in the music, which the movie audience, unlike the reader, can actually hear, and hear at length. As the scene unfolds, it assumes the character of a seduction, not to an erotic tie, but to Isabel's idealizing/narcissistic identification with Madame Merle as the embodiment of refined sensibility and emotional depth. The vehicle of these impressions—false ones, as events will prove—is once again the voice of Schubert, which comes to Isabel as the reward of a tacitly negotiated social and psychological exchange.

A scarcely audible tinkling at first, the music seems to summon Isabel from afar. It clarifies gradually as she turns her head, descends a staircase, and approaches the closed room from which the sound emanates. The piece proves to be the A-flat Impromptu of Op. 90. Its glittering upper-voice arpeggios and striving inner-voice melody accompany Isabel as she nears the door to the piano room, where she stands and listens by a mirror that gives us, but not her, a double image of her face (figs. 1–3). Just as this happens the music makes the transition to its middle section, an agitated, highly emotional episode in C-sharp minor. The juxtaposition of image and sound tells us that Isabel is reflected in the music: that the music, in Lacanian terms, is the imaginary, the specular image, by which she is captured, and in which she perceives her split, incoherent self as a single entity. Isabel is her own doppelgänger. Like someone singing the famous Schubert song to which the soundtrack will later allude, she plays the roles of both Death and the Maiden.

The music's own split personality mirrors, so to speak, this mirroring. The arpeggios and the striving theme are expressively worlds apart, yet they sound together; taken together they are an expressive world apart from the

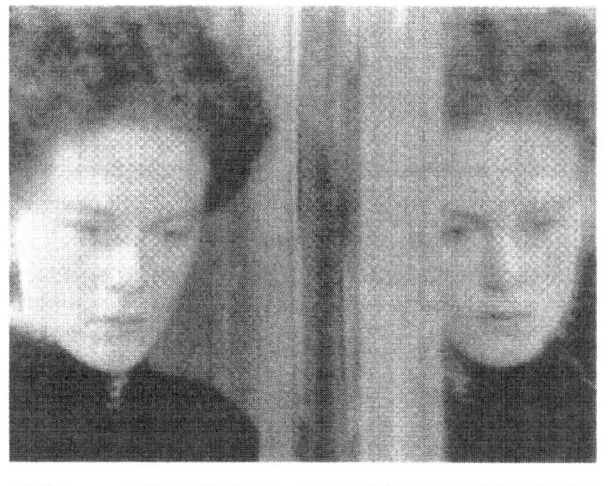

FIGURES 1–3.

Schubert in The Portrait of a Lady

impassioned music they envelop, yet they incubate the passion by the way they combine. The arpeggios descend in little iridescent bursts, rhythmically regular and broken by rests, while the theme extends itself continuously through repetition of a single syncopated figure along a rising trajectory (example 1). Reiterated incessantly, the two seem to be seeking, with mounting urgency, a point of convergence, of reconciliation and release—seeking, one might say, the threshold of their fate, like Isabel at the door. What they find, however, is not the expected A-flat-major cadence that eventually ensues, but its sudden, revelatory conversion into the transitional passage leading to C-sharp minor and the middle section (example 2). By adding a dissonant note—a routine dissonance, but one that sounds enormously transformative in this context—the transition recasts the tonic A-flat major as the dominant of Db minor, which is respelled as C-sharp.[6]

In so doing, the transition reverses, even revokes, the tendency of A-flat major to rise to its own dominant and thus to reach a satisfying cadence. (It so happens, though we only hear this by inference or memory, that the A-flat-major sections contain no cadences to the dominant.) The implication is that the melodic striving of the A-flat-major sections overruns the sectional boundaries toward a fulfillment that may not meet it in fully commensurate terms. The sources of this relocation can be traced to the opening measures of the work, which are in A-flat minor rather than A-flat major. Although the mode changes during the gradual evolution of the striving theme, the sense that the true destination of the music lies somewhere in the minor is never dispelled. (The predestined A-flat-major close, we might say, is only a supplement to the quite different destination reached in the middle of the piece.) We do not hear this in the film, only its repercussions, but we do hear the A-flat-major music pass through the looking glass into its C-sharp-minor double as the energy that sustains the arpeggio-theme combination of the one becomes a drivelike force in the pulsations—fully voiced chords in the bass continuously throbbing and changing—of the other.

As if compelled by that force, Isabel takes the next step in her story and opens the door, thus crossing a threshold both acoustic and symbolic. She enters the piano room slowly, suddenly taking the unmuffled music full in the face. Her gaze is riveted on the unseen player; she lets her hands creep

---

6. The dissonance is G-flat, the dominant an A-flat six-five chord. The transformative effect comes in part from the voicing of this chord. C, its third, appears in the deep bass an open sixth below the A-flat root; after two measures of murmuring, the rise of a semitone turns the C into the root of the C-sharp-minor triad. Apparently a force for stability (it had replaced C-flat to secure the major mode for the tonic), C turns out to harbor a secret unrest.

EXAMPLE 1. Schubert, Impromptu in A-flat, Op. 90. no. 4. Theme and arpeggios: mm. 46–65.

EXAMPLE 2. Schubert, Impromptu in A-flat, Op. 90. no. 4. Transition and opening of middle section in C-sharp Minor.

34

EXAMPLE 3. Schubert, Impromptu in G-flat, Op. 90. no. 3. Opening.

behind her back as if fearful of spoiling the moment (in a slightly earlier scene a shrill whistle has warned her not to touch a museum exhibit). As she closes in on the source of the sound, we see the player's back and partial profile. At this point the shadowy form of Isabel's back passes across the screen, a visual disruption that might be taken to reduce her subjectivity to a purely amorphous or potential state. When the shadow passes, Madame Merle abruptly stops playing and turns to face the onlooker—that is, both Isabel and us. She simply gazes intently; it is Isabel who supplies the verbal element of the interpellation by initiating the dialogue about the beauty of Schubert's music. She then makes her plea to hear more while taking her seat. Madame Merle begins to comply but interrupts herself to fix Isabel's identity ("'Are you the niece, the young American?'" [*PLS*, p. 23]), thus sealing the moment as interpellative. The music is now the intimate, sensibility-laden G-flat Impromptu of Op. 90 set, but it breaks off almost before it can be recognized. In order to get it, Isabel has to identify herself, offer a bit of her self to Madame Merle's construction ("'*C'est bon.* We're compatriots. I'm Madame Merle'" [*PLS*, p. 23]), which returns to her in the form of the music.

When the G-flat Impromptu resumes, its reflective self-containment offers a complement to the passionate intensity of the C-sharp minor passage and the associated suggestions of authenticity and subjective depth. A musical "portrait" of Isabel begins to take shape as both the reiterations of the theme-arpeggio combination in A-flat and the C-sharp-minor pulsations that serve as their hidden truth or core seek an idealized, sublimating echo in the gently undulating middle voices of the new Impromptu, which continue throughout the excerpt—and the piece (example 3). To this Isabel listens utterly transfixed, swaying slightly, her head resting on her folded upheld hands as the camera moves in slowly for a closer view of her. (One of the girls in the opening video is shown listening in much this way to a portable CD player.) The music overlaps into the shot of a blazing fireplace that starts the next scene, then fades away. But we have not heard the last of it.[7]

Counterturn: Mortal Wounds

The piano's interpellative scenes form the outer section of a three-part A B A pattern—a paradigmatically "musical" pattern that underlies and rearticulates the film narrative. The middle section consists of excerpts from the variation's movement of Schubert's String Quartet in D Minor (D. 810, 1824), a work known as "Death and the Maiden" because it takes the theme for this movement from Schubert's song of the same name (D. 531, 1817). The quartet music is not heard until much later in the film, but when heard it is heard four times, spaced at decreasing intervals, so that it decisively becomes Isabel's own music, the music of the "fate" she feels is not hers to escape. That fate is a classic ironic reversal of what she thought it to be. When she says, early on, "'It's not my fate to give up'" the chances that life offers, she gets her own story exactly backwards (*PL*, p. 118). Each segment of the quartet marks a chance surrendered. This music is superficially an auteurist commentary and has even been criticized for being obvious, but its role as commentary is mostly a pretext. Unlike the piano music, the quartet music is not diegetic, as the first excerpt will make a point of showing. But it is not extradiegetic, either, because it refers to the Schubertian subjectivity by which Isabel has so dramatically been interpellated.

Schubert's music, as the mirror at the piano room door has told us, and subsequent mirror images will tell us again, is Isabel's alter ego. It is a character, a doppelgänger, a directly embodied subjectivity that is half Isabel's and half Schubert's. The quartet music is the more uncanny in this respect both because Isabel never hears it when we do and because, with a single exception, it is never fully present in its own right. It is, as presented, a series of fragments that both intimates and in a larger sense contains the whole of which it is a part: the whole person and the whole story, which is to say, the whole film. Its fragmentation, which becomes increasingly pronounced after the first excerpt, becomes a realization of Isabel's subjective incoherence: bleeding pieces of an unarticulated whole. Taken together with the piano excerpts, the quartet sequence—the quartet quartet, so to speak—gives the essence of Isabel's story without its narrative elaboration. Like the theme of Death and the Maiden itself, the musical story assumes the role of an archetype, a deep home truth: that inescapable fate again.

---

7. My account of Isabel's interpellation by Madame Merle—and by Schubert—has been enriched by the contributions of my students in a graduate seminar on hermeneutics in nineteenth-century music, given at Columbia University in the spring semester, 2001.

36 *Schubert in* The Portrait of a Lady

FIGURE 4.

Like the A-flat Impromptu, the first quartet excerpt is snuck in faintly; it begins in the midst of variation 2, a lament sung by the cello amid quivering figuration in the violins and a hurried version of the death-march rhythm in the viola. The music proceeds to variation 3, where the same rhythm, twice as hurried, takes over the ensemble. This is a violent, heavily accented, continuously agitated piece, which is heard in a cut-and-spliced version as if in full. The expressive sequence reverses that of the piano scene, which passes from agitation to sensibility. The reversal intimates that Isabel's sensibility is the source of her derailed "fate": the Schubertian reverie, the dream of the exquisite, induced by Madame Merle has begun to play itself out as an unwitting repetition of Merle's own ruinous history with Osmond.

The quartet scene opens with a close-up of Isabel's naked arms and shoulders as she tenderly caresses a marble hand (fig. 4). Her head is on her own hand, as before, and as before she appears in proximity to a mirror in which she does not look. The music once again seems to come to her faintly from afar, but the music she "hears" turns out to be apparitional; it is, so to speak, falsely diegetic. A party is in preparation at which quartet music, presumably "Death and the Maiden," is to be played. We see the string players briefly—but they are not yet playing, though the music is, and now at full volume. Another time warp is in operation; the music actually ends at the point where the Osmond family sits down together to hear it begin.

Osmond himself (John Malkovich) dominates the scene once the camera moves away from Isabel and her reflection; he clearly stands in the presiding role of Death. But the initial association of the reflection and the music establishes that what we are hearing is Isabel's Schubertian subjectivity making itself known, the reflected image coming to uncanny life on the soundtrack. The music is obtrusively out of keeping with the party preparations. Its role is bluntly allegorical, except in the sense—which is effectively literal—that it embodies the spilling over of Isabel's still inarticulate surrender of her first set of life-chances. That surrender has been encapsulated in the opening mirror segment with the clustered images of pallid skin, the caress of the cold marble hand, and the reflection to which the subject reflected is oblivious or blind.

The second excerpt, a fragment of the agitated variation 3, comes as Isabel, contrary to her own strongest desires, helps separate Pansy from the young man she, Pansy, loves, but whose social status and wealth Osmond deems inadequate. Another chance—to prevent Osmond from ruining his daughter's life—is thus surrendered. The surrender, of course, is a symbolic recapitulation of Isabel's own, a coerced sacrifice of love. The setting for this scene is itself a place of sacrifice: the Roman Colosseum. As Isabel rushes Pansy to a carriage, the young suitor is left to plead and protest behind a closed grate, the prison or convent wall behind which Isabel has locked the possibility of love and from which even so she is compelled to flee in panic. It is worth noting in passing that not long before this scene Isabel has been shown at dusk in solitary contemplation. She stands in a bleak landscape described by the screenplay as "a grove of tall, dark cypresses"—hence a place of death—and "walks in [the] cold shade, contemplating the ruins of her happiness" (*PLS*, p. 105). The scene is accompanied by the melancholy solo of a solitary English horn, an echo of the melancholy *alte Weise* that Wagner's dying Tristan hears on the Cornish coast while he waits for Isolde, who will arrive too late. The scene suggests Isabel both as a pseudo-Isolde in relation to Osmond (who has seduced her with the false avowal, "'I am absolutely in love with you'" [*PL*, p. 263]) and an unrealized Isolde in relation to the rapidly declining Ralph, to whom she will eventually—arriving too late—bring a Tristanesque death.

The third excerpt, following closely on the second, shifts to the intensely expressive variation 5, of which we hear the first section (without repeat) and the first few bars of the second. In the former, the first violin abandons itself to stammering figuration that seems to protest hysterically at the steady gloom of the inner voices. The stammering comes in two waves, the

Schubert in The Portrait of a Lady

second and longer of which forms a despairing crescendo; the soundtrack cuts a transitional measure so that the peak of the crescendo carries directly over into the second section, where the stammering spreads to all three upper strings and the cello plunges grimly to the very bottom of its range. The gloom seems to grow stronger with each effort to resist it.

This music arrives along with a devastating message. Ralph is dying: another chance, that of sustaining an authentic human relationship, has been given up (given up, not lost, because Isabel has known all along that Ralph is to die young). Like its predecessors, this excerpt props itself on a surface thematic application that is both ironic and allegorical. Where Osmond played Death in the first excerpt, Isabel herself took the role in the second. Here in the third the role passes to a servant, someone like T. S. Eliot's eternal footman, who ascends a staircase (compare Isabel's descent in the interpellation scene) to deliver the message. ("I have seen the eternal Footman hold my coat, and snicker,/ And in short, I was afraid.")[8] The first part of the scene refuses the sight of faces to focus on hands, human to be sure but no more welcoming than the marble hand that Isabel caressed as the first excerpt started. These are the hands of destiny, which is handed to one on a plate but is, after all, out of one's hands. ("Though I have seen my head . . . brought in upon a platter,/ I am no prophet—and here's no great matter.")[9] There is, incidentally, a brief glimpse of another mirror in this scene, before which Isabel stands while her eyes—and our ears—are riveted on the message of death.

So far, the quartet sequence has constituted a kind of fragmentary statement of the variation sequence in Schubert's music. The fourth excerpt breaks this pattern, even as it brings Isabel's quartet-subjectivity to a culmination. The scene draws on the hitherto unheard variation 1, the origin of the diversified anguish of the others. That anguish emerges here as already fully present in a gapped, lamenting melodic line pieced together from offbeat phrases—hardly even phrases, just melodic splinters—and shadowed by the death-march rhythm on the pizzicato cello (example 4). The music begins (again snuck in, but quickly coming to sound full bore) as Isabel flees from Osmond's presence. He has sought to prevent her from returning to England to keep vigil at Ralph's deathbed, and the pressure he exerts seems impossible to resist. Still another chance has been given up, and this the most important one of all, the chance to be true at last to the only person Isabel really loves. The music accompanies extreme close-ups of her deathly

---

8. T. S. Eliot, "The Love Song of J. Alfred Prufrock," *Collected Poems, 1909–1962* (New York, 1984), ll. 85–86, p. 6.
9. Ibid., ll. 82–83, p. 6.

EXAMPLE 4. Schubert, String Quartet in D Minor, D. 810, "Death and the Maiden." Second Movement: Variation 1, first half.

pale face (the pallor is a frequent image throughout, a visual leitmotif) as she walks through a corridor weeping. The image of her face now once more divides against itself, this time separating as in double or even triple vision, seen as if blurred and multiplied by tears; the audience sees through Isabel's eyes what she again cannot see herself (fig. 5). No mirror is present this time to rationalize the division of identity. Throughout the film, mirroring has served to crystallize the desperation of self-division, the visual equivalent of which is the subject's—Isabel's—avoidance of her own mirrored gaze. In the final quartet scene, this avoidance becomes preemptive; the gaze shatters into an impossible visual object, an optical illusion that forms a true rendering of Isabel's psyche for the eye as the broken music does it for the ear.[10]

The excerpt continues as a new medium-long shot abruptly shows Isabel from behind as she passes like a condemned prisoner into the engulfing darkness of a doorway: the nadir of chances foregone. The screenplay quotes from James's text: "Her faculties, her energy, her passion, were all dispersed again. She felt as if a cold, dark mist had suddenly encompassed

---

10. On "impossible objects," see my *Music as Cultural Practice, 1800–1900* (Berkeley, 1990), pp. 84–83; on the gaze as object, see Jacques Lacan, *The Four Fundamental Concepts of Psycho-analysis*, trans. Alan Sheridan, ed. Jacques-Alain Miller (New York, 1978), pp. 67–122 and *Gaze and Voice as Love Objects*, ed. Renata Salecl and Žižek (Durham, N.C., 1996).

40 *Schubert in* The Portrait of a Lady

FIGURE 5.

her" (*PLS*, p. 112). Only when Isabel learns in the next scene (into which the music suggestively spills over) that Madame Merle is Pansy's mother does she find the strength to break the Schubertian mold that confines her—and to reclaim another one, musically, as her own.

The effect of the quartet excerpts can be clarified further by harking (or hearkening) back to the song on which they are based. The theme of the quartet's variations is the song's death motif, a gentle but implacable melody that combines the qualities of a funeral march and a chorale. First heard as a piano prelude, this theme gives way to the Maiden's pleas to be spared, then it returns to end the song in combination with the unsparing voice of Death. The vocal line for the Maiden's pleas is both anguished and cajoling, almost wheedling; its accompaniment is angular and agitated. Death's music envelops and depletes these qualities together with the subjectivity they represent; it effaces the Maiden's character from the song and thus prepares her for annihilation. Death's music enfolds the Maiden's in a smothering embrace. Gentle but implacable, his voice intones the notice of her fate in chains of unchanging pitches, extinguishing melody as her life will be extinguished (example 5). In the quartet, this drama is played out in a new form as each variation combines a return of the theme, often reduced to its distinctive rhythmic profile, with a high degree of melodic expressivity.

EXAMPLE 5. Schubert, "Death and the Maiden." D. 521. Start of Death's reply to the Maiden's plea.

What is consecutive in the song is simultaneous in the quartet; the quartet's melodic process allows the Maiden's subjectivity, generally entrusted to a very volatile first violin, to expand both in scale and scope. The end result, of course, is the same: the mortal voice is silenced and Death's, inevitably, prevails. But the story told is not quite the same. What the song presents as an allegory of cosmic or natural law becomes in the quartet a tragic drama; the Maiden's instrumental voice individualizes itself, expresses a desperation that presumes a personal history and psychology. The song's impersonal gravity becomes the quartet's angry pathos.

In the film this effect translates into a thwarted protest against Isabel Archer's moral and emotional, not physical, death, a cry on behalf of (and in that sense a prolongation of) life. The protest takes both visual and auditory forms.

First, the images accompanied by the quartet music parody or revoke Isabel's initial freedom. Staircases during the first and third excerpts recall the stairs down which Isabel was first drawn by Madame Merle's performance of the A-flat Impromptu; the marble hand from the first excerpt recalls the living hand of the title sequence, pointing to Isabel with the legend *The Portrait of a Lady* inscribed across its palm (thus turning us all into palm readers); the iron grate by the Colosseum in the second excerpt speaks for itself. In the final excerpt, with the multiple images of her face in extreme close-up, Isabel seems to be imprisoned or crushed by the film screen itself, which her face abrades as the music abrades it.

Second, the music in these scenes is warped—fragmented and exacerbated—in response to Isabel's predicament. Though all but one of the variations in the quartet movement are anguished or agitated, the movement sustains an underlying harmonic pattern that offers a degree of mitigation. That pattern is a recurrent rise from a beginning and continuation in the minor mode to a conclusion in the major, a recurrence, one might say, of chances for consolation that affirms a consoling potential even though it

42   *Schubert in* The Portrait of a Lady

ultimately fails to console. The film's quartet music is decisively cut off from this pattern. The only excerpts allowed to conclude are the fragment of variation 2, whose close in the major is immediately revoked by the onset of variation 3, and the semi-complete statement of number 3 itself, which is the only variation in the movement that ends in the minor. The excerpts from variations 1 and 5 are cut off before their conclusions in the major can be heard; variation 4, which is all major, is never heard. In addition, the retroactive turn of the last excerpt to the first variation suggests the workings of a cyclical rather than a progressive movement, the tightening of an emotional noose from which Isabel has only the most narrow and equivocal of escapes.

Third, the quartet music tends to overlap from the scenes it accompanies to those just before or after, as if to suggest that the subjective burden carried by the excerpts cannot be confined to a single place. Heard or unheard, the excerpts form the music of Isabel's married life. They snag the outer furnishings of a privileged domestic life on the coercions that furnish it inwardly.

Finally, the musical relationships between the impromptus and the quartet carry messages of their own. Of particular note is the way the agitations of the A-flat Impromptu's middle section become the distraught first-violin figuration and inexorable rhythms of the quartet excerpts, which lack—expel—the yearning melodic seconds that temper the piano music's turbulence. There is also the important contrast between the solo character of the piano pieces and the collective character of the quartet. The quartet excerpts first penetrate Isabel's psyche in or around a social event, and a forced social event at that, the party supervised by Osmond. Combining its own "social" character with this diegetic association, the quartet music figuratively identifies the mythographic meeting of Death and the Maiden with the destructive force of social rule or pressure. The voice of the song, though divided into the roles of Death and the Maiden, is always the voice of a single subject. The quartet contains such voices—the lamenting cello, the frantic violin—but subsumes them in the collective voice of the ensemble. If the collective speaks as one, it does so only in the form of something like the Freudian superego: an internalized social force, likened to fate by Freud himself, that repeatedly chastises Isabel and compels her to act against her own desires.[11]

---

11. The comments in this paragraph stem from questions posed by Vivian Ramalingan and Mark Slobin, respectively, when I read a shorter version of this paper in November 2000 at a panel organized by James Deaville representing six North American musical societies (mine being the American Musicological Society) at a joint annual meeting (with yet eight others) in Toronto.

The quartet episodes gain still further significance in relation to the film's standard extradiegetic music. Campion uses this music sparingly. Its dominant message (or trigger) is the pressure of sexuality, to which Isabel is highly sensitive but which she does not know how to enjoy and constantly seeks to repress. The first instance involves heavy, pulsating, erotic strings, bound to the minor mode and carrying overtones of both Puccini and the Baroque. The music materializes—as so often in this film, creeping up from the threshold of audibility—after a persistent suitor, whom Isabel both dislikes and desires, touches her face in her London room. The touch provokes a long, quasi-masturbatory scene that segues into an explicit sexual fantasy involving three different men, including Ralph. The pressure of sexuality translates literally here into the heavy stroke of bow on strings. The next instance, to the identical music, occurs in the underground passageway—symbolically the crypt or hellmouth—where Osmond first kisses Isabel, evoking a sexual response reminiscent of her earlier fantasy. (Isabel's arousal expresses itself in faint, half-suppressed moans that form a counterpoint to the music both here and elsewhere.) Osmond's kiss is explicitly the kind that "stops the mouth," cutting off speech with the direct oral production of desire. The film registers this oral leap, which seems to thrill Isabel and threaten her autonomy in equal measure, with the onset of sensuous music. Two scenes of kissing also conjure up such music at the film's conclusion. The die is cast, however, at or even before the very beginning, as "acousmatic" (that is, sourceless) female voices talk candidly about kissing over a black screen just before the opening "music video" begins.[12]

Osmond's kiss remains with Isabel as she goes on a world tour. The sequence that tracks her voyage is shot like an old-fashioned black-and-white movie on a screen-within-the-screen whose slightly rippled edges also suggest an old-fashioned picture postcard. The scene on this card-screen, introduced by piano music that sustains the silent-movie allusion at a certain remove, combines travel footage with erotic fantasy. One memorable sequence shows Osmond at the center of a Hitchcockian pinwheel (derived from his earlier twirling of Isabel's parasol) with a distinct Svengali look on his face, into which a tiny naked Isabel plummets. The tiny figure, seen from behind, is subsequently enlarged and seen frontally, now falling toward the audience. Isabel's memory of the words before Osmond's kiss, "I'm absolutely in love with you," begins with his offscreen voice, but gradually comes to be echoed antiphonally by hers as the Svengali spell completes itself. The subsumption of her voice by his carries the visual imagery of evil-magician

---

12. On the "acousmatic voice" ("voix acousmatique"), see Michel Chion, *La Voix au cinéma* (Paris, 1982).

Osmond and puppet-Isabel into the resonating subjective interior; both her memory and her desire become a mechanical repetition of his words.[13]

It is only a short step from here to the image of Osmond as the personification of Isabel's moral and psychological annihilation: Death to her Maiden. The quartet excerpts that punctuate the scenes from their marriage convey what happens, what it feels and sounds like, as Isabel gradually realizes that her subjectivity has become the unwilling but seemingly helpless host for Osmond's parasitic voice. That voice, in the guise of Schubert's music, inexorably metamorphoses into the image of the truth of her condition, her once-vaunted fate. But it can do so only because—as she did once before—she has opened the door to such music all by herself.

Return: Schubert, Woman to Woman

After the series of quartet excerpts ends—as we've seen, at the nadir and crisis of the diegesis—the film's musical frame structure closes. The soundtrack loops back to the deeper layers of Isabel's Schubertian identity by reprising the Impromptus. It does so at some length, as if to give the subjectivity-laden music, or music-laden subjectivity, room in which to resonate and grow. In musical terms, Isabel frees herself from the inexorability of the quartet music by revisiting and reversing the false promises of the piano music that first tied her story, through Madame Merle, to Gilbert Osmond's. But the relation of the piano music to Isabel is now equivocal—does it echo in her memory, consciously or not, or only in ours?—and it is by no means clear that her newfound autonomy can survive the deathbed reunion with Ralph that it makes possible.

Spurred by her new knowledge, Isabel travels in her carriage to the convent where Pansy has been immured and there unexpectedly encounters Madame Merle. The C-sharp-minor middle section of the A-flat Impromptu accompanies this sequence, beginning with the shadowy, funereal approach of the carriage from the depths of a darkened street. The music is now heard nearly in full, as if to complete the process of discovery curtailed by its earlier interruption. It continues through Madame Merle's fumbling effort to explain her presence, which Isabel rebuffs—undoing the old interpellation—by turning her back on the speaker. But the music does not quite reach completion, and its course spells out the hard truth sealed by this encounter. It does reach the point where the retransition to the more hopeful outer section would begin, but that point is marked by a repeat sign, and the music starts over to end at exactly the spot where it was first

---

13. The play of voices here forms a variant on the pattern described in Kaja Silverman, *The Acoustic Mirror: The Female Voice in Psychoanalysis and Cinema* (Bloomington, Ind., 1988).

interrupted in the piano room. This time, though, the interruption marks not a loss but a repudiation. The idea of a viable link between the two sections of the Impromptu, together with the feelings embedded in them, the idea of a coherent subjectivity grounded in that link and what it symbolizes, has been completely discredited.

Isabel's working-through of the fraught inner and outer journey underscored by the return of the C-sharp-minor music forms the nucleus of her Pyrrhic moral victory, which is sealed a few moments later by a second encounter with, and final rejection of, Madame Merle. Diegetically, this turning point coincides with Madame Merle's disclosure of the film's final secret, the fact that it is Ralph who has made Isabel rich, and with Isabel's biting refusal to rise to the bait. Musically, the moment coalesces with the reprise of the G-flat Impromptu, as if Isabel could be released from the effects of her original interpellation only by repeating its musical substance in full, but transposed to a register of memory that no longer beckons her subjectivity but assumes and reinterprets it.

The G-flat music is introduced behind the image of Madame Merle but appropriated by Isabel, who closes the carriage door in the face of her nemesis to cut off the latter's craven, self-excusing protestation of her own unhappiness. The music continues through the montage of Isabel's journey to Ralph, which mixes images of travel with the visual leitmotif of close-ups on Isabel's face—expressive but ultimately inscrutable, much as this Impromptu is in its mesmerizing appeal to Isabel's primary sense of self. The music ends only when Isabel returns to the piano room where the whole story of her "fate" began, where the piano lid is emblematically closed, and where she circles—gazing out a window, picking up a small dog—with her back constantly turned to the piano. Although the music does not carry over into her reunion with Ralph, Isabel's return to its origin allows her to make at least a temporary peace with the fate that it frames. She is thus able to do in this room something we have never seen her do before, something that Schubert's music has hitherto seemed to keep her from doing: she takes a good, long look at herself in a mirror.

The music for the film's concluding scenes prominently features both strings and piano in a concerto-like texture, thus combining the two sonorities that have guided Isabel's subjectivity throughout. The music, though, is no longer by Schubert, but by the film's own composer, Wojciech Kilar. The shift suggests that Isabel has passed into a new, if melancholy, identity that can no longer be sounded out from inside. Kilar's extradiegetic music acts at a telling remove from the images it would ordinarily be expected to saturate. For better or worse, Isabel has achieved an interiority that has become impenetrable, perhaps even to herself. No longer represented by Schubert, Isabel's subjectivity can no longer be represented at all. It can only be funneled into a convention that associates the piano, regarded as a deep, that is, self-harmonizing, solo voice, with the heightened individuality of a romantic protagonist and supports this pianistic persona on the swelling, collective surge of orchestral strings. (This is the terrain on which Tchaikovsky's First Piano Concerto becomes "Tonight We Love" and Rachmaninoff's Second, "Full Moon and Empty Arms.")

The distanced impression emerges as Isabel transforms her deathbed scene with Ralph into a full-blown *Liebestod,* drawing close to her cousin, kissing him, and lying down next to him, all the while releasing her long-suppressed devotion in a kind of enveloping verbal aria that expands to include his voice as well. Though it is hard to say whether the effect is deliberate, the "music" of her utterance, by which she tries to salvage something from her last lost chance, resists being absorbed in the romantic pathos of the non-Schubertian soundtrack, which begins just as the deathbed scene becomes decisively eroticized, combining the intense intimate dialogue with extreme close-ups of Ralph's and Isabel's faces as they kiss and embrace. This impression is both reinforced and darkened as the film approaches its final group of images. The music, gradually growing louder, continues through the scene of Ralph's funeral, then stops as Isabel wanders alone into the snowy woods. There she encounters her importunate suitor of old and the film renders the novel's most famous moment: a long, passionate kiss, here (though not in the book) initiated and multiplied by Isabel herself, from which she wrenches herself away and flees. The impending kiss is what cues the music, which resumes by picking up on its previous dynamic level and continuing to a climactic crescendo as Isabel races through the bleak snowscape (fig. 6). The romantic-concerto sound is at this point an exercise in pure futility, a failed symbolic continuation of the *Liebestod* with Ralph. At its peak, it leaves Isabel stranded, immobile, almost a fugitive, before a closed door whose knob—not the first of its kind—we have seen her hand turn but not pull.

Campion's use of Schubert in this film has a contemporary antecedent in Christopher Hampton's 1995 *Carrington,* where the slow movement of the String Quintet in C (D. 956, 1828) plays the role that Campion gives to "Death and the Maiden." Hampton's film dramatizes the real-life relationship between the painter Dora Carrington (Emma Thompson) and the Bloomsbury author Lytton Strachey (Jonathan Pryce). The mutual devotion of the pair was complicated, to say the least, by both Strachey's homosexuality and Carrington's heterosexual affairs, the paths of which sometimes crossed. But the devotion was real enough that Carrington shot herself to death shortly after Strachey died in 1931.

FIGURE 6.

Carrington quotes the quintet music three times: once as performed at a concert where Carrington and Strachey, in the audience, decide to live together; shortly thereafter at a happy moment in the new household, where Carrington is shown putting a record of the music on a gramophone; and finally on the soundtrack alone, at length, to accompany the closing sequence of Carrington's suicide. The music equivocates between encapsulating a romantic idyll that does occur and, as Philip Brett has suggested, lamenting the idyll that fails to occur, impeded by Strachey's homosexuality.[14] Unlike Isabel, however, Carrington is never interpellated by the Schubert she hears, even though she self-consciously takes it as the mantra of her union with Strachey. When the sound of the quintet migrates to the soundtrack at the close and there expands, it remains purely extradiegetic, a commentary on or at best an external reflection of Carrington's subjectivity. It is never a virtual form of that subjectivity, as is the case with Isabel. Where Campion's film supports the recognition of Schubert-in-Isabel by framing the sequence of quartet episodes with Isabel's face and filling in the frame with an inventory of bodily images, Hampton combines the music

---

14. See Philip Brett, "Piano Four Hands: Schubert and the Performance of Gay Male Desire," *Nineteenth-Century Music* 21, no. 2 (1997): 171–76.

with a visual sense of distance, even of chill. His film actually dramatizes the progressive disembodiment of the music, from the live players (an odd ensemble, like the Strachey-Carrington household, thanks to Schubert's use of two cellos rather than the usual two violas), to the scratchy gramophone (which we see in operation, clunky old needle apparatus and all, ironically juxtaposed to a medium close-up of Carrington's face—the music to which she comes closest is the most mechanical), and finally to the soundtrack, where the music becomes the auditory equivalent of the empty house, and emptied self, through which Carrington wanders before shooting herself. The point here is not that Campion's usage is superior—Hampton's process of disembodiment accurately comments on the nature of Carrington's "idyll"—but that Campion's rendition of subjectivity in relation to desire is different. In the end, whereas Carrington, too, is disembodied (at the point of her suicide she fades into both an external view of the house and into the music), Isabel becomes the embodiment of the music, or the music of her, as a desiring and despairing subject.

Despite these differences, Campion's Schubert and Hampton's are close cousins—like Ralph and Isabel. Both speak with special intensity at the nadir of the heroine's fortunes. Both closely associate Schubert with her doomed, alienated, sexually tormented subjectivity. That they do so is no accident. Both seem to reflect a changeover during the 1990s from the traditional to a postmodern image of Schubert: from Schubert as a cherubic, naive young man, a bit of a Schlemiel, happy in art if not in love, to Schubert as a socially marginal, syphilitic, workaholic, possibly homosexual man with a wicked temper.[15] The key point is that the second sequence of terms, which would once have served to lower Schubert's status, now serves to raise it. The same logic holds for Schubert's music, the traditional "faults" of which—a supposed tendency to let feeling override form and an indifference to hard-won, heroic resolutions—are now highly prized.

This "nouvelle" Schubert is consistent with a larger cultural tendency to reverse the standard relationship between margin and center: to find normative value precisely where it has most often been denied and conversely to deny it where it has most often been found. According to Slavoj Žižek, "In our permissive times when transgression itself is appropriated, solicited

---

15. Key texts in the construction of the latter-day Schubert include Maynard Solomon, "Franz Schubert and the Peacocks of Benevenuto Cellini," *Nineteenth-Century Music* 12, no. 3 (1989): 193–206; the eight essays collected in *Nineteenth-Century Music* 17, no. 1 (1993): 3–101, a special issue entitled "Schubert: Music, Sexuality, Culture," edited, with a brief introduction, by myself; Susan McClary, "Constructions of Subjectivity in Schubert's Music," in *Queering the Pitch: The New Gay and Lesbian Musicology*, ed. Brett, Elizabeth Wood, and Gary Thomas (New York, 1994), pp. 205–34; Elizabeth Norman McKay, *Franz Schubert: A Biography* (Oxford, 1996); and Brian Newbould, *Schubert: The Music and the Man* (Berkeley, 1997).

even, by the dominant institutions, the predominant opinion as a rule presents itself as a subversive transgression. If one wants to identify the hegemonic intellectual trend, one should simply search for the trend that claims to pose the unheard-of threat to . . . hegemonic power."[16] This formulation conflates a many-sided intellectual disposition with its most thoughtless or stereotyped forms, but it nonetheless marks the limit and difficulty of an important cultural tendency. Žižek is particularly concerned with the inversion of the relation between mourning and melancholy (the latter defined, following Freud, as the refusal to let go of a lost object), one context for which is the work of Butler, who has argued that melancholy may be less a local subjective abnormality than it is the origin of normative subjectivity.[17] The details of the argument are less pertinent here than its strategy of reversal, which accounts in part for its wide appeal during the 1990s. This strategy is also evident in Butler's argument that normative heterosexuality is a form of drag act.[18] In both cases, the reversal of priorities is not conceptually simple, though it is rhetorically brash; Butler qualifies carefully, identifying the indetermination between norm and deviation, not the topsy-turvy recasting of them, as the bearer of critical force. The result is nonetheless to shift a certain symbolic privilege from the standard to the nonstandard or queer, which now becomes the symbol of the true state of affairs.

Butler has also contributed to a third instance of margin-center reversal, the rise to eminence of J. L. Austin's concept of the performative utterance. For Austin, the capacity of language to exert "force" on and in thickly contextualized situations trumps its ability to formulate propositions, the standard by which it has traditionally been defined. What is done in saying, the production of "illocutionary force," exceeds and subsumes "locutionary" or "constative" meaning, the propositional content of what is said. The present familiarity of these distinctions testifies to the cultural power of their implicit hierarchy. Again the needed qualification is duly entered: Austin asserts that all utterances are both locutionary and illocutionary, performative and constative. Nothing is simple, or nothing as simple as it

16. Žižek, "Melancholy and the Act," *Critical Inquiry* 26 (Summer 2000): 658.
17. See Butler, *The Psychic Life of Power: Theories in Subjection* (Stanford, Calif., 1997); for a critique, see Dominick LaCapra, "Trauma, Absence, Loss," *Critical Inquiry* 25 (Summer 1999): 718–21. Butler's argument is a refined form of the reversal to which Žižek objects; it does not elevate the content of melancholy, but its formative role. The argument also occurs in several registers, one concerned specifically with the formation of normative heterosexuality, another more generally with the status of social power as a "lost object" incorporated as the superego.
18. See Butler, "Imitation and Gender Insubordination," in *Inside/Out: Lesbian Theories, Gay Theories*, ed. Diana Fuss (New York, 1991), pp. 13–31.

seems.[19] But the same shift of symbolic privilege occurs: the performative-illocutionary becomes the symbol of the true state of affairs. Butler goes two steps further. She not only stresses, along lines opened by Jacques Derrida, that performativity is "a renewable action without clear origin or end" so that "speech is finally constrained neither by its specific speaker nor its originating context"; she also proposes that "the speech act is a bodily act, and that the 'force' of the performative is never fully separable from bodily force."[20] Qualifications duly entered, even the performative harbors a margin-center structure that is subject to a symbolically powerful inversion.

The parallel to all this in musical iconography retains the simplicity that the philosophical examples avoid, though one may note that not everyone grants the avoidance, as Žižek does not. But musical iconography tends to work in broad strokes. It aims at creating a general orientation from which to listen to certain composers and so to identify them with a general semantic field. Thus in this arena we do get a direct reversal of the traditional polarity such that Schubert replaces his old familiar nemesis, Beethoven, as the musical voice of the universal, the subject qua subject. At least he does so when the *New York Times* publishes a lengthy article by Joseph Horowitz anointing the narrator of *Winterreise*, a figure of radical deprivation, as the true embodiment of that voice as opposed to the Beethoven of the Ninth Symphony, whose explicit claim to embody it has long been granted unreflectively.[21] One needn't assent to Horowitz's value judgments to grasp their symptomatic meaning: Beethoven is now becoming the exception (whom no one needs to emulate) rather than the rule (which no one can emulate) while for Schubert the tendency is the reverse. The agon between the two composers is an old chestnut, but one that refuses to go away. It is one of a series of such agons by which classical music establishes a certain worldly profile. To suggest that the music constantly churns up such deep-seated rivalries gives its history a built-in feeling of drama and importance. Classical music is not effete; it can be taken seriously, like business, sport, or war.

James can be said to have anticipated the iconographical reversal of Beethoven and Schubert when he revised *Portrait of a Lady*. In the first

---

19. See J. L. Austin, *How to Do Things with Words*, ed. J. O. Urmson and Marina Sbisà (Cambridge, Mass., 1962).

20. Butler, *Excitable Speech*, pp. 40, 141. See Jacques Derrida, "Signature Event Context," *Margins of Philosophy*, trans. Alan Bass (Chicago, 1982), pp. 307–30. See also Stanley Fish, "With the Compliments of the Author: Reflections on Austin and Derrida," *Critical Inquiry* 8 (Summer 1982): 693–722, and Gordon C. F. Bearne, "Sounding Serious: Cavell and Derrida," *Representations*, no. 63 (Summer 1998): 65–92.

21. See Joseph Horowitz, "A Journey through the Bleakest of Winters," *New York Times*, 12 Dec. 1999, sec. 2, p. 41.

version of the interpellation scene, it is Beethoven that Madame Merle is playing.[22] James's turning the job over to Schubert suggests a softening of his irony; Isabel may be no hero, but there is moral beauty in her failure. She knows not what she is, but she recognizes Schubert. Roll forward about a century, and the softening becomes a dissolve. Campion and Hampton invoke a Schubert who is a heroic figure precisely because he no longer needs to be a hero; he is a paradigmatic example of the wounded subject who has become the new ideal. And it is this Schubert whose music can speak for both Carrington and Isabel, speak *as* both Carrington and Isabel, neither of whom can find love in the right place. The music refuses to judge them for this, and in the refusal lies its latter-day meaning.[23]

In Campion's film, the music's embrace of the broken self, or more exactly of the break that it takes to constitute selfhood, is confined neither to the narrative specifics of the diegesis nor even to the invocation of the postmodern Schubert as Isabel Archer's alter ego. The musical vicissitudes of Schubert in Isabel's story all reenact the core trope of center-margin reversal, which they invest with the full force of musical affect and impulse. In other words, the music repeatedly translates a conceptual indeterminacy into a symbolic priority. The process begins with the movement, literally tracked by Isabel's following the sound of the A-flat Impromptu to its source, from aesthetic recognition to interpellation, and more particularly from the compelling Beethovenian traits of autonomy and veracity to the seductive Schubertian ones of intimacy and illusion. Thereafter the symbolic priority goes to the Schubertian soundtrack itself in excess of the narrative image, and this at several levels, though without overtly disrupting the image's conventional centrality.[24] Thus we have the general displacement, the synoptic compression, of Isabel's narrative into Schubert's music; into music that both does ("Death and the Maiden") and does not (the Impromptus) have textual associations that reproduce that narrative as an allegory of her fate; and into a musical "form" that is both narratively open (all made of excerpts, most lacking cadences) and musically closed (the A B A cycle from Impromptus to Quartet to Impromptus).

---

22. See the textual appendix to *PL*, p. 517.

23. On Schubert's own contribution to the ideal of the wounded self, see my *Franz Schubert: Sexuality, Subjectivity, Song* (Cambridge, 1998), esp. 1–38. The elements of the ideal were already in play in Schubert's day, which, however, sought to contain them (and even to value them by containing them) through the exercise of social and aesthetic judgment. Schubert's songs can often be understood as attempts to bypass or forestall that exercise.

24. This shift in priority can be understood as a marked, reflexive form of the constitutive relationship between music and the nexus of words and images. On the general topic, see my *Musical Meaning: Toward a Critical History* (Berkeley, 2001), pp. 145–93.

52 *Schubert in* The Portrait of a Lady

For Campion, it would seem, the force of this music is ultimately affirmative, grim as Isabel Archer's fate may be. The Isabel of the soundtrack structure, the closed Schubertian A B A, may achieve a self-sufficiency that negates, though it does not efface, the deprivation of the Isabel who finishes the diegesis. Each of these Isabels has a music of her own. Like the protagonist of *Winterreise*, which the wintry close of the film may well evoke, the Schubertian Isabel has chosen unsatisfied desire as the mark of her authenticity. As in the song cycle, that lack of satisfaction finds a paradoxically nourishing form in the music that expresses it—not the romantic-concerto music we hear while we watch Isabel race through the snow, but the music of Schubert in which she has consummated her choice and cocooned her lovelorn identity. The shift of musical styles during this episode thrusts the Schubert medley decisively into the past, towards which Isabel can be said to be running, seeking again the now empty room to which the sound of the A-flat Impromptu first drew her.

But she is also running into the future. Surrounded by the snows of yesteryear, Isabel is more a paradigm than a person, as much so as the postmodern Schubert who is her tutelary spirit. The cocoon the two have woven together is, like all cocoons, a liminal space. Isabel's story is over, but it could be just beginning: "She could be today's girl, but she happens to live in 1870." So her story is not quite over because the stories of her heirs, the girls in the opening video, have scarcely begun. Campion's Schubert defines the space of vital marginality from which those stories can be imagined, not least by their appointed heroines, even if he has nothing to say to them. His music becomes the medium in which Isabel's thwarted fate survives as a possibility for others because it alone has not been given up. The music secures this survival not simply by giving symbolic priority to the figure of the tormented outsider but by establishing both the historical distance and the contemporary nearness of that figure in the same breath, at the same time. The film's postmodern voice belongs to Schubert. And the Schubert it belongs to is above all a figure of relocated social power, the bellwether of a change not just in musical politics but in the politics of subjectivity.

CHAPTER 13

Haydn's Chaos, Schenker's Order; or,
Musical Meaning and Musical Analysis: Can They Mix?

For most of the twentieth century, meaning was regarded as a hindrance to understanding music. Good listening was supposed to be based on close attention to the articulation of style, form, and structure. Music theory and its sibling, musical analysis, assumed the role of describing these fundamentals of technique and training listeners to perceive them; musicology constructed the history and taxonomy of technique and made aesthetic judgments on it. There was no place in this system for a critical or critical-historical hermeneutics. Musical expression could, of course, be talked about--how could one avoid it? – but it was widely regarded as problematical and often left at the level of cliché or worse (how do we know that the Funeral March of the ›Eroica‹ is sad?). Historical trends and events could be invoked as a general background (Napoleonic politics for the ›Eroica‹) but not discerned at the heart of the music itself. Meaning, dismissively qualified as programmatic or extramusical, was understood to attach superficially to what was truly musical about music, which it also misrepresented or trivialized. Although music is obviously saturated with meanings ascribed to it in practice by its listeners and listening practices, performers and performance practices, these meanings were not recognized as an intrinsic and legitimate part of musical experience. Instead they were relegated at best to the dialectic of what Carl Dahlhaus called »formalization«, the process whereby some semantic content finds expression in music but is eventually discarded as the music reaches ever higher stages of purely internal elaboration.[1] »The meaning of a piece of music,«

---

1 Dahlhaus: Beethoven, p. 34-42. The notion of formalization stems ultimately from Wagner's 1857 essay on Liszt's program music. See also James Hepokoski's review of Werbeck: Tondichtungen, p. 603-24, esp. 605-612.

as Roger Scruton formulated the prevailing principle in the century's closing decade, »is what we understand when we understand it as music«.[2]

These ideals, of course, were neither accepted by everyone nor everywhere enforced with the same degree of rigor. Nor were they often applied to the less prestigious, i.e., popular, forms of music. Nonetheless, the overall trend was very dominant until the turn of the 1990s, at which point a counter-tendency emerged, in the first instance among American musicologists. Sometimes labeled »the new musicology«, this development was prompted both by a recognition of the concern with critical theory, along with the quarrel between theory and history, that had been preoccupying scholarship in the humanities for the previous two decades, and by a desire to come to grips with the social dimensions of music, particularly as a branch of the broader social construction of subjectivity.[3] By the time the century ended, the whole field of Anglophone musical scholarship had been transformed by a reorientation toward meaning and its problems. (For proof, just examine the programs of the annual meetings of the American Musicological Society across the 1990s.) But the transformation was not accomplished evenly, nor without controversy, nor, even more to the point, without certain received ideas managing to survive more or less intact via a process of subtle retrenchment.

One of the most important of the latter concerns the relationship between musical meaning and musical form, or, what amounts to the same thing at an institutional level, between musical hermeneutics and musical analysis. Many musical analysts would nowadays be glad to concede that music has what would still probably be called extramusical meanings, but most would also still insist that such meanings, to be valid, must be strictly derivable from the musical structures that it is the province of analysis to specify. Many historical musicologists would still agree. The result is to limit the range and richness of musical meaning, to perpetuate its secondariness, and also, in reaction, to generate a certain impatience with analytic interests on the part of those more concerned with meaning. The wider quarrel between theory and history thus plays itself out anew. And though it is no more likely to be settled to everyone's satisfaction in this venue than in any other, the musical version of this quarrel is potentially instructive because it is so explicit. A look at it may be useful both within and beyond the narrow – but it turns out not to be so narrow – arena of musical understanding.

---

[2] Scruton: Aesthetics of Music, p. 344.
[3] For overviews of these developments, see Williams: Constructing Musicology, and Cook: Musical Meaning, p. 170-95.

488

In what follows I will try to show that musical meaning is not extramusical, not secondary, and not, as it is often unreflectively claimed to be, merely »subjective« in an invidious sense. Some degree of musical analysis remains indispensable in the process of critical interpretation, but analytically specified structures can neither determine nor control meaning. Nor can they automatically claim to be meaningful in themselves simply because they can be analytically specified. This should not, however, be taken as an argument against analysis itself – as I just observed, some degree of analysis is indispensable – but only against the conceptual and institutional claims that have traditionally been made on behalf of analytic knowledge and its (theoretical) objects.

The focal point of this argument is a classic analytic study by Heinrich Schenker of the introduction to Haydn's oratorio ›The Creation‹ (1799), »The Representation of Chaos«. This text has been chosen not just because of Schenker's dominant role in music analysis in the English-speaking world, but also because it represents an explicit attempt by Schenker himself to move from analysis to interpretation – something he did more often than was once acknowledged. This focus on Schenker involves a certain restrictiveness, in that only one type of analysis comes under scrutiny. This is both linear analysis (its common designation) and depth analysis, meaning, on the one hand, any analytical approach that engages, strictly or loosely, with the Schenkerian conception of »free composition« (der freie Satz) as the continuous elaboration (or »prolongation«) of elemental contrapuntal patterns, and, on the other hand, any approach that grants constructive power to background patterns that are not themselves music, that is, are not sounded as such, but may be heard only »through« rather than »as« the musical foreground or »music itself«. This orientation clearly carries with it a preference for certain musical repertoires as well as for certain analytical methods. Much of what follows, however, should apply mutatis mutandis both to other approaches and to other musics. It may also, or so I hope, open up lines of communication between the problem of musical meaning and the broader discipline of hermeneutics, which has too often tended to give music short shrift, if any at all.

For those not schooled in Schenker's system, the next two paragraphs should provide a sufficient basis to follow the subsequent discussion.

Schenker claims that the masterpieces of tonal music are »composed out« from a contrapuntal skeleton consisting of a simple bass progression, tonic to dominant to tonic, supporting a scalewise descent of three, five, or eight tones (the first of which is denominated the head tone [*Kopfton*]) to the first scale degree. This descent, *die Urlinie*, combined with the bass, gives the background structure of the composition, *der Ursatz*; it has become customary in English-language analysis not to translate the terms given here in German. The composing-out process takes the form of the »prolongation« of these elemental background features through several layers of »middleground« structure until the »foreground«, the acoustic »surface« of the piece, is reached. An important role in this process is played by »linear progressions«, ascending or descending sequences of three, four, or five notes that guide the musical action of one structural layer from the layer(s) beneath. These progressions sometimes act like musical motives, and sometimes like small-scale versions of the *Urlinie*.

Schenker developed a system of graphic notation to represent these relationships. The basic key to reading the graphs is that, except at the foreground level, note-values do not indicate duration, as in normal musical notation, but structural importance. Linear progressions are indicated by slurs; scale-degrees by careted numerals; background relationships by beams. In the course of analysis, it is sometimes necessary to specify the exact registral position of a note. In the present essay, this is done by means of superscripts. The note c^1 is middle C; c^2 and c^3, respectively, the C's an octave and two octaves higher. The notes in the lower octave are designated by lower-case letters without superscript. In cases where registral specification is unnecessary, notes are designated by upper-case letters.

The particularities of Schenker's system can be, and have been, subject to endless dispute, and the version of it under discussion in this essay was later refined and revised by Schenker himself. The core concept, however, the intelligible dynamic relationship between a surface and a depth, has considerable historical resonance and for many people still seems to carry intuitive conviction. It may be wrong in many ways, but there is something right about it, too. Why, then, does it, and the mindset to which it appeals, have such a troubled relationship to the question of meaning?

1.

The bone of contention between linear analysis and critical hermeneutics is the cardinal point that the deep structures proposed by analysis are, as just noted, not normally heard as such, heard as music. They are both inaccessible to immediate perception and qualitatively neutral. One can, of course, learn to hear through to them, at least some of them, but even so it makes little sense to assign them an expressive character apart from the surface presentations they are felt to organize. In a sense, they remain closed off from – one might say deaf to – these surface presentations, to which they remain impervious, impermeable, incapable of being changed or affected by them.

490

From the critical standpoint, this faceless character renders deep structures useless, even a hindrance. Critical interpretation must pay constant attention to the foreground details of expression, representation, texture, and lyric or narrative impetus from which analysis necessarily abstracts. In the literary and cultural theory of the 1980s and 90s, such attention to what might be called signifying surfaces became a means of challenging the very concept of deep structures, even when the operative theoretical base – deconstruction, psychoanalysis, new historicism, cultural studies – accorded with Schenkerian analysis in treating surface phenomena as symptomatic of something less immediate. The same imperative grounds a famous witticism by Arnold Schoenberg, who joked that his favorite parts of Beethoven's ›Eroica‹ Symphony turn up only as the inessential little notes in Schenker's graphic analysis of the piece. Being faceless, deep structures can have nothing to contribute to the interplay of values, representations, and communicative acts which forms the matrix of critical interpretation.

The same territory looks very different from an analytic standpoint. True enough, linear analysis is striking, and problematical, for its ability to consume signifying surfaces: to consume them, indeed, in the very process of accounting for them. Analysis posits deep structures that are elaborated into a signifying surface--the musical foreground – without being contingent in any way on what that surface might signify. The foreground of the Funeral March in the ›Eroica‹ may try to confront human mortality in the light of modern warfare; the middleground and background do not. From the classical analytic standpoint, this independence – a version of the imperviousness I spoke of earlier – is a strength; it gives the deep structures their universalizing power.

Even so, other depth-surface theories do not require severances of this order. Take classical psychoanalysis, for example, a product of the same cultural milieu as Schenkerian analysis. For Freud, the structural effect of a repressed thought is inextricable from its worldly bearing, the nexus of desire, law, and circumstance that impels its repression. Traces of this nexus always mark the dreams or symptoms to which the thought contributes, and from which it can in turn glean new derivatives. Psychoanalysis may have owed part of its immense mid-twentieth-century impact on social thought to just this persistence of worldly connections. Freud's ›Interpretation of Dreams‹ and ›Psychopathology of Everyday Life‹ read in part like in-depth surveys of Viennese customs, habits, and quirks.

Classical accounts of the linear analysis of music do not allow for such continuities between structural levels, and make it hard to say just where or how the elaboration of a musical structure acquires a worldly bearing, or, indeed, is even consistent with one. For Schenker himself, it is precisely the »mystery« of the composing-out process from »background-depth« to »foreground-breadth« that produces the »complete independence of music from the outside world, a self-containment which distinguishes music from all the other arts«.[4]

Few present-day analysts would go that far, at least in theory, but most analytical practice still devalues – normatively devalues – the communicative action of the foreground. The rationale for this devaluation stems partly from the artistic ideal of organic form and partly from the conceptual ideal of »hard« knowledge. These are the legacies, respectively, of nineteenth-century aesthetics and science, disciplinary areas that may originally have appealed to different interests and values, but that nevertheless share a surprising number of assumptions. There is a covert alliance between the critic's (if not the artist's) quest for unity-in-variety in art and the researcher's quest for lawlike regularities in positive science. Music analysis, both Schenkerian and otherwise, has tended to combine these two quests, setting itself an arduous task that can claim to be pursued with rigor and even a kind of epistemic heroism. In particular, the linear analysis of music locates the coherence of a variegated discourse in relationships of underlyingness or subsumption. Aesthetically, the deep structures that articulate these relationships testify to the immanent presence of organic unity and to the consequent identity of structure and expression. Epistemologically, the same structures provide a distinctively musical mode of intelligibility and ground it in what Schenker, invoking (all too aptly) the preestablished harmony of Leibnizian monads, calls a »final immutable nucleus« for surface transformations.[5]

Deep structures both authorize and embody sameness amid difference, stability amid change, simplicity amid complexity. Binary oppositions of this type are a familiar topos in what can by now be called classical deconstruction, which examines the aims and outcomes of the »metaphysical« orientation that seeks to make the first, centripetal term the foundation, truth, or governing principle of the second, centrifugal one. It seems fair to say that the tradition of musical analysis, in its modern forms, has been unblushingly metaphysical in this sense, ripe for the Derridean plucking.[6] The tradition might even be said to be moved by a desire to secure music as a metaphysical preserve in a world increasingly alienated from metaphysical positions. From this standpoint, the facelessness of musical deep structures is a sign of their authenticity. The aim of linear analysis, as

---

4 From Schenker: Das Meisterwerk, v. 3; translation from Kalib: Thirteen Essays, p. 512. Subsequent translations from ›Das Meisterwerk‹ are my own unless otherwise indicated.
5 Schenker: Das Meisterwerk, v. 1, p. 194.
6 On Derrida and binarism, see Culler: On Deconstruction, pp. 85-134, 150-56.

Whittall and Jonathan Dunsby put it, is to »identify some kind of fundamental structure [*Ursatz*] which can be said to determine, through composing out, the entire surface of the piece in question«.[7] Schenker, writing less coolly, is more explicit about what this determination entails:

> [Musical] content [...] emerges out of a clairvoyantly-perceived connection which is at the outset in the depth of a background. Only the connection of depth from the background to the foreground constitutes connection of breadth in the horizontal direction of the foreground. Only such a connection, even taken biologically, constitutes the actual organic connection, the synthesis of a musical composition, its living breath.[8]

Inexpressive in itself, the *Ursatz* supplies the underlying vital principle, the living interconnectedness, on which the expressivity of the foreground ultimately depends.[9]

With so much to divide hermeneutics and analysis, any mixing of the two might seem like an exercise in futility. Each seems to render the other incoherent as a matter of principle. Yet the suppositions that underwrite this division are highly questionable.

On the critical side, the apparent qualitative neutrality of deep structures is not sufficient to distinguish them from foreground structures that are supposed to be qualitatively rich. Considered in isolation, a sforzando or a pungent dissonance, a melodic shape or a rhythmic profile, is just as neutral as a middleground linear progression. Signifying surfaces cannot simply be decoded; they must be interpreted before their signifying and expressive power can be released.[10] And once one starts interpreting, there is nothing, literally nothing, that cannot assume a qualitative, signifying value. By its own standard of omnivorousness, criticism cannot dismiss the results of analysis.

Even less, perhaps, can analysis dismiss the results of critical interpretation. On the analytical side, the fact that the deeper structural layers are independent of the expressive character of the foreground does not forbid the surface and depth to interact: to mirror, qualify, contradict, clarify, or obscure each other. The dynamism between layers may have qualitative

---

7   Dunsby / Whittall: Music Analysis, p. 109, parentheses omitted.
8   Kalib: Thirteen Essays, p. 510.
9   Compare John Rothgeb's pungent statement that »surface associations . . . would be almost trivial without the foil provided for them by the underlying tonal configurations«, cited in Cohn: Autonomy, p. 164. Cohn calls for a partial deprivileging of the *Ursatz* within Schenkerian analysis, in order to show »how motive, form, rhythm, and other aspects of ›design‹ interact with harmony and counterpoint, in a complex mutual feedback of autonomous forces« (pp. 169-70). This is surely a step in the right direction. But why should »autonomous« forces resign themselves to a »mutual feedback«? And why should we suppose that musical forces are »autonomous« in the first place?
10 For discussions of interpretation that bear on this point (and the next), see Fish: Circumstances; Kramer: Outline; Mailloux: Interpretation; and de Man: Semiology.

value even if the deeper layers have none. The dynamism itself may be a means of disseminating qualitative value from surface to depth. The deep structures may lose, even sooner rather than later, their incapacity to be affected by the surfaces above them; they may even wriggle out of their abstract, theoretical existence in the direction of some sort of sensuous life. And the fact that one structural layer is more stable than another does not automatically make the more stable layer more primary or foundational. There is no self-evident reason why deep structures (perhaps several of them in a single composition, rather than just one) cannot be understood to be generated from the top down, foreground to background, and this in any number of ways: confidently, deceptively, perfunctorily, desperately, and so on. In such cases, the dynamism between layers will once again act both to produce and to transmit qualitative values. Meaning can shape structure no less, perhaps more, than structure can shape meaning.

To illustrate these last points in a preliminary way, we can turn to a first consideration of »Representation of Chaos«. As Schenker's graphic analysis shows, the *Urlinie* of this piece completes its descent at an early moment, only two-thirds of the way through (example 1).

494

As the graph does *not* show, the foreground realization of this completion – »the Great Tattoo«, as I have called it elsewhere – is brutal and disruptive, by all odds the most violent moment in the piece (example 2).

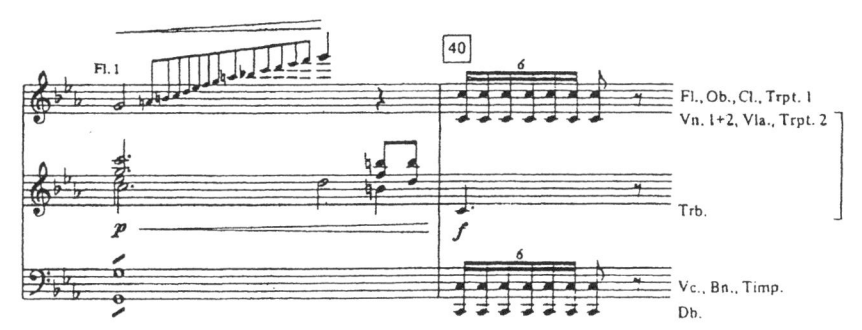

[Musical example: measure 40, showing Fl. 1, Fl., Ob., Cl., Trpt. 1; Vn. 1+2, Vla., Trpt. 2; Trb.; Vc., Bn., Timp.; Db.]

Since Haydn is representing primordial chaos here, the possibility arises that the descent of the *Urlinie* should be regarded as premature, as a failure of structural integrity prompted by the expressive and representational values of the foreground. The representation of chaos in the Classical, Biblical, and cosmological sources available to Haydn all agree that chaos is not only the antithesis of order in general but of music – consonant music – in particular; the creation of the world coincides with the passage from discord to concord. Haydn draws on this tradition to represent chaos at its worst as a violence done to the consonant essence of music, a violence that, imparted to this essence, renders it monstrous. Whatever the background here may be, it is not qualitatively neutral, not unaffected by the foreground.

The conclusion seems clear: the logic by which hermeneutics and analysis seek to depreciate each other is untenable. Its failure, a fortunate one, opens the possibility that works of music may establish a continuity, a running dialogue, between their deep structures, their signifying surfaces, and their cultural, historical, and discursive fields of affiliation. Deep structures may thus become accessible to critical interpretation.

As an object of interpretation, however, a deep structure will not be the kind of foundational truth it has customarily been taken to be. Though it may have foundational value on one occasion, on another it may be significant primarily as a response to some value or representation given in the foreground, or as itself a kind of foreground elaboration of a nonmusical deep structure given in the cultural field. If theory and criticism are to mix, criticism must learn to love abstractions, but theory must do something harder: it must loosen its claims to epistemological authority. Epistemological authority itself must become a decentered and migratory term, circulating everywhere but at home nowhere.

2.

Schenker's analysis of Haydn's »Representation of Chaos« furnishes a useful test case for these claims. As we will see, the analysis goes very well with a hermeneutic approach, but only if we step back from Schenker's foundationalist assumptions. The analysis itself need not be challenged. Instead, it needs to be appropriated on behalf of a looser, more pervasive, and more historicized process of interpretation than Schenker was willing or able to allow.

Since the music itself is explicitly representational, one can argue compellingly that an adequate understanding of it must include an account of its representational value. This point is not lost on Schenker. Haydn, he claims, was intent on »stretching and straining [the] means [of musical art]« so far that their »riddles« would recall the »riddles of creation«.[11] These riddles turn on the »inextricably linked« concepts of chaos and »the genesis of light and life«,[12] concepts that find their musical projections, respectively, in vertical stasis and linear motion. For Schenker, Haydn's chaos corresponds to a series of monolithic »thrusts« [Stösse]: dramatic unison or chordal attacks by the full orchestra. The thrusts occur as clearly isolated foreground events at structural turning-points (e.g. mm. 1, 9, 40). Gradually, chaos as embodied in these thrusts is »mollified« or »appeased« (besänftigt) to the point of negation.

The work of appeasement is carried out by a continuous chain of three large-scale linear progressions extending from the midpoint to the end of the movement (mm. 31-40, 40-49, 50-59). The track of these progressions manifests itself in the foreground by a continual »sinking« (*Senkung*) in the register of structural tones. The sinking leads from eb^3 – not coincidentally the *Kopfton* – all the way to c^1. When c^1 is reached, »the registral tension is over, chaos expires (*atmet aus*), light appears«.[13] Example 3 outlines this process and at the same time amplifies Schenker's account of it. The registral action at first cuts across and finally coalesces with the tripartite division of the movement determined by the grand linear progressions, a division further demarcated by the recurrence of the chord a^{1b6}, the »chaos chord« that acts throughout as a referential sonority. With each sinking in structural register, melodic activity in the register(s) left behind becomes

---

11 »Deshalb ergibt sich auch Haydn bei der Darstellung des Chaos durchaus den Grundsätzen seiner Kunst, ist aber freilich beflissen, ihre Mittel so weit zu strecken, zu spannen, daß sie wie in Rätseln an die Rätsel des Chaos gemahnen«, Schenker: Meisterwerk, v. 2, p. 161.

12 »Mit der Vorstellung des Chaos ist untrennbar ein Werden von Licht und Leben verknüpft«. Schenker: Meisterwerk, v. 2, p. 161.

13 Schenker: Meisterwerk, v. 2. p. 168.

496

notably transparent in its prolongational character, a process that culminates in the more perfect transparency of octave doubling in the measures just preceding the closing cadence.

Reasonably enough, Schenker's hermeneutic practice is guided by his foundationalist assumptions. He generates meaning from the bottom up, constructing a parallel in which interpretive unfolding follows compositional unfolding. First, he selects important elements in the deep structure as the sources of meaning. Second, he scans the foreground realizations of those elements for qualitative values. Third, he projects these values rhetorically onto an *ad hoc* image of chaos. Then – and the point is important – he stops.

The problem with this approach is not the projective use of rhetoric, which is necessary to any hermeneutic effort. It is not even the reliance on ad hoc imagery; virtually all interpretation has an informal, improvisatory dimension that supplies part of its energy and often has good results. The problem, rather, is Schenker's assumption that the structural background is foundational in the strongest sense, that it supplies the essential truth to which all further knowledge of the music can be subordinated. The effect of this assumption is to impoverish interpretation. The background must be richly specified; its meaning can be relatively threadbare without serious loss. The specific meaning matters far less than the relationship that allows some meaning or other to be »composed out« of the background along with the *Ursatz*.

Both conceptually and historically, Schenker's hermeneutic makes tunnel vision a virtue; it blanks out the semantic complexity of meaning on one side, and the historical particularity of meaning on the other. For Schenker, deep structure gives meaning but cannot receive it. Descriptions of the deep structure, however derived, thus acquire too much interpretive power. They transfer meaning to the foreground while remaining impervious, indeed indifferent, to the conceptual and imagistic resources of the traditions supporting the representational or expressive character of the foreground. In the representative case of Haydn's chaos, Schenker's order precludes more meaning than it confers. Although his own resources happen to overlap with Haydn's at several points – for instance the emphasis on enigma and the link between chaos and light – Schenker sees no reason to reflect on this relationship, and thus gives up the chance to benefit from it.

To illustrate the loss that results, we can return to the »Representation of Chaos« and Schenker's problematical treatment of its *Urlinie*. As the graphic analysis shows (example 1), the descent of the fundamental line forms the first of the three grand linear progressions by which chaos, for Schenker, is mollified. Schenker's commentary on this descent celebrates its unifying effect. The descending progression e^{b2}-d^2-c^2 (mm. 37-40), he writes, not only leads to the cadence that resolves the tension surrounding e^{b3}, the *Kopfton* (m. 9, prolonged at m. 31), but also answers the ascending motive c^3-d^3-e^{b3}, which completes the initial ascent to the *Kopfton* and forms, besides, the first melodic passage in the movement (mm. 7-9).

As we have seen, however, what is structural resolution in the background of this music is violent disruption in the foreground. Schenker does not fail to notice this problem, but he does fail to be sufficiently startled by it, to be moved to interrogate it. He simply remarks that »Chaos is not yet mollified – suddenly a new thrust surprises us«.[14] He does not acknowledge the sharp, not to say blatant, contradiction in the fact that the center of the musical structure should be realized, not as a mollification, but as a thrust. It does not occur to him to read this contradiction in other than formal terms, in this case as a demand for registral »sinking« imposed by the e^{b3}, and it emphatically does not occur to him to ask whether the contradiction alters the status of the *Ursatz* itself. For Schenker the foundationalist, the claims of structure always take precedence over the claims of meaning. With Haydn's ›Chaos‹ movement, Schenker heeds this imperative to the point of correcting the music. At m.40, where the *Urlinie* completes its descent, structural levels a and b of Schenker's graph align the first scale degree with a structural phantom: the tonic triad, *not* notated in the parentheses that would indicate implied rather than actual presence, that Haydn carefully left out.

On the historical side, Schenker's scheme of rough thrusts and gradual sinking suggests a kind of Big Bang theory of creation in which chaos proves to be self-limiting. Chaos on this model is doomed to ebb away, to yield itself *decrescendo* to natural or divine law as embodied, by Haydn, in the laws of tone. Chaos, we might say, yields to law much as the confusions of a musical foreground yield to the clarity of the background.[15] For Haydn to have followed such a model, however, is almost inconceivable. The representation of chaos in Western discourse is remarkably consistent from antiquity through the Enlightenment. Examination of the standard sources, most notably the Bible, Plato's ›Timaeus‹, and Ovid's ›Metamorphoses‹, clearly interdicts any idea of self-limitation. The chaos of traditional cosmogony can never simply expire. Instead, it must be mastered, wrested into cosmos from without by a divine creator. The creation from this perspective is the primordial instance of the sublime, and its magni-

---

14 Schenker: Meisterwerk, v. 2. p. 167.
15 Schenker himself used this metaphor in ›Free Composition‹ (trans. Oster, p. xxiii), identifying the temporality of the present with »the whole of the foreground, which men call chaos«.

tude – the clash of divine power and resistant materiality – sounds out clearly in the violence of the unavailing cadential thrusts that end the first two of Schenker's three grand linear progressions.

Mastery over chaos begins when the primordial tract of boundlessness is tranformed into intelligible space. This process involves both the division of matter into the four elements (earth, air, fire, and water) and, what concerns us more, the circumscription of the whole. The Biblical image for this circumscription occurs in Proverbs (8.27) in words ascribed to Wisdom: »When [God] prepared the heavens, I was there: when he set a compass [i.e., a circular boundary] on the face of the deep«. Plato concurs; the eternal god, he claims, fashioned the world »in a rounded spherical shape, with extremes equidistant in all directions from the center, a figure that has the greatest degree of completeness and uniformity«.[16] A printer's ornament familiar through the seventeenth century shows the divine hand tracing a circle in chaos; Milton's account in ›Paradise Lost‹ does likewise, construing the Biblical compass in a modern, rationalist sense:

> He took the golden Compasses, prepar'd
> In God's Eternal store, to circumscribe
> This Universe, and all created things:
> One foot he center'd, and the other turn'd
> Round through the vast profundity obscure,
> And said, Thus far extend, thus far thy bounds,
> Thus be thy just Circumferance, O World.[17]

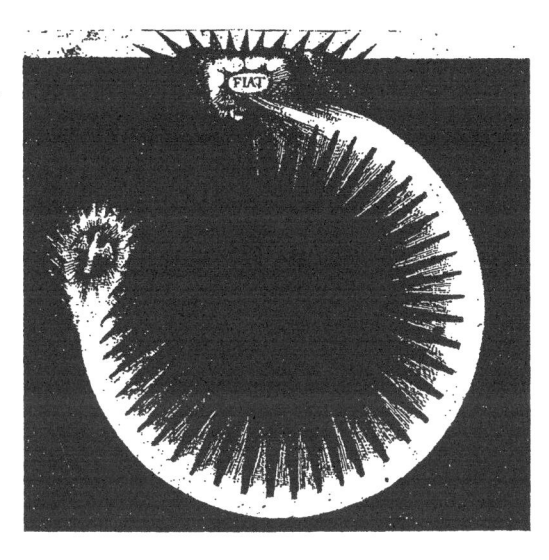

An illustration in Robert Fludd's cosmogony, ›Utriusque Cosmi Historia‹ (›The History of both Worlds‹, 1624, figure 1), shows this first act of creation becoming intelligible as the light of the first day traces out the cosmic sphere and begins to fill it. Finally, in a critical rather than reverent spirit, William Blake's Milton-inspired etching of 1794, ›The Ancient of Days‹ (figure 2), polemically links the

---

16   Plato: Timaeus, p. 44.
17   Milton: Paradise Lost.

ideals of divine mastery and scientific rationalism by extending the creator's left, or »sinister«, hand into a pincer-like pair of compasses.

With this field of affiliation in view, we can return to the question of how to interpret the linear motion that Schenker finds in Haydn's »Representation of Chaos«. The first item to consider, or consider yet again, is the one that raises the interpretive question most acutely, the descent of the *Urlinie* in mm. 39-40 (example 2). A hermeneutic window is offered here by a fairly drastic foreground event: the sharp contrast between g^3 in m. 39 and c^1 in m. 40. The g^3 sounds at the top of a run on the solo flute and marks the registral apex of the movement; the c^1 is the weightiest tone in the orchestral thrust, the Great Tattoo, that invokes the first scale degree, a role c^1 also plays in the famous unison (the *Urklang*) with which the movement opens.[18]

In this setting, the registral sinking that traverses the chain of grand linear progressions might be understood as the symbolic filling-in of a void: the musical space between g^3 and c^1. The filling-in reaches its goal, a goal as much qualitative as structural, with the quiet cadence to c^1 that ends the movement (mm. 58-59). Technically, the concluding c^1 is no more than a prolongation of the first scale degree of the *Urlinie*, reached as c^2 in m. 40. So strong, however, is the foreground contrast between disruption at m. 40 and closure later on that this technical truth is put into question.[19] At best, we might say that the c^2 of m. 40 is reconfigured by subsequent events so that it assumes its structural value only in retrospect. The weight and continuity of the registral process that envelops m. 40, however, suggests that the reconfiguration is more radical: that the true structural tone is the cadential c^1. Chaos is subdued (not »mollified«) when c^1, extracted from the core of the *Urklang* and Great Tattoo, stands alone as the Archimedean point of creation. This shift in value is enhanced by the fact

---

18 The unison at m. 40 covers an e^{b1} on the horns which sounds for half a beat after the unison ends. This e^{b1} is omitted from ex. 2; its significance is suggested in ex. 4.
19 A friction, it should be added, even a contradiction, arises in m. 40 itself between the sonoric weight of c^1 and the structural value of c^2.

that the last of Schenker's grand linear progressions (mm. 50-59) leads to the cadential c^1 from g^1, a structural correlate of the earlier foreground g^3. This last progression sounds with a clarity that gradually spreads from the depth to the surface. Perhaps it should be taken as a corrective, a kind of idealized *alter ego* to the less-than-ideal *Urlinie*.

As the filling-in of an intervallic abyss, Haydn's registral/structural sinking sounds the way Fludd's and Blake's pictures look. The music makes up in breadth what it necessarily lacks in pictorial exactitude. In returning to – and thereby unveiling – its point of origin by moving methodically across musical »space«, it, too, gives a »just Circumference« to the world. And in so doing it represents, not a chaos in spontaneous recession, but a chaos being mapped and mastered, an always-incipient locale being delimited and enclosed by the drawing of a continuous boundary. At the level of musical structure, this process manifests itself in two ways: figuratively, in the quasi-spatial image produced by the sinking, and conceptually, in the reconfiguring of foreground disruptions as elements of deep structure.

As Blake's ›Ancient of Days‹ suggests, the traditional imagery of creation acquires new meanings in the era of modern science. In the influential formulations of Descartes and Bacon, the boundary that makes nature intelligible is the one that divides the subject of knowledge from the object known. In turn, in the form of detachment, impartiality, objectivity, this division is the vehicle of mastery over nature and authority over culture.[20] Conceptually, such mastery involves reducing the apparent chaos of natural phenomena to law, something that Blake suggests by the continuity between the compasses and the powerfully muscled body of his creator. As Kant put it, the modern scientist understands that reason must not let itself »merely toddle along, as it were, in Nature's leading strings«, but must instead »take the lead with principles of judgment based on fixed laws and compel Nature to answer its [reason's] questions«.[21] Kant's imagery plainly identifies the mastery of the scientist-subject over Nature as object with the attainment of manhood and an associated independence from maternal guidance, or even from feminine entanglement. The identification is typical. From the Renaissance on, mastery over nature is recurrently figured as the triumph of heroic masculinity, something that Blake suggests by drawing his muscular creator as a patriarch rimmed with light,

---

20 On this subject see Treitler: Introduction.
21 Kant: Kritik, p. 16. In full: »Sie [the scientists] begriffen, daß die Vernunft nur das einsieht, was sie selbst nach ihrem Entwurfe hervorbringt, dass die mit Principien ihren Urteile nach beständigen Gesetzen vorangehen und die Natur nötigen müsse auf ihre Fragen zu antworten, nicht aber sich von ihr allein gleichsam am Leitbande gängeln lassen müsse«. I have chosen to translate this passage myself because the several standard translations that I consulted all prettified and neutralized Kant's language.

and that Kant suggests further by postulating a mythic-heroic paradigm of revolutionary science based on the »happy thought of a single man« on whose mind »a new light flashe[s]«.[22]

Like Blake's picture, but with a reversal of its values, Haydn's music conflates the traditional basis of creation with the early-modern basis of scientific knowledge. In pairing the curve of a figurative boundary with the conceptual turn of reconfiguration, the musical structure of the »Representation of Chaos« paraphrases sacred history in the purportedly virile and objective terms of heroic epistemology. The structure, indeed, can be said to arise from and embody the paraphrase. As example 3 shows, a conjunction of the pitches c^1 and e^{b1} begins the movement, marks the end of the first two grand linear progressions, and returns doubled at the lower octave to mark the end of the third grand progression and of the whole. The musical structure is therefore cyclical, and lucidly so. The lucidity even extends to the length of the cycles, which come close to being governed – imagistically *are* governed – by whole-number ratios. From a religious standpoint, this cyclical structure forms a temporal projection of the perfect physical and spiritual order traditionally symbolized by the circle. From a scientific standpoint, the same structure effects a heroic reduction of chaos to lawlike, quasi-mathematical regularity. Under compulsion from reason, chaos proves not to be nature's opposite, but its prototype.

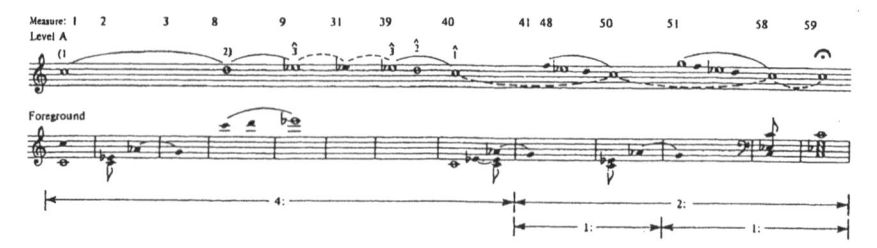

The cyclical structure of the »Representation of Chaos« forms a deep image, as it might be called, that epitomizes a primary concern of ›The Creation‹ as a whole. In representing a plenteous and lawlike nature that continuously reveals divine agency, ›The Creation‹ becomes an esthetic projection of the theological argument from design. This argument, which holds that natural order manifests the existence of a benevolent God, was of signal importance during Haydn's lifetime. Ironically, part of its appeal

---

22 Kant: Kritik, p. 15. For a historical and philosophical overview of objectivist science with special attention to its gendered character, see Bordo: Cartesian Masculnization of Thought. A complementary account appears in Jordanova: Natural Facts. For an account of the ideology of Baconian objectivism, see Albanese: ›The New Atlantis‹.

502

derived from a growing loss of intellectual authority – a loss, as Kant admiringly observed, to which it is quite impervious.[23] Under attack from the likes of Kant, Hume, and the materialists La Mettrie and D'Holbach, the argument from design flourished, as Kant said it should, as a feeling of amazement and admiration. Like other highly popular works of its time – say James Thomson's ›The Seasons‹ (1726-30), a poem in its fiftieth printing by the end of the century, when it became the textual source of Haydn's ›Die Jahreszeiten‹, and Christoph Christian Sturm's ›Reflections on the Works of God in Nature‹, a favorite book of Beethoven's, ›The Creation‹ offered a venue for this feeling of wonder, masking argumentative weakness with esthetic strength. At the same time, in a separate development, the image of a benevolently hierarchical nature was widely used to support the social power of higher-bourgeois and aristocratic men.[24] This ideological trend is consonant with heroic epistemology, and ›The Creation‹ provides a venue for it, celebrating Kant's »happy thought of a single man« in Adam's benevolent assumption of authority over nature and Eve.

3.

Haydn's »Chaos« movement does not limit its engagement with issues like these to a single deep image. Interpretive opportunities crisscross the movement and extend into its sequel, the setting of the first verses of Genesis. Four of these opportunities are particularly notable:

The commencement of Biblical narration. The cadential c^1 reached in m. 58 leads to a recitative for Raphael, a bass, who proclaims: »Im Anfange schuf Gott Himmel und Erde« (In the beginning, God created the heavens and the earth). As Schenker observed, the foreground vocal line for this phrase constitutes a prolongation of the underlying motive C-D-E♭, which arises in the foreground unadorned during the »first melody-creating passage in chaos« to complete the initial ascent to the *Kopfton* (example 4).

---

[23] Kant: Transcendental Dialectic, pp. 518-524.
[24] For an account of the eighteenth-century interplay of hierarchy and benevolence, see Markey: Sentimentality.

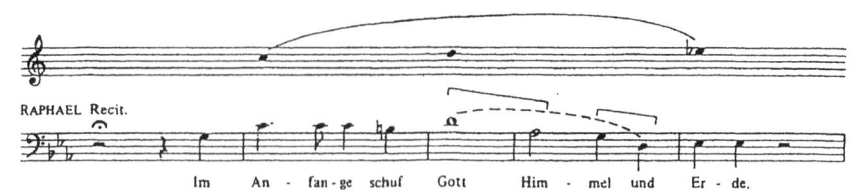

[Musical example: Raphael Recit. "Im An-fan-ge schuf Gott Him-mel und Er-de."]

A double-dotted statement of the motive, in both its original form and in transposition, is the most prominent melodic feature of the »Chaos« movement. This »chaos motive« consistently acts as an engine of instability, churning up foreground tensions through its sequential or contrapuntal elaborations (mm. 22-24, 31-40, 45-47).

In appropriating the C-D-E♭ motive, Raphael's recitative once again represents the mastering of chaos, and this time both voices and dramatizes it, by reconfiguring »chaotic« foreground elements as elements of structure. The foreground vocal line accentuates this reconfiguration by setting the emblematically charged word »Anfange« to the structurally charged pitch c^1. More accentuation quickly follows. The foreground line splits the structural D of the motive into the tones of a descending octave; the octave is filled in quasi-symmetrically as the augmented fourth d^1-a^b is followed by its rectification in the shape of the perfect fourth g-d. Emblematically bridging the distance between the words »Gott« and »Erde«, this well-balanced octave-descent mirrors in little the registral/structural sinking that, like a compass, traverses the »Chaos« movement. In so doing, the descent also establishes the middle range of the bass voice, conventionally virile and authoritative, the range befitting an epistemic hero, as the primary vocal level for scriptural narration. What we hear from Raphael's mouth is the voice of Truth: the voice in whose utterance the divine or natural or symbolic law appears as presence.[25]

2. *The flute descent*. Raphael's use of octave coupling to connect God and the inchoate earth is prefigured during the last of the three grand linear progressions. The third scale degree of this progression, realized as e^{b1} on first violins, meshes with a lyrical foreground descent on solo flute from d^3 to e^{b2} (example 5).

---

25 As always, my use of the term »symbolic« carries a Lacanian sense. Suggesting common sources, the musical imagery of this passage is reminiscent of Raphael's account of the early phases of creation in Milton's ›Paradise Lost‹: »Silence, ye troubl'd waves, and thou Deep, peace, / Said then th'Omnific Word, your discord end [...] / Thus God the Heav'n created, thus the Earth, / Matter unformed and void: but on th ewat'ry calm / His brooding wings the spirit of God outspread, / And vital virtue infus'd [...] , / conglob'd / Like things to like, the rest to several place / Disparted, and between spun out the Air, / And earth self-balanc't on her Centre hung« (V. 217-18, 231-36, 239-42).

504

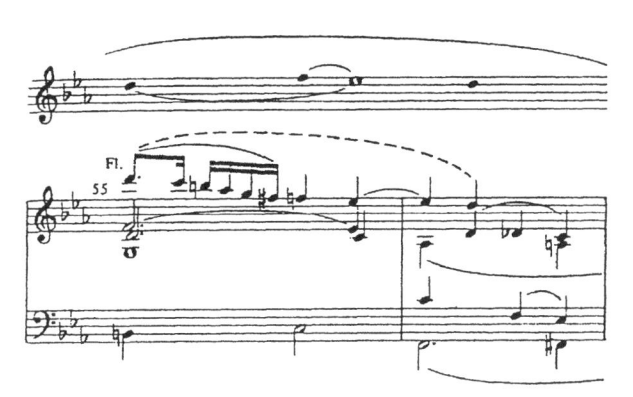

The violins' subsequent movement to d^1, the second degree, is doubled by the flute at the upper octave, as is the final descent to the cadential c^1. The flute's initial D is linked to Raphael's D on »Gott« in a cluster of ways: by registral prominence, common texture (solo against string background), a common bass (B), and comparable harmony (chords with identical roots, an actual G for the flute, an implied one for Raphael).

The simplest way to interpret this pairing is to suggest that the flute descent, like the *incipit* of Raphael's narrative, traces in the foreground the same image of divine circumscription which is traced in the middleground by registral/structural sinking. It remains, however, to account for the qualitative difference fostered by the two foreground images, the one lyrical, the other declamatory. Raphael's recitative associates cosmos with mastery; the flute descent, its lyricism without parallel in the »Chaos« movement, recalls the association of cosmos with musical concord. A term of power (mastery) is thus paired with a term of pleasure (concord), a pairing that may be read equally well as either synonymy or antinomy. This interpretive crux encapsulates a larger tension, running throughout ›The Creation‹ as a whole, which poses the spontaneous joys of paradise against the need to enforce (and not just in paradise) the regime of natural and social hierarchy.

An important moment in the introduction to the third and final part of the oratorio allows this tension to crystallize. The recitative (no. 29, for Uriel, a tenor) renews the idea of a cosmic music linking heaven and earth:

Von himmlischen Gewölbe
strömt reine Harmonie
zur Erde hinab.
[From the vault of heaven
streams pure harmony
to earth below.]

The vocal line for this figure of pleasure, allusively preceded by a pastoral serenade on triple flute, finds its expressive center in a purely lyrical gesture, a melisma at »Harmonie«. Yet the vocal line as a whole recalls nothing so much as Raphael's earlier figure of power (example 6).

[Musical notation: Uriel's vocal line with text "Vom himm-li-schen Ge wöl-be strömt rei - ne Har - mo - nie zur Er - de hi - nab."]

Once again, the words designating heaven and earth are split between registers under the aegis of an octave coupling. As the first scale degree of E Major, e² rules the setting from within the key words »himmlischen« and »Harmonie«; e¹, with help from the subsequent string cadence, rules the closing phrase, »zur Erde hinab«. The falling seventh at »Erde« supplies both a foreground image of the space thus »compassed« and a foreground recollection of two other sevenths: the structurally charged d³-eb² of the flute descent and the intervallic space between Raphael's »Gott« (d¹) and »Erde« (eᵇ).

Like its precursor, this passage can be taken equally well to project either a meshing or a teasing apart of power and pleasure as the first principles of cosmos. The terms of the meshing are clear enough, but they should not be granted too credulously. Unlike Raphael's, Uriel's gesture of mastery needs a voiceless supplement from the strings to complete its structural work. It is as if the lyrical efflorescence on »Harmonie« were too distracting, too seductive, even too feminized to be fully consistent with, fully subsumed by, Uriel's will to mastery; such effusions themselves count among the things that must be mastered. (Compare the subsequent duet, no. 30, in which Eve takes the lead in praising the greatness and wonder of the world. Her vocal line is marked by a florid tendency that Adam generally resists except where he can emphasize mastery – and at that only in a partly covered inner voice – by elaborating the »masculine« term »Handwerk« [handiwork]. The awkward foreground contrast between the fluid melisma and the stiff cadence formula that follows it, between »Harmonie« as sensuous immediacy and harmony as structure, reiterates this same uncertainty. The refreshing stream of pure harmony turns out to be partly a sign of potency – a play on the Classical image of »Father Aether«, the sky, fertilizing the earth – and partly a sign of excess.

The dynamics of linear progression. The chain of grand linear progressions that Schenker finds in the »Chaos« movement is both cumulative and goal-directed. By expanding the breadth of its components from three to four to five tones, the chain evolves a final linkage of the fifth and first scale degrees from an initial linkage of the third and first. The circumscription of chaos is represented as complete when the dominant and tonic tones have come to be bound together across a single linear unit, the end of which coincides with the only real tonic cadence in the movement. This binding reconfigures as structure both a distended foreground emphasis on the key of E♭ Major (mm. 9-31) and the recurrent failure of apparently precadential C-Minor dominants to produce a satisfying cadences (m. 4-5, 39-40, 46-50; the dominant of E♭ mirrors this floundering at mm. 20-21). The emergent linkage of the fifth and first degrees also constitutes a dynamic deep image that identifies the overcoming of chaos with the coming forth of musical order in what for Haydn would be its quintessential forms: the relationship of dominant to tonic and the primacy of perfect over imperfect consonance.

The Passage from Chaos to Light. The »Chaos« movement famously achieves closure, not through the C-Minor cadence that precedes Raphael's recitative, but through the C-Major »creation cadence« that concludes the setting of the sentence, »Und es war Licht« (And there was light). The turn to C Major occurs at the last in a series of possible C-Major/Minor cadence-points. This series both provides a supplement to the movement's ›Ursatz‹ and asserts the principle of reconfiguration – the conversion of foreground instabilities into structural elements – on the largest possible scale.

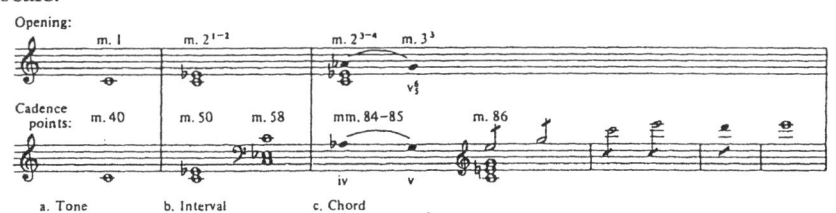

As example 7 shows, the foreground of measures 1-2 consists of a unison C, followed by the interval C-E♭, followed in turn by the chord A♭6. The series of cadence-points both composes out this expansion from tone to interval to chord and reorients the expansion from chaos to cosmos by resolving the initial A♭ chord (the inverted C-E♭-A♭) to the C-major triad (the root-position C-E-G). The first C-Major chord thereupon becomes the fulcrum of an extended foreground arpeggiation; the chord itself expands into cosmos, rising, as Schenker observes, to sublime heights in a decisive transformation of minor to major: »Overtopping the e♭³ of measure 9, the e³ of light lifts itself aloft in measure 89« (»Das es³ in T. 9 übergipfelnd, erhebt es das e³ des Lichtes in T. 89«).[26] This arpeggiation is a supremely energetic gesture, well served by Schenker's decidedly phallic

---

26 Schenker: Das Meisterwerk, v. 2, p. 168. In context, Schenker's use of the verb »erheben« suggests an invocation of »das Erhabene«, the sublime, as well as »Erhebung«, exaltation, elevation.

imagery. Proclaiming the triumph of structure with throbbing repercussive attacks on the notes of the triad, the arpeggiation represents light as a creative energy in which the the aimless and violent energies of chaos are sublimated. Consistent with both the grandeur and authority of Biblical narrative and with a heroic ideal of masculinity, this energy is both the esthetic and social mainspring of ›The Creation‹.

Both formally and ideologically, therefore, the passage from chaos to light consists of a crowning moment of transparency, a coincidence of structure and expression which is as plain within Haydn's frame of reference as within Schenker's, and which, within both, depends on the sonoric value of the tone e^3 as the third scale degree of C Major. For Haydn and his contemporaries, who were famously carried away by it, this moment encapsulated the Enlightenment dream of the perfect coincidence between signs and their meanings and, more broadly, between representation and truth.

As Foucault has shown, this coincidence was identified with the image of order produced by arranging signs into »an immense network« (p. 65-66), each element of which displays »the pure and simple connection between what signifies and what is signified« (p. 67), and the totality of which shows representation, or »thought as a whole« (p. 65) to be »illuminated by the fact that it releases the continuity of being« (206).[27] Haydn offers a wittingly naive version of such a network, »a spontaneous grid for the knowledge of things« (p. 304), in the taxonomic tone-painting that punctuates his narrative of the six-day's work of Creation. In so doing, he also conflates the cognitive map of what Foucault calls the Classical *episteme* with traditional associations linking prelapsarian bliss, natural wisdom, and Adam's transparent naming of the animal creation.[28] The more exalted representational network supporting the passage from chaos to light makes a similar conflation, the *episteme* in this case intertwining with the associations, noted earlier, linking cosmic harmony, the laws of tone, and mastery over nature. These terms coalesce most fully in the structural and expressive climax of the cadence on »Licht«, which supplies the representational network with a central, Archimedean point at which its transparency is paradigmatically – in figurative terms, primordially – grounded.

The C-Major arpeggiation arising out of the cadence is at pains to connect the plenitude of the sign for light with the coherence of the encompassing network. E-naturals frame the musical action; the pulsating first violins ascend through the tones of the triad from e^2 to e^3 and mark the

---

[27] Foucault: Order.
[28] On the privileged role of naming in the Classical *episteme*, see Foucault: Order, pp. 115-20.

508

revelatory arrival at e^3 with emphatic lower-neighbor motion (example 7). This gesture is multiform. It at once actualizes the metaphorical identification between the birth of light and the modal shift from minor to major, parallels that identification with the dynamic »overtopping« of Schenker's *Kopfton*, and projects the image of a light that, brilliant to start with, brightens to incandescence. On every count, Haydn annexes the charisma of the light signified to the musical image that signifies it.

Yet the annexation is not secure: not fully. It is possible to hear Haydn's arpeggiation, though not the cadence that it elaborates, as a little overstated, a little coercive. This is especially so in the interior of the four-measure phrase: in m. 88, where the superimposition of tonic and dominant sonorities suggests a brimming over or momentary knotting up of luminous energy, and in m. 87, when the massed instrumental forces take over after only a single choral measure on the grand word »Licht«. It is as if the word, despite the climactic cadential voicing that allies it with the scientific and religious Word, were in need of an instrumental or tonal supplement: as if some external authority, or rather some external power, were being introduced to support a truth that ought to need no support but its own self-evidence.

This conflation of expressive energy with ideological force occurs because the triumphant conjuncture of divine revelation, structural completion, and representational totality is not just an innocent abstract idea. It is also a vehicle of worldly power, which circulates it, and which it helps circulate, through an »immense network« of institutional, discursive, economic, and social practices. Not for nothing did the educational reformer Heinrich Stephani complain in 1797 that »the sciences [Wissenschaften] are there only for certain classes, and are not to be seen as a store for all mankind«; indeed, the protocols of eighteenth-century natural philosophy explicitly required evidence to be reported by a gentleman observer, never a woman or common man, even when the object under observation was the gentleman's own body.[29] Not for nothing did a French »police dictionary« published in 1787 describe the magistrate-general of Paris as the figure who centers »all the radiations of force and information that spread from the circumferance«, the master »who operates all the wheels that together produce order and harmony[, t]he effects of [whose] administration cannot better be compared than to the movement of the celestial bodies«.[30] And not for nothing did the reviewer for the ›Allgemeine Musi-

---

29 Stephani's remark is quoted by Kittler: Discourse Networks, p. 70. On scientific evidence and the »Cartesianism of the genteel«, a detailed example of the circulatory process to which I've alluded, see Schaffer: Self Evidence.
30 Des Essartes: Dictionnaire, cited in Foucault: Discipline, p. 213.

kalische Zeitung«, reporting on the first public performance of ›The Creation‹ in 1799, begins his notice with a series of suggestive juxtapositions:

> Not to report immediately [...] were to display too little feeling for the Art, or too little for Friendship. This masterpiece of the new musical age was given in the National Theatre next to the Burg. The audience was exceptionally large and the receipts amounted to 4088 fl., 30 kr., [...] a sum that has never been taken in by any Viennese theater. [...] Apart from this, the aristocracy paid the by-no-means inconsiderable costs (the singers and the orchestra consisted of more than 180 persons). One can hardly imagine the silence and the attention with which the whole Oratorio was heard.[31]

To the extent that Haydn's climactic musical image enforces an ideology while it embodies an ideal, it does so because the stakes placed on it were too high to let well enough alone.

4.

Interpretive claims like those just issued *seriatim* are, I realize, necessarily problematical. »Flute descents and cadence points aside«, someone might argue, »Raphael's recitative is the anchor of your argument and it really gives your game away. Haydn's »Chaos« movement is text-connected, atypically supplied with clues to meaning. How are we supposed to deal with music in its own right – with absolute music? And besides, even granting your textual clues, how can we be sure that the music really conveys the meanings you ascribe to it?«

To answer the second objection first, the problem of whether ascribed meaning is or may be conveyed meaning is not unique to music; it is intrinsic to the interpretive situation as such. Meanings are not more transparent in texts than in sonatas; they are only more articulate. We might argue, with no pretense to closing the issue, that a cultural product of any complexity can »convey« meaning only after its receivers have, in however small a way, done conscious interpretive work on it. Meanings are always retrospective; they can only be conveyed *after* we have learned to expect them. The real question is how fully and concretely a work meets our expectations of it. In musical terms, I would suggest, such fullness and concreteness are best grasped dynamically, in the interplay of deep structure, foreground expression, and field of affiliation.

As for the first objection, clues to meaning are everywhere. So are texts, even if only implicitly. As a product and practice of culture, a work of music, *any* work of music, is amply text-connected. Put more strongly: music, insofar as it signifies at all, is not only texted but textual. From a

---

31 Allgemeine Musikalische Zeitung (March 24, 1799), quoted in Landon: Haydn, p. 454.

510

hermeneutic standpoint, »absolute music« is not an obstacle but an opportunity, a historical idea that needs to be interrogated both as a theoretical construct and as an ideological fiction. Particularly to be questioned is the notion that absolute music is the musical thing-in-itself, unencumbered by »extramusical« meaning. As I noted at the outset of this essay, extramusical meaning, so often written off as a mirage, a superfluity, a triviality, is precisely the issue on which the changing climate of musicology made its wager at the close of the twentieth century. Once musical form and expression have been sufficiently historicized to provoke and receive culture-based interpretations, the meanings that result, even those that accrue to the deep structures envisioned by analysis, can no longer reasonably be called extramusical.[32]

Bibliography

Albanese, Denise: ›The New Atlantis‹ and the Uses of Utopia. In: English Literary History 57 (1990), pp. 503-28.

Bordo, Susan: The Cartesian Masculnization of Thought. In: S. B.: The Flight to Objectivity: Essays on Cartesianism and Culture. Albany 1987, pp. 97-118.

Cohn, Richard: The Autonomy of Motives in Schenkerian Accounts of Tonal Music. In: Music Theory Spectrum 14 (1992), pp. 150-170.

Cook, Nicholas: Theorizing Musical Meaning. In: Music Theory Spectrum 23 (2001), pp. 170-195.

Culler, Jonathan: On Deconstruction. Ithaca/N. Y. 1982, pp. 85-134, 150-156.

Dahlhaus, Carl: Ludwig von Beethoven. Approaches to his Music. Trans. Mary Whittal. Oxford 1991.

Dunsby, Jonathan / Arnold Whittall: Music Analysis in Theory and Practice. New Haven 1988.

Fish, Stanley: Normal Circumstances and Other Special Cases. In: S. F.: Is There A Text in This Class? The Authority of Interpretive Communities. Cambridge/Mass. 1980, pp. 268-292.

Foucault, Michel: The Order of Things. An Archaeology of the Human Sciences. New York 1970.

Foucault, Michel: Discipline and Punish. The Birth of the Prison. Trans. Alan Sheridan. New York 1979.

Jordanova, L. J.: Natural Facts. A Historical Perspective on Science and Sexuality. In: Carol MacCormack / Marilyn Strathern (Eds.): Nature, Culture, and Gender. Cambridge 1980, pp. 42-69.

---

[32] This essay is an updated version – partly revised and partly rewritten to accommodate ten years of changes in the field – of an article published in ›19th Century Music‹ 15 (1992), pp. 3-17 as ›Haydn's Chaos, Schenker's Order; or, Hermeneutics and Musical Analysis: Can They Mix?‹. The change in subtitle is meant solely to mark the difference between the two versions.

Kalib, Sylvan: Thirteen Essays from the Three Yearbooks. ›Das Meisterwerk in der Musik‹ by Heinrich Schenker: An Annotated Translation. Ph.D. diss., Northwestern University 1973.

Kant, Immanuel: Kritik der Reinen Vernunft [1781]. Ed. Erich Adickes. Berlin 1889.

Kant, Immanuel: Transcendental Dialectic, Chapter III: The Ideal of Pure Reason, Section 6: The Impossibility of the Physico-theological Proof [of God's Existence]. In: Critique of Pure Reason. Trans. Norman Kemp Smith. 1929; rpt. New York and Toronto 1965, pp. 518-524.

Kittler, Friedrich A.: Discourse Networks. 1800/1900. Trans. Michael Metteer, with Chris Cullens. Stanford 1990.

Kramer, Lawrence: An Outline of Musical Hermeneutics. In: L. K.: Music as Cultural Practice: 1800-1900. Berkeley 1990, pp. 1-20.

Kramer, Lawrence: Haydn's Chaos, Schenker's Order; or, Hermeneutics and Musical Analysis: Can They Mix? In: 19th Century Music 15 (1992), pp. 3-17.

Landon, H. C. Robbins: Haydn: Chronicle and Works. Vol. 4: The Years of The Creation, 1796-1800. Bloomington/Ind. 1977.

Mailloux, Steven: Interpretation. In: Frank Lentriccia / Thomas McLaughlin (Eds.): Critical Terms for Literary Study. Chicago 1989, pp. 121-134.

Man, Paul de: Semiology and Rhetoric. In: P. M.: Allegories of Reading: Figural Language in Rousseau, Nietzsche, Rilke and Proust. New Haven 1979, pp. 3-19.

Markey, Robert: Sentimentality as Performance. Shaftesbury, Sterne, and the Theatrics of Virtue. In: Felcity Nussbaum and Laura Brown (Eds.): The New Eighteenth Century: Theory. Politics. English Literature. New York, London 1987, pp. 210-230.

Milton, John: Paradise Lost. Ed. Merritt Y. Hughes. New York 1962.

Plato: Timaeus. Trans. H. D. P. Lee. Harmondsworth, Middlesex 1965.

Schaffer, Simon: Self Evidence. In: Critical Inquiry 18 (1992), pp. 327-362.

Schenker, Heinrich: Das Meisterwerk in der Musik. Trans. Ernst Oster. New York 1979.

Schenker, Heinrich: Rameau oder Beethoven. In: H. S.: Das Meisterwerk in der Musik, 3 vols. Munich 1925, 1926, 1930.

Scruton, Roger: Aesthetics of Music. Oxford 1997.

Treitler, Leo: Introduction. In: Music and the Historical Imagination, pp. 1-18.

Werbeck, Walter: ›Die Tondichtungen von Richard Strauss‹. Review of James Hepokoski. In: Journal of the American Musicological Society 51 (1995), pp. 603-624.

Williams, Alastair: Constructing Musicology. London: Ashgate 2001.

CHAPTER 14

Speaking Melody, Melodic Speech

This essay seeks to conceptualize a familiar but little-studied phenomenon, the intermediate form of expression between song and speech that arises when a melody associated with words is sounded without the words being sung. This 'singing melody' is interpreted in its historical context and illustrated with reference to works in three disparate genres drawn from the past two centuries: instrumental works by Schubert, Britten's opera *Billy Budd*, and the film *Casablanca*.

In memoriam Steven Paul Scher

The relationship between music and the spoken word is usually conceived in terms of actual sound: a segment of music supports, enhances, subverts, or obscures a speech act. But one of the most common types of relationship is more virtual than actual. It happens when music itself 'speaks': that is, when a musical phrase associated with certain words is used motivically, but without the words being either uttered or sung. Such 'speaking melody' is songlike but not song, not speech but still speechlike; there is nothing else quite like it. The melody, precisely, does not sing; it speaks, and what it says is definite and understood, as if a virtual voice had uttered the substance of the words without their sound. Speaking melody is a device basic to accompanied song, to musical theater, and even to instrumental music, but there has been virtually no theorizing about it. This paper proposes to start some.

One basis for this initiative is a recent effort by Slavoj Zizek to theorize the relationship of words and pictures to what he, following Jacques Lacan, calls the Real, the unsymbolizable substrate of reality in the usual sense of the term. Voice figures importantly in this model but music does not, a defect I hope to rectify. A second basis is the anatomy of speaking melody itself, a kind of triple counterpoint involving the

128

melody per se, the words virtually enunciated by it, and the "melody" of intonation – the palette of timbres, breath sounds, pitch contours, vibrations, inflections, and so on – available to speech as material support and to music as an object of imitation. Starting from the last, these elements form a continuum running from inarticulate vocal substance to full articulation to the 'spiritualized' form in which melody absorbs articulate speech, only to rejoin, at this upper limit, the sheer materiality of the intonational matrix. This encounter at the limit entails the recognition of a material or musical excess, sometimes slight, sometimes more. My theorization will accordingly dwell on the concept of excess, surplus, or remainder, and this in two distinct, partially opposed senses. But before we arrive at that point the stage of theory will need some historical setting, for this is a theory that will try to keep firmly within a historical horizon.

Music is constantly singing songs without words. Singing that way is how music speaks. Once words have been joined to a melody, the words seem to saturate the music so that the music can voice them afterwards even in their absence. Their absence even seems preordained by the thoroughness with which their presence is assimilated; the music is saturated, but the words have been absorbed. This process, to be sure, occurs within certain limitations. The words involved tend to be simple – just a phrase or two, sometimes memorable, sometimes not – and when sung they tend to come at the beginnings of melodies or in refrains, the segments of music most likely to be recalled or repeated with the words unvocalized. The remarkable thing is how articulate those unvocalized segments are.

Such musicalized speech in the absence of words – speaking melody – conveys the verbal utterance as an intentional object rather than as an object of perception. We know the words but do not hear them; they bypass the senses that the music addresses. The language is distilled to a kind of essence, a term meant here in the double sense of a core of spirit or meaning and of a volatile liquid known by the penetrating aroma it leaves behind when it has seemed to vanish. Speaking melody channels the semantic flux of music into a definite but transient form, something not just nameable but named. In so doing, it both reveals and protects against a dread of meaninglessness that lurks at the fringes of much musical experience. Speaking melody highlights both the charismatic value of the musical aphorism – the mystique of the Proustian "little phrase" – and the vacuity potentially created by its repetition.

From one point of view, widely held in the eighteenth century, speaking melody is best understood as an explicit or reflexive form of the basic condition of melody itself. For Jean-Jacques Rousseau, melody is precisely an imitation of speech; its expressive contour mimics the intonational flow of expressive verbal utterance.

> By imitating the inflections of the voice, melody expresses plaints, cries of suffering or joy, threats, moans; all the vocal signs of the passions fall within its province. It imitates the accents of [various] languages as well as the idiomatic expressions commonly associated in each one of them with given movements of the soul. [...] This is where musical imitation acquires its power, and song its hold on sensitive hearts. (282)

At best, of course, this claim takes a historically limited repertoire of melodies as a universal norm, but its obsolescence as a proposition does not exhaust its force. The underlying notion that melody distills expressive speech to its essence has great durability. And it is not always tilted in favor of speech: rather the reverse. Even for so unmusical a thinker as Sigmund Freud, it is the musical element of speaking melody that makes it compelling.

In his reconstruction of the experiences behind his famous "Revolutionary Dream", the analysis of which takes up several discrete sections of *The Interpretation of Dreams*, Freud recalls humming Figaro's defiant aria "Si vuol' ballare, signor Contino" from Wolfgang Amadeus Mozart's *The Marriage of Figaro* after witnessing some imperious behavior at the railway station by the reactionary minister Count Thun (226). The words not uttered establish a frame of reference. But it is the music, into which the words have been absorbed, that carries the force of impudence, resentment, and rebelliousness. Freud's text quotes the words, but the reader who eyes them without hearing the music in the mind's ear will miss more than half the point. The hearing even has to go beyond the melody per se to the way it was performed. Freud is a little dubious that anyone else at the station would have recognized the familiar tune, implying that he may have been humming it off-key or with some other changes that would indicate his resentment. In other words, he was in all likelihood distorting the tune under the pressure of his feelings. The distortion forms a surplus of expression, a remainder, that marks the rage

130

of a liberal against political reaction and a Jew against anti-Semitism. Meanwhile, the melody per se identifies Freud with Mozart's Figaro as a figure of triumphant impudence, and perhaps also with Mozart himself as a figure of resistance by genius to aristocratic privilege.

The same balance of force and signification occurs every time a vocal phrase is picked up by an instrument or ensemble, whether in an abstract composition or in musical theater, on a movie soundtrack or in everyday life: Freud was hardly alone in humming, singing, or whistling an accompaniment to events in the process of living them. Film especially, or video more broadly, makes constant use of speaking melody, so much so that it seems basic to video forms not only as an auditory supplement, but also as an element of visuality. One can, it seems, see more, see better, in both the visual and conceptual senses, when speaking melody is somewhere in the picture.

But speaking melody is not a neutral form. Whether because it involves the absence of word and voice, or because its historical development connects that absence with the imagery of disembodiment and the uncanny, of distance in time and remoteness in space, speaking melody above all exists in a modality of pathos. It is nostalgic; it suggests mourning and memory; it hangs on to bits of the past that need to be let go. In so doing it acts like a material-aesthetic form of "melancholia" in the classic psychoanalytic sense of clinging to the past by internalizing lost objects and reproaching them inwardly for the loss they represent. Of course this is only a tendency, not a law. It is not hard to find exceptions. But the tendency is strong: no law, but perhaps a rule, a model with a long shadow.

Freud's dream analysis is a case in point because it does seem like an exception: "Si vuol' ballare" is defiant, not mournful. But in Freud's account it is really both, its aggressiveness a scant disguise for political and personal nostalgia. The melody harbors a longing for the hopefulness of Freud's happy childhood in the time of the liberal "Bürger" ("Bourgeois") Ministry of which he writes elsewhere in the dream book. "It began to dawn on me", he says there, "that [another, thematically related] dream had carried me back from the dreary present to the cheerful hopes of the days of the 'Bürger Ministry', and that the wish that it had done its best to fulfill was one dating back to those times". Symbolized by the pleasure ground of the Prater, the famous park on the city's outskirts, the Vienna of the "Bürger" Ministry conjoined the love of Freud's parents for their son, a fortuneteller's prophecy of a great future for him, and the hope of full assimilation for Austria's Jews (226)[1]. Without the loss of that fair early world the music in the "Revolutionary" dream is pointless. Figaro's defiance at the train station is the hopeless defiance of an exile in his own land.

What gives speaking melody such power? Freud's narrative suggests that one answer lies in the gap between the expressiveness of the melody and the meaning of the words. The words tell us, or would if we could hear them, what the melody says, but the message thus delivered is always incomplete. We know that the tune in the slow movement of Gustav Mahler's First Symphony is saying "Frere Jacques" or "Brüder Martin", but what we are to do with this information the melody does not say. If one subtracts what the words say from what the melody expresses there is always an expressive remainder, a surplus or excess to deal with. And that remainder is the heart of the matter. With sung melody, the remainder tends to be veiled by the fullness of voice; speaking melody takes the veil away. How does this remainder act, and to what end?

The short answer is that it acts by distorting the texture of ordinary reality – the lifeworld governed by the norms of law and language, Lacan's symbolic order. It does so either to create an incitement to new acts of symbolization or to insist on the presence of something unsymbolizable. To continue with the Lacanian vocabulary, the remainder is either an enhancement of the symbolic or an eruption of the Real.

Zizek's model concerns the latter. His essay "Grimaces of the Real" focuses on the human face as a primary locus of symbolic reality and examines how the Real – the terrible enjoyment of living substance devoid of rule or reason – makes its appearance

---

[1] The other dream involved here is goes by the sobriquet "Uncle with the Yellow Beard"; its latent content overlaps that of the "Revolutionary" dream in an extensive network of associations. Freud traces his wishes all the way back to his mother's pride, shortly after his birth, at a fortuneteller's statement that she had brought a great man into the world; to childhood revisitations of the scene of the prophecy in the Prater, where another prognostic said that Freud would become a cabinet minister – the image on which the whole pattern converges; and to the hopes for full assimilation of the Jews that the Bürger Ministry inspired: "My father had brought home portraits of these middle-class professional men [of the Ministry] – Herbst, Giskra, Unger, Berger and the rest – and we had illuminated the house in their honor. There had even beeen some Jews among them. So henceforth every industrious Jewish schoolboy carried a Cabinet Minister's portfolio in his satchel." (225-26)

132

by agonized facial distortion. Many of Zizek's examples also involve the voice, which produces a grimace when it cannot come to utterance. The voice in such cases is an object that gets stuck in the throat; it is "what cannot burst out, unchain itself, and thus enter the dimension of subjectivity", which is also the dimension of symbolic reality. "The first association here", writes Zizek,

> is Munch's Scream [...] [where] it pertains to the very essence of the depicted content that the scream we perceive is mute, since the anxiety is too stringent to find an outlet in vocalization. [...] [This] structural muteness is indexed within the painting itself by the absence of ears from the homunculus's head: as if these ears, foreclosed from the (symbolic) reality of the face, return in the Real of the anamorphotic stain the form of which recalls a gigantic ear." (117)

Ana/morphosis: form as de-formation, deformity. The remainder of mingled desire and repulsion left over by any act of symbolization here returns by indelibly disfiguring the act of symbolization itself[2].

But not all remainders are anamorphotic stains. An alternative type is one of the topics canvassed by my book *Musical Meaning*. One of the commonest notions about music is that one cannot express what it means in words; something, and that the most important thing, is always left over. Yet these musical remainders have nothing monstrous about them; quite the contrary. And Edvard Munch's "Scream" looks like the very antithesis of music. So what would happen, I wondered, if instead of treating the musical remainder as either an ineffable *je ne sais quoi* or as a negative principle, an abstract curb on articulate meaning, we tried to regard it as a positive phenomenon, a concrete involvement with the problem of meaning? The remainder in that case would not be what disqualifies me from speaking about music or from finding new contexts in which the music becomes meaningful. On the contrary, it would be the rationale and the motive for me to keep on speaking and contextualizing. The remainder would deny a

---

[2] Zizek's initiative can be understood as an effort to extract the kernel of truth from the truism that no act of symbolization is ever complete. Lacan defines the Real, to the extent that he defines it at all, as that which resists (evades, escapes) symbolization. Taking this resistance psychoanalytically rather than metaphysically, he understands the Real as pertaining to (being "of") the subject's unspeakable desire. Zizek regards the Real as a kind of agency, and a powerful one at that. Rather than forming a negative, indiscernible limit on the power of the symbol, it intervenes continually in symbolic processes, marking its presence obtrusively with its signature stain or deformity. And because these extrusions of the Real are indeed linked to desire, they can never be escaped. For Zizek, reality (the symbolically constructed world) is pockmarked by them.

portion of meaning in the present only in order to promise it, though never all of it at once, in the future. The anamorphotic remainder that impedes the hermeneutic would be joined to a metamorphic counterpart that promotes the hermeneutic. And these two different remainders would actually be one and the same.

Of course texts and pictures have such remainders, too; the grimaces of the Real have opposites in every medium. What makes the musical remainder special? And what, more particularly, is special about it in the case of speaking melody?

Where the Real appears, there is probably no point in making distinctions; all the remainders are breaks in the skin of perception, whether they are blots, garbles, or noises. But where meaning hovers just out of reach, distinctions are possible. The hermeneutic remainders of texts and images are relatively abstract and immaterial, the faint traces of the unsaid or unseen. Our everyday confidence in the force of meaning rests to some degree on this faintness. In music, however, the remainder is material and sensuous. Grasping it is fundamental to both musical pleasure and musical power. Music does more than 'have' a remainder; it embodies its remainder. Indeed, one way to define music is as the material-sensuous remainder of interpretation.

Speaking melody is a hybrid of the musical and verbal instances; it combines the material consistency of music with the symbolic value of words, but without merging them together as sung melody tends to do. In the sphere of utterance, the remainder tends to appear as a reduction of articulation to pure phonic substance, intonation denuded of speech. This reduction, like the remainder itself, is subject to a duality whose tensions determine its precise effect in any given instance. On one hand, the reduction may occur when words are choked back, garbled, smeared together; at its outer limit, this verbal implosion would be the equivalent to the sickening distortions of face and voice described by Zizek. On the other hand, intonation may simply replace all or part of a speech act as an overflow of some immediacy or nuance; its distortion would be hermeneutic, at worst enigmatic, and at the extreme a token of intimate, virtually unmediated communication. There is, of course, an endless variety of mixed instances between the two extremes.

Speaking melody belongs to this intermediate domain. Or perhaps one ought to say that the intermediate domain belongs to it. When a melody gives us to apprehend the

134

words we do not hear, it acts as like a detached form of the intonational substrate of speech. The process is like an unveiling of the living substance of the words, the rich materiality that the articulateness of speech regularly obscures. Like the words themselves, this substance is purely virtual. When the unuttered speech is incorporated in the sensory richness of the music, the music tends to assume the status of the terrible but fascinating Real, the unsymbolizable kernel of forbidden/ecstatic pleasure/repulsion at the core of subjective life. Beneath any specific distortion that may mark this effect lies the innate distortion produced by the simultaneous occurrence of verbal understanding and verbal absence, which renders the music palpably but imperceptibly different from what it would otherwise be. The notes aren't different; the melody is. Each of these distortions magnifies the other. This mutual resonance helps explain the emotional force of speaking melody.

But the Real thus made manifest is not the standard Real. Rather it is a Real partly recuperated for the symbolic order, a Real allowed to enter the symbolic as something other than a blot or grimace, something that does not repel meaning but, by assuming an aphoristic, enigmatic, oracular character, attracts it. Speaking melody undoes the grimace of the Real. Its anamorphotic remainder fuses with its hermeneutic remainder. It gives the Real a haven in reality.

Zizek's descriptive terms blot, stain, smear, grimace, let alone phallic anamorphosis, are too extreme in this context. Speaking melody typically trades in slighter distortions, shimmers, or flickers of misperception; if the distortion is too great, the speaking melody turns into travesty – for which, of course, there any many uses – and becomes a device of alienation, as, once again, in Mahler's "Frere Jacques". We need a term for the distortion characteristic of speaking melody, so I will speak here not of blot but a blur, something at the edges of perception rather than "in your face": the smudge of the real.

Thus far, however, both this smudge and the element of pathos in speaking melody describe only general effects; they are points of theory. But such general effects are never, or let us say rarely, realized in their generality. They respond, rather, to particular circumstances; they mark their materiality, their distortion, and their nostalgia in highly particular ways. Speaking melody is a historical form, even a form that insists on rather than insinuates its own historical character.

A useful profile of speaking melody must therefore be historically resonant. To meet that requirement, I propose to examine a series of examples spanning several media across two centuries: an opera and a movie from the 1940s, and a pair of instrumental compositions from the 1820s.

The opera is Benjamin Britten's *Billy Budd* (1951). In this adaptation of Herman Melville's novel, Billy, the innocent "Beauty" or "Baby" aboard a British man-o-war, is falsely accused of mutiny by Claggert, the master of arms. The accusation may be a distorted form of Claggert's desire for Billy, which must not be symbolized; Billy, who stutters under stress, replies in distorted form as well, striking and inadvertantly killing Claggert in lieu of speech. Remainders are thus at the heart of this story, which ends as the ship's captain, Vere, orders Billy's execution despite his obvious innocence. Britten and his librettists, E.M. Forster and Eric Crozier, were primarily interested in Vere, whose dilemma is exposed early in the opera by means of speaking melody.

Talking with his officers about the danger of mutiny, Vere draws attention to a chantey being sung below decks as the crew retires for the night. He takes the chantey as a sign of contentment; it is exactly the opposite. The words express a deep longing to be elsewhere, anywhere but here: "Blow her away, / Blow her to Hilo, Hilo, Hilo […] ." At the end of the scene, Vere, now alone, is distracted by the chantey as he tries to read. The song is already halfway to becoming voiceless, smudged by the distance of its off-stage, below-decks source. Part of it is submerged in the darkness of the low voices singing together. Part of it fades into the distance with the repetitions of "Hilo", which turn the exotic place-name into pure vocalization, more smudge than utterance: a becoming-inarticulate of speech under the pressure of desire[3].

The metamorphosis completes itself a moment later as the orchestra picks up the chantey and makes it the basis of an extended fantasy. What is truly at stake becomes fully apparent when the fantasy takes up the speaking melody of a second chantey, introduced on solo flute. The words will not come until later. Britten wrote this tune

---

[3] Hilo is a port in the Sandwich (i.e., Hawaiian) Islands, as remote as possible from the Atlantic setting of the opera. On another reading, the nonsense that "Hilo" becomes through repetition makes another kind of sense. In the opera's Anglicized pronunciation, it forms a synoptic statement, unrecognized by the singers, of the social (and would-be metaphysical) difference mapped onto the ship's decks: high/low.

136

before he had words for it – words, he told their author, that should be "as gloomy, homesick, and nostalgic as you like"[4]. The words he received convey a deep longing for release, even for the peace of death: "Over the ocean, over the water, into the harbour, carry me home." Taken together, the two speaking melodies universalize the feelings of which they speak. The men's longing ceases to arise from the circumstances of the narrative and becomes the circumstance from which the narrative arises. The longing becomes manifest as the unfathomable substrate that the opera, at best, can symbolize only in part.

Just a few years before "Billy Budd", Hollywood produced a legendary instance of speaking melody in *Casablanca* (1942). The story has become legendary, too: separated when the Nazis occupy Paris, the lovers Rick and Ilse (Humphrey Bogart and Ingrid Bergman) meet again in Casablanca; Ilse is now married to a resistance leader, and Rick must renounce her so that she, in turn, can support her husband in his struggle. The song "As Time Goes By", as sung at the piano by Rick's employee and emotional minder, Sam (Dooley Wilson), embodies the lost romance.

On separate occasions, first Ilse and then Rick insist on hearing the song, but with a subtle difference. Ilse starts by asking for the music (with the famous "Play it, Sam") but she also wants the words ("Sing it, Sam"). Rick reencounters Ilse for the first time when he interrupts Sam's singing – an interruption that cannot hold up. Alone with Sam later, Rick, too, asks for the song ("Play it!" he says, turning Ilse's plea into an anguished command), even though he cannot bear to hear it; we can see as much in the grimace on Bogart's face. But what Rick asks for is speaking melody, not song, and the film complies. As Sam plays, the orchestra backs up the melody before shifting to the underscore for what follows, a flashback to the lovers' life in Paris[5]. Most of this interpolated narrative is fragmentary; music holds it together, especially "As Time Goes By". Fragments of the melody recur as underscore at all the key romantic moments, each more haunted by impending loss than the last. But it is precisely these moments

---

[4] Cooke and Reed, 65.

[5] Berthold Hoeckner has drawn attention to the song's transitional role here and to its eventual embedding in the flashback it introduces. His reading sees lost time less fatefully than mine, but there is no need to choose between them; they deal with different modes of memory.

that the song, as speaking melody, is bringing most vividly back to life. When Sam actually plays and sings the song for the lovers in Paris, no one suspects its power to do that.

The flashback ends with a return to Rick, still listening as Sam plays. (The playing breaks off at the musical phrase for "and still say", leaving the music for "I love you" to hover somewhere between something still to be said and something no longer sayable.) Far from just invoking a lost time, the song is what refuses to let the time be lost. That, after all, is what the melody says when it speaks: "The fundamental things apply / As time goes by." The fundamental things are those that remain as time goes by, and in this case the most fundamental thing of all is the song itself. If Rick, if Ilse, could forget the song, they could let the past be past. But they cannot forget. The song will not let them; it smudges their every thought with the Real of their love.

The close of the film is haunted by the logic of the song, which it can neither accept nor escape. In the penultimate scene, Rick has firmly resolved to let Ilse go; he will send her away himself. To end the story he will end **their** story. He explains his renunciation with one famous line after another: "We'll always have Paris," "The troubles of three little people don't amount to a hill of beans in this crazy world," "Here's looking at **you**, kid." As he speaks, the orchestra on the soundtrack weaves together phrases from "As Time Goes By"; when he finishes, the strings fill the ensuing silence with a melting rendition of the song's refrain as the camera lingers on a closeup of Ilse's face. The effect is to contradict the narrative ending. It puts the audience in the position of the old Rick, the Rick who refuses to let go of Ilse and Paris – a refusal measured precisely by the original version of the song. The quivering strings of the closing version impart the smudge of the Real and create a complex pattern whereby Rick says one thing and the speaking melody that supports him says something else: the very thing he would like to say, but cannot. The pattern culminates with an epiphany at the level of speech genre: melodrama (that is, music joined to the spoken word, but with a play on the sense of highly wrought narrative) resolves itself in lyric.

Perhaps this outcome is why some people go back to *Casablanca* over and over, as if hoping to meet – just once – with the ending announced by the music, not by the plot. The song, of course, has been heard on the soundtrack before, even heard too often, but

138

it becomes decisive here because Rick is repeating the separation from Ilse that gave the song its power in the first place. In this context the absence of the words becomes the presence of the unspeakable desire that will not permit itself to be renounced. The speaking melody clearly says that the problems of three little people – especially two of them – amount to far more than a hill of beans even in this crazy world.

A lesser world, if not a crazy one, is Franz Schubert's topic in portions of two major instrumental works, his Octet in F Major (D. 803) and String Quartet in A Minor (D. 804), composed during the same two-month period in 1824. Both works quote a song he had composed five years earlier, "Schöne Welt, wo bist du, Fragment aus Schillers Die Götter Griechenlands". The short text bears full quotation:

Schöne Welt, wo bist du? Kehre wieder,	Fair world, where are you? Turn back again,
Holdes Blütenalter der Natur!	Sweet blossom-age of nature!
Ach, nur in dem Feenland der Lieder	Ah, in the fairyland of songs alone
Lebt noch deine fabelhafte Spur.	Still lives your legendary trace.
Ausgestorben trauert das Gefilde,	The died-out meadow mourns,
Keine Gottheit zeigt sich meinem Blick.	No godhead comes before my eyes.
Ach, von jenem lebenwarmen Bilde	Ah, of that life-warm image
Blieb der Schatten nur zurück.	Only the shade remains behind.[6]

In both octet and quartet, the only phrase reproduced as speaking melody involves the two words "schöne Welt" ('fair world'). But the two works invoke this phrase to markedly different effect. We need to go back to the song to see how and why.

The passage quoted is less 'in' the song than appended to it by the piano alone. Repetitions of a single three-note figure, static and forlorn, frame the song proper; they also intrude on it about two-thirds of the way through. (Examples 1a and 1b show the framing statements, mm. 1-5 and 50-55.) At each occurrence, this refrain sounds over unchanging 6-4 harmony in A-minor – afloat, as it were, in the no-world of the present. Between the framing statements, we hear a disrupted A-B-A pattern: two A-major sections enclose an A-minor middle section that ends with the intrusion of the refrain. The first A-major section carries the verse to the point where the gods are said to live on only in song; the A-minor section begins with the transition to the fraught word "ausgestorben" ('died-out') and goes on to the end, marking the dismal consequences

---

[6] German text from Schubert's score; my translation.

for latter-day reality. The second A-major section recapitulates the first section's first half, consisting of a double statement of "Kehre wieder, / Holdes Blümenalter der Nature" ('Turn back again / Sweet blossom-age of Nature'). This recapitulation is ironic at best, both in its major key and in the incompleteness of its utterance; its structural inevitability only darkens its implications. The invocation is one that can never be answered, as the closing return of the refrain declares. Deprived of the gods, Nature cannot even say "No." The static futility of the refrain figure expands to envelop the form of the song as a whole.

Example 1a. Schubert, "Die Götter Griechenlands", opening, mm. 1-5

Example 1b. Schubert, "Die Götter Griechenlands", close, mm. 50-55

140

The dotted rhythm of this figure anticipates that of "Schöne Welt" in the voice, which is, however, sung to different pitches. The speaking melody provides an alternative intonation that is never realized vocally because it is too despairing; its minor mode and harmonic instability too fully confirm the loss that the voice, hoping against hope, still questions with its "kehre wieder". As the song proper begins (ex. 1a), the voice cuts across the piano's oscillating E-D-E with the rising figure C-D-E. The voice and piano do coincide on E, though, at the word "Welt", and again on A at "du" as the harmony finally shifts – though one cannot really say it resolves – from the second inversion to root position. At the end of the song, this alignment, the balance of hope and despair, is lost. The voice reaches its A with the 6-4 harmony still in effect, then falls silent. The piano is left to conclude by repeating its own more melancholy version of the refrain figure. Only after this does the harmony shift again – again not really resolving, and with the voice no longer involved (ex. 1b). The effect is similar to that of the more famous frame structure in the later "Am Meer", another song of loss, where the 6-4 harmony does not even bother to shift. In "Schöne Welt", therefore, it is the forlorn alternative voice that has the last word, and the true word, in a speaking melody rather than the sung one of which it is the shadow, the shade that remains behind[7].

The instrumental quotations in the Octet and Quartet revive this alternative voice, in which the question 'where' cannot really be asked because it has already been answered by 'nowhere'. The third movement of the quartet counteracts this answer precisely by catching the little phrase up in its genre, the minuet, an antique form that fulfils the subsequent statement in Schiller's poem that the fair world survives in fable, though only there. The tight, static shape of the phrase acts as a smudge on the richly wrought minuet theme, but the theme has little trouble coping with it. Or rather, just a little; there is nothing glib about the process. The solo cello begins the movement with a deep, groaning statement of the "Schöne Welt" phrase, the last note of which refuses to let go and draws the other instruments to it in somber-hued imitations. But the overriding lyrical impulse is already at work even as these echoes chime in, and the graceful lilt of

---

[7] It is worth noting that the original version of the song has no shift to root position at the voice's first "du". By adding the shift, Schubert converts its subsequent absence at the last "du" from the restatement of a settled condition to the enactment of a loss.

the minuet emerges from them seamlessly and irrefutably (ex. 2). If the fair world survives only here, we can still be assured that it survives well enough.

Example 2. Schubert, Minuet from Quartet in A Minor, D.804, opening

Example 3. Schubert, Finale from Octet in F Major, D.803, opening

This is an assurance that the octet will not allow. Here the smudge becomes a smear in the guise of wrenching string tremolos that envelop the little phrase (ex. 3). The

142

feverish quivering of the ensemble forms an extended slow introduction to the finale, which it defines precisely as an attempt to seek in original composition the consolation that the minuet claims to have found in genre. The movement is superbly equipped to succeed in this. Its indefatigable first theme frames a sonata exposition unusually rich in melodic variety, and itself varies prolifically and irrepressibly during a development section that it wholly engrosses. But the attempt to recall a vanished world by these means is compromised by its very definition, and the movement nearly founders on it when the introduction returns, briefer but more feverish than before, just prior to the coda. The coda itself seems oblivious, but the listener can hardly be that in good faith. Where the quartet stresses the consolations of fable, the octet dwells on the emptiness of the shades – the ghosts and figments – that the fair world has left behind. Both pieces repeat the little phrase like a forlorn cry, but the quartet follows the text by ritualizing and therefore rationalizing that cry, substituting the generic conventions of the minuet for the rhetorical figure of apostrophe. The octet lets the cry erupt and fade without the intervention of ritual or rationale. Its little phrase is a noisy remainder that the effervescence of the finale cannot assimilate.

The little phrase, then, has larger implications, and not in this one piece alone. What are the larger implications of speaking melody itself? What might its role be in a broader auditory culture?

On the evidence of our examples, the phenomenon of speaking melody would seem to mark the limit of an important hermeneutic principle, as formulated by Hans-Georg Gadamer: "Language is not just one of man's possessions in the world; rather, on it depends the fact that man has a world at all. The world as world exists for man as for no other creature that is in the world. But this world is verbal in nature." (441) Against this, as an exception to it, is the fact that there are many moments in life when language is silent, suspended, but world is not. What we experience at such moments cannot be the verbal nature of the world. Rather we must come into contact with something prior to the world as word, cosmos as logos, and yet something consistent with it. We must experience the imprintability, so to speak, of phenomena by language.

Listening to instrumental music often falls into this category. Such listening can suspend language without at all suspending world; rather the reverse, for the music 'worlds' us very powerfully. When that happens, we can hear the world's latent imprintability as a positive form, but still prior to the realization of any actual imprint. And this is a condition that shows us the world in a special light, perhaps one less susceptible than usual to rationalization and distanced perception. The world thus disclosed is pleasurably smudged by the Real. In this context we can speculate that what speaking melody does is capture the otherwise imperceptible movement between symbolic imprintability and the imprint: the lapse of meaning by which meaning is replenished, a moment inflected by both reason and magic, both surplus and loss.

References

Cooke, Mervyn and Philip Reed. *Benjamin Britten: Billy Budd*. Cambridge: Cambridge Univ. Press, 1993.

Freud, Sigmund. *The Interpretation of Dreams*. James Strachey, trans. New York: Avon, 1965.

Gadamer, Hans-Georg. *Truth and Method*. 5th German ed., 1986. Joel Weisheimer and Donald G. Marshall, trans. Rev. 2nd ed. New York: Continuum, 1989.

Gras, Vernon W., ed. *European Literary Theory and Practice*. New York: Dell, 1973.

Hoeckner, Berthold. "Audiovisual Memory: Transport and Transportation". Paper presented at the conference *Beyond the Soundtrack: Representing Music in Cinema*. Univ. of Minnesota, April 2004.

Kramer, Lawrence. *Musical Meaning: Toward a Critical History*. Berkeley: Univ. of California Press, 2002.

Rousseau, Jean-Jacques. *The First and Second Discourses and Essay on the Origin of Languages*. Victor Gourevitch, trans. New York: Harper and Row, 1990.

Zizek, Slavoj. *Enjoy Your Symptom! Jacques Lacan in Hollywood and Out*. 2nd ed. New York: Routledge, 2001.

CHAPTER 15

"Longindyingcall"

Of Music, Modernity, and the Sirens

——bewitching fatal singers, the nixies and naiads, the Lorelei and (combers of combers and of hair in waves) the mermaids singing each to each, all the undulant forms of femininity calling from across the spray or under the wave, of the Rhinemaidens and the fair Melusine and Undine, the aspiring little mermaid of Hans Christian Andersen and the down-drifting one of Edward Burne-Jones, the one longing after the world of culture in the guise of love but struck dumb and no more able to walk on land, really, than she was underwater, the other rejecting the world of culture in the same guise, blank-faced and simpering, her arms tightly enwrapped about the naked man doubly castrated (loins and arms effaced) by her grasp and brought down to a cavern that contains, precisely, nothing:

Of these strange beings and their stranger spheres of being transvalued as means of making alternative worlds, home of lost continents, strange treasures, and sunken cathedrals, of shipwrecks and the dice of drowned men's bones that never abolished chance and of course those pearls that were his eyes, each and all scattered and changed yet purified and recognizable in the iris of the undulant watery lens, enhanced with the fluidity of the imaginary yet still contained within the gyres of the sym-

"LONGINDYINGCALL"

bolic, dangerous, to be sure, but also emancipatory, revealing the possibility that ordinariness may yet be bathed in wonder and desire:

Of watery forms as a mode of philosophizing, a condensation and dream displacement of Hegel's proposition that the ocean gave humanity its original idea of the infinite, an *Aufhebung* in reverse whereby the high epic masterplot of civilization-building is destroyed yet invaluably preserved in a lower register, hard-headed and hard-hearted masculine aspiration both softened and fantasticated by immersion in the opalescent translucent medium identified with the feminine, the origin, and the end.

But perhaps it's time to break the surface of the waves and reason of these things more slowly.[1]

Loreleis, naiads, sirens, mermaids, and other undulant forms of dangerous femininity return in the nineteenth century to the waters from which the Enlightenment had banished them. They ply their seductive trade thereafter as projections—so the standard explanation goes—of masculine anxiety in a world of changing gender roles. The more women want, the more they demand access to public spheres and private pleasures, the more men worry about being lured by them into a fatal immersion:

> A mermaid found a swimming lad,
> Picked him for her own,
> Pressed her body to his body,
> Laughed; and plunging down
> Forgot in cruel happiness
> That even lovers drown.
>   W. B. Yeats, "The Mermaid"[2]

This explanation cannot be gainsaid, especially with regard to the flood tide of fin-de-siècle paintings epitomized by Edward Burne-Jones's famous *The Depths of the Sea* (1887; fig. 6.1).[3] But fatal attraction is not the whole story. Burne-Jones's painting pretends nothing else is involved by the simple device of showing exactly that. It gives us virtually nothing but a male form in the fatal grip of a female one. Yeats's little poem does much the same. But this nothing is not a mere absence; it signifies. The loving but mindless grip of the mermaid's femininity effaces not only her victim's masculinity but also the symbolic foundation of his identity, his whole familiar world of signs, projects, and possessions. The painting makes this explicit in the bareness of the cavern to which its couple sinks, and it all but explicitly presents this effacement as a double castration—his arms gone, his loins a slot for the crook of her elbow. But far more is being

[195]

"LONGINDYINGCALL": OF MUSIC, MODERNITY, AND THE SIRENS 283

Figure 6.1. Edward Burne-Jones, *The Depths of the Sea.* Watercolor. Courtesy of the Fogg Art Museum, Harvard University Art Museums. Bequest of Grenville L. Winthrop. Photo: Katya Kallisen. Image copyright © 2004 by the President and Fellows of Harvard College.

[196]

"LONGINDYINGCALL"

effaced here than simple masculinity. Culture itself is stripped bare. Perhaps that's the point of the Venus de Milo arms: man is no longer *homo faber,* man the maker. The painting's mode of representation exceeds—but thereby also expands—its mythic content.

Numerous literary and, especially, musical treatments go even further in this direction. Not confined to or by seductive visualization, these media can suggest the rhythm, the timbre, the melodious strangeness of the sirens' song; they can listen better, be heard better. On that basis many of them suggest that post-Enlightenment sirens represent more than the *reductio ad absurdum* of the standard modern forms of gender construction, and more, even, than an alternative to them. To be sure, both the *reductio* and the alternative do matter; they can matter a great deal. But they matter as they do in the painting: in a form that exceeds, and thereby also expands, their mythic content. They range over the full field of ideology while pretending to inhabit only its fissures and edges. With alterative gender construction as a symbolic basis, the sirens, along with their watery sisters, represent an alternative to the standard modern forms of world construction. The sequence of evocations in Debussy's *Nocturnes for Orchestra* (1899) got the rhythm of it exactly right: a continuum runs from the cloud-world of shape-shifting fantasy ("Nuages") to the festive play of antinomian energy ("Fêtes") to the uncharted pursuit of the sirens' song ("Sirénes")—to which Debussy adds a wordless women's chorus, the undulant line of which literalizes the metaphor in the listener's ears. Fixed in his seat at the concert hall, the listener becomes the modern form of Odysseus tied to his mast, for whom the enchainment of the body makes possible the enchantment of the mind.

The sirens were called back to life in the nineteenth century not simply to help cope with modern forms of identity and desire, but to help cope with the form of modernity itself. In a multiplicity of versions and variants, the sirens and their song represent precisely what modernity and modern subjectivity have lost, precisely that which they must lose or alienate from themselves to become modern. For that very reason, the sirens also represent that which the modern must fantasize about regaining, even only in treacherous glimpses, and why, as Kafka tells us in his parable "The Silence of the Sirens," they are closest to the modern subject when he thinks he knows no more of them.[4]

These tropes are far from exhausted. As recently as 2000, Joel and Ethan Coen's film, *O Brother, Where Art Thou?*, made a loose transposition of *The Odyssey* to Depression-era Mississippi. Here one Ulysses Everett McGill and his companions are diverted from the road where they're driving—the archetypal action of modern American odysseys—to

[197]

a wooded stream where the sirens, country girls in white shifts, sing while they wash their clothes. The soft-focus landscape bears no trace of the modern except the invisible presence of the camera that renders it. Shot in slight slow motion to accord with the singing, the scene might almost be imagined as set in the depths of the song, as if under water.

Or take the show planned for Las Vegas by *Cirque du Soleil* in 2003, as reported by the *New York Times*. The underwater scene here is not imaginary:

> The contortionist perched at the edge of a transparent basin like a nymph on the rim of a cocktail glass. She peeled off her bra and slid into the water, followed by a woman who was her near mirror-image. The two began a submerged dance less acrobatic than erotic: their backs arched, their arms twined, their legs moved in anatomically improbable ways....
>
> Then, abruptly, the women shot to the surface and gulped at the air. "That will give you an idea of where we're going," explained Lyn Heward, the creative president of *Cirque du Soleil*, matter of factly.[5]

The leap from fantasy to, and as, the business of modernity could hardly be clearer. It is like a splash of cold water—in reverse.

The world below or beyond the waves, to which the sirens' or the mermaid's song beckons the voyager, is typically represented as the Nether Nightmare of misogynist fantasy, home of the subject as devoured or drowned. Stéphane Mallarmé's "Un Coup de dés" (A Throw of the Dice, 1895), a poem whose lines are strewn irregularly across successive pages in imitation both of the look of an orchestral score and the spread of debris after a shipwreck, plays darkly on Shakespeare's famous "Of his bones are coral made; / Nothing of him that doth fade / But doth suffer a seachange / Into something rich and strange" (*The Tempest*, I.ii.398–401). The drowned master mariner, for whom "une stature mignonne ténebreuse / en sa torsion de sirène" (a delicate shadowy shape with the twist of a siren) has lodged within the plume of the fatal wave, finds

> son ombre puerile
> caressée et polie et rendue et lavée
> assouplie par la vague et soustraite
> aux durs os perdus entre les ais
> his childish shadow
> caressed and polished and rendered and washed
> suppled by the wave and withdrawn
> from the hard bones lost between the timbers[6]

"LONGINDYINGCALL"

In "Death by Water," the fourth section of *The Waste Land* (1922), T. S. Eliot displaces the sirens' song into the cry of gulls and describes the process of dissolution in a phrase packed with echoes of Shakespeare and Mallarmé both: "A current under sea / Picked his bones in whispers."[7]

But the water that thus transforms substance into shadow, leaving only the hard bones behind, also serves as a medium that jumbles, blurs, and transforms the constituents of the world above while still preserving their intelligibility. The preservation is both dangerous, because irrational —fluidity here belongs as much to categories as to bodies—and transfiguring. Borne on the sea swell, Eliot's drowned sailor enters a new mode of reflective awareness: "As he rose and fell / He passed the stages of his age and youth / Entering the whirlpool."[8] The dissolution of Mallarmé's mariner is followed by

> Fiançailles
> dont
> > le voile d'illusion rejailli leur hantise
> > ainsi que le fantome d'un geste

> [a] Betrothal
> whose
> > illusory veil splashed up its obsession
> > like the ghost of a gesture.

Betrothal as the upper world knows it finds its ghostly equivalent in betrothal to a siren, the play of whose illusory bridal veil is like the splash of a cresting wave. To trace such undulations across the page as both verbal music and visual image is the work of the poem's modernity. For Homer's Odysseus, the sirens' song is a lure to simple dissolution; for his modern descendants, the dissolution is the sirens' song itself, the pleasure of which is its own fatality. As Rilke puts it in his poem "Die Insel der Sirenen" (The Island of the Sirens, 1907), there is no defense against the knowledge that "es dort auf jenen / goldnen Inseln manchmal singt" (there on that golden island it sometimes sings).[9] "It" sings: just what or who does the singing scarcely matters. Whoever hears is immersed in the sea of fantasy.

Such immersion recalls an overrationalized modern mundanity to the fabulous time of legend and marvel. For Robert Schumann, Mendelssohn's concert overture *The Fair Melusine* (1834) should evoke a fairytale world in every listener, especially with the shimmering siren song that seems to immerse both the listener and the tale in an imaginary depth that restores a chastened reality to the condition of romance: "Here might grow vivid to everyone those happy images with which youthful fantasy delights to linger, those legends of life deep down on the ground of the waves, full of darting fish with golden scales, of pearls in open shells, of buried treasures that the sea has taken from men, of emerald castles towering up one atop another."[10] The depths of the sea systematically shift nature (the darting fish), art (those are pearls that were his eyes), commerce (the sunken treasure), and architecture (the emerald castles) into the register of enchantment. The multiplication of emerald castles is both comprehensive and climactic; it gives the suggestion not just of world-fragments, but of an alternative world with its own logic. To paraphrase in terms of a later, similar depiction, a great building—say a cathedral—in a modern city is a tourist site, an anachronism, and a familiar landmark. But a great building like the one evoked by Debussy's piano prelude "La Cathedral engloutie," the "engulfed cathedral" rising out of the waves and sinking beneath them again in a long, slow, endless rhythm—Mont-Saint-Michel as it looks, not as it is: a cathedral of which the musical image is built from processions of parallel chords rising or sinking over basses that plumb the depths of the keyboard in hollow resonant tones or murky undulations, occasionally relieved by splashes of high treble: a cathedral in the sea is a wonder.

This construal of the siren/mermaid trope in the modern era appears at its most explicit in two famous segments of Theodor Adorno's and Max Horkheimer's *Dialectic of Enlightenment* (1947). In the pages that follow, I will read backward from this text through its precursors in Kafka and Nietzsche, then forward through a series of musical instances of the modern siren from Mendelssohn through Wagner to Ravel. This sampling, in the shape of a wave that in breaking releases the siren within its plume, will survey the form taken by the watery trope in response to the rationalizing demands of modern enterprise culture, as Mary Douglas calls it.[11] Typically for the music of this era, this response embodies a reversion to an allure that has apparently been refused or at least contained. That reversion appears in its most restricted, resentment-laden form in Horkheimer and Adorno. With each step backward in textual time, it becomes looser and more rewarding, in alliance with musical imagery and a musicalized style. This retrospective tendency intensifies and plays forward when the narrative shifts to actual music and the image of the sirens' song becomes a symbolic rendering of its sound. What impels the tendency toward reversion is not just nostalgia for a beauty or pleasure not yet denuded of mystery, but the still more seductive call of critical intelligence: the exposure as ideological illusion of the need to resist such beauty or pleasure.[12]

In no case, however, will I suggest a comprehensive reading of any of

"LONGINDYINGCALL"

these texts or pieces, and not just because of space constraints. As I've suggested elsewhere, "meaning, hermeneutically regarded, is not diffused evenly throughout a work of music (or anything else) but distributed unevenly in peaks and valleys. The peaks are the points of endowment"—installed by explicit sense-giving gestures, semantic performatives—"from which meaning extends to 'cover' the work as a whole."[13] My aim here is to trace the wavering course of the siren trope from peak to peak; to profile the trope by noting a series of open, obvious points at which its potentials for meaning are activated. The result should suggest an interpretation of the trope, at least within the limited horizon of my examples, while leaving the interpretation of the examples themselves incipient and underdetermined. In some cases what the work actually "says" or represents will be less important than the allure of a detail, a way of proceeding, a shift of expressive focus. This approach seems particularly appropriate for the sirens, whose paradigmatic effect is to appropriate all meaning and value to their song, so that the traveler who hears them wants—like Odysseus tied to his mast—only to leave the depleted shell of a world behind and deliver himself up to whatever the song portends.

Horkheimer and Adorno take Odysseus as the prototype of the alienated, overrationalized subject of Enlightenment, and the sirens episode of *The Odyssey* as his prototypical moment.[14] The allure of the sirens is the prospect of losing oneself in a past prior to the social and technological domination of nature; the sirens' song inevitably destroys the alienated subject who hearkens to it by promising, falsely, a "happy return" to the pre-enlightened state. Odysseus ratifies his identity as a—the—modern subject by creating a triple distance between himself and the beckoning song. First and foremost, he mobilizes the force of social domination, plugging his crew's ears with wax so that they can row him past the island of the sirens without themselves being touched by their singing. He is the master; he alone will be the hearer (*der Hörende*) who avoids bondage (*die Hörigkeit*). Second, he uses his famous wiliness to find the technical means to listen unharmed. He will be chained to the mast of his ship, unable to move, unable to order his deafened crew to turn back. With his arms bound, his ears will be free. His faith in this device comes from the third mechanism of distance, the use of his reason to find "a loophole [Lücke] in the contract [of his subjection], which enables him to fulfill the statute while evading it. The primeval contract does not anticipate whether the passing traveler listens bound or unbound to the song."[15] Purely a creature of instrumental reason, Odysseus feels entitled to heed the letter and break the spirit of the "contract" with neither regret nor scruple.

Horkheimer and Adorno are not impressed. Odysseus, they argue, degrades the sirens' song with the means he finds to hear it: "Odysseus recognizes the sublime archaic power [*archaisiche Übermacht*] of the song even as, technically enlightened [*technisch aufgeklärt*], he has himself bound. He yearns towards the song of pleasure and thwarts it as he does death [*Er neigt sich dem Liede der Lust und vereitelt sie wie den Tod*]."[16] Recognizing the song's primordial power is not the same as feeling it, and Odysseus can find no more in it than entertainment, a proto-bourgeois reduction of the song's unique enchantment to the "longing of the passerby [*Sehnsucht desser, der vorüberfärt*]". Or, as they also put it, he reduces the song from a compelling immediacy to "a mere object of contemplation, to art"; he treats the sirens' song like a casual concertgoer.[17] Worse yet, this fortunate-unfortunate (*glücklich-misglückten*) encounter has sickened (*erkrankt*) all subsequent song, so that "the whole of Western music labors against the contradiction of song in civilization, that nevertheless again proclaims the emotional power of all art music."[18] What we know as music is at best a parody of the sirens' song, a defensive appropriation of what we dare not hear.

Kafka's parable "The Silence of the Sirens" (ca. 1920) is less stringent. Like Horkheimer's and Adorno's, his Odysseus, here called Ulysses, is a technocrat proud of his wiles, a figure too competent for his own good, an allegorical embodiment of modern enterprise and concurrent lack of spirit. Perhaps because Kafka made an error, perhaps because he didn't, this Ulysses differs from Homer's original. He not only has himself bound to the mast, but also stops up his own ears with wax, not those of his crew; he does not want to hear the sirens at all. The parable puts a series of ironic spins on the fortunate-unfortunate results. The sirens know that "though admittedly such a thing has never happened, still it is conceivable that someone might possibly have escaped from their singing; but from their silence certainly never."[19] So they do not sing at all. Ulysses, hearing nothing, but not knowing that there is nothing to hear, mistakenly believes that his trick has worked. Yet he may not be wrong, because the look of bliss on his face seduces the sirens; it makes them forget their singing.

The ironies do not stop here, but cutting across their proliferation is a classic moment of epiphany that belongs both to the content of the parable and to its language. Ulysses sees for a moment the siren song he cannot hear, and the parable turns for a moment from detached reflection to absorbed lyricism: "For a fleeting moment he saw their throats rising and falling, their breasts lifting, their eyes filled with tears, their lips half-parted, but believed that these were accompaniments to the airs which died unheard around him."[20] Regardless of what Ulysses believes, the text

[202]

"LONGINDYINGCALL"

presents the "accompaniments" as surrogates for the absent airs, the music of which sounds in the lyricism of the prose and underwrites the images that depict the moment as rhythmic, erotic, affecting, and enraptured. Admittedly, this is not the last word. Ulysses sails away and the ironies resume. Besides, the moment is an illusion. But so is Ulysses's triumph, even if we accept a "codicil" stating that he knew the sirens were silent and only pretended to mute the song they only pretended to sing. Either way, the sirens win as well as lose. Their silence, which is equivalent to the modern condition, is also the condition of possibility for imagining their song. As Rilke put it, the song is only the other side of the silence.

Silence is also the condition of the sirens' appearance in a key passage from Nietzsche's *The Gay Science* (1888). Acting in his own person as a modern subject rather than through a mythical deputy, Nietzsche comes too late to encounter the sirens themselves. But he can still find allegorical value in the material and symbolic forms that would once have made up such an encounter. He finds them in displaced bits and pieces of the imagery traditionally associated with them, or with their cousins the mermaids. And in displaced form, too, he hears them, even though, like their sisters in Kafka, they do not sing.

The passage begins with questions of hearing posed as Nietzsche wades amid the "burning of the breakers" [*inmitten des Brandes der Brandung*]: "Do I still have ears? Am I all ears and nothing else?" Then a ship sails by, mantled in "ghostly beauty":

> When a man is in the midst of his noise [*Lärm*], in the midst of the breakers of his plots and plans [*Würfen und Entwürfen*], perhaps he sees there calm enchanting beings glide past him, for whose happiness and retiringness [*Zürückgezogenheit*] he longs—*they are women*. He almost thinks that there with the women dwells his better self; that in these calm places even the loudest breakers become as still as death and life itself a dream of life. Yet! yet! my noble enthusiast, even in the most beautiful sailing ship there is so much noise, and so much petty, pitiable noise! The enchantment and the most powerful effect of woman is, in philosophical language, an effect at a distance, *actio in distans;* but there belongs thereto first and foremost—*distance.*[21]

Distance, it might be said, is the essential medium of the sirens' song. What is at stake in it here?

Overtly the passage seeks to reject the sirens, to affirm the Odyssean life of plots and plans regardless of the noise it makes. With Nietzsche, of course, the plots and plans are not willingly those of modern enterprise but those he requires to overcome it. The sirens represent an alternative that he would like to regard as regressive. But he cannot make the charge stick. The exclamatory "Yet! yet" that marks the turning point of his effort also marks its futility. The more pervasive effort of the passage is to enact the impossibility of rejecting the sirens, an action that cannot be carried out no matter how hard one tries, not least because one never tries as hard as one might. The sirens are still enchanting, too enchanting to let pass; they can be rejected only in terms that preserve their enchantment. This is implicit in Derrida's important reading of the passage:

> Woman's seduction works from a distance, the distance is the element of her power. But from this song, from this charm, it is necessary to keep one's distance, it is necessary to keep at a distance from distance, not only, as one might think, to protect oneself against this fascination, but also very much to succumb to it. It's *wanted*, this distance (which is wanting). *Il faut* la distance (qui faut).[22]

Derrida's comments are notable for restoring the sirens to Nietzsche's text, which makes no mention of their song or its charm, and for adding the implicit suggestion that for Nietzsche "siren" and "woman" are essentially synonyms. But they are not so much synonyms for each other as for the failure of critical reflection to unravel their enchantment. If distance enchants, then keeping one's distance from distance can only enchant the more.

But why do these sirens not sing? Their silence is not a stratagem like that of Kafka's sirens, but part of a broader pattern of reversal, or reversion, that endows the Odyssean quester with the sirens' own character. The quester in this passage is a centered figure, not a voyager; a figure of the shore, not of the ship; and a figure who does not hear, but sees, the object(s) of his desire. In each of these respects, the quester trades places with the sirens. Their song is his dream of silence, a dream that can never be fulfilled and that can be dreamed at all only amid the noise, the plots and plans, of the dreamer. The song is enchanting precisely because it must thus be dreamed. It is not the sailor who must elude the sirens, but the sirens who must elude the beached sailor—but who do so precisely so that, paradoxically, in their distance he can be moved by them, in their silence he can hear their song, and more, can, in the very texture of his prose, sing their song.[23]

A similar reversal underlies Mendelssohn's *The Fair Melusine,* a musical recounting of the legend of a mermaid who can assume human form

"LONGINDYINGCALL"

and even marry, but only if she revisits her true shape by submerging herself once a week. According to Schumann, the overture consists of three types of music, representing in turn the "charming, yielding Melusine," her "proud, knightly" husband, Lusignan, and the rippling water, represented by a "magical wave figure" [*zauberischen Wellenfigur*], which alternately seems to envelop and divide the embracing couple.[24] All of these elements form complete sectional units, which the overture weaves into something like a sonata form. But this is a form that sounds the way a submerged object looks, drawn, so to speak, into a mermaid's "delicate shadowy shape" by the expressive allure of its topic. Form and expression continually vie with each other; the sections are arranged so as increasingly to problematize the impression of sonata, eventually to the point of dissolution. It is as if the archaic identification of music with feeling—that siren song—were drawing the ear away from the modern enterprise of reconciling feeling with form.

(Here the reader stops to hear the music. Failing that, to hear its silence.)

The overture begins tranquilly with reiterations of the justly famous wave figure; these apparently constitute the "first theme" of a standard sonata form in F major. The turbulent knightly music follows in F minor, at which point the formal trouble begins—in triplicate. In the standard form, energy precedes lyricism, not the other way around; the second theme is virtually never in the minor; and the two themes belong to different keys, not the different modes of the same key. The situation seems to right itself when Melusine's lyrical music subsequently enters in A-flat major, the key appropriate for a second theme when the first is in F minor. It now appears that the knightly and lyrical themes make up such a pair, expressively as well as tonally in the right order. They really do make a couple, with the music of the "charming, yielding" siren in her secular, domestic form presented as an adjunct to her husband's knightly pride, or knightly bluster, which returns to envelop the lyrical theme before the ensuing development. The wave music seems in retrospect like an introduction. Expressively primary, its evocative texture is formally secondary, setting the scene for a process it can adorn but not control.[25]

The development, where more knightly hubbub drives the lyrical theme to assume a turbulent form, would seem to confirm this impression were it not prefaced by a return of the wave music. This, the music of Melusine's other form—the form of her otherness—not only mimics the rippling of waves but also sets up a wavelike rhythm that ripples across the entire overture. Each time it appears the music seems self-sufficient, serenely unaffected by either the mood or the formal drama of the music around it. It next arises when the recapitulation flatly declines to bring back the supposed first theme with its knightly regalia, and puts a full restatement of the "introductory" wave music in its place. One result is to juxtapose this music with the return of the lyrical "Melusine" theme in its original "yielding" form, as if Melusine and her proper element were blissfully reuniting. The knightly music tries to intervene but washes harmlessly away. The scene of formal resolution dissolves the logic of the couple into the charm of the singular being who escapes all logic but her own. As if in protest, the knightly music makes one last appearance in the guise of a coda. But it is only a *faux* coda, or a failed one; the real coda belongs to the wave music, which returns yet again, expands to form a frame for the whole overture, evolves a group of exquisite farewell gestures, and quietly ebbs away.

In the end the siren prevails. Her song, the music of her element, sluices through and over the elements of a sonata form until the form blurs and fades. Yet it does not entirely fade; it does not even threaten to. The overture wants to overturn Odyssean illusions about the shipwreck of form, not to perpetuate them. Like the silence of the sirens in Kafka, the framing effect of the "magical wave figure" becomes significant only in relation to the form it eludes, the submerged and finally the absent presence that never stops mediating it. The wave-figure increasingly opens a utopian space outside the modern, progressive narrative embodied in the sonata-form couple, but, like a freshet, it takes its shape from sluicing along the contours of that narrative. The form is not destroyed; it is transformed. Polished and suppled, it suffers a sea-change.

Mendelssohn thus issues the claim that modern cultural anxieties about fluidity are groundless, or rather too earthbound. They are, he suggests, tied to a defensive sense of pragmatic rationality masquerading as an outdated nobility. The contrast between the wave figure and the knightly theme encapsulates this point. The wave figure varies but does not develop; mutable but continuous, it leads only to itself and luxuriates in its own presence. Its "magical" quality is the first thing we hear in it, as its throaty warble on solo clarinet becomes the murmuring of the strings in a collective dream. The knightly figure develops but does not vary. For all its motivic and developmental activity, it is rigid in its gestures and unable to escape the rigid codes that govern it. In context, its trumpet-and-drum rhetoric sounds in part like a proclamation of its own conventionality. The change of mode that unites and divides it from the wave music is something like a fall into modernity from a timeless or primordial realm. This is a modernity diminished by the transparency of its codes and techniques, the noise of its knightly enterprise. But the noise leaves the

"LONGINDYINGCALL"

wave music undisturbed as, magical as ever, it calls from and recedes into the distance later celebrated by Nietzsche and Derrida.[26]

The opening of *Das Rheingold* (1854) is often thought to owe a resentful debt to the opening of Mendelssohn's overture. Wagner seems to recompose Mendelssohn's magical wave figure in order to invert its values; his version will be ambivalent, not merely attractive; complex, even tortuous, rather than simple; and deep where (from Wagner's fraught ideological perspective) Mendelssohn's is superficial.[27] These differences are particularly pointed with respect to the fall into modernity, which in Wagner cannot be divided neatly between masculine purpose and feminine temptation. To be sure, when the Nibelung dwarf Alberich renounces love in favor of the gold cared for by the Rhinemaidens, he embodies—among other things—the heartless spirit of modern enterprise as Wagner conceived it. But his action also reenacts a fall already traversed by the Rhinemaidens themselves, and in the place one would least expect for such sirens: in their song.

The action of the *Ring* cycle begins with that song. More exactly, it begins with the Rhinemaidens' transition to song from amid a rippling stream of soft, undulant nonsense syllables. Voice emerges from the instrumental Prelude to initiate the drama by progressing into speech. But to venture a reading of this event we need to immerse ourselves in the time before voice.

According to Wagner himself, the *Rheingold* Prelude is based on an evocation of "rapidly flowing water" represented by "the musical sound of the E-flat major chord, which continually surges forward in a figured arpeggiation; these arpeggios appear as melodic figurations of increasing motion, yet the pure E-flat triad never changes, and seems through its persistence to impart infinite significance to the [watery] element."[28] The music unfolds slowly in a continuous additive pattern that begins with a single E-flat at the bottom of the orchestra and ends with what Warren Darcy calls "a collage of six different ostinati" swirling simultaneously.[29] The evolution from a single, murky, unmeasured tone, reinforced by audible overtones, to a complex, transparent, measured texture suggests a passage from the static condition of primordial harmony to the rhythm of historical time. This movement, however, is not yet that of a fall or alienation, as the unchanging harmony, with its "infinite significance," affirms. Each new phase in the music reinscribes the primordial unity at its origin. The rupture that designates modernity has not yet occurred.

That begins to change when a Rhinemaiden's voice enters the scene, bringing with it the first change of harmony. Woglinde makes the pivotal

[207]

utterance, mingling her nonsense syllables with phonetically similar words so that, for a moment, there is little distinction to be made between articulate speech and pure vocalic wave motion without meaning:

> Weia! Waga! Woge, du Welle!
> Walle zur Wiege! Wagalaweia!
> Walala weiala weia!
>
> Weia! Waga! Well up, you wave!
> Waft to a womb-bed! Wagalaweia!
> Wallala weiala weia![30]

The mingling of liquid utterance with lyrical melody creates a new form of magical wave figure that leaves any sense of rupture with the origin unacknowledged. To make it so is perhaps the very definition of a siren song. But when the Rhinemaidens thereafter move from voice to speech, when they begin to discuss who they are and what they ought to do, they introduce at a stroke all the elements of modernity that have so far been held in suspension: narrative, history, responsibility, law, the possibility of transgression, the seeds of retribution. When Alberich comes along, as he does all too quickly, an inevitable intruder, he simply initiates the repetition as action of the alienated condition that informs the siren song as irony. The one is as implicit in the other as the E-flat triad is implicit in the overtones of the originary tone.

Wagner thus gives a dark new turn to an old idea. The identification of the transition from voice to speech as the mark of the human dates at least back to Aristotle and had been revived by Jakob Grimm as recently as 1851.[31] The wave music of Mendelssohn's Melusine can also be heard as a revival of this idea; the rippling phrase that flows through it is heard most often passing between solo instrumental voices, primarily the two clarinets and first flute, before spreading to the strings, as if it were a wandering voice whose domain is the liminal space between the vocally articulate and the verbal.[32] The siren in this context represents the original power and pleasure of voice apart from the speech to which voice is drawn as powerfully as it draws the desire of those who speak.

But this is very far from the end of the story. For Wagner the origin and its echo in the siren song do not so much belong to the past as to the depths beneath the present, represented by the depths of the Rhine. That the *Ring* ultimately returns to those depths, ending where it began, is one of the most famous things about it. That this ending involves an extended reprise of the "Weia! Waga!" melody suggests that the reinscription of the origin, or at least the smallest of departures from it, is a permanent pos-

"LONGINDYINGCALL"

sibility even when the consequences of the fall into modernity are catastrophic. "Yet! yet"—and here the weight of Wagner's ambivalence can be felt—that the melody returns only in the orchestra, not in a Rhinemaiden's voice, suggests that to voice it, to realize the perennial possibility of reinscribing primordial harmony in historical time, would be to risk catastrophe all over again. It is only, Wagner seems to say, in the fleeting moment of its first—or last—utterance that the siren song can keep the promise it cannot keep from making.

This implication is perhaps anticipated in the first act of Wagner's *Tannhäuser* (1845), which begins by representing the song of the classical sirens themselves: an unaccompanied, and quite ravishing, lyric for a small group of women's voices. This instance is exceptional with respect to the trope described in this essay, thanks to a contradiction between the dramatic and musical "plots" of the opera. Tannhäuser's relationship to modernity is conceived along lines current among the German Romantics around the turn of the nineteenth century: he is caught between the finitude of the classical world and the Christian discovery of the infinite. His antithetical beloveds, Venus and the saintly Elisabeth, personify the choice between these alternatives, which he is never unequivocally able to make; the sirens represent the essence of what holds him back. Musically, however, the sirens are seductive precisely for their modernity, which offers the hero—who is also, of course, a minstrel—a different mode of infinity: the infinite ambiguity of a five-note chord that resolves only to a discord and has no fixable identity, and which, perhaps for that very reason, is possessed of an extraordinary sensuousness and sweetness. This allure, like that of the women on Nietzsche's passing ship, depends on action at a distance. Once heard, the sirens' voices recede into the "far distance," presumably offstage, from which they are heard again later in the act in a fragmentary reprise, thereafter to be heard no more. Fading away is their mode of being. Proximity would destroy the promise of these voices, as the events set in motion when Alberich accosts the Rhinemaidens will later prove. The *Ring* concludes by receding into the distance of the sirens' song—and of their silence. It returns to the space of promise apart from fulfillment.

German composers, of course, were not the only ones interested in that promise, as my earlier references to Debussy acknowledge. Like their counterparts in Debussy's slightly earlier *Nocturnes*, the three movements of Ravel's piano suite *Gaspard de la nuit* (1908, based on poems by Aloys Bertrand) form an allegorical sequence, one reading of which turns on the wish to escape the stringencies of modernity.

As its title suggests, the central movement, "Le Gibet" [The Gallows],

[209]

evokes a scene of punishment, fatality, the imposition of reason by law; the inexorability of these constraints finds its musical correlative in an ostinato on a single note that tolls throughout the piece. The outer movements lie beyond the boundaries of law and reason. The first, "Ondine," is the siren song. Although the associated poem represents a failed temptation—the narrator, betrothed to a mortal woman, rejects the water-nymph's call to rule in her moonlit palace beneath a lake—the music concentrates entirely on evoking the temptress. Ravel's Ondine is a creature of shimmering impalpability. She is associated primarily with high-treble tremolos, glissandi, and arpeggios that swirl around the melodic line and, at climactic moments, obliterate it, releasing more turbulent wave figures that span the keyboard. The process is continuous, and in its continuity seems completely unmoralized; the charm and the turbulence simply come and go, inextricably folded into each other.[33]

Neither, however, seems a match for the *Grand Guignol* horrors of the gibbet. For that the third movement is required, a portrait of the malicious imp known as Scarbo. A kind of punk Puck, Scarbo is a figure of pure antinomian energy; the music that depicts him is spiky, burly, scurrying, and belligerent. His special affinity is for the deep, growling bass, in pointed contrast to Ondine's shimmering treble; the depths he comes from are visceral, not glassy. And yet—another yet!—even Scarbo is susceptible to the charms of Undine. At about its two-thirds point, after a protracted spell of deep-bass growling, the imp's musical profile reverts to the siren's. Despite some efforts to turn the reversion to parody, the music clears and softens, evoking Ondine's rippling texture and slipping for a moment into a distant paraphrase of the wave-caressed melodic tracery of the earlier movement. There is nothing so definite—nothing so crude—as a quotation; the moment is already dissolving even as it forms; but its effect, imbued with a Mallarméan aura of precise but nebulous suggestiveness, is just for that reason the perfect reminiscence of a siren song.

The impalpability of this reminiscence may stem not only from Symbolist aesthetics, but also from the kind of anti-narrative impulse already noted in Mendelssohn and Wagner. After all, sirens exist to interrupt a voyage, the most ancient of templates for narrative. By avoiding literal quotation, Ravel can have Ondine interrupt Scarbo's narrative without regressing to a counter-narrative. The siren song thus defines itself by, or as, music's reflective withdrawal from the narrativity that is one of its chief links to the work of culture.

For the listener who yields to its charm, the song's action at a distance casts a shape-shifting spell. The apparition of Ondine in "Scarbo" turns

"LONGINDYINGCALL"

Gaspard de la nuit into a reflection on the grim consequences of rejecting Ondine and her world, or rather of trying to reject them, since the rejection proves impossible. "Scarbo," to be sure, moves on from this moment of reversion and reflection and finishes with its raw, vital energy intact. But the reversion cannot be undone, only ignored, and the ignoring of it may seem to give Scarbo's rampages an edge of panic that is harder to ignore. Where the energy of Debussy's "Fêtes" seems to liberate a responsiveness to the sirens' song, the energy of Ravel's "Scarbo" tries and fails to compensate for the song's receding. To the charms of the watery world, it can oppose only a great deal of Nietzschean noise: for Scarbo, too, is a creature of plots and plans, even if only in travesty. In him the bullying of Mendelssohn's Lusignan, the grasping of Wagner's Alberich, and the violence that Horkheimer and Adorno saw in instrumental reason, all find their inverted image. Ondine tells us so, the phantoms of her siren song and magical wave figure still acting at a distance, in the voice of another reason.

The watery world is attractive as a liminal medium because the boundaries of the masculine body and body-ego, the appointed vehicle of the modern subject, Odysseus updated, must continually be reaffirmed, traced against the solid impalpability of water as by the spindly figure of the stooped, sickly Nietzsche wading an imaginary Mediterranean, willing his way into the water or the thought thereof because the masculinity he inherits is defined as the will and the willingness to risk the mixing, the improper existence signified and enacted by fluidity, in order to become once more unmixed, a process that is also a political economy because water has no proper, observes no propriety, cannot be property, a dispossession that is the constant theme, the melos and melody, of the siren song that he both hears and ventriloquizes, song and wave and woman alike signifying and enacting the pleasures of mixing (Melville's Ishmael and Queequeg in the slippery union of squeezing lumps of whale sperm into fluid, the shoppers at Zola's department store The Ladies' Paradise drifting away on the liquescent fantasies induced by their softing silks), melting pleasures that in the masculine libidinal economy must (but can't) be disavowed because they are the pleasures (yes, of course, the pleasures, since we are speaking here of imaginary bodies, no more capable of being wounded than an animated cartoon) of castration (which must not, lest we honor the fantasy too much, be the last word, from the absence of which the sirens may infer that there should be no last word at all, absolutely no la

NOTES

1. Evocative language or no, academic protocol requires the identification of several of the allusions in these paragraphs. The mermaids calling and combing allude to T. S. Eliot's poem "The Love Song of J. Alfred Prufrock" (1909) and "the dice of drowned men's bones" to Hart Crane's "At Melville's Tomb" (ca. 1926), which itself may allude to Eliot's *The Waste Land* (1922) and to Stéphane Mallarmé's "Un Coup de dés jamais ne abolira le hasard" (A Throw of the Dice Will Never Abolish Chance, 1895), also alluded to (and subsequently discussed) here. G. W. F. Hegel's statement about the sea is from the Introduction to his *The Philosophy of History* (1830–1831), trans. J. Sibree (New York: Dover, 1956), 90. The allusions to Herman Melville and Emile Zola in the final paragraph of this essay refer to chaps. 94 and 4, respectively, of their novels *Moby-Dick* (1851) and *The Ladies' Paradise* (1883). The "Longindying call" of the title is from the "Sirens" chapter of James Joyce's *Ulysses* (New York: Random House, 1961), 256, an epitomizing phrase that is also an homage to a text too complex to be discussed in these pages.

2. No. III of "A Man Young and Old" from *The Tower* (1928), in *Collected Poems of W. B. Yeats* (London: Macmillan, 1967), 250.

3. For a comprehensive survey, with illustrations, see Bram Djikstra, *Idols of Perversity: Fantasies of Feminine Evil in Fin-de-Siècle Culture* (New York: Oxford University Press, 1986), 35–271.

4. The literature on modernity is too vast for citation. Classic starting points for its definition (especially for the tradition canvassed by this essay) include Max Weber, "Science [Wissenschaft] as a Vocation" (1917) and "Religious Rejections of the World and Their Directions" (1915) in *From Max Weber: Essays in Sociology*, ed. H. H. Gerth and C. Wright Mills (New York: Oxford University Press, 1958), 129–58 (esp. 138–49) and 323–59 (esp. 333–57); see also Charles Taylor, *Sources of the Self: The Making of the Modern Identity* (Cambridge, Mass.: Harvard University Press, 1989); and Anthony J. Cascardi, *The Subject of Modernity* (Cambridge: Cambridge University Press, 1992).

5. From Guy Treblay, "After Nice, a Return to Vice," from *The New York Times*, Sunday, June 8, 2003, sec. 9, 1.

6. Translation of this and the subsequent passage modified from Mallarmé, *The Poems: A Bilingual Edition*, trans. Keith Bosley (Harmondsworth: Penguin, 1977), 272.

7. T. S. Eliot, *Collected Poems, 1909–1962* (New York: Harcourt, Brace and World, 1963), 65.

8. Compare Arthur Rimbaud, "Le Bateau ivre" (The Drunken Boat), ll. 21–24: "je me suis baigné dans le Poème / De la Mer . . . ou, flottaison bléme / Et ravie, un noyé pensif parfois descend" (I bathed in the Poem / Of the Sea . . . where, flotsam pale / And enraptured, a pensive drowned man sometimes sinks); from Rimbaud, *Complete Works, Selected Letters*, trans. and ed. Wallace Fowlie (Chicago: University of Chicago Press, 1966), 117; translation modified.

"LONGINDYINGCALL"

9. From Rainer Maria Rilke, *New Poems, The German Text with a Translation, Introduction, and Notes by J. B. Leishman* (New York: New Directions, 1964), 168, my translation.

10. From Georg Eismann, ed., *Robert Schumann: Ein Quellenwerk Über Sein Leben und Schaffen* (Leipzig: Breitkopf und Härtel, 1956), 77, my translation.

11. Mary Douglas, "The Person in an Enterprise Culture," in *Understanding the Enterprise Culture: Themes in the Work of Mary Douglas,* ed. Shaun H. Heap and Angus Ross (New York: Norton, 1992), 41–62.

12. On reversion and music in the post-Enlightenment era, see chap. 2 of my *Classical Music and Postmodern Knowledge* (Berkeley: University of California Press, 1995), esp. 43–51. It is worth noting that the most explicit theorization of reversion and its troubles, Horkheimer and Adorno's rereading of the Homeric sirens, is also the latest. An implicit part of my argument here is that, in a typical effect, the belated theorization crystallizes a discourse that has already circulated for a long time, and that in this case—and this is *not* exceptional—all but begins in actual music. It might even not be going too far to speculate, given Adorno's preoccupation with Wagner, that the mythography of the sirens in *Dialectic of Enlightenment* is in part a response to Wagner's *Ring* cycle, to which this essay will turn at an important juncture.

13. From my "Yesterday's Moonlight: Chopin, Beethoven, and the Hermeneutics of Resemblance," in *D'une herméneutique de la musique,* ed. Christian Hauer (forthcoming).

14. On the relation of these paradigms to the general project of Horkheimer and, especially, Adorno, see Richard Leppert's Introduction to Theodor W. Adorno, *Essays on Music,* selected, with introduction, commentary, and notes, by Richard Leppert (Berkeley: University of California Press, 2002), 27–31.

15. Max Horkheimer and Theodor W. Adorno, *Dialektik der Aufklärung: Philosophische Fragmente* (1947; reprint, Amsterdam: Verlag de Munter, 1989), 76; my translation.

16. Horkheimer and Adorno, *Dialektik,* 76.

17. Horkheimer and Adorno, *Dialektik,* 48.

18. Horkheimer and Adorno, *Dialektik,* 76.

19. "The Silence of the Sirens," trans. Willa and Edwin Muir, in Franz Kafka, *The Complete Stories,* ed. Nahum N. Glatzer (New York: Schocken, 1971), 430–32.

20. Kafka, "The Silence of the Sirens," 431.

21. From section 60 of *The Gay Science;* the translation here is adapted from that of Barbara Harlow in Jacques Derrida, *Spurs: Nietzsche's Styles / Eperons: Les Styles de Nietzsche* (Chicago: University of Chicago Press, 1979), 47. Derrida begins his discussion of this section with the provocative observation that "All of Nietzsche's investigations, and in particular those which concern women, are coiled in the labyrinth of an ear" (43).

22. Derrida, *Spurs,* 48, my translation.

23. In section 310 of *The Gay Science,* "Will and Wave," another marine encounter reanimates the mermaids much as section 60 does the sirens. Nietzsche

[213]

again represents himself as standing amid the breakers, but this time his interest goes to the bodies of the waves themselves. The result is the creation of a subaqueous world in which erotic-romantic energy is indistinguishable from unconstrained enjoyment of the will to power: "arch your dangerous green bodies as high as you can, raise a wall between me and the sun—as you are doing now! Truly, even now nothing remains of the world but green twilight and green lightning. Carry on as you like, roaring with overweening pleasure and malice [Übermut]—or dive again, pouring your emeralds down into the deepest depths, and throw your infinite white mane of foam and spray over them: Everything suits me, for everything suits you so well, and I am so well-disposed toward you for everything." From *The Gay Science,* trans. Walter Kaufmann (New York: Random House, 1974), 247–48.

24. Eismann, *Quellenwerk,* 1956), 77, my translation.

25. For a more detailed account of the formal design of the movement, together with information about the genesis of the overture, see Thomas Grey, "The Orchestral Music," in *The Mendelssohn Companion,* ed. Douglass Seaton (Westport, Conn.: Greenwood Press, 2001), 475–83.

26. The expressive contrasts of Mendelssohn's overture might be said to return, on a larger scale and with an infusion of a postwar melancholy, to organize Hans Werner Henze's romantic ballet *Undine* (1957). Here the plot takes a siren's twist and celebrates the hero's death by water as a triumph of love that unites him with the water nymph.

27. Wagner might be said to treat Mendelssohn himself here as a kind of siren, but one who can, so to speak, be outsung by the Odyssean artist-voyager whom he tempts. In the background of this song contest (shades of *Tannhäuser,* of which more below), Wagner chose to resist Mendelssohn's siren song by identifying it as Jewish within an anti-Semitic discourse, most pungently in the infamous pamphlet *Judaism in Music* (1850). But Mendelssohn for that very reason remains a presence in this music, while a figure such as E. T. A. Hoffmann—whose opera *Undine* (1816), based on the novella of that name by Friedrich de la Motte Fouquet, is another of Wagner's sources—does not.

28. From Wagner's *Mein Leben* [My life], 1869; translated by Warren Darcy in his "*Creation ex nihilo:* The Genesis, Structure, and Meaning of the *Rheingold* Prelude," *19th-Century Music* 13 (1989): 79–100, at 79. I have changed the tenses here from past to present.

29. Ibid., 97.

30. To preserve the alliteration, I've fabricated "womb-bed" as a translation of "Wiege," cradle.

31. Aristotle's formulation appears in the *Politics,* 1253a, 10–18; for a discussion, see Giorgio Agamben, *Homo Sacer: Sovereign Power and Bare Life,* trans. Daniel Heller-Roazen (Stanford: Stanford University Press, 1998), 7–8. Grimm's statement is in his "On the Origin of Language," trans. Ralph R. Read III in *German Romantic Criticism,* ed. Leslie Willson (New York: Continuum, 1982), 262–69.

"LONGINDYINGCALL"

32. On the trope of wandering voice, see the Epilogue, "Voice and Its Beyonds," to my *Opera and Modern Culture: Wagner and Strauss* (Berkeley: University of California Press, 2004).

33. In her playful self-sufficiency, Ravel's Undine may look forward to the narrator of Laurie Anderson's *Blue Lagoon* (from Anderson's album *Mister Heartbreak*, 1984), a figure who, instead of attracting men, merges the traditionally masculine persona of the castaway into the figure of the mermaid. This is a woman's mermaid—one of the few. My thanks to Paul Attinello for calling my attention to the song.

CHAPTER 16

"Au-delà d'une musique informelle": Nostalgia, Obsolescence, and the Avant-Garde

The musical avant-garde has long since become the routine it wants to overthrow. A half-century ago, in his essay "Vers une musique informelle," Theodor Adorno already found its output formulaic, and therefore in default of music's aesthetic mission (as he saw it) to register and resist the administered world of instrumental reason. At the time, this charge might plausibly have been called regressive, symptomatic of Adorno's nostalgia for the high modernism that the avant-garde thought of itself as discarding. (Schoenberg was dead, or so Pierre Boulez had infamously declared.) Today, with the world arguably more administered than ever, and fitted out with a soundtrack on which any and every style becomes a parody of itself, the charge seems not only pointed but also prescient. The very concept enshrined by the phrase "avant-garde," a quasi-military advance along a single line of progress or conquest, has the feel of a cultural relic. New works of avant-garde music fail to shock; we know their tricks too well. Worse yet, many older avant-garde works have become endearing—even, in the digital age, quaint.

This historical irony overshadowed the 2005 New York premiere of *Shadowtime*, a "thought opera" by the composer Brian Ferneyhough and the poet Charles Bernstein. First performed at the Munich Biennale in 2004, *Shadowtime* is based on the life of Walter Benjamin. The choice of protagonist is emblematic: who better than Benjamin could embody the avant-garde's rejection of the false normality of modern life or better embody the concept of the artist-hero self-exiled amid the detritus of history? The opera begins with Benjamin's suicide in 1940 (when he decided—mistakenly—that his attempt to flee Nazi Europe had failed) and proceeds through a non-linear, non-narrative sequence of six further scenes exploring different facets of Benjamin's thought. Benjamin himself appears less as an agent than as a personification of the critical consciousness "presiding," in Ferneyhough's words, "over the sublimely catastrophic demolition of Enlightenment values taking place around him as he wrote."[1]

The music is characteristic of its composer, unremittingly dense and difficult. The text is obscure in its own right and further obscured by its setting, with phrases both sung and spoken simultaneously throughout. At one point, a figure with two heads, one of Karl Marx, the other of Groucho, questions Benjamin about the future of memory. At another, in an underworld modeled on a Las Vegas nightclub (had someone been watching the popular television series

---

[1] Ferneyhough, quoted by Jeremy Eichler, "A Secular Messiah Gets His Own Opera," *The New York Times*, Sunday, 17 July 2005, section 2, column 2.

CSI: Crime Scene Investigation?), "a Liberace-type entertainer plays a violently difficult and mesmerizing piano work of nearly 20 minutes while reciting a text that mixes droll philosophical questions with gibberish."[2]

The idea that this work would upset its audience seemed to please both the composer and librettist, who also seemed to take it for granted. Good avant-gardists both, they cast themselves as the enemies of a complacency based on a thoughtless clinging to those demolished Enlightenment values. "Listeners," Ferneyhough informs them in a program note, "must let go of a fixed notion of what constitutes musical form" if they are to grasp *Shadowtime*. "Many," says Bernstein, "will no doubt be befuddled," but although "there have been a lot of very clear books written on the subject of this catastrophe ['the blank space of what happened to Europe between 1940 and 1945'] . . . can anyone say that they truly understand what happened?"[3]

Maybe not. But the befuddlement never materialized. Neither did the antagonism. Judging from the reviews, those who didn't like *Shadowtime*—apparently the majority—were respectful but lukewarm. Boring the opera may have been; shocking it was not. It would have been far more shocking as a number opera. As an avant-garde production, it was merely predictable. Ferneyhough and Bernstein seemed to harbor nostalgic hopes of re-enacting the 1913 premiere of *Le Sacre du printemps*; what they got was the equivalent of a dud at the movie box office.

What went wrong?

I've permitted myself what amounts to a long prologue for two reasons. The first is to suggest that the avant-garde has become a second-order phenomenon. Where it once sought radical immediacy, its principal effect is now to signify its own operation from a reflective distance. Where it once sought to break through the traditional norms of artistic, rational, and social order, it has become a normative practice for the depiction of such breakthrough. The avant-garde has become as stylized as classical ballet. It is a fiction of transgression, often directed against norms that have already become depleted not only in art but also in everyday life. In a sense much stronger than the "classic" one proposed by Peter Bürger, the avant-garde has become historical.[4] Its historical character has become the medium of its perception.

What went wrong in *Shadowtime* is that the opera did not figure this out, and therefore failed to figure it in. The avant-garde, historically regarded, had a certain cultural mission. Amid considerable ideological diversity, most avant-garde programs could take as a motto Rimbaud's famous imperative of 1873, "Il faut être absolument moderne"—one must be absolutely modern.[5] The hallmark of this mandatory modernity was a relentless negation of the authority of the past. As Malcolm Turvey has argued, however, actual avant-garde

---

[2] Anthony Tommasini, "For a New Operatic Type, Complexity Rules," *The New York Times*, Saturday, 23 July 2005, section B, column 1.

[3] Ferneyhough, quoted by Tommasini, "Secular Messiah"; Bernstein, quoted by Eichler, "New Operatic Type."

[4] Peter Bürger, *Theory of the Avant-Garde*, trans. Michael Shaw (Manchester: Manchester University Press, 1984).

[5] From "Un saison en enfer," in Wallace Fowlie, ed. and trans., *Rimbaud: Complete Works, Selected Letters* (Chicago: University of Chicago Press, 1966), 208.

practice was less monolithic than this program.[6] Especially as the avant-garde aged, it showed elements of nostalgia for inherited forms, even reversion to them. Apparently, the real necessity was to be *relatively* modern. The use of Karl and Groucho Marx as twin icons in *Shadowtime* is a good latter-day example. It is a fairly tired joke that the opera's creators seemed not to recognize as such.

But there is more at stake here than the invocation of a familiar narrative in which radical beginnings wind down ignominiously to conservative ends. The heteronomy of form, the ambivalent dialectic of absolute modernity and renascent tradition, is immanent in the very idea of the avant-garde, built into its underlying logic. The problem is that this logic is not infinitely extendible. After a century or so of repetitions, it has become obsolescent, dulled by familiarity and overtaken by events, both stylistic and technological, in the popular media. The question today is not how to continue the avant-garde as an open tradition but how to continue appreciating it as a closed one.

That brings me to the second reason for my prologue: to smuggle Walter Benjamin into the picture. Of course in doing so I risk the same self-mystified avant-gardism I have been criticizing in *Shadowtime*. Benjamin has become one of those pop-idol equivalents that the intellectual world insists on manufacturing, replacing one with another at regular intervals like a product line: Foucault out, Adorno in, Derrida out, Benjamin in, and so on. Calling on Benjamin now is almost a cliché. But clichés, as the cliché goes, are clichés for a reason, and Benjamin can offer real help toward a fresh appreciation of the avant-garde by offering a basis—only seventy-five years old!—for a fresh articulation of its logic.

That logic is my true subject here. I will primarily be looking at its operations in the two cornerstone figures of avant-garde experimentation in American music, Charles Ives and John Cage. Benjamin could not have known of the one and died too soon to know of the other. Besides, he had little interest in music. Yet his observations, which were prompted by surrealism in literature, can be adapted to fit Ives and Cage and many others—a broad range of instances outside the art and the era that grounded them.

Writing in 1929, Benjamin thought of surrealism in the spirit of another Rimbaudian principle, the disordering of all the senses. He was looking for an antidote to bourgeois subjectivity and found it in artistic practices that simulated the purported ecstasies of drug-induced delirium: "In the world's structure dream loosens individuality like a bad tooth. This loosening of the self by intoxication is, at the same time, precisely the fruitful, living experience that allowed [the surrealists] to step outside the domain of intoxication."[7] Intoxication here is a means, not an end, and even as a means it is only a metaphor. By writing *as if* intoxicated, the surrealists left the domain of intoxication for a higher, non-corporeal mode of ecstasy. Benjamin thinks of this new state of being as a replacement for religious fervor, and more particularly for mystical illumination. Aesthetic intoxication is ecstasy without the sacred and ecstasy *against* the sacred. It is half mimicry and half parody (but the halves do not make a whole). Surrealism

---

[6] Malcolm Turvey, "The Avant-Garde and the 'New Spirit': The Case of *Ballet méchanique*," *October* 102 (2002): 35–58.

[7] "Surrealism: The Last Snapshot of the European Intelligentsia" (1929), in Walter Benjamin, *Reflections: Essays, Aphorisms, Autobiographical Writings*, ed. Peter Demetz, trans. Edmund Jephcott (New York: Schocken, 1986), 179.

arose from a "bitter, passionate revolt against Catholicism [by] Rimbaud, Lautréamont, and Apollinaire. ... But the true, creative overcoming of religious illumination certainly does not lie in narcotics. It resides in a *profane illumination,* a materialistic, anthropological inspiration, to which hashish, opium, or whatever else can give an introductory lesson."[8]

The concept of profane illumination already both contains the logic of the avant-garde and describes what is at stake in it. On the one hand, the experience induced by avant-garde practice is a quasi-sacred illumination forged by profane means. Its effect is the penetration of a mystery: not a sudden solution of the mystery but the experience of suddenly finding one's way into and around the space of the insoluble, a breakthrough to a realm of mystery that is comprehended only in being experienced thus. Reflection will do no good there. Yet on the other hand, the avant-garde experience is an illumination *of* the profane, both a transcendent clarification of worldly matters and an infusion of them with an ecstatic light. "We penetrate the mystery," Benjamin writes, "only to the degree that we recognize it in the everyday world. ... [T]he most passionate investigation of the hashish trance will not teach us half as much about thinking (which is eminently narcotic), as the profane illumination of thinking about the hashish trance. The reader, the thinker, the loiterer, the *flaneur* are types of illuminati just as much as the opium eater, the dreamer, the ecstatic. And more profane."[9]

On this model, the avant-garde artwork is always contradictory. It is always anamorphic, free of the traditional burdens of form, intelligibility, and social compliance; and it is always retrospective, looking back on those burdens with a gaze that sheds new light on them and perhaps endows them with new life. For the most part, the anamorphic aspect strikes the perceiver first, only to be encroached on, at least a little, and often more, by the structuring force of perception.

This encroachment holds the key both to the logic of the avant-garde and to its history. One might surmise that the delirium sought by avant-garde works is an antidote to the violence that lurks beneath the veneer of civilized (read: bourgeois) life: for Rimbaud, perhaps, the violence of the Paris Commune; for Apollinaire and others of his generation, the far worse catastrophe of the Western front. (Of course this antidote could itself take the form of violence, as the example of the Italian Futurists famously illustrates, as does Benjamin's linking of fascism to the aestheticization of politics.) The musical avant-garde after the Second World War, especially perhaps in the Darmstadt of Boulez and Karlheinz Stockhausen, was in part motivated by a similar impulse in the face of a still larger catastrophe. So the stakes in the avant-garde enterprise are high, even when its surface manifestations are frivolous, witty, or clownish, more Cage's 4' 33" than Stockhausen's *Klavierstücke.*

The mark of the avant-garde is thus a release of the specific negation that haunts the standard forms of thought and representation, of selfhood and sociality: the giddy or delirious or ecstatic manifestation of the unformed substance that underlies or underwrites all form but that can appear only as a kind of deformity. And the question raised by the avant-garde is how far, for how long, it can sustain this appearance, this negative epiphany, before investing it with symbolic value and therefore "re/forming" it in a double sense: re-forming it, forming it anew; and reforming it, correcting its excesses or defects.

---

[8] Ibid.
[9] "Surrealism," 190.

For an example, consider Apollinaire's calligrammes, picture poems composed by deforming standard typography so that the text forms the picture that illustrates it. One of the best known of these is entitled "Coeur" (Heart, 1918) for reasons immediately obvious; it consists of the letters that spell out the phrase—pointedly not a sentence—"Mon coeur pareil à une flame renversée" [my heart like a flame upside-down] arranged in the familiar shape of a heart:

```
          N                    N
        E   V                o C
      R       E R           
    E           s É E M        Œ
    M                          U
    M                          R
     A                        P
      L                      A
       F                    R
        E                  E
         N                I
          U              L
                   à
```

From the visual perspective, nothing could be more conventional, even banal; the image illustrates the sentiment with the literal-mindedness of a greeting card. (Or an epitaph; it is inscribed on Apollinaire's grave in the Pére-Lachaise cemetery in Paris.) From the linguistic perspective, the phrase has been deformed in fundamental ways. It lacks spacing between words and it lacks the neutrality of ordinary typography. What is more, it cannot be read from left to right. The phrase begins and ends with left-to-right movement along the wavering line that forms the top portion of the image, although the lack of punctuation between "versée" (poured; *not* a word in the text) and "Mon" suggests that "beginning" and "ending" have been suspended here; the eye is invited to rotate in perpetuity around the heart, as if to feed its flame. After "Mon," the shape of the image draws the eye continuously from right to left until the top line is regained with the completion of "renversée."

To traverse the text is thus to enact the inversion of the natural-seeming order of reading, at least to Western eyes, just as the heart inverts the flame. The image is immediately legible but the text, though it can be deciphered, can never be read. The words have regressed toward the garbled and the random, the void of which peers through the empty center of the image even as the image denies it. And the same may hold good for the words' meaning. It remains unclear whether the likeness postulated by the phrase is to be taken as a metaphor or as a literal description of the inversional effects of the image and the typography.

The text of "Coeur" is an ideal example of the negativity typically sought by the avant-garde. This quality is perhaps best described by the term *informe*, borrowed from Salvador Dali by the art historian Rosalind Krauss to characterize what she calls the "optical unconscious" of modernity.[10] As Krauss observes, the *informe* is not a negativity or a lack that stands as the opposite of form, but a positive consistency without identity, a "splitting of every 'identity' from itself into that which it is not" (166). The *informe* is the substance of what categories and boundaries cannot delimit, yet it cannot appear without them; it is a thing without a self "that form itself creates, as logic acting logically to act against itself within itself, form producing a heterologic" (167).

As the term "heterologic" suggests, it is tempting to assimilate the *informe* to the category of the Other that plays a key role in several influential schools of late modern thought—Derridean deconstruction, Lacanian psychoanalysis, Levinasian ethics. But to do so would be misleading. The *informe* is not a vehicle of difference. It subtends both difference and identity, difference and likeness; it is too nonspecific to form the concrete opposite or antagonist by and against which a style or genre or identity defines itself. Moreover, unlike the Other, which is postulated as forever irreducible, the *informe* is vulnerable to a historical undertow. It is not supposed to be, but it is. That which is *informe* in one generation becomes a mere difference in the next. A grinding noise eventually acquires an alias and becomes an expressive construction: the *Tristan* chord, the *Petrushka* chord. This reducibility of the *informe* may help motivate the demand for continual disruption in avant-garde art, the call for a normative iconoclasm: not for a break with tradition but for a break with history, or rather the circumvention of history, the continuation of non-tradition and non-identity.

But as the story of *Shadowtime* indicates, this process cannot go on forever. What happens to each instance of the *informe* also happens to its concept. Eventually history will overtake—will have overtaken—the production of the *informe* as such and bring it to closure. At that point we may be able to recover the sense in which avant-garde works once encountered (that is, produced) the *informe*, but we can no longer recover the perceptual impact of the encounter. The *informe* becomes a trope.

The historical process mirrors the internal logic of the avant-garde work, but it does so with a telling difference. If the era in which it could shock has not wholly expired, the work can sustain and even enhance its presentation of the *informe* in dialectic with the structuring traditions it cannot escape, however much it may travesty them. But the historical process progressively alienates and finally brackets the perceptual shock. What begins as an offense ends as an icon. As it ages, the urinal that Marcel Duchamp signs "R. Mutt" and christens "Fountain" in 1917 becomes easygoing, comfortable, almost comforting; by 1964, eight authorized replicas of the lost original find their way into museums and private collections; in 2004, five hundred British art experts vote "Fountain" the twentieth century's most influential work of art, just ahead of another once-shocking work, Picasso's "Les Demoiselles d'Avignon" (1907). Against this effect of domestication, we are left to rely on critical interpretation to recover the sense of the *informe* in historically avant-garde works. At best their manifestation of the *informe* will replenish its diminished power with the force of the imagined past.

---

[10] Rosalind Krauss, *The Optical Unconscious* (Cambridge., MA: MIT Press, 1993), 149–68.

This process, however, is not only historical. It is also immediate, a property of the present of the avant-garde work as well as a prophecy of its future. Avant-garde works present themselves from the outset in a condition of implicit ruin. They contain the narrative of their own decline and subsist by resisting it. It is this synchronic logic of the avant-garde that the historical revival of once-unformed phenomena seeks to recover.

To facilitate the recovery, we need to describe this logic, presented earlier as a simple conflict between the manifestation of the *informe* and the encroachment of structuring perception, with greater precision and at a further theoretical remove. The *informe* initially appears as a pure lack in positive form, a consistency of negation. It induces a kind of vertigo, the first moment of the delirium in which Benjamin finds—or seeks—profane illumination. This impression, however, fades with time, and sooner rather than later. For the *informe* can appear at all only within a gap, an aperture, in a formal framework. At first the consistency in the gap threatens to envelop its former container; the white space in Apollinaire's heart dwarfs the little letters that enclose it. But eventually the situation is reversed. The image limits the white space within it and organizes the white space around it. The *informe* becomes manifestly what it always (already) was, a perspectival effect, the burned-out illusion of which is meant to be re-ignited by the next avant-garde "breakthrough." What remains thereafter is the mutual relationship of form and the *informe*, which, without necessarily signifying anything, may nonetheless be or become significant. Thus some avant-garde works incorporate and in part escape their own future nullification. The avant-garde work survives its inevitable obsolescence, if it does survive, to the extent that it can be understood to decline any nostalgia for the purity of the original *informe*.

Charles Ives raises the question of this nostalgia explicitly in the final movement of his *Orchestral Set No. 2* (1909–1915), a work that carries the *informe* as far as it can go within Ives's musical discourse—and that is quite far, indeed—only, apparently, to subsume it in the end under the most familiar of melodic forms. John Cage carries the *informe* even further in his *Imaginary Landscape No.* 4 (1951), "composed" for an ensemble of radios. The sounds produced, as no one will be surprised to learn, are entirely random and not subject to perceptual regulation. Yet as its title half admits, Cage's composition is open to the same nostalgia that it gently and playfully rejects.

Like many of Ives's major works, the *Orchestral Set No. 2* broods over the question of American national destiny by associating it with the question of advanced versus traditional musical technique. The first movement, "An Elegy for Our Forefathers," sustains a static background texture throughout. The elegy materializes on solo trumpet out of the brooding atmospheric mass and disappears back into it. Both the melody and its sonority are traditional—nostalgic and hymn-like; the trumpet solo carries overtones of solemn Civil War memorials. The background divides against itself in a way that both enhances and undermines these values. On the one hand it serves the function of a formal ostinato; on the other, it appears as the formless presence of something unknown, dim, and primordial, not music at all by traditional definitions. Memory writes itself on this texture as medium, questions the shape of the future, and then dissolves as the shapeless background persists.

The middle movement is a high-spirited collage of hymnody and ragtime, but for all its vitality (sometimes touched by nostalgia) it is essentially an interlude, an interval of distraction between one elegy and another. The real heft of the piece comes in the last movement, "From Hanover Square North, at the End of a Tragic Day, The Voice of the People Again Arose." This finale commemorates an incident following the sinking of the passenger liner *Lusitania* by a German U-boat in 1915. With the news still fresh, commuters on an elevated train platform in lower Manhattan, Ives among them, spontaneously began to sing the old Protestant hymn "In the Sweet Bye-and-Bye" after the sound of it on a hurdy-gurdy drifted up to them from the street. The random crowd thus momentarily transformed itself into a tight-knit community with a specific national identity.

Ives represents the transformative hymn-singing with a fortissimo brass chorus recalling the solo trumpet of the first movement. The rest of the orchestra moves in swirls of dense, multi-layered dissonance that have been building up throughout the movement. This vast polyphony, the component parts of which can be heard only in random flashes, the lines of which cannot be followed at such, has up to this point been the whole of the music; we have been listening to a progressive unfurling of orchestral sound into the *informe*. Then, at a stroke, this *informe* becomes a mere background, a foil against which the spiritual authority of the traditional rural hymn can present itself as a bulwark against chaos. The music, because there is need for it, revives a world that Ives thought he had lost forever to urban modernity, the homogenous world of the New England countryside, rugged and spiritual and quintessentially American. The voices of the crowd, unheard in themselves, have taken up the sound of the hurdy-gurdy, the sound of the city street par excellence, and raised it to the level of the sublime by simulating the sound of a small-town brass band.[11]

"In the Sweet Bye-and-Bye" momentarily translates the ruthlessness of total war, fought without borders and without quarter, into the communal, well-governed sphere of American pastoral. Yet the sternness of the sound also suggests a resolute face turned toward the war, which Ives's patriotism would endorse when America joined the Western alliance in 1917. In this context the music looks forward to a triumph of American virtue as the only means of preventing a Europe gone mad from unchecked destruction. (It is one of history's little ironies that the situation seems to have reversed itself today.) But this is not yet the music of empire, in which Ives had no interest; however triumphalist, it is profoundly and deliberately parochial.

The conclusion comes immediately afterward: a long, slow fade-out based on a static texture recalling the first movement's underlying sound-mass but changing its character. The texture is no longer dark and heavy with the burden of the past but soft and shimmering, a musical mist that slowly drifts away toward the horizon of an unknown future. Elegy becomes prophecy in the medium of memory; the image of national community dissolves into an intimation of spiritual communion. For a moment, and just for a moment, the hymn has torn away the veil of the material world. It has let the aura of spiritual reality take over the scene at Hanover Square, though perhaps this happens only in memory—only, indeed, in the music. Or perhaps two scenes have been involved, blended together so that they cannot be told apart: one from the urban present, the other from the rural past. The combination allows

---

[11] The displacement of voice into instrumental sound is essential to the process of sublimation, which corresponds to the passage of the event from the phenomenal world to the symbolic order. Ives underscores this necessity by placing an actual choir singing a *Te Deum* at the beginning of the piece; after a few moments, the voices fade into the orchestral texture, not to be heard from again.

a glimpse of ideal community both in time (the unison hymn) and beyond it (the ethereal background).

It is important that the impact of the Hanover Square incident does not become fully present until the place and the moment have been re-created musically. By adding memory and also serving as its expressive vehicle, the music makes permanent and transcendental the incident's fleeting moment of solidarity. Ives's musical technique serves not just to record or represent a moment of transcendence, but to perpetuate it acoustically. Each performance rises to the point of the music's self-abolition, the point at which the *informe* breaks through in the guise of a shout, and then a whisper, of eternity.

But the breakthrough is unstable, and not only because it, too, is fleeting. In an earlier study of this movement I suggested, along the lines just traced, that "In the Sweet Bye and Bye" is repressive as well as triumphant when it subordinates the dense swirl of music from which it emerges. It reverses the rising tide of that music and forces it back toward the horizon; it makes the pungent, multi-layered texture into a musical melting pot in which the diversity of the urban crowd disintegrates and reforms itself in obeisance to the old-time hymn. The hymn works ideologically more than it does formally or aesthetically.[12]

I would still say so. Ives himself described the music in these terms, and to ears brought up on the contours of tonal melody—still most Western ears today, and all the more so in 1915—the melodic Gestalt stands out like a rock against a stormy sea. The storm is the storm of the *informe*, immensely powerful but set on the verge of its disappearance. Form prevails in the guise of spontaneous spirit; the collage technique that defines the avant-gardism of the movement collapses into a texture that is both musically and ideologically regressive, a broken-down version of old-fashioned melody-with-accompaniment.

But I would also suggest something else. The musical whirl and swirl brought to heel by this last trump becomes audible as *informe* precisely through the ear-trumpet of the hymn. Bits and pieces of the hymn have been heard amid the orchestral mass all along. Once the hymn breaks forth, the ear is split between hearing these fragments teleologically, as anticipations of a predestined outcome, or hearing them contingently, as sonic material that the brass choir appropriates as the same time as it wrestles the acoustic mass into a semblance of form. Only with the presentation of this choice—a choice that cannot be made—does the *informe* manifest itself fully.

In saying this, I am not making the banal suggestion that order and chaos can only be heard relative to each other. On the contrary: the point is that what one hears at this moment becomes radically indeterminate, caught specifically in a contradiction between accident and event. The result is that the *informe* persists and permeates the musical texture more fully than does the acoustically more powerful hymn tune, and that it does so precisely *because* the hymn tune is more powerful. Instead of a convenient acoustic image for the local chaos of the urban crowd, the orchestral music becomes, or wants to become, a tangible manifestation of pure spirit. It presents itself as something like the voice of the all-embracing Over-Soul conjectured by Ives's beloved Transcendentalist philosopher, Ralph Waldo Emerson. The brassy hymn tells a familiar tale, but it sounds out over a long thunderclap from the unfathomable world beyond. The hymn is helpless to paraphrase this sound, before which it

---

[12] Lawrence Kramer, *Classical Music and Postmodern Knowledge* (Berkeley: University of California Press, 1995), 190–92.

is nothing but ideology. All the hymn can do is to make the sound audible as the sound of the *informe* as such.

Like Apollinaire's calligrammatical heart, the sound of this climax is from one perspective perfectly legible, even sentimental and conventional, and from another perspective permanently inscrutable. The release of the *informe* that negates the idea of purity and disrupts all finite systems of thought assumes its own terrible version of purity that demands total adherence even though there is no known way to hear it. The sound can no longer be contained even by the trope of transcendence. In its rustling, whirring, buzzing, and the like it approaches the negative transcendence that Gilles Deleuze and Félix Guattari associate with the "plane of consistency" of the insect world, the becoming-insect of music in which the music's free-form "molecular flows" are set loose.[13] This limit-condition threatens to captivate the listener even as it tempts the listener to flee: to grasp the ideological anchor—here that old-time hymn—in sheer self defense.

From this perspective the ethereal fadeout that ends the piece is not a consummation that the hymn makes possible. On the contrary, it is an almost involuntary confession that the hymn is no more than a prop, in the double sense of a means of support and a device used to sustain a theatrical illusion. The vanishing trace of the *informe* does not inherit the place of memory, but marks the place to which memory cannot pass.

The kind of critical interpretation I have just performed on Ives's "Hanover Square" is not possible with Cage's *Imaginary Landscape No. 4* because there is nothing to perform it on; in traditional terms, Cage's music lacks content. Where Ives understands the *informe* as the horizon of memory, Cage understands it as the erasure of memory. His work—and it *is* a work—is scored for twelve radios, operated by twenty-four players under the direction of a conductor. At each radio, one player controls the volume, another the frequency; a form of traditional staff notation strictly prescribes the changes in both parameters. This carefully constructed order will, however, remain inaudible, while the sound that it produces will form a random assemblage entirely contingent on the place and time of performance.

No doubt there is an element of lighthearted mockery here, a gentle satire on the traditional symphonic ensemble. But as always with Cage the playful lack of solemnity serves a serious purpose. To regard the turning of the radio knobs as a form of musical performance is to defamiliarize the natural-seeming mechanical actions, the fiddling on strings, the blowing into tubes, which customarily produce musical sound. To see and hear an ensemble "playing" the radios fosters the recognition that, in the long historical view, it is just by chance that the sounds produced by actions such as fiddling and blowing count for us as music and not as something else. The fact that other forms of sound count as noise becomes equally arbitrary. The result is to smudge the difference between officially musical sounds and sounds produced at random, as by twiddling the knobs of a radio to see what's on the air.

But more is at stake here than the apparent freedom we may find in chance. The point is not simply to immerse oneself in random sound events, but to grasp the production of the *informe* by the precise following of a score, thus creating a perspective in which the familiar forms of musical sound assume a quality of accidental formation, the way a rock formation

---

[13] Gilles Deleuze and Félix Guattari, *A Thousand Plateaus: Capitalism and Schizophrenia* (1980), trans. Brian Massumi (Minneapolis: University of Minnesota Press, 1987), 308–309.

might resemble a face. Like Apollinaire's heart, *Imaginary Landscape No. 4* constructs a traditional image of authentic, indeed "heartfelt," expression by means that render what is expressed ultimately inscrutable though not indiscernible. Like the letters that spell out, but do not articulate, "Mon coeur pareil à une flame renversée," the acoustic detritus produced and assembled by the radio ensemble is decipherable—one can make out the static, the voices, the snatches of music—but it is not readable or, as one might say, not listenable.

What do these pieces by Ives and Cage have in common?

The initial answer would seem to be: nothing. Nothing, that is, except their avant-garde status, the mark of which is their willingness or eagerness to admit noise into the sphere of music, or, more precisely, to redraw the boundary between music and noise. It is probably fair to say that the privileging of this mark came only with, and only became articulate with, the music of Cage around mid-century. No matter what audiences may have thought, it is clear that Schoenberg, for example, never thought of his music as resembling noise, much less incorporating it, even though the First Viennese School has a claim to be considered the first self-identified musical avant-garde. The noise idea is already present in certain works of early modernist music, such as Henry Cowell's "Banshee" (1925), played directly on the strings inside a piano, and Edgard Varese's "Ionisation" (1931), scored for percussion and sirens, but there is no category or context for it until later. Pieces like these and like the Ives become avant-garde in retrospect; no such category was available when they were composed.

This absence is itself as much a historical contingency as any random event in an aleatory piece. It is worth noting that by the time Ives composed the *Orchestral Set No. 2* and Cowell (still a teenager) had started experimenting with the piano, Luigi Russolo, in association with the Futurist movement of Filippo Marinetti, had already tried to create a noise aesthetic. Russolo wrote a manifesto on "The Art of Noise" (1913) and actually gave two concerts with a "noise orchestra" composed of sixteen newly invented instruments. The sounds are lost, but the manifesto gives the flavor of his enterprise: "Let us cross a huge modern capital with our ears. ... We will delight in distinguishing the eddying of water, of air or gas in metal pipes, the muttering of motors that breathe and pulse with an indisputable animality, the throbbing of valves, the bustle of pistons, the shrieks of mechanical saws."[14] The imagery of machines that mutter and throb locates the *informe* qua noise at the point of the pleasurable collapse between the boundaries of the animate and the inanimate. But the First World War, the war the Futurists had foolishly longed for as the consummate expression of modernity, interrupted Russolo's efforts, and when he tried to resume them after the war was over, the moment of noise as art had, for the time being, passed.

In a sense, then, it is Cage and his associates who make Ives avant-garde and realize the latent significance in his noise as well as theirs. Noise is all that links our Ives and Cage exemplars, and all that is needed to link them. But this sense is too limited.

On closer inspection, the Ives and Cage pieces turn out to be closely parallel in both their immediate character and their underlying logic of the *informe*. On the first point: both are deeply invested in the sense of place, conceiving music as they embody it as acoustic landscape. And this landscape is not general; it is national—ideologically so in Ives, by

---

[14] Quoted by Emily Thompson, *The Soundscape of Modernity: Architectural Acoustics and the Culture of Listening in America, 1900–1933* (Cambridge, MA: MIT Press, 2002), 136.

perhaps unconscious allegiance in Cage's. As the musicalization of radio noise, Cage's piece intersects what was still the primary broadcast medium of its time (television being still young); the radio airwaves—the hum of news, weather, talk, music, static—was the primal stuff knitting together the national landscape both at home and in the car, the same sort of jellylike medium that Hart Crane had imagined a few decades earlier when radio itself was still new:

> And from above, thin squeaks of radio static,
> The captured fume of space foams in our ears. ("Cape Hatteras," 23–4)[15]

On the second point: the scoring and conducting of the radio manipulations serves the same function as Ives's hymn tune; it makes the *informe* audible as such. It does so as much visually as acoustically, by reversing the locus of order and disorder. The normally casual, even random, act of turning a radio dial becomes the basis of a precise choreography while the music normally produced by such choreography never rises above the level of noise, or rather, raises noise to the level of music.

The result is an avant-garde version of the music of the spheres. The actual sound of the radio collage in any given performance is absolutely particular, purely and simply itself in the present moment. Yet at the same time it has no distinguishing features, nothing to differentiate it from any other realization at any other moment. It is both full and empty, an acoustic tapestry and a blank page. To a sympathetic ear, this union of opposites endows the sound with a mystical value. It produces a fusion of immanence and transcendence, the ascetic and the ecstatic, that justifies the scoring and conducting without ceasing to reduce them to a travesty. In so doing, it perhaps brings aesthetic intoxication to a limit, a point of aporia, which is also one of the principles of its logic. Just as the *informe* is released, it threatens to assume a fetish-like character incompatible with the very idea of the *informe*. The avant-garde does not consist of a resolution of this dilemma, but in a persistent reproduction of it—under the illusion that each new instance is precisely the resolution that it undercuts.

A further way to think about the interrelationships of form and the *informe* is in terms of Deleuze and Guatari's distinction between smooth and striated space. The latter is the milieu of the "metrical," "arborescent" music of tradition, the former of the rhizomatic movement of the avant-garde. (Traditional music organizes itself like a tree—the paradigmatic metaphor of organic form; the avant-garde runs every which way, like weeds.) For Deleuze and Guattari, the pivotal avant-garde composer is Boulez who, they say, was the first to situate music systematically in a movement between these spaces (477). But the two also think of music in general as essentially rhizomatic, and take Olivier Messiaen along with Boulez as an exemplar. As they hear it, music as such is avant-garde regardless of its formal consistency, for which their model is the refrain: "Music is a creative, active operation that consists in deterritorializing the refrain. ... Music dispatches molecular flows. Of course, as Messiaen says, music is not the privilege of human beings: the universe, the cosmos, is made of refrains;

---

[15] From *The Bridge*, in Marc Simon, ed., *The Complete Poems of Hart Crane: The Centennial Edition* (New York: Liveright, 2000), 77.

the question in music is that of a power of deterritorialization permeating nature, animals, the elements, and deserts as much as human beings" (300, 309). Beyond the formal grid of the refrain the infinitely smooth space of the *informe* stretches away on all sides.

Nonetheless, as Deleuze and Guattari never tire of repeating, the distinction between smooth and striated space is a transient one. There is perennially a becoming-smooth of the striated and a becoming-striated of the smooth. The authors' own tendency, however, disclaimers aside, is to re-solidify the distinction after its every dispersal: "[T]he simple opposition 'smooth-striated' [always] gives rise to far more difficult complications, alternations, and superpositions. But these complications basically confirm the distinction" (481). Deleuze and Guattari are in the last instance partisans of the smooth against the striated. Although they deny that smooth spaces "are in themselves liberatory," they affirm that it is in these spaces alone that "life reconstitutes its stakes" (500). A prominent sign of this orientation is the privilege that the authors grant to music, or rather the trope they institute of a music that, in its essence, insofar as it *is* music, always moves along lines of flight from the striated to the smooth. They think of this phenomenon in the spirit of Baudelaire: "Music sometimes takes me like the sea!"—for, as they observe, "the sea is a smooth space par excellence" (479).

In this context, re-solidifying the distinction, it would seem fair to define traditional music as that which, at any given moment, minimizes the becoming-striated of the smooth, and to define the avant-garde as that which maximizes the becoming-smooth of the striated. Traditional music arrests the flows of sound through smooth space and draws them as much as possible back to the striated. The avant-garde loosens and scatters the sound lodged in the striated and sluices it as much as possible into the space that, as rendered available in a particular historical moment, counts as smooth. But the boundaries of these spaces constantly change, in most cases irreversibly. The space that seems smooth today tends to seem striated tomorrow.

And here a problem arises. This way of thinking works well enough up to a point, then stalls. The model of spaces in mutual becoming is descriptively strong, but conceptually it is too strong for its own good. It blocks the full-throttle, epiphanic manifestation of the *informe*; it limits delirium by dialectic and thus takes the *informe* as such out of the equation. The noise of smooth space is merely the negation of traditional music, which excludes it altogether or includes it by imitation; as soon as actual noise is heard, traditional music is silenced. The order of striated space is the parallel negation of avant-garde music, which excludes it by design but includes it by accident, or rather by the propensity of performers, listeners, or even of random occurrences to fall into striated patterns. When the patterns appear, the avant-garde collapses back into tradition. There is a kind of drab homeopathy at work, a closed system that works on a kind of toggle.

To think the avant-garde more radically it is necessary to think the *informe* without reference to the accidents of form. To do that, it is necessary to conceive of a condition in which the distinction between smooth and striated makes no sense, or doesn't matter, or simply fails to apply. (This leaves open the question of how to think the presence of the *informe* in traditional music, but that question lies outside the scope of this essay.)

The key point here is that order may occur at random, in which case it cannot be said to be order at all. As Stéphane Mallarmé famously put this principle in the title of an avant-garde poem meant to illustrate it, "A Throw of the Dice Will Never Abolish Chance." Consider an imaginary musical example: an imaginary landscape number—fill in a six-digit prime. One is listening to Cage's silent three-movement composition 4' 33" and hears someone on the street outside whistling the *Habanera* from *Carmen*. Or, since the stake here is pure chance, for some reason all the radios in *Imaginary Landscape no. 4* simultaneously begin to broadcast *The Ride of the Valkyries*. Neither outcome is foreign to Cage's design, even though both are, to say the least, unlikely. But that is what chance is like. If we were to describe either of these situations as a becoming-striated of the smooth, we would be right in a phenomenological sense; the soundscape would indeed fall into the striated pattern. But we would also entirely miss the point.

The point is to hear the tunes as noise: to hear them, not as patterns, but as random assemblages; to hear them, so to speak, as if they were not there. And to hear them thus is also to hear the sound of random presence in all apparent design. The tunes would not be the negation of the prevailing noise, but a part of it. The *informe* of the imaginary landscape would be the enveloping negativity that is the landscape's condition of possibility. This condition would become audible as such through the random fluctuations of sound that realize the landscape as a soundscape.

The problem posed by this outcome, the outcome paradoxically determined by the *informelle* logic of the avant-garde, is the temptation to treat this negativity as the substance of a negative aesthetic theology, as a secret wisdom before which the listener becomes an initiate. Delirium is addictive, as Benjamin's drug-tinged language indicates. One might just as well worship a canonical masterpiece in quest of aesthetic illumination: it amounts to the same thing. In this context the presence of an audible scrap or tune or a hint of pattern might actually be helpful, precisely in deferring the moment of an always false initiation.

Conversely, with the Ives finale: the hymn tune demands allegiance; it denies the *informe* character of the sound mass by giving its own latent presence in that mass a platform on which to come together. It literally trumpets itself as a theological and a national solution. But it speaks too loudly not to strain credulity. And its subsequent disappearance uncovers the trace of an *informe* that neither the hymn nor the sound of the crowd can encompass: a positive presence this time, but one so opaque that it resists all attempts to name or rationalize it.

This ending suggests, in whispers, that the reframing of the *informe* by the hymn tune is no more than virtual, an illusion wrought by ideological desire. The problem is that the reframing is so overwhelming, both acoustically and dramatically, that the lesson of the ending may go unheeded. Perhaps the music even wants it to go unheeded, and allows it to sound only the better to silence it. We may be supposed to hear the ending as a dissolution, a disappearance, the ebbing away of the *informe* as an echo of resurgent form. Whether the music succeeds in giving this impression—a success that would be its failure—depends on just how much delirium the ear, like a vessel, can retain after the brass choir has scoured it out. Just a little may be just enough. Although the ending is no more than a residue, it may be sufficient to pose a question in the spirit of Walter Benjamin, who deserves the last word (182): "What form do you suppose life would take that was determined at a decisive moment precisely by the street song last on everyone's lips?"

Index

Abbate, Carolyn, 40
Abrams, M. H., 23
Adams, John, 165
    "The Wound-Dresser," 164, 172–4
Adorno, Theodor, 303, 305
    Dialectic of Enlightenment, 287, 288, 298
Agamben, Giorgio, xiii
Alighieri, Dante
    Inferno, 167
Althusser, Louis, 213
Anamorphosis, 268–9, 306
Andersen, Hans Christian, 281
Anderson, Laurie
    Blue Lagoon, 302n
Apollinaire, Guillaume, 306
    "Coeur," 307–8, 312, 313
Ariès, Philippe, 198, 203
Aristotle, 295
Austin, J.L., 6–7, 7n, 9, 15, 38, 233

Bacon, Sir Francis, 251
Badiou, Alain, xiii
Bakhtin, Mikhail, 48
Balzac, Honoré de
    Le Père Goriot, 197, 198
Baraka, Amiri, 64
Barber, Samuel
    Adagio for Strings, 170, 172
Barthes, Roland, xiii, 14, 60, 191, 191n
Baudelaire, Charles, 315
    "L'Héautotimorouménos," 24
Beardsley, Aubrey, 24
Beethoven, Ludwig van, ix, 19, 21, 69, 199n, 204, 235, 253
    Coriolan Overture in C Minor, op. 62, 70–93
    Piano Sonata no. 5 in C Minor, op. 10, no.1, 109, 120, 128, 129–32, 133
    Piano Sonata no. 8 in C Minor, op. 13, "Pathetique," 109, 120, 128, 129–32, 133
    Piano Sonata no. 12 in A-flat, op. 26, "Funeral March," 101, 109, 198–200
    Piano Sonata no. 17 in D Minor, op. 31, no. 2, "Tempest," 70, 109–43
    Piano Sonata no. 23 in F minor, op. 57, "Appassionata," 70, 109, 110, 112, 115–120, 132, 133, 139–40, 145, 151
    Piano Sonata no. 26 in E-flat, op. 81a, "Les Adieux," 101
    Piano Sonata no. 32 in C Minor, op. 111, 151
    Piano Sonatas "Quasi una fantasia," op. 27, 109
    Piano Sonatas ops. 54, 78, 90, 111 (as group), 109
    The Ruins of Athens, 102, 103
    Sonata no. 6 for Violin and Piano in A, op. 30 no. 1, 160
    Sonata no. 9 in A for Violin and Piano, "Kreutzer," op. 47, 145–60
    String Quartet no. 1 in F, op. 18, no. 1, 70
    Symphony no. 3 in E-flat, op. 55, *Eroica*, 83, 101n, 205, 237, 241
    Symphony no. 9 in D Minor, op. 125, 18–19, 20, 41n, 95–107, 234
    Trio no. 1 in D for Violin, Cello, and Piano, op. 70, no. 1, "Ghost," 69–70
Bekker, Paul, 71, 82–4
Benjamin, Walter, 303–6, 316
Bennett, Richard Rodney, 159
Bentham, Jeremy, 57
Berg, Alban
    Lulu, 24
Bergeron, Katherine, 57, 58, 65–6
Berlin, Irving, 63
Berlioz, Hector, 72, 74, 91n
    Grande messe des morts, 18–20
    Symphonie funèbre et triomphale, 199
Bernstein, Charles
    Shadowtime, 303–6
Big Other (Lacan), 92n, 183
Blake, William
    "The Ancient of Days," 249–50, 251, 252
Bloom, Harold, 199n
Bohlman, Philip, 57–8, 62
Borodin, Alexander
    String Quartet no. 2 in D, 159
Boulez, Pierre, 303, 314

Bourdieu, Pierre, 10–11
Bowdler, Henrietta, 73
Bradley, A. C., 74
Brahms, Johannes
    Alto Rhapsody, 84
    Intermezzo, op. 119, no. 1, 35–43
Brett, Philip, 231
Breuer, Josef, 33
Brinkmann, Reinhold, 18, 19
Britten, Benjamin
    Billy Budd, 271–2
Brown, Marshall, 39n
Browning, Robert
    "Apparent Failure," 191, 193n, 194
    The Ring and the Book, 42
Burne-Jones, Edward, 281
    The Depths of the Sea, 282–4
Bussoni, Ferrucio, 203
Butler, Judith, 213, 233–4, 233n
Byron, George Gordon, Lord, 23, 102, 106, 118–19
    Don Juan, 102–3

Cage, John, 305
    4'3", 306, 316
    Imaginary Landscape No. 4, 309–10, 312–13, 316
Cahill, Sarah, 172
Calderón de la Barca, Pedro, 75
Campion, Jane
    The Portrait of a Lady (film), 209–36
Carter, Elliott, 18
Casablanca, 272–4
Chopin, Frédéric
    Piano Sonata in B-Flat Minor (Funeral March), 179–205
Clarke, Mary Cowden, 74
Coen, Joel and Ethan
    O Brother, Where Art Thou?, 284–5
Cohn, Richard, 58–9
Coleridge, Samuel Taylor, 71–3, 91n, 134–5n
    The Rime of the Ancient Mariner, 146, 147, 151
Collin, Heinrich von
    Coriolan, 71, 75–93
Condillac, Étienne de, 124–8
Cook, Nicholas, 95–6n, 96
Cowell, Henry
    "Banshee," 313
Crane, Hart
    "Cape Hatteras," 314

Czerny, Carl, 110, 112, 115, 117–18

Dahlhaus, Carl, 114–15, 139, 237
Dalí, Salvador, 308
Davis, Miles, 57, 64
Debussy, Claude, 287, 298
    "La Cathedral engloutie," 287
    Nocturnes for Orchestra, 284, 296
Deleuze, Gilles, 312, 314–15
Delille, Jacques, 185
Delius, Frederick
    "Sea Drift," 164
de Man, Paul, 22
Dempster, Douglas, 58–9
Derrida, Jacques, xiii, 8n, 8–9, 15, 54, 113, 127, 134, 234, 242, 291, 305, 308
Descartes, Réne, 251
Dickens, Charles
    A Tale of Two Cities, 119
Douglas, Mary, 287
Duchamp, Marcel
    "Fountain," 308
Dunsby, Jonathan, 243
Dvorak, Antonin, 74

Eliot, T. S., 154
    "The Love Song of J. Alfred Prufrock," 222, 299n
    The Waste Land, 286
Ellington, Duke, 179
Emerson, Ralph Waldo, 311
Enlightenment, the, 85, 100, 120–1, 124–8, 134–5, 258–60, 288–9
Ernst, Heinrich Wilhelm
    "Elegy," 158

Ferneyhough, Brian
    Shadowtime, 303–6, 308
Flaubert, Gustave
    Madame Bovary, 24
Fludd, Robert
    Utriusque cosmi historia, 249, 251
Forster, E. M., 145, 271
Foucault, Michel, 48, 51, 57, 65, 258, 305
Freud, Sigmund, 2, 14, 29n, 37, 73, 182, 226, 233
    Interpretation of Dreams, 33–4, 241, 265–7, 267n
    Psychopathology of Everyday Life, 241

Gadamer, Hans-Georg, xiv, 16, 278

Geertz, Clifford, 13, 48
Géricault, Théodore, 119
Gilly, Friedrich, 100
Goethe, Johann Wolfgang, 96, 97n, 101
    Faust, 18, 24
    "Harzreise im Winter," 84
    Wilhelm Meisters Lehrjahre, 21, 22, 24–31
    "Winckelmann and His Age," 99, 105
Gossett, Philip, 59–60
Grimm, Jakob, 295
Guattari, Félix, 312, 314–15

Habermas, Jürgen, 46, 203n
Hampton, Christopher
    Carrington 230–32, 235
Hanslick, Eduard, 2–3, 5, 5n
Haraway, Donna, 52
Harrison, Robert Pogue, 167
Haydn, Franz Joseph, xvi
    "The Creation," 239–60
    "The Seasons," 253
Hazlitt, William, 73
Hegel, Georg Wilhelm Friedrich, 52, 61, 96, 101–2, 103, 112, 119–20, 282
Heine, Heinrich, 181n
Henze, Hans Werner
    Undine, 301n
Herder, Johann Gottfried von, 96
Hermeneutic windows, 6, 9–10, 86, 250
Hermeneutics, xi, xiv–xv, 1–20, 41–3, 88–90, 110–11, 191, 193–4, 237–8, 260–61, 278–9, 287–8
Hindemith, Paul
    "Lilacs" Requiem, 164
History, speculative (universal history), 96, 110, 120–21, 124–8
Hitler, Adolph, 168
Hoeckner, Berthold, 272n
Hoffmann, E. T. A., 5, 5n, 71, 74–9, 82, 88, 92n, 126, 128, 214, 301n
Hölderlin, Friedrich, 149
    Hyperion, 101, 105
Homer, 149
    The Odyssey, 286, 288–9
Horkheimer, Max
    Dialectic of Enlightenment, 287, 288, 298
Horowitz, Joseph, 234
Huneker, James, 180, 194

Ibsen, Henrik, 24
Ideology, 66, 89–90, 213–14, 259

Illocution, 7, 9, 67, 233
Imaginary, the (Lacan), 53
Impossible objects, 223
Interpellation, 213–14, 218, 219, 235
Ives, Charles, 305
    Orchestral Set No. 2, 309–12, 313–14, 316

James, Henry
    "Owen Wingate," 35–43
    The Portrait of a Lady, xvi, 209–36
Janacek, Leos
    String Quartet no. 1, "After Tolstoy's Kreutzer Sonata," 160
Jander, Owen, 121
Jean-Paul, 24
Jordan Roland, 35 et seq.
Joyce, James
    Ulysses, 299n

Kafalenos Emma, 35 et seq.
Kafka, Franz, 287
    "The Silence of the Sirens," 155, 284, 289–90
Kallberg, Jeffrey, 185, 200
Kant, Immanuel, 3–6, 9, 16, 23, 72, 121, 134, 251–3
Keats, John, 41
    "Ode on a Grecian Urn," 39
Kennedy, John F., 179, 204
Kerman, Joseph, 17, 66
Kermode, Frank, 40–41
Kern, Jerome
    "Smoke Gets in Your Eyes," 159
Kilar, Wojciech, 229
Kinderman, William, 95n
Klimt, Gustav, 24
Kotzebue, August von
    The Ruins of Athens, 102, 103
Kramer, Lawrence
    "Three Poems of Walt Whitman," 174–6
Krauss, Rosalind, 308

Lacan, Jacques, 53, 80, 92n, 103, 182–3, 254n, 263, 267, 308
Lamb, Charles and Mary, 74
Language, music and, ix–x, 22, 97–8, 112–15, 117–18, 260–61, 263–5, 267
Lawrence, D. H., 164
Leadbelly (Huddie William Ledbetter), 53
Leibniz, Gottfried Wilhelm, 242
Lenz, Wilhelm von, 112, 187–8, 194

Leonard, Nancy, 90n
Leppert, Richard, 148, 156, 300n
Lessing, Gotthold Ephraim, 96, 99
Levinas, Emmanuel, xiv–xv, 308
Liszt, Franz, 63, 74, 179, 180, 194
Love-death (*Liebestod*), 154, 230
Lyotard, Jean-François, 46
Lyriic, 39

MacCannell, Juliet Flower, 100
Mahler, Gustav
    Symphony no. 1 in D, 267, 270
Mallarmé, Stéphane, 24, 299n
    "Un coup de dés," 285–6, 315
Mann, Thomas, 37
    Tonio Kröger, 37–8
Marinetti, Filippo, 313
Marx, Adolph Bernhard, 93n, 110, 112, 115, 120, 157
Marx, Groucho, 303, 305
Marx, Karl, 303, 305
Massenet, Jules
    Thais, 158
McClary Susan, xvi, 157, 160
Meaning, musical, x–xi, 1–20, 88–90, 117–19, 237–8, 260–61
Melville, Herman, 298
    Billy Budd, 271
Mendelssohn, Felix, 74, 287, 297–8, 300n, 301n
    The Fair Melusine Overture, 286, 291–4, 301n
Messiaen, Olivier, 314
Michaelis, Christian Friedrich, 122n, 126
Milton, John, xii
    "Lycidas," 163
    "On Shakespeare", xii
    Paradise Lost, 249, 254n
Monteverdi, Claudio, 53
Morgan, Robert, 62–3
Mörike, Eduard
    "Nachmittags," 39–40
Mozart, Wolfgang Amadeus, 48, 50, 53, 59, 61, 63, 102
    Divertimento for Violin, Viola and Cello in E-flat, K. 563, 54
    The Marriage of Figaro, 265–6
Munch, Edvard
    The Scream, 268

Nadar (Félix Tournachon), 184, 186
Narrative, 39–41, 93n, 191–4, 297

Nettl, Bruno, 57, 61
New Musicology, x–xi
Newcomb, Anthony, 18, 19
Newman, Ernest, 21–2
Niecks, Frederick, 194
Nietzsche, Friedrich, 14–16, 20, 24, 42, 113, 287, 296
    The Gay Science, 290–91
Nohl, Luwig, 120
Novalis, 23

Offenbach, Jacques
    Tales of Hoffmann, 158
Other, otherness, 53, 57, 62, 67, 101–2, 106, 308
Ovid (Publius Ovidius Naso)
    Metamorphoses, 36, 248

Paër, Fernando
    Achilles, 101
Performative utterance, 6–9, 38, 51–2, 233–4
Petty, Wayne, 199n
Picasso, Pablo
    Les Demoiselles d'Avignon, 308
Plato
    Timaeus, 248–9
Plutarch
    Lives, 77
Pope, Alexander, 72
Postmodernism, 48–9, 53, 65
Poussin, Nicolas
    The Arcadian Shepherds, 187n
Prendergast, Christopher, 184
Proust, Marcel, 214

Rachmaninoff, Sergei, 203–4
    Piano Concerto no. 2 in C Minor, op. 18, 230
Ragon, Michel, 183
Randel, Don, 60
Ravel, Maurice, 287
    Gaspard de la nuit, 296–8
Real, the (Lacan, Žižek), 103, 263, 267–9
Reynolds, Christopher, 18–19
Reynolds, David, 166
Rilke, Rainer Maria
    "Die Insel der Sirenen," 286
Rimbaud, Arthur, 304, 305
    "Le Bateau ivre," 299n
    A Season in Hell, 46
Rimsky-Korsakov, Nikolai, 158
Rolling Stones, the, 63
Romanticism, 23–4, 71–3

Rorem, Ned, 165
  War Scenes, 170–72
Rosen, Charles, 147, 150
Rossetti, Dante Gabriel
  "Parted Love," 33
Rossini, Gioacchino, 57, 59
  La gazza ladra, 198n
Rothgeb, John, 243n
Rousseau, Jean Jacques, 125, 127, 133, 134, 265
Rubinstein, Anton, 203
Rushdie, Salman, 214
Russolo, Luigi
  "The Art of Noise," 313

Schenker, Heinrich, xvi, 5, 239–59
Schering, Arnold, 70
Schiller, Friedrich, 126
  "Die Götter Griechenlands," 12, 274
  "Ode to Joy," 95–107
  "On Naïve and Sentimental Poetry," 99
Schindler, Anton, 110, 117, 118n
Schinkel, Karl Friedrich, 105–6n
Schlegel, August, 71–2, 91n, 97, 97n
Schlegel, Friedrich, 21, 24–5
Schmalfeldt, Janet, 114, 139
Schoenberg, Arnold, 241
  Book of the Hanging Gardens, 24
Schubert, Franz, ix–x, 209–36
  "Gretchen am Spinnrade," D. 118, 30
  Impromptu in A-flat, op. 90, no. 4, D. 899, 214, 217, 220, 228, 235
  Impromptu in G-flat, op. 90, no. 3, D. 899, 218, 229
  Octet in F, D. 803, 274–7
  Rosamunde (incidental music), op. 26, D. 797, 12
  "Schöne Welt, wo bist du" ("Die Götter Griechenlands"), D. 677, 274–6
  String Quartet no. 13 in A Minor, D. 804, 11, 274–7
  String Quintet in C, D. 956, 230, 231
  String Quartet no. 14 in D Minor, D. 810 ("Death and the Maiden"), 219, 220, 223–6, 235
  Symphony no. 8 in B Minor, "Unfinished," D. 759, x
  Wilhelm Meister songs, 21–32
  Winterreise, D. 911, 23, 234, 236
Schumann, Clara, 43, 158
Schumann, Robert, 21, 90n, 193, 193n, 286, 292
  Symphony no. 4 in D Minor, op. 120, 158

Scruton, Roger, 237–8
Seuss, Dr. (Theodore Geisel)
  The Five Hundred Hats of Bartholomew Cubbins, 45
Shakespeare, William, xii, 69–93
  Hamlet, 7–8, 9, 37, 73, 75–7, 92n
  Macbeth, 69, 70, 75–7
  The Tempest, 70, 110, 112, 117, 117–18n, 285
Shaw, George Bernard, 36
Shelley, Percy Bysshe, 23
  "Adonais," 11, 163
  "Ode to the West Wind," 11, 119, 120
  Prometheus Unbound, 36
Sibelius, Jean, 160
Solie, Ruth, 58, 65
Solomon, Maynard, 95n, 99
Spinoza, Benedict de, 72
Stalin, Joseph, 180
Stephani, Heinrich, 259
Stockhausen, Karlheinz
  Klavierstücke, 306
Stone, Oliver, 170
Strauss, Richard, 74
Stravinsky, Igor
  Le Sacre du printemps, 304
Sturm, Christoph Christian
  Reflections on the Works of God in Nature, 253
Subjectivity, x, xv–xvi, 23–4, 42, 52, 73, 111, 124–8, 134, 143, 213–14, 219, 228–32
Sublime, the 121–7
Subotnik, Rose, 199n
Swinburne, Algernon Charles, 24
Symbolic order, the 182–4, 267–8

Taruskin, Richard, 107
Tchaikovsky, Peter Ilyich, ix
  Piano Concerto no. 1 in B-flat Minor, op. 23, 230
  Romeo and Juliet, 67
Thomson, James
  The Seasons, 253
Tieck, Ludwig, 24
Todorov, Tzvetan, 40–41
Tolstoy, Leo, 102, 214
  "The Kreutzer Sonata," 145–60
Tomlinson, Gary, 17, 45–55, 58, 64–5
Tovey, Donald Francis, 71, 81–2, 84, 85, 95–6, 112, 149
Treitler, Leo, 17, 95n

Tropes, cultural, 88–9, 164, 166–8, 183–4
Tropes, structural, 10–13
Turvey, Malcolm, 304–5

Varese, Edgard
    "Ionisation," 313
Vaughan Williams, Ralph, 165, 175
    "A Sea Symphony," 164
    "Toward the Unknown Region," 164
    Dona Nobis Pacem, 168–70
Vaughan Williams, Ursula, 168
Verdi, Giuseppe, 74
Vernet, Joseph, 121, 123, 135
Voice, 106, 133–4, 158–9, 173–4, 228, 230, 263, 270, 294–6

Wagner, Richard, xii, 24, 34, 37–8, 59, 71, 74, 77–82, 85, 88, 287, 297, 300n, 301n
    Die Meistersinger, 37
    Parsifal, 61
    Das Rheingold, 294–6, 298
    Tannhäuser, 296
    Tristan und Isolde, 221

Weber, Carl Maria von, 59
Welles, Orson, 179
White, Hayden, 48
Whitman, Walt, 163–77
Whittall, Arnold, 243
Winckelmann, Johann Joachim, 99, 100, 149
Wittgenstein, Carolyne, 180, 194
Wittgenstein, Ludwig, xiv, 38
Wolf, Hugo
    Wilhelm Meister songs, 21–34
Wordsworth, William
    The Prelude, 23, 107
Work, musical, x, xii–xiii, 46, 51–2, 54, 60–62

Yeats, W.B.
    "The Mermaid," 282

Žižek, Slavoj, xiii, 103, 182–3, 232–4, 233n, 263, 267–8, 268n, 269, 270
Zola, Émile, 191, 298
    The Debacle, 176n
    Thérèse Raquin, 193